INSIDE MULTIMODAL COMPOSITION

NEW DIMENSIONS IN COMPUTERS AND COMPOSITION

Gail E. Hawisher and *Cynthia L. Selfe*, editors

INSIDE MULTIMODAL COMPOSITION

edited by

Andrew Morrison
InterMedia, University of Oslo, Norway

HAMPTON PRESS, INC.
CRESSKILL, NEW JERSEY

Printed in the United States of America

Library of Congress Cataloging-in-Publication Data

Inside multimodal composition / [edited by] Andrew Morrison.
    p. cm. -- (New dimensions in computers and composition)
  Includes bibliographical references and index.
  ISBN 978-1-61289-000-5 (hardbound) -- ISBN 978-1-61289-001-2 (paperbound)
  1. English language--Composition and exercises--Study and teaching--Computer-assisted
instruction. 2. Creative writing--Computer-assisted instruction. 3. Language
arts--Computer-assisted instruction. 4. Educational technology. I. Morrison,
Andrew, 1960-
  LB1576.7.I674-20H 2010
   372.3--dc22

                                              2010052860

Hampton Press, Inc.
23 Broadway
Cresskill, NJ 07626

CONTENTS

v

FIGURES AND TABLES

PART I

FRAMING

1

VIEWS FROM THE INSIDE OUT

Andrew Morrison

MOTIVATIONS

Mixed Views, Multiple Mediations

The image in Figure 1.1 has two of the book's contributors engaging with Kazuhiko Hachiya's award-winning electronic artwork from the early 1990s (Hachiya 1993, 1996). The work is a mediating artifact that encourages embodied interaction. It comes into being only through the attempts of the two participants to 'see' one another's point of view. The participants are linked by radio waves, clad in head-mounted displays with in-built cameras and winged power packs containing antennae. In this work, it is the sensory, kinetic, and perceptual transposition of another person's

Figure 1.1. Synne Skjulstad (foreground) and Martin Havnør (background) using the *Inter Dis-Communication Machine* (Kazuhiko Hachiya 1993), foyer Lentos Museum of Modern Art, Linz Austria, 2004.

perspective or intersubjectivity that allows us to toy with experience and concepts of connectedness and shared sensibility in a digital age.

The title of this work is the 'Inter Dis-Communication Machine.' It is clearly a piece that plays with virtual reality technology fashionable at that time. Entering into it raises questions. When I am myself, how am I the other, when does being merge, and what affordances does the technology enable and exhibit? Through this mediated transposition, viewers are emboldened to move, devoid of their usual shared sight lines. Their access to the work is technologically embedded and yet realized in their own performativity as a multimodal composition. Whereas the artist sees this work as creating a sense of double and mutual identity (Hachiya 1996: online), those watching and perhaps asking and guiding these two switched players may also wonder at what is being processed, through the technology and by and between the users. At a more intimate level, the artist alluringly says he designed the piece 'to allow for the possibility of kissing and making love.'

We encountered this work in a public domain: We joined a queue of eager users in a busy gallery setting at the *ars electronica* festival in Linz, Austria, which over several years a group of contributors to this book has been attending. In some way or another, this festival challenges us to don a set of metaphorical wings and reach for different understandings of digitally mediated communication and the intersections between art, technology, media, and interpretation.

This book is also about reaching for new knowledge through engaged, experimental, and transdisciplinary inquiry. Individually, together, and transversally, the chapters collected here investigate the potentials and limits of a variety of perspectives as they intersect in the compositional activities of mediated making meaning. This mediated meaning making— itself a dialogical composition—is increasingly realized through the inter- relationship of different sign systems and sociosemiotic and multimodal discourse modes. For Stöckl (2004: 9), . . . multimodal refers to commu- nicative artifacts and processes which combine various sign systems (modes) and whose production and reception calls upon the communica- tors to semantically interrelate all sign repertoires present.

Multiple Perspectives

The collection offers multiple perspectives on changing multimodal and mediational practices often in the form of detailed analyses of case-based design experiments developed collaboratively by the authors. Close hermeneutical analyses are also included. We situate multimodality het- erogeneously, after Bakhtin (1986), within experimentation into the mak- ing and analysis of multimediational compositions across a variety of modes, types, settings, participants, and disciplines. We include, for example, a focus on learners' discourses and media histories, the study of commercial web texts, processes of making an art installation, blogging choreographic processes, and questions of archiving an ethnologist's digital video of making a Viking boat. The collection includes material on students' engagement with film editing in an online environment and their production of their own cultural history learning resources, alongside experiments with wikis and multiple activities of mediated meaning making. Taken together, we see that these contributions may be applied within an extended view of digital multiliteracies and creative practices.

Our mediated compositions are moving off the desktop and the attention there to written composition (Sirc 1999). Although we treasure writing and its many facets, our notion of composition takes up the emerging activities involved in communicating with new tools in mixed contexts and across a variety of mediating activities. *Multimodal composition* refers to the changing practices and analyses of such multiple mediations that are often enacted collaboratively and across established domains. Practice and analysis here influence one another in what is increasingly mediationally dynamic discourse in an interplay between tools and signs (i.e., discourse that is constructed by its generation yet also constructs its significations by being situated in mediated activity).

Inside Multimodal Composition draws together research, development, and teaching from composition studies and digital media and communication, studies in technology-enhanced education, information systems, mediated cultural history, electronic arts, and contemporary art history. For the most part, the book focuses on the interrelations among digital systems, tools, and multimediational articulations. We connect cultural and communicative perspectives to mediated communication to those of 'new' media and electronic art, and also to object-oriented and system design in informatics. Several chapters make closer reference to Human–Computer Interaction (HCI) and, more specifically, embodied interaction (Dourish 2001), tangible interfaces, and aesthetic computing (Fishwick 2006). Perspectives on social semiotics and the Systemic Functional Linguistics (SFL), which lie behind many of the recent writings on multimodality, are also covered.

Across these chapters, the authors have stretched their own interdisciplinary wings and tried to find some degree of cohesion in their creative designs and applied studies of composition in the making. A sociocultural perspective on mediated meaning making, drawing on the work of Vygotsky (1962, 1978), underpins much of the research reported here. At the same time, reference is made to the theory of multimodal discourse (Kress & van Leeuwen 2001) and related work in Systemic Functional Linguistics (SFL) and critical discourse analysis. However, research in these areas seldom makes extensive reference to 'new' media or digital design and informatics outside of computational linguistics.

In addition to approaches from SFL and studies of discourse in learning, this collection of chapters attempts to make clearer connections to new media and hermeneutics while drawing on research in informatics. We argue that greater attention needs to be given to forms and functions of digital multimodality while keeping in view its antecedents and the mediated meaning making across and within modes that surround it and help our understanding of what encompasses multimodal composition. The wider contexts for multimodal discursive innovation and construction are therefore central. This is to perform a social semiotics that analyzes how texts are constructed, denotatively and connotatively, and how they are part of a wider culture industries sector. It is also to reach outward for perspectives that study the activities of mediated meaning making, whether through students' own appropriations of specialist discourses or via practice-based collaborative constructions of works that involve art and technology that include audiences as active participants.

Parts and Wholes

One of the major challenges in making and analyzing multimodal discourse, especially the digital, is how to account for the relations between among diverse parts, variant relations, and summative wholes. This is a central issue in framing transdisciplinary research and digitally mediated productions in particular. However, what is at issue here is not simply a matter of developing notions of convergence but ways of making and unpacking sets of relations between among disciplines, concepts, and communicative constructs embedded in practice. Remaining within disciplinary knowledge domains provides security and the robustness of well-tried approaches. However, when the research processes and objects are plastic, we are challenged to find practical and theoretical frames that enable us to sew together the known and given—to acknowledge the legacies of earlier inquiry—while delving into ways of finding, designing, applying, and analyzing new relationships. In a sense, this is to build a form of multimodal theory—not merely an interdisciplinary one but one that is transdisciplinary. It is one that is informed by changing practices involving our engagement with new tools and articulations. Ultimately, this is to center on communication and its social and cultural composition, in design, via use and through analysis. Martin and Stenglin (2007: 235), two writers on SFL and multimodality, in their reflections on positionality and perspective in transcolonial exhibition design in terms of both spatial and cultural grammars, are still '. . . pining for the intermodal theory which will in time reconcile one grammar with another and explain how the meaning of the two or more modalities is so much greater than the sum of their parts.'

Understanding the potential for communication and its many intersecting modes and mediations, in both production and analysis, demands that we relate diverse parts to complex wholes. A recently published essay by the Russian semiotician Yuri Lotman (2005) reminds us that this is a complex process. Lotman developed the concept of the semiosphere to account for the intricate relations of parts and wholes in meaning making: For Lotman (2005: 215)

> . . . the semiosphere repeatedly traverses the internal borders, assigning a specialized role to its parts in a semiotic sense. The translation of information though these borders, a game between different structures and sub-structures; the continuous semiotic 'invasions' to one or other structure in the 'other territory' gives birth to meaning, generating new information.

> The internal diversity of the semiosphere implies its integrity. Parts enter the whole not as mechanistic details, but as organs in organisms. The essential feature of the structural formation of the core mechanisms of the semiosphere is the fact that each of its parts creates its own whole, isolated in its structural independence. Its connections with other parts are complex and are characterised by a high level of deautomatisation. Moreover, at higher levels, they acquire a behavioural character, i.e., they gain the ability to independently choose programmes of activity. Relative to the whole, located at other levels in the structural hierarchy, they reveal an isomorphic quality. Thus, they are, simultaneously, the whole and its likeness.

Inside Multimodal Composition argues and demonstrates by way of applied research and transdisciplinary theorizing, not only the grammars of social semiotics, but also multiple activities and mediations at the level of discourse.

MULTILITERACIES

Multimodality, Complexity, and Meaning Making

In developing the many chapters gathered here, it has been important to remind ourselves, as Baldry and Thibault (2006: 149) note, that 'In spite of the pioneering work of Bateson, Birdwhistell, Hall and others in the 1950s, the multimodal study of social meaning-making remains in its infancy.' More than a few of the authors of *Inside Multimodal Composition* demonstrate that the phenomenon of multimodality is increasingly realized across a variety of domains—of work, learning, and leisure—in which digital tools and culturally situated signs systems intersect in complex significations. The ensuing technologically mediated artifacts (Wartofsky 1979), or compositions, are expository and expressive. They are imbued with historical, cultural, and developmental qualities. They also challenge our given analytical frameworks and practices by virtue of their complex relations of discourse modes, media types, and mediational articulations.

In this collection, we direct our attention to these artifacts as processes and products. For us, they are realized by way of discourse in action (Norris & Jones 2005) and the role of mediated action in particular (e.g., Lemke 2005). Our interest, then, is in the complexity of multimodally and multimediated communication and its relationships to collaborative creativity, expression, and articulation that together may be seen as compositions. In addition to the focus on language and other modes characteristic of many of the main publications on multimodality originating in applied linguistics and social semiotics, we place weight on digital textuality, the uptake of digital tools, and rhetorical experimentations and articulations involving various media and participants who have different needs related to a diversity of contexts.

This complexity of composition has more and more to do with understanding relations between multiple elements and constructions (see Figure 1.2). These elements may be published in cross-media texts, or they may come to be circulated through shared authoring and distribution through social networks. The production and consumption of multiple

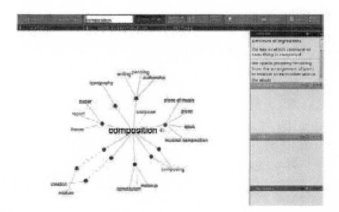

Figure 1.2. Search result for word 'composition' at http://www.visual thesaurus.com/

media and modes and the role of collective making point to the centrality of activity. Many modes may be threaded into multimediational texts that may include a span of activities in their design and a diversity of enactments by participants, whether individually or in various configurations of shared meaning making (Wertsch 1991).

Multimodality, Multiliteracies, and Multimediational Composition

Rhetoric and Composition Studies have undergone major changes and challenges in the past two decades that are widely reported. This book argues that we are increasingly working within what we may term a *multimodal rhetoric*. Stand-alone desktop machines and word processing by individual writers have been extended to networked and distributed communication using a variety of applications and modes of articulation. Teachers of academic, technical, and professional communication have generated a body of research into the changing character of not just writing but increasingly how a diversity of media types and modes of articulation may be incorporated within 'composition' (e.g., Ulmer 2003). This too has been connected to the wider application of computers in writing, learning, and the generation of computer-mediated communication in the shape of situated and multimediational multiliteracies (Snyder 1998; Ulmer 1998; Cope & Kalantzis 2000; Hawisher & Selfe 2000; Kress 2003; Buckingham 2003). A considerable body of work now exists in multimodal literacies in schools (Jewitt & Kress 2003, Jewitt 2005) and higher education, in which information communication technologies and multiple contexts of learning are covered (e.g., Hawisher & Selfe 1999). In these studies, whether explicitly stated or not, it is the meaning making by participants in discourse events that is the central concern. Further, meaning making in multiple contexts (e.g., Lund 2006) and with multiple media may be understood as meta-literacy (Lemke 1998).

One of the main arguments coming from computers and composition has been not to let the technology 'write' us, but that we write through the technology (Haas & Neuwirth 1994; Haas 1996). Learning to communicate in digitally mediated environments and with an array of tools demands that we pay attention not only to the how of composition but also what we do inside its unfolding and shaping through use (e.g., Wysocki et al. 2004). As the opening vignette demonstrates, the enactment of individual and shared composition may be extended to a variety of discourse modes not traditionally housed within written, expository rhetoric. These discursive modes are now mixed with elaborate multimodal digital environments and articulations. Much of the current writing on multimodality does not address the digital.

Our movement inside the multimodal character of composition has crossed domains, such as in an analysis of visualisation strategies in the persuasive constructions of online advertising. In our journeying into the depths of multimodal composition, our research has looked at the spread of multiliteracies and the creative and collaborative articulations of digital design professionals and media-rich discourse expressions. In conveying this diversity of material, we include a range of modes of representation and analysis. In travelling inside multimodal composition, we present and analyse two aspects: multiliteracies and multimediation. Multimodal, multimediational multiliteracies are increasingly being realised across formal tasks and contexts of learning (e.g., Rasmussen et al. 2003) and the participatory flux of popular culture (e.g., Anderson 2003; Jenkins 2006). Students and the wider public meet tools applied to genres in formal corporate web mediation, and, in accessing these texts, they are exposed to innovations generated out of earlier conventions and practices that are reapplied and situated in new contexts of narration and information representation.

Concerning our own production of mediated text, in the daily contexts of work and learning, core commercial applications have a pervasive and reproductive presence as genres are recirculated and potentially alternative expressions often stifled by the mediation of given presentation modes. Mediated meaning making in a digital age demands that we learn conventions and skilled uses and formulations with tools; however, it also asks that we take these up in reference to earlier mediated histories and see their uses in wider developmental learning frames, thereby situating mediated meaning making historically, not simply as form and function but as mediated, networked expression.

It is important that we also study texts that have been composed. Redström (2006), writing from an informatics background, reminds us that, although user-based studies enrich our understanding of designs in use, without attention to the texts—in our view as utterances—there is a danger of reifying user perspectives while missing a major part of their computational and indeed textual reference. At the same time, however, studying students' early uptake of new tools and modes of communication allows us as educators and researchers to engage with new modes of collaborative enactment that sit between the 'page and the screen' (Snyder 1998). *Inside Multimodal Composition* argues that all of these aspects contribute to a wider understanding of multimodal multiliteracies and in a variety of domains characterised by multiple practices and motivating related transdisciplinary analysis.

TRANSDISCIPLINARY FRAMES

A Sociocultural Approach to Communication, Design, and Learning

Many writings on multimodal discourse are within linguistics. However, these studies are also connected, in part, to the domain of social semiotics (see Chapter 2 for further details). Until recently, social semiotics has been concerned with developing 'grammars' of sign systems that allow us to analyze discourse products and processes. Yet in the application of this approach in educational and mediational contexts, for example, in changing multiliteracies or visual communication, little mention is made of underlying learning theories or the transdisciplinary linkages that characterize much of the research into 'new media.' In addition, the influence of critical discourse analysis on social semiotics is also often not fully acknowledged. In our view, a sociocultural approach to communication—that includes design, production-based inquiry, situated use, and transdisciplinary analysis—is needed to account for the complex texts that we meet and our roles in mediated environments within which we encounter and, indeed, contribute to the process of their complex composition.

Social semiotics has an important place in a sociocultural approach to communication. However, a sociocultural approach to communication is not only concerned with the mapping of the syntagmatic. It also has as its main concern the ways in which tools and signs are related in what we articulate—that is what and how we communicate with and through tools and signs. Without also attending to paradigmatic relations and situating them in a wider meta-theoretical framework, it is difficult to account for the emergence and expression of complex, multimodal discourse in which the digital may be a key component. Such complex communication may also be more fully understood not only by detailed studies within specific domains, important as they are to building wider understanding, but also be enriched by relating aspects from the humanities, social sciences, and computer science. This allows us to draw on fields such as aesthetics, poetics, rhetoric, narrative, and visual studies. Developments in anthropology and the learning sciences, for example, may contribute to a richer understanding of collective and collaborative processes of communication and composition. Informatics allows us to address matters of system design, such as object-oriented programming, semantic relations, and users and use.

Tools, Signs, and Mediation

In the remainder of this subsection, two key approaches to understanding complex relations, networks, and practices of mediated meaning making are mentioned: activity theory and actor network theory. Although there is debate about what these approaches offer and do not (see Chapter 2), our sociocultural approach to communication incorporates aspects of both these approaches.

Analytically, the concept of activity, central to activity theory (Engeström et al. 1999b), allows us to explore the nature of relationships between tools and signs (e.g., Kaptelinin & Nardi 2006; see Chapter 2). By focussing on activity, we have been able to investigate ways that tool-sign relations are patterned. In our compositions—practically and theoretical-ly—we have engaged with new tool sets and their situated uses and embodiments in a variety of texts that prime us to take them up and make meaning with them. By seeing multimodal discourse in action, and indeed as an activity in dialogue with others in the here and now as well as in lis-tening to utterances long spent, we have moved into new articulations of our own competencies (e.g., Miles 2003) and those of our students.

Alluding to the work of Leont'ev (1978, 1981) in activity theory, it is necessary to see these as both vertical and horizontal layers. Connecting layers of activity and the alignment of roles within and between them is needed to allow and account for work among designers, implementers, users, and managers. This is most important because a single artifact or group of artifacts can mediate in several ways, at different times, and in varied aspects. Wikis, for example, can function as tool, sign, site of con-flict or conflation, and mode of communication.

The concept of 'knotworking' (Engeström et al. 1999a) helps frame this. Knotworking refers to the activities of complex organisations with fluid boundaries, characterized by collaborative work whose task is orga-nized by its related actors who have not been previously linked. In the context of work, this activity is often of a short-term nature, centered on a task, and it demands participants to coordinate themselves around com-plex emergent objects. This is a matter of co-configuration. We see activi-ty as a central concept in making sense of what may seem to be a tangle of multiples in the realisations of complex, dynamic, and collaboratively fashioned texts and situated communication.

Assemblages and Spaces

This chapter looks from the inside out, giving an orientation as to what the collection covers and some of the coherence it achieves. Latour (2005) expresses clear distrust of critical, reflexive approaches, preferring to advance into a flatland where an unpreconceived topography of concepts may be traced. This is in keeping with the formulations of Actor Network Theory (ANT) (Law & Hassard 1999). In this view, different actors have their own perspectives that come into being through negotiation and the alignment of views with others. It is these assemblages that are central. Latour insists that we attend to not just the threads and knots that bind nets of such coherence, but that we acknowledge the importance of the spaces that lie in between.

> Contrary to substance, surface, domain, and spheres that fill every centimeter of what they bind and delineate, nets, networks, and 'worknets' leave everything they don't connect simply *unconnected*. Is not a net made up, first and foremost, of empty spaces? . . . If knowledge of the social is limited to the termite galleries we have been traveling, what do we know about what is outside? Not much. (Latour 2005: 242)

In our design and research into multimodal composition, we have not simply looked outward from secure footholds in known disciplines. The many contributors—through their individual and joint compositions—have been motivated to examine not just shared spaces but also ones unknown to one another (e.g., Sullivan & Porter 1997).

Making connections takes considerable effort and some risk. In our inquiries, we have also been open to investigating the practical and theoretical gaps between the well knotted and the elaborately networked. This has involved us in laying out our individual, shared, different, and common interests and views. However, although we have been interested to viewing such networked relations, we have also held onto a variety of critical insights and steered our analyses and interpretations conceptually on the basis of their specificities.

In this inquiry, our stance becomes one that is less declarative and denotative, more tentatively connotative, and participatively explorative. Following the approach of ANT, we may see these as 'worknets.' However, (as Latour does not quite articulate), there are spaces 'inside' that are also under construction, spaces to which we have returned and reassessed (Johnson-Eilola 1998). These too were present as part of investigating emerging and changing connections as they are shaped and as we reflect on them and the pathways that they permit.

Flying Critically

The authors here show that multimodal composition may be approached as situated meaning making that is mediated via different modes in various assemblages. Traditions and legacies of sociosemiosis are part of the practice of the conceptual development of the works and systems presented, developed, and analyzed by the contributors, as well as those to which they refer. To engage with digital tools and technologies in mediated meaning making, in part, and especially in humanistic inquiry, which is an interplay of heuristic and heuretics or methods of artistic invention (Ulmer 1994), is to move without clear maps. However, writing on hypertext, Johnson-Eilola (1997: 13–14) reminds us of the importance of maintaining a critical view on new technologies and their apparent promise:

> In hypertext, we are like angels without maps, suddenly gifted with wings discovering not only that we cannot find heaven, but also that walking made us fell less dizzy, that our new wings snag telephone wires and catch in door frames. We recognize the apparently radical enactment of nonlinearity inherent in the node-link structure of all hypertext; we proclaim in various ways that revolutionary potential; and then we immediately rearticulate those potentials in terms of our conventional, normal practices. Although I understand that it is impossible to somehow completely step outside of the discourses in which we operate, we should make critical inquiry into the ways in which we rearticulate such technologies a primary interdisciplinary project.

Again and again, we have found it necessary not only to make connections across disciplines, but to identify and relate elements from within one domain to sections of another. By doing this, we have had to examine some of the major shifts in practices and their related conceptualizations and patternings. These patternings too have not necessarily been

Figure 1.3. Sorting, knotting, and swinging: Screenshot from the musician Beck's website. www.beck.com

simply additive; in many instances, they have been metonymic, a brico-lage of potential ingredients, an ongoing engagement in a seemingly penumbral zone. Nevertheless, we have grounded our investigations in an overall sociocultural perspective that places the communicative at the center of multimodal composition and mediatized discourse in action.

A PROJECT ACROSS PROJECTS

Project-Based Research

Project-based inquiry is becoming prominent in research that is motivated to investigate the application and uptake of emergent and new technologies. How we function as knowledge organizations—embroiled in the vicissitudes of funding and effecting teaching and researching—demands that we engage with matters of multimodal composition that draw on multiple competencies and collaborative meaning making. In research today, doctoral degrees are increasingly attached to projects; national-level research projects demand an amalgam of local experts and developers, and participants engage in networks of international scholars and specialists. This too has been the case in researching *Inside Multimodal Composition*. This collection of chapters includes a group of colleagues who have worked with one another over many years alongside others who have collaborated afresh for the book; others have embarked on new projects in wholly new linkages and also written them up as part of these new partnerings. As a whole, we offer theoretical perspectives that are prevalent in analyses of technology, communication, and learning in Scandinavia and through projects developed in partnerships with colleagues from southern Africa. The chapters have also been developed from within an interdisciplinary research center, InterMedia, where practice based inquiry is often linked with conceptual analysis in facing innovation and exploring emerging technologies and their design and use.[1]

The MULTIMO Project

The book is built around a core research and development project called MULTIMO.[2] The project aimed to examine the construction and exchange of multimodal discourse across different domains and across several related projects. Ultimately, MULTIMO was concerned with experimentation with the mixed materialities of meaning making and the means for analyzing them. MULTIMO has benefited from being connected to three other projects running in tandem with it at InterMedia: *Designing Design, ICT-UCT,* and *gRIG.* Several related projects were also connected as is mentioned later.

Links to Related Projects and Partnerships

Designing Design aimed to draw together international and local designers, educators, and researchers in a seminar series.[3] The seminars were to be mediated online and functioned as one of the points of contact and debate for the growth of design research at the University of Oslo. Looking at genres of online mediation was also a feature in the seminars. Related publications appear in journals, conferences, and books (Wagner et al. 2010).

The application of mixed media and methods in cultural composition was also central to the *gRIG* project (Guild for Reality Integrators and Generators). With a focus on mixed reality arts and research by design, *gRIG* drew together expertise and fostered an ecology of experimentation with a range of artistic and research partners from across Europe.[4]

On a different tack, ICT-UCT has looked at supporting the uptake of information communication technologies by educators in the human sciences supported by the Centre for Educational Technology (CET), the University of Cape Town (UCT), South Africa and InterMedia at the University of Oslo, Norway. In a more recent project, in South Africa, research has examined the introduction of wikis as part of undergraduate pedagogy in political science (Carr et al. 2007), one part of a wider cross-center project into building communities of practice around teachers' uses of technology in the humanities (Carr et al. 2008) and workshop-based methods for building situated, online pedagogical resources and relations (see Chapter 7).

This collection includes earlier project-based work and student-based productions in Zimbabwe on multimodal multiliteracies (e.g., Morrison 2001, 2003) related to underlying research into computer-supported learning and concordancing based at the Communication Skills Centre, Linguistics Department at the University of Zimbabwe. Research into critical discourse analysis (Morrison & Love 1996) was also part of a wider view on language and context developed there that contributed to the later focus on multimodal multiliteracies. This has extended to projects based in Norway involving Zimbabwean students of dance and choreography, as well as composition of digital scenography and online mediation of research (see Chapter 12, this volume; Morrison 2003a, Skjulstad & Morrison 2005).

In this collection, there are also two chapters that touch on issues to do with interfaces and communication design. They are the outcome of shared work into digital media and communication design. Part of this has been realized in the MULTIMO project with Synne Skjulstad at InterMedia, funded by a project called Aesthetics at Work. We have also collaborated on earlier projects in interface design and mediated scenography. This collaboration has extended more recently into research on digital advertising and modes of mediated persuasion (Chapter 5) and the inclusion of publics in producing and consuming products and services through new forms of viral, self-, and group-circulated marketing (Morrison & Skjulstad 2007), both part of the Persways project.

The research presented by Gunnar Liestøl (Chapter 3) is the outcome of several intersecting projects into innovation-invention, genre, and digital media, also based at the Department of Media and Communication.[5] The work reported by Anders Fagerjord (Chapter 4) results from his doctoral research at the Department of Media and Communication at the University of Oslo. His interest in multimodality has been furthered by a project called Participation and Play (PaP).[6] Wenche Vagle (Chapter 15) joined the book after working on several of her own. We first co-taught a master's-level course in Oslo in critical discourse analysis in 1992. Thus, her contribution to my understanding of multimodality spans more than a decade of research and discussion.

In addition to the original MULTIMO project group, Andreas Lund (Chapter 12), earlier a postdoc researcher at InterMedia, is a co-author of one of the chapters. His contribution is connected to research into changing collaborative practice and wikis in an Oslo school related to two EU-funded projects: *Kaleidoscope* and *Knowledge Practices Lab*.[7]

The collection also includes Prefaces by colleagues who over the years have contributed greatly to discussions and understanding of multimodality across the disciplines and contexts of communication, from Cape Town to Croatia. A number of the chapters are written with developers and designers: They have not only contributed greatly to the composition of multimodal expressions and a variety of works and their mediations but also to their analysis. *Inside Multimodal Composition* also benefits from the exploratory nature of two interdisciplinary master's theses, as well as four doctoral level studies.

Several other projects are also represented in the book. The authors who report on them from the Department of Media and Communication at the University of Oslo also collaborated with the editor of this book in the early 1990s, and were connected to a joint research and education program between the Department of Media and Communication at the University of Oslo and the Media Programme at the University of Zimbabwe, including the academic communication one in the Linguistics Department. Together these collaborations have spanned critical discourse analysis for Media Studies (with Wenche Vagle); development and research into design, hypermedia, and learning (with Gunnar Liestøl); and music, rhetoric, and web media (Anders Fagerjord). Research based in Norway has also been connected in different ways to joint educational and media projects in southern Africa as part of longer collaboration processes.

OUTLINE OF THE BOOK

Parts and Chapters

The book has five main parts: Framing, Mediating, Making, Documenting, and Reflecting. Each part begins with a short Preface that refers to some of the main issues raised in that grouping of chapters. Many of the chapters could have been placed under more than one of these parts.

Part I: Framing

In Chapter 2, 'Scrabble in a Conceptual Toolbox,' Andrew Morrison presents an overview of some of the major concepts and perspectives taken up in the collection. This chapter extends material covered in Chapter 1. It suggests that, especially in digital domains, multimodal composition needs to account for the emergent and unfolding in the interplay among tools, technologies, and articulations as mediated meaning.

Part II: Mediating

This part of the book aims to take up perspectives on multimodality originating in media and communication studies. The authors have all been closely involved in the production and analysis of 'new media' and here analyze digitally mediated texts through humanistically informed textual analysis.

In Chapter 3, 'PowerPoint Beyond Hardware and Software,' Gunnar Liestøl proposes that, in the understanding of digital media, we attend to an additional level of construction and analysis he calls meaningware. Taking PowerPoint as his case, he demonstrates how the invention of digital genres, not often apparent in learning, needs this level of meaningware because hardware and software alone cannot provide a level of mediated meaning making. Liestøl refers closely to the arguments of Edward Tufte on the limitations of the presentational uses of PowerPoint, but he argues that what is needed is attention to genre design through the classical rhetorical approach of invention. He uses a variety of visuals to show how relationships between showing and telling may be alternatively framed and thereby enrich our notions and practices of multimodality in and as genre design.

In Chapter 4, 'Multimodal Polyphony: Analysis of a Flash Documentary,' Anders Fagerjord carries out a detailed textual analysis of a documentary film on the website by *National Geographic* made in the software Flash. Taking up polyphony as a metaphor from music, Fagerjord explores how different modes and media are used in a multimodal ensemble. He draws on musical terms, such as 'harmony' and 'dissonance,' in analyzing multiple voices and their combinations in online multimodal text.

In Chapter 5, 'Mediating Hybrid Design: Imaginative Renderings of Automotive Innovation on the Web,' Andrew Morrison and Synne Skjulstad examine how a leading commercial automaker uses digital visualization and metaphors from neurology as a means to market a hybrid sport utility vehicle online. Persuasion is achieved through the projection of design innovation via the aesthetic and communicative use of digital tools and associations to popular technoculture.

Part III: Making

This part discusses the processes of multimodal design and construction in production-based research that cover the experimental design of electronic art and experience-driven installation works, as well as shaping of digital resources for online learning by large groups of university students.

In Chapter 6, 'Reactive and Responsive Artifacts in Discourses of Multimodal Embodiment,' Andrew Morrison and Even Westvang examine the relations between the responsively and embodied actions of users to reactive artifacts in the tangible interface of a purposively built electronic installation. From this case, they pose a causative mode that stretches multimodal discourse into the kinetic and the machinic, where the user is asked to fathom out the internal workings of the artifact and incorporates these into their active engagement with it.

Chapter 7, 'Behind the Wallpaper: Multimodal Performativity in Mixed Reality Arts, is by Andrew Morrison, Idunn Sem, and Martin Havnør. Here a blend of the live and mediatized in a mixed reality installation work is explored in terms of multimodal performativity. The work plays with relationships between surfaces, in the form of wallpaper and multiple layers of mediation through back projection and the overlay of the live participants with stored video clips of a dancer.

Chapter 8 by Andrew Deacon, Andrew Morrison, and Jane Stadler is titled 'Multimodal Production and Semiotic Resources for Learning About

Film Narrative.' Large film theory and analysis courses are traditionally lecture- and text-based. The chapter describes an online learning activity, *Director's Cut*, developed to invite undergraduates to apply their under-standings of theory and to edit a short sequence of their own in an educa-tional context where they have little practical experience of this. Related teaching and assessment components support students' 'reading between the lines' filmically and their appreciation of decisions made by the direc-tor, the editor, and others involved in film production. The chapter demonstrates that designing for learning concerns transformation, a con-cept drawn from Engeström's expansive learning model—here the design of the automated feedback mechanism used in guiding students' under-standings of cinematographic conventions.

Part IV: Documenting

Emerging digital technologies permit modes of iterative design and reshaping, as well as storage and distribution that have not only changed our means of making and distribution, but also how we document processes and construct archives. In this part of the book, we focus on issues that lie inside realizing changes in document description, processes of accounting, and mediation of professional digital discourse.

Chapter 9, 'Digitizing Cultural Historical Research,' by Dagny Stuedahl and Ole Smørdal offers a theoretical framework for seeing how multi-modality may be applied to help understand the meaning making of actors in a network of qualitative research mediation. This framework is developed with reference to a wider collaboration related to a project by an ethnologist into the reconstruction of a Viking boat. In an account of the multiplicity of elements and their combinations in composing research into cultural history, the authors draw together concepts and per-spectives from ANT—alignment, negotiation, and translation—and demonstrate how a multiplicity of digital media are involved in the com-position of a network of digital research.

'Blogging the Ephemeral' is the title of Chapter 10 by Andrew Morrison and Per Roar Thorsnes. A review of literature on blogging is linked to the concept of mediated action and applied to a blog case on the development of the collaborative and creative processes of choreography. Drawing on Bakhtin's concept of polyphony, extracts from the related *Docudancing* blog are included as part of the chapter text.

In Chapter 11, 'What Are These? Designers' Websites as Communica-tion Design,' Synne Skjulstad studies web design from a communication design perspective, arguing that existing approaches from HCI and aes-thetics neglect the mixing of media and modes in multimediational designer texts. She refers to the sites of two design companies where attention to the interface forms the content of mediation and promotion of design talent. Skjulstad has devised three concepts that she applies to the material chosen: navigation, layering, and visual density. She relates each of these concepts to their heritages and shows how, through their co-presence and co-articulation, they provide us with analytical tools for the closer examination of websites as more than surface or structural design. She argues that multimodality may be enriched theoretically and analytically from a communication design perspective.

Part V: Reflecting

The chapters in Part V reflect on issues of empirical research into situated meaning through students' and researchers' participation in shaping and interpreting multimodal discourse, as well as its historical and mediated emergence.

'Multiple Activity-Multiple Mediation' is the title of Chapter 12 by Andrew Morrison, Ole Smørdal, Andreas Lund, and Anne Moen. They present a conceptual framework for approaching the phenomenon of wikis as underdetermined tools for collaborative communication that are also mediating artifacts that permit shared meaning making through their enactment. The lens of knowledge building is presented as an aid to the analysis of changing practice. Three projects are presented as a means to opening out discussion of the communicative, technical, and pedagogical design and configuration of activities in wikis that are conducted by multiple actors with varying speaking positions in the nexus of discourse.

In Chapter 13, 'Border Crossings and Multimodal Composition in the Arts,' Morrison discusses developmental and development-oriented learning with digital media. Three case studies relating to Zimbabwe are presented: one in fine arts and two in performing arts. A cultural, historical activity theory frame is adopted drawing on Engeström's model of expansive learning that is critiqued. Multimodal discourse and activity theory are shown to be enriched through the study of students' production of mediating artifacts from the humanities.

In Chapter 14, 'Guiding Meaning on Guided Tours: Narratives of Art and Learning in Museums,' Palmyre Pierroux inquires into narratives of meaning where there is an interplay between given, structured, and guided interpretation and students' independent meaning making. She outlines two main perspectives in the intersection of art and museum education: contextualist and essentialist. She places her study firmly within a sociocultural approach to learning, drawing on Wertsch's concepts of mediation, appropriation, and 'mastery.' Empirically, using discourse and interaction analysis, Pierroux shows how the study of students' discourses on artworks reveals their own processes and awareness of meaning making.

'In the Beginning There Was Only Electricity, Together With Words, Music, and Sounds' is the title of Chapter 15 by Wenche Vagle. Adopting a historical linguistic analysis of the development of semiotic resources in the first 15 years of Norwegian radio, Vagle places these in relation to changing practices of using sound to re-create context and communicability. The chapter is part of a much larger study of Norwegian radio. Drawing on the work of Goffman, Hjelmslev, and Halliday, Vagle proposes models for understanding the emergence of genre in the early compositions of broadcast radio. Her chapter challenges us to reconsider the assertions of the 'new' in digital media and to delve deeper into reflecting on their developmental character.

ONWARD AND UPWARD

'Inter Dis-Communication Machine'

The title of the immersive artwork pictured at the start of the chapter is somewhat unwieldy at first reading: 'Inter Dis-Communication Machine.' However, it points to one of the main paradoxes facing networked and technology-enhanced communication today. Communication is increasingly networked, messages are shared, and our meaning making is collaboratively effected.

Relationships between production and consumption of mediated communication now involve us in an array of digital tools and competencies that are realized increasingly as and through multimodal composition. We not only draw on but also generate the resources involved in the production of communication and its electronically distributed exchanges. The study of such discourse in action points to the importance of activity, and increasingly, its realization via 'social media.' It is the dynamic nature of our mediated meaning making as and in activity that becomes prosthetically acute as embodied interaction and tangible interfaces continue to become additions to earlier modes of verbal and visual communication. Collaboration and shared meaning making become critical, as do the assemblages of mediated articulations and their realizations in multiple activities.

ACKNOWLEDGMENTS

Thanks Ole Erstad, Ole Smørdal, Gunnar Liestøl, Sten Ludvigsen, Synne Skjulstad, and Dagny Stuedahl for invaluable discussions.

NOTES

1. This includes research into technology-enhanced learning and work by other colleagues at InterMedia, an interdisciplinary research center at the University of Oslo (e.g., Rasmussen et al. 2003, Ludvigsen & Mørch 2005) and related research in the region (e.g., Engeström et al. 1999b) including design research (e.g., Löwgren & Stolterman 2004).
2. MULTIMO was part of a national research program into communication, ICT, and media (called KIM in Norwegian). For details, see: http://www.forskningsradet.no/servlet/Satellite?cid = 1088789326338&pagename = kim%2FPage%2FHovedSide. For more details on MULTIMO, see http://www.intermedia.uio.no/projects/research-projects-1/multimo
3. The research project seminar series Designing Design website is available at http://www.intermedia.uio.no/projects/designingdesign/
4. *gRIG* was funded by the EU Culture 2000 Programme. See: http://www.intermedia.uio.no/display/grigsite/Process
5. See Internet in Transition III (site in Norwegian): http://www.media.uio.no/prosjekter/internettiendring/
6. Participation and Play: http://imweb.uio.no/pap/index.php?page_id = 31
7. Kaleidoscope: http://www.intermedia.uio.no/projects/research-networks-1/kaleidoscope-1/kaleidoscope and KP-Lab: http://www.intermedia.uio.no/projects/research-projects-1/kp-lab-knowl edge-practices-laboratory

REFERENCES

Anderson, Daniel. (2003). 'Prosumer approaches to new media composition: consumption and production in continuum.' *Kairos*. Vol. 8, No. 1. Available at http://kairos.technorhetoric.net/8.1/index.html

Bakhtin, Mikhail. (1986). *Speech Genres and Other Late Essays*. Emerson, Caryl & Holquist, Michael (Eds.). McGee, Vern (transl.). Austin: University of Texas Press.

Baldry, Anthony & Thibault, Paul. (2006). *Multimodal Transcription and Text Analysis*. London: Equinox.

Buckingham, David. (2003). *Media Education. Literacy, Learning and Contemporary Culture*. Cambridge: Polity Press.

Carr, Tony, Morrison, Andrew, Cox, Glenda & Deacon, Andrew. (2007). 'Weathering wikis: net based learning meets Political Science in a South African university.' *Computers and Composition*. Vol. 24, No. 3, 266-284.

Carr, Tony, Deacon, Andrew, Cox, Glenda, & Morrison, Andrew. (2008). 'Teaching with technology: a multifaceted staff development strategy.' In Kimble, Chris & Hildreth, Paul. (Eds.). *Communities of Practice: Creating Learning Environments for Educators*. Charlotte: Information Age Publishing. 103-125.

Cope, Bill and Kalantzis, Mary. (Eds.). (2000). *Multiliteracies: Literacy Learning and the Design of Social Futures*. London: Routledge.

Dourish, Paul. (2001). *Embodied Interaction*. Cambridge, MA: The MIT Press.

Engeström, Yrjö, Engeström, Ritva, & Vähäaho, Tarja. (1999a). 'When the center does not hold: the importance of knotworking.' In Chaiklin, Seth, Hedegaard, Marianne & Jensen, Uffe. (Eds.). *Activity Theory and Social Practice: Cultural-Historical Approaches*. Aarhus, Denmark: Aarhus University Press. 345–374.

Engeström, Yrjö, Miettinen, Reijo, & Punamaki, Raija-Leena. (Eds.). (1999b). *Perspectives on Activity Theory*. Cambridge: Cambridge University Press.

Fishwick, P. (Ed.). (2006). *Aesthetic Computing*. Cambridge, MA: The MIT Press.

Haas, Christina. (1996). *Writing Technology: Studies on the Materiality of Literacy*. Mahwah, NJ: Lawrence Erlbaum Associates.

Haas, Christina & Neuwirth, Christine. (1994). 'Writing the technology that writes us: research on literacy and the shape of technology.' In Hilligoss, Susan & Selfe, Cynthia. (Eds.). *Literacy and Computers: The Complications of Teaching and Learning With Technology*. New York: MLA Press. 319–335.

Hachiya, Kazuhiko. (1993). 'Inter Dis-Communication Machine.' [artwork]

Hachiya, Kazuhiko. (1996). 'Inter Dis-Communication Machine.' Honorary mention. *Prix Ars Electronica 1996*. Ars Electronica, Linz, Austria. Available at http://ww w. aec.at/en/archives/prix_archive/prix_projekt.asp?iProjectID = 112 64

Halliday, Michael. (1985/1994). *Functional Grammar*. 2nd edition. London: Edward Arnold.

Hawisher, Gail & Selfe, Cynthia. (Eds.). (1999). *Passions, Pedagogies and 21st Century Technologies*. Logan: Utah State University Press.

Hawisher, Gail & Selfe, Cynthia. (Eds.). (2000). *Global Literacies and the World Wide Web*. London: Routledge.

Jenkins, Henry. (2006). *Convergence Culture*. New York: New York University Press.

Jewitt, Carey. (2005). *Technology, Literacy, Learning: A Multimodal Approach*. London: Routledge.

Jewitt, Carey & Kress, Gunther. (2003). *Multimodal Literacy*. New York: Peter Lang.

Johnson-Eilola, Johndan. (1997). *Nostalgic Angels: Rearticulating Hypertext Writing*. Norwood, NJ: Ablex Publishing Corporation.

Johnson-Eilola, Johndan. (1998). 'Negative space: from production to connection in composition.' In Taylor, Todd & Ward, Irene. (Eds.). *Literacy Theory in the Age of the Internet*. New York: Columbia University Press. 17-33.

Kaptelinin, Victor & Nardi, Bonnie. (2006). *Acting With Technology. Activity, Theory and Interaction Design*. Cambridge, MA: The MIT Press.

Kress, Gunther. (2003). *Literacy in the New Media Age*. London: Routledge.

Kress, Gunther & van Leeuwen, Theo. (2001). *Multimodal Discourse: The Modes and Media of Contemporary Communication*. London: Arnold.

Latour, Bruno. (2005). *Reassembling the Social*. Oxford: Oxford University Press.

Law, John & Hassard, John. (Eds.). (1999). *Actor Network Theory and After*. Oxford: Blackwell.

Lemke, Jay. (1998). 'Metamedia literacy: transforming meanings and media.' In Reinking, David, McKenna, Michael, Labbo, Linda & Kieffer, Ronald. (Eds.). *Handbook of Literacy and Technology: Transformations in a Post-Typographic World*. Mahwah, NJ: Lawrence Erlbaum. 283–301.

Lemke, Jay. (2005). 'Place, pace, and meaning: multimedia chronotopes.' In Norris, Sigrid & Jones, Rodney. (Eds.). *Discourse in Action: Introducing Mediated Discourse Analysis*. Routledge: London. 110-122.

Leont'ev, Alexei. (1978). *Activity, Consciousness, and Personality*. Englewood Cliffs, NJ: Prentice-Hall.

Leont'ev, Alexei. (1981). *Problems of the Development of the Mind*. Moscow: Progress Publishers.

Lotman, J. 2005. 'On the semiosphere.' *Sign System Studies*. Vol. 33, No. 1, 205-229.

Löwgren, Jonas & Stolterman, Eric. (2004). *Thoughtful Interaction Design: A Design Perspective on Information Technology*. Cambridge, MA: The MIT Press.

Ludvigsen, Sten & Mørch, Anders (2005). 'Situating collaborative learning: educational technology in the wild.' *Educational Technology*. Vol. XLV, No. 5, 39-44.

Lund, Andreas. (2006). 'The multiple contexts of online language teaching.' *Language Teaching Research*. Vol. 10, No. 2, 181-204.

Martin, James & Stenglin, Maree. (2007). 'Materialising reconciliation: negotiating difference in a transcolonial exhibition.' In Royce, Terry & Bowcher, Wendy. (Eds.). *New Directions in the Analysis of Multimodal Discourse*. London: Routledge. 215-238.

Miles, Adrian. (2003, Spring). 'The violence of text.' *Kairos* 8.1. Available at http://english.ttu.edu/kairos/8.1/binder2.html?coverweb/vot/index.html

Morrison, Andrew. (2001). *Electracies: Investigating Transitions in Digital Discourses & Multimedia Pedagogies in Higher Education. Case Studies in Academic communication from Zimbabwe*. Unpublished doctoral dissertation. Department of Media & Communication, University of Oslo. 450 pp & 2 CD-ROMs.

Morrison, Andrew. (2003). 'From oracy to electracies: hypernarrative, place and multimodal discourses in learning.' In Liestøl, Gunnar, Morrison, Andrew & Rasmussen, Terje. (Eds.). *Digital Media Revisited*. Cambridge, MA: The MIT Press. 115-154.

Morrison, Andrew & Love, Alison. (1996). 'A discourse of disillusionment: letters to the editor in two Zimbabwean magazines 10 years after independence.' *Discourse & Society*. Vol. 7, No. 1, 39-75.

Morrison, Andrew. & Skjulstad, Synne. (2005). 'Movement in the interface.' *Computers and Composition*. Vol. 22, No. 4, 413-433.

Morrison, Andrew & Skjulstad, Synne. (2007). 'Talking cleanly about convergence.' In Storsul, Tanja & Stuedahl, Dagny. (Eds.). *The Ambivalence of Convergence*. Göteborg: Nordicom. 217-335.

Norris, Sigrid & Jones, Rodney. (Eds.). (2005). *Discourse in Action: Introducing Mediated Discourse Analysis*. London: Routledge.

Rasmussen, Ingvill, Krange, Ingeborg & Ludvigsen, Sten. (2003). 'The process of understanding the task: how is agency distributed between students, teachers and representations in technology-rich learning environments?' *International Journal of Educational Research*. Vol. 39, No. 8, 839-849.

Redström, Johan. (2006). 'Towards user design? On the shift from object to user as the subject of design.' *Design Studies*. Vol. 27, No. 2, 123-139.

Sirc, Geoffrey. (1999). '"What is composition ...?" after Duchamp: (Notes toward a general teleintertext).' In Hawisher, Gail & Selfe, Cynthia. (Eds.). *Passions,*

Pedagogies and 21st Century Technologies. Logan: Utah State University Press. 178-204.

Snyder, Ilana. (Ed.). (1998). *Page to Screen: Taking Literacy Into the Electronic Era*. London: Routledge.

Stöckl, Helmut. (2004). 'In between modes: language and image in printed media.' In Ventola Eija, Charles, Cassily & Kaltenbacher, Martin (Eds.). *Perspectives on Multimodality*. Amsterdam: John Benjamins. 9-30.

Sullivan, Patricia & Porter, James. (1997). *Opening Spaces: Writing Technologies and Critical Research Practices*. Greenwich, CT: Ablex.

Ulmer, Gregory. (1994). *Heuretics*. Baltimore, MD: The Johns Hopkins University Press.

Ulmer, Gregory. (1998). 'Foreword/forward (into electracy).' In Taylor, Todd & Ward, Irene. (Eds.). *Literacy Theory in the Age of the Internet*. New York: Columbia University Press. ix-xiii.

Ulmer, Gregory. (2003). *Internet Invention: From Literacy to Electracy*. New York: Longman.

Vygotsky, Lev. (1962). *Thought and Language*. Cambridge, MA: The MIT Press.

Vygotsky, Lev. (1978). *Mind in Society: The Development of Higher Psychological Processes*. Cambridge, MA: Harvard University Press.

Wagner, Ina, Bratteteig, Tone, & Stuedahl, Dagny. (2010). (Eds.). *Exploring Digital Design*. Vienna: Springer.

Wartofsky, Marx. (1979). *Models: Representation in Scientific Understanding*. Dordrecht: D. Reidel Publishing Co.

Wertsch, James. (1991). *Voices of the Mind. A Sociocultural Approach to Mediated Action*. Cambridge, MA: Harvard University Press.

Wysocki, Anne, Johnson-Eilola, Johndan, Selfe, Cynthia & Sirc, Geoffrey. (2004). *Writing New Media*. Logan: Utah State University Press.

2

SCRABBLE IN A
CONCEPTUAL TOOLBOX

Andrew Morrison

THE IMPORTANCE OF POLYPHONY

As consumers and producers of discourse in a digital age (Jenkins 2006), we move between given designs (platforms, interfaces, etc.) for communication and the enactment of communicative moves that entail a selection of discourse modes and moves. We engage in what Mikhail Bakhtin refers to as speech genres or social languaging, which means anticipating the responses of others in our every *utterance* while participating in the unfolding of the dialogical among texts, contexts, tools, and participants over and in time (Bakhtin 1981, 1984, 1986; Wells 1999; see also Chapter 10 on blogging, and Chapter 15 on radio history). At the level of utterance, argued Bakhtin, every enactment in discourse has in its act of issuing an addressee. Utterances, in turn, are linked with those of others: The multi-accentual or polyphonic character of discourse is realized through the interplay between different 'voices' in texts and in speech (see Chapters 3 and 10).

This chapter offers a range of perspectives and concepts that may help further frame an emerging understanding of multimodal composition as mediated utterances in action. This is a composition that is not declarative: Its 'stance' is transitory, unfolding, and experimental. This unfolding character resonates with the thinking of Gregory Bateson (1979/2000: 7), in that it is a 'living' composition, or *creatura*, one that is built on the emergence of difference and distinctions. Bakhtin also argues that we reach for the dialogical in action, through the enactment of collaborative exchanges that constitute the communicative, or in the case of the chapters gathered here, the multimodally compositional.

How this may be achieved with respect to multimodal texts, exchanges, and their movement in time (i.e., chronotopically; after Bakhtin 1981), also demands that we examine how various perspectives for construction and analysis may be negotiated and combined, not simply converged. This can be seen, for example, in the transposition of prior genre and communicative events from classical rhetoric into emerging practices through presentational tools such as *PowerPoint* (Chapter 3). Across the chapters and in iterative and reflexive relations between making and reflection, in a sense this is to begin to build a transdisciplinary and multimodal approach to matters of both epistemology and ontology, in which an abductive logic is also in play.

'Communication design' is a term taken up in a number of the chapters in this book, some explicitly (e.g., Chapter 11) and others less directly (e.g., Chapter 8). Communication design provides an important overarching perspective on mediated communication and mediated meaning making that transverses disciplinary domains and linkages between technologies and learning, art and design, and culture and context. It enables us, for example, to connect social semiotics with the learning sciences and to situate 'new' media studies in relation to cultural contexts of prior and emerging use (e.g., Ross 2003).

Multimedia Messaging Services (MMS) . . . on TV

On a pragmatic and discursive plane, as 'situated play' (e.g., Turner 1982), Figure 2.1 from the interaction designer Timo Arnall's website shows his design for multimodal messaging from mobile phones to a Norwegian television channel. These functionalities are shown in the various windows: At the top are images of participants, the main large window can function as a photo space for large or thumbnail images, and the column to the right has a roll of text messages that may also include visual components. Different mediations, generated from mobile phones and also computers, may appear on the large high-definition TV screens in homes and bars late into the night and early in the morning. The messaging tends to be generated by teens and young adults; short text entries may lead to voice contact on mobile phones and to online chat.

Figure 2.1. Three screengrabs from the design for MessTV, TVNorge, Norway (Timo Arnall): http://www. elasticspace. com/2003/12/mess-tv

Multiple Senses of 'Scrabble'

In the following sections, a number of core perspectives and concepts are presented that may assist us in the making and analysis of multimodal compositions. These sections form a conceptual toolbox from which further 'multimodal theorizing' may be generated. The metaphor of scrabble offers several senses that may be related to this framing of multimodal composition. Scrabble may refer to a drawing or a doodle. In the processes involved in developing this collection, we have drawn an array of representations, from concept maps to choreographic flows. We have also tried to visualize our enframings of transdisciplinary research.

In a different sense, to scrabble is to actively dig about for something with one's hands. This too has taken place in a 'toolbox' of perspectives and concepts. Our activity has often been to find ways to interrelate inquiry and insights generated by both practice and theory. The concepts and perspectives advanced may be related to the commercial board game *Scrabble* that involves composing words from letters that form patterns that in turn generate scores. The main difference is that, in the game, letters are selected randomly from a large pool, whereas in our 'language game', we offer a number chosen of conceptual artifacts (Bereiter 2002) and perspectives that they may be reordered, combined, and juxtaposed. Ours is a language game that does not aim for triple scores; it is an additive, cross-connotational activity of theorizing a game play between concepts and practices. Through this game play, we offer an extended view of multimodal discourse to what is already precisely formulated within applied linguistics.

In following this cross-connotational patterning, readers are invited to make connections of their own, just as the various contributors have done in their chapters. This is to align with the proposals of Shaffer and Clinton (2006) that we look further into a theory of distributed mind, based on a sociocultural perspective on learning (as outlined in Section 5), that asks that we engage with the generation of the cultural and symbolic aspects of digital culture. This engagement is realized in our contextual interactions with multiple tools and semiotic resources that intersect in the generation of polyphonic discourse in which utterance, unfolding meaning making, and the emergence of new articulations and reflections on them are critical (Bakhtin 1981, 1984, 1986). The multiple activities and mediations involved in these unfoldings—and their intersections, legacies, and distinctions—are central to the realization of multimodal composition. At a meta-level, in this chapter, *'The pattern which connects is a metapattern. It is a pattern of patterns. It is that metapattern which defines the vast generalisation that, indeed, it is patterns which connect'* (Bateson 1979/2000: 11, original italics).

CREATIVITY, COLLABORATION, AND SEMIOSIS

Tapping in

In designing, learning, teaching, and researching with new tools—online, offline, and blends of the two—we need to remain open to both the new and the emerging. In engaging with multimodal and digital composition, what is a challenge is how to tap into collaboration and creativity (Greene 1995; Czikszentmihalyi 1996; Carter 2004; Sawyer 2006). In fashioning and unpacking multimodal composition, we need to find ways to draw on creativity and build it sensibly and carefully into mediated design, semiosis, and research. As many of the chapters demonstrate, research from the humanities may inform studies into digital design and socioculturally framed meaning making. In this respect, relationships between creative production and the reflected analysis may be 'phrased' reflexively, each inflecting the other.[1] Shotter's (2003: 21) reference to orchestral music holds here: '. . . all its participant parts have a living relation with each other; that is . . . they constitute a *dynamically* emerging or *growing* structure, *a structuring structure* one might say' (original italics).

Here Stuart Hall's concept of articulation is useful (Morley & Chen 1996; Hall 1997). He argues that articulation refers to both the giving of a view and the linkages between elements in modes of representation and communication. This concept is seldom taken up in multimodal discourse studies or in ones into mediated meaning making from a sociocultural approach to learning. Concerning changing multiliteracies as utterance and articulation, how we engage with creativity in making meaning is also not often discussed in relation to polyvocal and multimodal enactments that connect the individual with the collective. Where 'third-generation' Activity Theory does this (see e.g., Chapter 13), mediated meaning making that draws on knowledge and experience from the humanities (rhetoric, poetics, narrative, and performance) is largely not discussed.

Creativity occurs across domains and disciplines, and it should not be misconstrued as lying only in the creative arts and industries. Creativity is a resource and a quality that each person and group brings to a dynamic engagement with multimodal and technology-enhanced communication, design, learning, and work. The chapters gathered here have attempted to address these issues of creative design, articulation, and use by engaging with meaning making that is multiply made, multimodally and multimediationally. We have been motivated to generate works and analyses that entail meaning making on the part of the individual and the collective (Moran & John-Steiner 2003). This may be seen at the interpersonal and intersubjective levels. However, it also may be seen at a conceptual level, where 'scrabble' is played out through the laying down of potentially contiguous, even metonymic, formulations onto and through which related utterances may be articulated, in Hall's representational terms, as specific 'views' and linkages (see Figure 2.2).

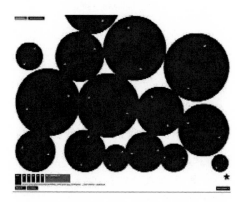

Figure 2.2. Screengrab of interface from electronic art site: www.yugop.com

This is not a matter of simply building semantic cross-references; it involves elaborate meta-perspectives that draw on inductive processes of inquiry but, in a transdisciplinary frame, also abductive ones. Bateson argues that, in thinking about thinking, we include abductive reasoning (drawing on the notion from the semiotician Peirce) and also study relations between elements in and as patterns. For Bateson (1979/2000: 18), 'What has to be investigated and described is a vast network or matrix of interlocking message material and abstract tautologies, premises and exemplifications.' In this collection, we also relate this thinking to the rhizomatic patternings conceptualized by Deleuze and Guattari (1987). What is critical here is not only patterns of information but our patternings in and of them, in effect as nomadic movement. In Bateson's phrasing, the map is not the territory.

Multimodal Discursive Activity

In a series of recent papers, John Shotter (2003, 2006) took up this question of creativity and unfolding with reference to a string of scholars (Bakhtin, Wittgenstein, Vygotsky, Goffman, Bateson, Bergson, and Goethe). Shotter, who has his disciplinary roots in psychology, argues that we need to actively engage with the dynamic, relational unfoldings of our own polyphonic discourses that avoid the boundaries of Cartesian logic that cannot adequately account for the extraordinary that occurs *within* reality. It is this focus on investigating what is within (see Chapter 1) that challenges us to engage with the chiasmic or dynamically intertwined (see also Chapter 6). The responsive, embodied, and situated aspects of our being in the world are therefore in flux, and it is this state of the transitional that places new pressures on us to find as well as be open to finding (Wittgenstein 1953/2001) ways to 'language' relationally. This needs to take place with respect to our surroundings and experience, in the arts and in design, as well as inside our practices and concepts.

This is not a matter of us each retaining a private language for the 'beetles in our own boxes', as Wittgenstein (1953/2001: §293) exemplified in his scenario, in which we are asked to imagine we each have a box containing an object we name beetle, but we cannot see inside one another's boxes. Our inability to see inside (multimodal composition) what we 'hold' makes problematic the relation between sense and reference, and each object we hold thus becomes 'invisible' in our internal languaging. Seeing mediated meaning making as situated in contexts that entail the inscription and activation of communicative and cultural resources highlights the importance of shared composition in finding and collaborating on resemblances between what is within. This is to move, as Vygotsky argues, from the implicit to the explicit, from tacit knowledge to levels of multiple articulation, *in and as multimodal discursive activity*.

For the individual, this is a matter—as a participant or contributor to design, implementation, articulation, and reflection—of entering into active and productive dialogue with others: persons, artifacts, and articulations. At the collective level, such dialogue in technology-enhanced composition and communication requires shared effort that works toward understanding emerging activities and their coordination as collaborative, digitally mediated discourse (Arnseth & Ludvigsen 2006). We take this up, for example, concerning wikis and the unfolding processes of their situated use (Chapter 12; see also Carr et al. 2007).[2]

Sociocultural Semiosis

Drawing on the work of Vygotsky and other sociocultural theorists, studies in mediated learning have taken up the relationship between tools and signs in contexts of communication. Electronic literacies, or electracies as I have called them following the work of Greg Ulmer (see Chapter 13), force us to engage with both the given and the emergent in our classrooms, homes, and professional and public selves (e.g., Burn & Parker 2001). Jay Lemke (1998: 286-287) suggests that:

> Instead of theorising causal relations from one autonomous domain to another (technologies to literacies, literacies to minds, minds to societies), if we unite all these domains as participants in the myriad subnetworks of an ecosocial system, we can give detailed accounts of their interdependencies and the self-organising dynamics of this complex system. We need to break down the artificial boundaries we have tried to create between the mental and the material, the individual and the social aspects of people and things interacting physically and semiotically with other people and things.

Such interdependencies have been the concern of social semiotics (e.g., Lemke 1995; van Leeuwen 1999, 2005a, 2005b; Kress 2003) that has veered away from the functionalism and syntagmatics of structuralist formulation. Still strongly influenced by the work of Michael Halliday, researchers in social semiotics now amplify the importance of multimodal meaning making and accentuate relations between among tools, signs, and significations (connotative and denotative). van Leeuwen (2005a: xi) outlines social semiotics as moving beyond structure and system in its reappointment to the ways people use semiotic 'resources' (in production and consumption). He demarcates how semiotic modes may be compared, contrasted, and integrated in multimodal artifacts and events. He further argues that social semiotics today is concerned with the importance of use in regulating these resources, and how social semiotics is also practice for finding new ways of generating resources and ways of using them (van Leeuwen 2003).

Yet given this reorientation, literature on social semiotics has not taken up many of the challenges of developing such resources in digital domains as is the concern of many of the chapters here. Today, transdisciplinary resources include new media studies, sociocultural approaches to learning and work, information systems and communication design, studies in digital textuality from the humanities, and situated poststructuralist studies in the social sciences. Many of the contributors to this collection also position themselves as design researchers who are engaged in transdisciplinary research into precisely these intersections, in and through action (Morrison et al. 2004). We find social semiotics to be a rich and challenging approach. However, in making and confronting new expressions, we see a need to further connect to related traditions from the humanities also, such as rhetoric as *inventio* in digital domains (see Chapter 2; Fagerjord 2005; Prior et al. 2007) and the changing relations between performance and performativity (see Chapter 7).

Shaffer and Clinton (2006: 292) argue that their meta-concept of 'toolforthoughts' allows us to see tools in social contexts and the consequences that accrue therein. This is important for complex relations among information systems, software, authorship, agency, and social environments in the articulations and exchanges of multimodal composition:

> A theory of distributed mind posits that the fundamental unit of analysis for cognition is not a system composed of human beings and tools but is rather the systematic effects of individual toolforthoughts and the particular forms of social interaction they foster. For each toolforthought, the task is to understand its particular constraints and affordances—and thus how it participates in particular kinds of social interactions at the expense of others.

It is important to stress that without attention to both the design and enactments of mediated communication, the important links between social semiotic resources for making meaning and the processes for enacting semiosis (also in relation to genres, norms, and emerging articulations) are often overlooked. A sociocultural approach to mind, culture, and communication takes mediated activity as its unit of analysis. However, it is the *complexity* of multimodal mediation and its relations to multiple activities—in and over time—that present us with challenges for design, documentation, analysis, and reflection.

The next section looks at the current topography of research on multimodal discourse and points to a need to connect it further to new media studies and to intersections between tools and meaning making in socio-cultural approaches to learning and work. However, what is also important is that research into mediated culture and to the culture industries more broadly is often missed in studies of meaning making in learning at a time when participatory and multimodal composition is rapidly expanding online in networking applications, and zones such as *MySpace* and *FaceBook* and relations between production and consumption are being activated by advertisers in engaging us in persuasive mediated meaning making (Morrison & Skjulstad 2007). In this collection, digital multimodality is connected to earlier studies of multimodal discourse, and links are made to related domains of research and production, making, and analysis that move between meaning potential and our negotiation of affordances for mediated meaning making.

MULTIMODAL DISCOURSE

Expanded Scope

Within applied linguistics and discourse studies, a string of recent book-length publications have addressed the issue of multimodality (e.g., Kress & van Leeuwen 2001; Ventola et al. 2004; O'Halloran 2004; Baldry & Thibault 2006; Machin 2007; Royce & Bowcher 2007). These works largely remain lodged in studies of language, albeit the social semiotics of systemic functional linguistics (SFL; e.g., Halliday 1985); few connections are made to work in critical discourse analysis (e.g., Fairclough 1992; Morrison & Love 1996) to sociocultural perspectives on learning and technology or to multisequential and digital tools and systems in 'new media' other than concordancing. However, there are insightful studies that have addressed visual, auditory, and spatial aspects of multimodality although still within a 'grammatical' frame (e.g., van Leeuwen 1999, 2004, 2005b; van Leeuwen & Jewitt 2001; Stöckl 2004; Matthiessen 2007).

One of the core concepts that has been advanced as a means to meet our changing multiliteracies that span media types, tools, and our sociosemiotic resources is that of multimodality (see Figure 2.3). Kress and van Leeuwen, well known for their publications in social semiotics and visual communication (Kress & van Leeuwen 1996; Kress 1998, 1999), have more recently centered on multimodality (e.g., Kress & van Leeuwen 2001). They define multimodality as '. . . the use of several semiotic modes in the design of a semiotic product or event, together with the particular way in which these modes are combined . . .' (Kress & van Leeuwen 2001: 20). This then also refers to how these modes may reinforce and complement one another or be hierarchically ordered.

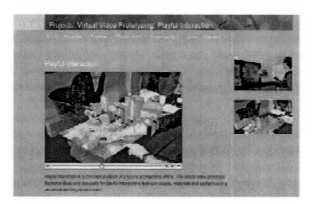

Figure 2.3. The virtual architect, spatial tools for design in a shared work-space a component of the Virtual Video Prorotyoping project at CAVI, Aarhus University, Denmark. http://www.cavi.dk/vvpindex-va.php

There are now works in multimodality and literacies (e.g., Jewitt & Kress 2003), multimodal concordancing (e.g., Baldry 2004; Bateman et al. 2004), and frameworks for multimodal transcription and analysis (Baldry & Thibault 200). Diverging from language-driven approaches to multi-modal discourse, Kress and van Leeuwen (2001: 4) accentuate '. . . the multimodal resources which are available in a culture used to make mean-ings in any and every sign, at every level, and in any mode.' However, despite their powerful sociosemiotic and discourse frames, writings on multimodal discourse seldom feature references to digital domains and the now substantial research publications on 'new' media and digitally mediated design and communication. Most recently, research has begun to be extended to comparisons of print and electronic media, for exam-ple, news (Bateman et al. 2007) and to cartoons (Fei 2007), although the latter still concentrates on sequential structures, media, and reading. In this book, in facing the challenges of making and analyzing multimodal composition, we broadly adopt a *discourse in action* approach that empha-sizes that discourse is created and composed, exchanged, and circulated through its enactment in contexts of use and collaboration (e.g., Wertsch et al. 1995; Scollon 1998, 2001; Norris & Jones 2004; Scollon & Wong Scollon 2004) that also encompasses the digital.

Text and Context

Ventola et al. (2004: 1) characterize text and discourse researchers' attempts to understand communication as responses to two main dis-placements. The first displacement has been that of text from context.

Applied linguists, discourse scholars, and language teachers have all been motivated to connect text and context in approaches to communication that have valued the role of situatedness, or socially shaped meaning making and of adding contextual information to studies of language. The second displacement refers to the separation of language from other means of meaning making. Attempts to investigate, analyze, and theorize multiply made semiosis are now being addressed by linguists such as Ventola et al. (2004). Most often, they argue, disciplinary boundaries and boundedness have kept the study of multiply made discourses within specific frames and means of inquiring about them. Their collection, as is the case with that edited by O'Halloran (2004), moves outward from a base in SFL to examining how discourse may be made and analyzed multimodally.

These collections, however, do not stray from a core SFL focus. Even where they connect to developments in digitally mediated communication, for example, on simulation and temporality (e.g., Lemke 2005,) they make sparse reference to a wider literature that may enrich our understanding of multimodality. Approaches such as these, and indeed those of Kress and van Leeuwen (1996, 2001), are invaluable additions to our research into multimodality. However, their reach inside the making and shaping of multimodal discourse is constrained by the predominance of an underlying grammaticalization and lexicalization linked to SFL. Despite this criticism, Ventola et al. (2004: 1) note that

> . . . it is relatively recent that the developments of the various possibilities of combining communication modes in the 'new' media, like the computer and the Internet, have forced scholars to think about the particular characteristics of these modes and the way they semiotically function and combine in modern discourse worlds.

O'Halloran (2004: 1) too observes that, 'To date, the majority of research in endeavours in linguistics have tended to concentrate solely on language while ignoring, or at least downplaying, the contributions of other meaning making resources.' van Leeuwen (2004) has offered a concise list of reasons as to why linguists need to pay attention to the visual in particular. Where we focus on visual textual analysis of the web (e.g., Chapter 4) and spoken discourses on visual art (Chapter 14), we also include contextual analysis of spoken discourse and the development of radio (Chapter 15).

Communication Ensembles

For Kress and van Leeuwen (2001: 111), '. . . meaning is made in many different ways, always, in the many different modes and media which are co-present in a communicational ensemble.' Our interest in the digital and its design in relation to multimodal discourse is with how it can allow us, rhetorically and poetically, to reach for new patternings and permutations of texts and their situated uses. The notion of the ensemble thus also translates to our collective text and its approaches. The chapters show that multiply made configurations and expressions are realized through and as discourse in action.

Where the transcoding of material from the print paradigm of earlier magazines and textbooks (Kress 1998) has been discussed in terms of a contemporary preponderance for the visual over the verbal, attention has also shifted to representation, enactment, and interpretation in three-dimensional spaces such as galleries (O'Toole 1994, 2004; Pang 2004; van Leeuwen 2005b). Despite these studies, there has been little published on the relations of multimodal discourse theories (originating in social semiotics) to the multilayering of hypertextual and hypermediated texts (e.g., Kok 2004) and dialogical communication presented in websites, blogs, and wikis. These are not only environments in which meaning making is being made collaboratively, but also where its character, stylistics, and textures are realized through incremental discourse re/production conducted by participants using a diversity of media and expressions.

Design and Production of Multimodal Discourses

Attending to a diversity of now intersecting text types, media, exploratory production, and mediated meaning making is important for studies in rhetoric and composition and for investigations into the changing character and practice of multiliteracies (e.g., Buckingham et al. 1995; Buckingham 2003; Wysocki et al. 2004). It highlights the role of activity in the productive discourses of participants to formal and informal learning settings. It allows us to examine relations between text and their contexts of construction and the ways in which they become part of situated meaning making. Attention to the role of design in the forging of these relations is now appearing in writing on multimodality and multiliteracies. However, as we show, this is more complex than to argue that participants to discourse refer at an abstract level to 'available designs' (Kress and van Leeuwen 2001: 5-6). In digital arenas, it is also a matter of designing for participation and thus collaborative composition by users.

In their volume *Multimodal Discourse*, Kress and van Leeuwen (2001) argue that we attend to a variety of modes of communication—sound, image, music, and gesture—in addition to language.[3] Kress and van Leeuwen go so far as to argue that modes and media now pervade both the design and production of discourses. Our aim has been to see how this might be realized in the intersections of media, technology, and collaborative composition and the layers of meaning making involved in their construction and uses. However, we show that this is a complex endeavour whether in technology-enhanced collaborative learning in wikis or the elaborations of the roles of software and 'choreography' in performatively shaping an art installation. This is because the composition of multimodal discourses is more than a combination of modes. It is about complex relations of modes as well as elements within them. These are not simply recombinations or remediations (Skjulstad 2007).

Fei (2004a: 222) proposes a multilevel model for describing and analyzing multimodal texts. He calls this the Integrated Multisemiotic Model (see also Fei 2004b, 2007). His model is designed to account for both composite and componential aspects of multimodal discourse. Fei argues that we may extend Halliday's meta-functions to communication planes. These planes make it possible to look beyond the notion of 'grammatical metaphor' proposed by Halliday to 'semiotic metaphor.' Fei's work offers a complex model that draws together meta-functions and links them to three planes of communication: expression, content, and context (after Martin 1992). As several chapters in our collection argue, however, such an approach to multisemiosis needs to be further repositioned to account for dynamic discourses and texts that entail mixed media activated and realized in multiple activities (Bødker & Bøgh Andersen 2005). Royce (2007) suggests how this might be developed concerning verbal-visual relations in print (not digital) text through co-occurrence of these modes in relations of intersemiotic complementarity. However, as, for example, an analysis of designers' webtexts (Chapters 5 & 11) indicates, these relations may be both complementary and contrasting, where the medley of 'language functions' (not only 'textual' ones) transverses information and communication designs for multiple activities in nonsequential discourse structures and their multimediational reading paths and uses.

For the most part, our studies do not apply a formal SFL frame; what they offer instead is a trajectory of multimediational, multimodally framed inquiries into some of the interdisciplinary challenges that face multimodal composition. In many senses, we argue that these inquiries still await further linkages with research in a wider systemic functionalist view that has multisemiosis as its core. Fei's model may offer a boundary object for this purpose—the three communicative planes might be connected to communication design, and his space of integration among medium, materiality, and 'language' functions that span language and image may be extended to other areas of multimodality, such as spatial ones in exhibition (Martin & Stenglin 2007) and via multimodal, electronic installation arts (e.g., Chapter 7). The challenge that confronts many transdisciplinary scholars, however, is how to access the complex, rich potential of SFL without considerable background in this field. The work of

Kress and van Leeuwen offers considerable means toward deciphering and developing studies in multimodal discourse, not only language. In transdisciplinary studies into multimodality, the distinction between and across definitions of the 'object' of inquiry is likely to continue (e.g., Activity Theory and Actor Network Theory [ANT]). At a meta-level, multimodal discourse studies may well be enriched by reexamining discourse and power relations grounded in critical discourse analysis and them further to the rapidly emerging complex of production and consumption of multimodal composition in digital domains (e.g., social software and its transference to mobile communication that is now beginning to be enacted, technically and discursively; see Morrison et al. in press).

As Martin and Stenglin (2007: 236) argue, we need to pay close attention to context because a major challenge for a 21st-century social semiotics is '. . . how to reconcile genesis and systematicity (diachrony with synchrony as it were). Focusing multimodal analysis on sites where people try to make the world a better place may be one useful way of spurring this dialectic along.' For many of the contributors, this leads us to what we refer to as communication design, which is based on transdisciplinary, production-based inquiry. Our research covers text analysis, developmental and participatory design, and the study of contexts of situated use. Our view on Communication design is a sociocultural one—situated meaning making is built through shared design processes, via the tools and resources we apply, and in our collaborative encounters in fashioning mediated meaning making—and reflections on it.

COMMUNICATION DESIGN

Linking Multimodalities and Mediated Meaning Making

In this collection, we pay close attention to the importance of sociocultural perspectives on design, multimodal discourse production, and analysis and their relations to technology-enhanced pedagogies and the emerging practices of multiliteracies. We extend this to the notion of 'communication design.' We have developed this term as a means of framing design processes and developmental aspects of sociosemiotic and situated approaches to mediated meaning making. Communication design is a plastic term. It moves between the deliberate and unfolding iterations of design activity. It may be moved to suit specific contexts and needs as the focus shifts from form and function to articulation. This dynamic is important in our research. It informs the application of concepts and the selection of methods. As the pursuit of design reaches for what is not yet quite in place, a focus on communication works to situate that grasping in contexts of development and use. In contrast to other influential approaches, such as interaction design (Löwgren & Stolterman 2004) and participatory design, as well as representations in learning (e.g., Ivarsson & Saljö 2005), communication design strives to integrate a variety of modes and means of mediation in the production and uptake of mediated meaning making.

The well-framed design of resources for meaning making in discourse events and artifacts provides participants with the potential for developing their competencies, articulating their intentions, and, in the case of both of these, sharing these in dialogue with others. Concerning multimodal composition, focusing on communication design allows us to cross disciplinary boundaries and the necessary points of passage in various yet related approaches to the study and practice of mediated meaning making, whether in language, visual rhetoric, media-specific articulations, or explorations with new tools (Morrison et al. 2004; Morrison & Skjulstad 2007; Skjulstad Chapter 11).

Digital Textualities

In a wider communication design view, what is crucial is to see how various elements to mediatized discourse texts, events, and enactments form an overall entity (see Figure 2.4). For example, one of the contributors to this volume has argued elsewhere that we pay close attention to the role of montage as a motif in dynamic digital discourse (Skjulstad 2007) that is nonetheless connected to understanding overall textual coherence. Developing coherence across and between different modes—whether spoken or written, visual or kinetic—in multimediational texts places demands on our involvement with them (Halliday & Hasan 1976). This refers to our potentially multiple activities in roles as designers and developers, educators and students, and critics and researchers, to mention a few.

Figure 2.4. *Listening Post* (Hansen, Mark & Rubin, Ben), Ars Electronica 2004 (Photographs: Andrew Morrison)

'New' media studies into digital textuality often argue that we need to recognize two aspects that may also intersect with one another. The first is the argument that one is always composing the new in relation to the prior (e.g., Gitelman 2006). The second aspect is that digital textuality is marked by the generation of hybrid-composed texts (e.g., Bolter & Gromala 2003). Both these approaches inform our practices of designing and developing mediated communication. They assist us in developing analyses of multiply mediated texts and their uptake in diverse and multiple contexts. However, what these approaches miss are the *transpositional and metonymic aspects* of multimodal discourses, in which complex, dynamic characteristics are in play. This complex, as we argue, is very much to do with the intersections of multiple media and information systems with multiple communicative activities. These are significant in the design and uses of mediated communication.

Electronic Art and the Enactment of Multimodal Composition

To date, there are few studies of multimodality and electronic art; rarely too do studies of multimodality reference the now extensive literature on 'software aesthetics' or aesthetic computing (Fishwick 2006). Studies in multimodal communication need to be extended to these domains, and this is what we argue in Chapters 6 and 7, which are explicitly connected to electronic installation works. In these chapters, we cite a large body of publications and suggest that attention is needed to codesign the computational, and the gestural, and ways in which kinetically framed engagement and enactment are already moving into the mainstream. The wand-like *Wii* from Nintendo merges the embodied gestures of physical, tangible interfaces of arcade games with the wearily worn gyrations of joystick and mouse click of laptop and desktop gaming.

Investigations and expressions in electronic art have stressed the potential and significance of breaking known barriers and conventions by repurposing and reassigning affordances and conventions in and through the computational and its recodings. This differentiates it from the major commercial domain of gaming and even the often freely available interpersonal networking of social software sites and applications. Electronic art may be seen as adding to multimodal mediation through its expressive innovations (see Figure 2.5). Ultimately, these are poetic; they are crafted to engage us in a variety of interplays with the digitally mediated, often in a medley of media and modes, and increasingly in the form of installations. These installations are cast as mixed reality works, a mix of the materially here and now and the digitally stored and generatively emergent. As we argue and show, this is also a matter of moving from

Figure 2.5. Gallery visitors in the Young Tate programme for young adults run by young adults. Tate Modern, London, U.K. PDA and sound information on a painting (left): active table and related projection (right). (Photographs: Palmyre Pierroux)

earlier notions of interaction and interface design as reactive to more responsive stances. The concept of performativity is being developed to explain the complex relations between the machinic in the design of computational art environments and our human endeavours and actions in completing or realizing these works kinetically. In Chapter 7, we take this up in detail and suggest it may be framed in what we term *multimodal performativity*.

This is to acknowledge and yet extend the concept of discursive performance developed by Judith Butler (1993) that importantly placed focus on genre, gender and embodiment. Terry Threadgold (1997: 1, 103-109), also writing from a feminist perspective, however, suggests that, advancing stories and perspectives on positionality, we also need to include meta-linguistic and discursive critiques of the stories we rewrite. This too demands that we engage with their materialities and contexts of enactment (Threadgold 1997). In moving to a notion of multimodal performativity, we follow this direction: We nurture the unfolding complexities by arguing that these meta-critiques are even more important precisely because they are embedded and enfolded in multiple valencies. They come into being via cross-mediations and in the dynamics of twingled systems design and their polymorphous enactments between among the textual, the social and cultural, and the technical.

The Importance of Articulation

In unpacking the processes and products of mediated meaning making as artifacts (including electronic discourses), a communication design approach needs to understand the relationships between among tools, signs, and their significations (i.e., as articulations). It is this latter point that we are motivated to highlight, especially the role of media and communication in multimodal discourse. The articulation, or composition, of meaning making in modes and media—in multiple relations, intertextually and interpersonally—is often overshadowed in studies into 'interaction design' where media, mode, and mediation are not the focus.

SOCIOCULTURAL PERSPECTIVES

Multimodal Compositions and Meaning Making

With the many and rapid changes in technology-enhanced design, learning, and communication, it is important to be able to situate emerging texts, mediations, and shared articulations (i.e., as multimodal compositions) in relation to theories of individual and collective development and understanding. A sociocultural perspective on mediated meaning making, following Bakhtin (1981, 1986), Vygotsky (1962, 1978), and later Leonte'v (1978, 1981), among others, offers a diverse yet substantial and robust means for conceptualizing and analyzing the changes in personal and collective meaning making with respect to tools, signs, and mediation.

A sociocultural perspective asserts that design, learning, transformation, meaning, and communication are realized through social relations and mediated activity that take place in developmental processes and situated contexts. (Engeström 1987; Wertsch 1991; Engeström et al. 1999). These scholars provide rich conceptual frameworks within which to investigate and analyze multimodal discourse in the making. We also refer to Activity Theory and its formal apparatus for unpacking relationships between these aspects in developmental communication. In addition to most of the influential Activity Theory studies of work, informatics, and learning, we also focus on art, communicative and creative design, and a mix of analogue and digital media.

A sociocultural perspective tackles the relationships between the historical and institutional contexts and situations of discourse and the ways in which we process and contribute to understanding them though action (Wertsch et al. 1995). This action is realized not only in the mind, but in social interaction through which both individual and collective meaning making are constituted and taken up in action (Wertsch 1998, 2002). The dynamic of social interaction is also part of the semiotic resources on which we draw to fathom new problems and elaborate existing knowledge (Engeström 1999, 2001). It is the attention to the dynamics of meaning making as socially and culturally generated that is also important to analyze. In addition to attention to digital textuality (see e.g., Chapter 11 on communication design in websites), a richer view of a sociocultural approach to communication design and mediated action includes the processes and realizations embodied in design, as well as those articulated through situated use and refined through reflection on action.

Drawing on studies in the learning sciences, a sociocultural perspective encompasses various views. These include distributed and situated cognition (Lave & Wenger 1991) and community of practice (e.g., Wenger 1998; Wenger et al. 2002), Cultural Historical Activity Theory (CHAT), and approaches to mediated action. A sociocultural perspective has been widely applied in studies of learning, including recently the emerging domain of Computer Supported Collaborative Learning. Many studies have concentrated on vertical developments in linkages between tools and meaning making. In this collection, we argue for the importance of horizontal relations and transdisciplinarity, through which the complex of multimodally mediated communication may be enacted and studied. CHAT not only draws on the work of Vygotsky and the concept of mediation but extends this through Leont'ev to the study of collective activity in addition to individual action. Here a three-level model allows us to distinguish between activity, action, and operation (Leont'ev 1978). Activity is oriented toward the object or motive, actions are driven by goals related to the object and may be both individually and collectively framed, and operations are geared toward tools and the conditions through which they are routinized. In activity, tensions and contradictions arise, and these are forces for change and transformation. Taken together, these concepts allow us to look inside mediated action.

Mediated Action

Central to a sociocultural perspective is the concept of mediated action (Wertsch 1991). This allows us to examine relationships between tools and signs as culturally shaped and shaped by culture (Wartofsky 1979). Tools and signs in the views we cover are realized in and as multimodal texts as artifacts and in multimodal discourses via 'dialogue' at the level of articulation. Mediation is therefore not static but part of the emerging and changing character of meaning making in action. However, mediation needs to be understood not only in terms of language but the interplay of a range of modes of making meaning that encompass bodily, temporal, stylistic, and expressive domains (see Figure 2.6). Bakhtin (1981, 1986) saw this as 'social language' that is built up through a web of earlier texts and articulations and always directed toward an audience or addressee. For us, this is part of a wider communication design view. Genres, modes of address, and the means we employ to realize them as messages are part of what is a mediating activity, This is constantly being negotiated through social interaction and the roles and 'speaking' posi-

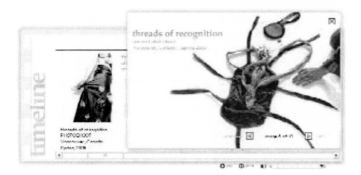

Figure 2.6. Website on whisper/s project, Simon Fraser University, BC Canada. With scrollable project windows and overlays. http://whisper.iat.sfu.ca/

tions we adopt and are able to access and articulate with respect to cultural and institutional conventions and formations.

One educational model approached to account for this complex of mediations is that of expansive learning by Engeström (1987). This model is concerned with the developmental and transformative aspects of learning. In Chapter 7, we take this up on students' engagements with an online learning environment designed to guide them in the fundamentals of film editing and genre composition. The model is also applied across three projects that involved cultural and contextual study of mediated activity in the arts relating to southern Africa (Chapter 13). Mediated action also needs to be seen in relation to historicity, argues Engeström. More recent versions of CHAT have taken up the challenge of understanding multiple systems of activity and their intersections around potentially shared objects. Here work is ongoing in developing an apparatus to help account for the meaning making that is made through multiple activities. One core concept is that of multivoicedness of these intersections. We discuss this further in Chapter 10 on blogging and choreography and the work of Bakhtin in particular.

Meaning Making and Discourse in Action

With the changes and challenges that technology-enhanced communication present to us and we ourselves enact, a sociocultural perspective allows us to examine mediated discourse as events and in and as action. However, it also leaves room for looking into the unfolding of activities and the temporary, tentative, piecemeal, complex, and recursive turns we may take in reflecting on those activities when they are in flux. Meaning making is framed ultimately via the meta-tool of language, which allows us access to a shared mode of articulation so as to more closely reflect on the moves from appropriation to mastery (Wertsch 1991) and the shift from everyday to scientific concepts (Vygotsky 1978).

In these and other chapters, we are interested to make linkages, not separations, between analyses of problems and the zones or spaces they constitute by way of tools, signs, and mediating artifacts. CHAT is an approach that has not been widely adopted in media studies or in the humanities, although it has been applied in information sciences (e.g., Nardi 1996). This collection, therefore, aims to show that, in conjunction with other approaches and through selections and argumentations, a sociocultural perspective may be fruitfully applied to understand the complex, collective mediations and multiple intersections in mediated communication that is increasingly multimodal.

Mixed Mediations With Multiple Activities

In summary, we take composition to be a multiply made process and product. For example, in the chapter that looks at the processes of creative construction in choreography via a blog, we present the multiple views of participants involved in the process who using written words, still images, video, and hypertext to construct a selective auto/ethnography of composition. It is the situatedness of meaning making that is central. In a further link, however (and one not commonly made), we situate medium-based approaches to new media (e.g., Manovich 2001; Bolter & Gromala 2003) in relation to sociocultural perspectives (largely applied to learning and work) that is informed by notions of mediated action and the interplay of tools, signs, and mediations. In the next section, mention is made of the need to look at the socially and machinically assembled networks of the multimodally mediated that the sociocultural perspectives originating largely in psychology given here do not address to the same extent.

NETWORKS AND ASSEMBLAGES

Actants, Networks, and Negotiations

What we see as needed in studies of multimodality in a digital age is inquiry into the cross-mediation of semiotic resources in and as communicative practice. Our view is that resources are simultaneously present in texts and are realized in dynamic and intersemiotic shifts (Iedema 2003: 42) that are realized, to refer back to Halliday, through activity in situations. Here we also extend activity from its largely social meaning-making focus on human languaging to include the dynamics of Human-Computer Interaction (HCI). However, it is digital discourse that concerns us, but not just the technological or humanist determinism of early studies of 'new' media or HCI.

Actor Network Theory (ANT; e.g., Law & Hassard 1999) has ascribed symmetrical agency to humans and machines in technologized communication. Latour (2005: 237) encourages us to follow the actors and flow and not to separate object and subject views. He refers to what he terms circulating entities as mediators, thereby extending his earlier notion of actants:

> Mediators have finally told us their real names: 'We are beings out there that gather and assemble the collective just as extensively as what you have called so far the social, limiting yourself to only on standardized version of the assemblages: if you want to follow the actors themselves, you have to follow us as well.' (Latour 2005: 240)

However, these agencies may also be seen to be less symmetrical than earlier proposed by ANT, in that as designers, developers, artists, educators, students, and researchers, we are interested in the purposes or motivations of our activities in deploying the machinic in the compositional in which we are the primary meaning makers (Kaptelinin & Nardi 2006).

In these unfoldings, negotiations and translations of different perspectives take place. These too may be understood as crossing domains and interests. In an ANT approach (e.g., Latour 1996, 1999, 2005; Law 1997), such transactions involve us in partnerings with technologies that are 'actants.' We also argue that it is the relations between actors—human and machine—in networks of relations, negotiations, and translations (e.g., Law 1997) that are important in understanding our changing multi-literacies and mediated practices (see Chapter 8). Following the work of Latour, we may argue that the sites of composition and the assemblages and relations of the actors are also a part of changing agencies between technologies of communication and our mediated articulations.

Building a Patchwork of Links

Latour (2005: 253) suggests to us as analysts that 'Critical proximity, not critical distance, is what we should aim for.' However, as is mentioned later, in human-machine negotiations, questions arise about ascribing agency and intentionality to the machinic, and thereby the articulation of meaning. This too extends to artistic domains, which are included in our research. Links between ANT and Activity Theory are still being framed, and this collection does not claim to elaborate them definitively. Hanseth (2007) reminds us that ANT too is in flux, especially concerning complex systems and information communication technologies. He points out that a new set of terms are now being taken up, namely, multiplicities, inconsistencies, ambivalence, and ambiguities (Hanseth 2007: 84).

The contributors to *Inside Multimodal Composition*, each interested in technologically enhanced discourse as both marked by social and cultural inheritances yet contemporaneously contingent on the emergent and potentially inconsistent, see human activity as the primary driver of mediated communication. Meaning making, as creative construction and as interpretation, is first and foremost situated in our embodied interactions (e.g., Dourish 2001) and shared hermeneutics. These are realized individually and collectively within and across multimodal discourses.

Work in production-based inquiry and close textual analysis has encouraged us to see how the articulation of multimodal compositions may be influenced by the unexpected through generative computing that offers us unseen and unexpected permutations and configurations. These too, in turn, may further unsettle, alter, or confirm our expectations and influence our ongoing acts of composing. In short, it is the dynamics of multimodal mediational communication that continues to engage and challenge us.

Composition in the Making

These interdisciplinary linkages, some more tentative than others, are also about the texturings of boundary object and crossings (e.g., Star 1989) and inquiry into changes in representations that concern the emergent and the nomadic (Deleuze & Guattari 1987). Despite their necessary sequential presentation, the chapters may be seen to constitute a rhizome of topics and 'structures' that is concerned not only with the mutable, but the work within. This has to do with shared compositions in the making. In making these compositions—iteratively and increasingly as part of complex interdisciplinary digital design processes—it has been important to pay attention to the dynamics of co-construction and their collaborative communicative use.

CHAT and ANT have now been widely applied to the study of organizations, networks, and technoscience. However, they are rarely seen as complementing one another (e.g., Miettinen 1999), nor are they predominantly applied in relation to the domains of rhetoric, art, and design. To some degree, it may be fruitful to pursue interdisciplinary theorizing that is ontologically multimodal so as to open up a plane for identifying passage points (Latour 1999) as dialogical zones for transdisciplinary convergence between among mode, medium, articulation, and expression.

In our creative and critical engagement with project and production-centered inquiry, inductive and abductive logic have repeatedly appeared almost within grasp as we have struggled to take hold of our own changing electronic multiliteracies or electracies (Ulmer 1994, 2003; Morrison 2001, 2003). So often we write about these on the part of our students. Here we include these as part of a wider and ongoing transformation of multimodality in mediated communication in which various participants—students, researchers, designers, programmers, and choreographers—are involved in 'learning to write the technology.'

TOWARD TRIPLE SCORES?

Moving With the Polyphonic

The screengrab shown in Figure 2.7 has been chosen to draw together the perspectives presented above. It is taken from a new social network site in Norway called *Origo* developed by Bengler media, to which one of the contributors of this book, Even Westvang, belongs. *Origo* is based on an earlier and still lively invitation-only social calendaring service for Oslo called *Underskog*. Meaning undergrowth in Norwegian, *Underskog* realizes many of the features now so widely used in *FaceBook*. In contrast to other ethnographic studies of social networking (e.g., boyd 2004; boyd & Heer 2006), we have analyzed the design and performative discourse of

Figure 2.7. Screengrab of start page with global view from social networking site, Origo, Norway.

Underskog in a jointly authored polyphonic study that acknowledges multiple contributions between among design and analysis, key events in development processes of the system, and emerging needs and wants from users drawn from use (Morrison et al. in press). *Origo* takes this approach further into the public domain and in its mediated representations and articulations, not only as discourse across links (Kolb 1996) but as *multimodally relational discourse*.[4]

Such a polyphonic process of design and mediated expression may be 'cast' as a *digitally performative discourse*. This is one in which multiple 'players' engage in an online environment that is framed to allow for participation, event sharing, and collaborative and dialogical processes or mediated meaning making. What is now already being realized through this communication design—as platform and as shared discursive process—is similar to what Shaffer and Clinton (2006: 297) envisage in applying their concept 'toolforthoughts' to the building of distributed cognition: 'A theory of distributed mind suggests what what matters instead is what students will be able to accomplish in collaboration with toolforthoughts.'

To return to the earlier discussion on approaches to emerging multimodal discourse, as Shaffer and Clinton (2006: 297) argue, we need to distinguish between things that move and our human actions in digital culture. The many related projects that make up *Inside Multimodal Composition* each in their own way, and as a composite, address the unfoldings and dynamics of mediated meaning making. We take up, review, and suggest a variety of concepts and related theories in order to do this. At a macrolevel, these include, among others, multiple activity and multiple mediation, mediating artifacts, reactivity and causality, multimodal performativity and enactment, expansive learning, nonlinear and chronotopic text, multimodal ensembles and multimodal persuasion. They extend to meaningware and invention, complex relational structures and patterns, alignment and negotiation, developmental and historical genre, and mediated meaning making and appropriation.

Multimodal Composition on the Move

Understanding multimodality in the composition of mediated action and the mediation of composition in design and use have been our concerns. We have looked into how to design for dynamic interfaces, where and when to use which media, and what to move between different modes and shared communicative spaces in our situated discourses.

In these moves, the monumental and the ludic are copresent, iconically and indexically. In the contexts of learning about art in museum settings, there is an interplay between institutional discourses and those of individual learners (Chapter 14). Laughter and a playful physicality of responding to an installation work as it unfolds draw us into a wider multimodal staging and mediated performativity on the part of participants in and as embodied interaction (see Chapter 7).

In Figure 2.8, toy balloons are a cipher for mediated dialogue that is 'on the move.' This dialogue is realized in the context of wider cultural and creative industries, alongside those of deliberative design and unscripted popular use. Following Bakhtin, it is one that is polyphonic, more than a ring tone, or a call waiting signal. The dialogical in mediated meaning making is about collaborative communication that may be more complex than the sequentiality of a single conversation. At the level of utterance, recent developments in social software applications allow us to realize how networks of mediated discourse, linking sets of tools and articulations, have developed in tandem. Educationally, and in creative expressive communication, this allows us to move from the notion of discourse across links to linking discourse in and as mediated action across media types and in communication.

Deleuze (1993/1997) argued in *Essays: Critical and Clinical*, his last publication while alive, that we need to examine the imminent conditions concerning what our philosophizing is addressing, as movement. This is likely to become even more critical as developments in handheld communication are already making it possible to generate and comment on discourses that are made on the move. This marks a further shift for multi-mediational, multimodal literacies as they slither off desktops and laptops, into our hands, across multiple and wireless contexts, enacted by the gestural swipe of an RFID marker or the unsolicited beckoning of a GPS-driven service. We need to follow these movements not only empirically, but philosophically too.

Figure 2.8. Semiotic resources on sale. Mobile phone balloons, Florence Italy. (Photograph: Andrew Morrison).

'Clearing a Path for Composition'

In the pages that follow, there are echoes of student voices from museums, shards of former boats lying alongside paper models, and the hewing of wood for new voyages today recorded on video and now troubling categorization digital archives. We have included websites that accelerate in their own time of mediation and via the dynamics of designers' own expert compositions, as well as those dancing different processes. We have shown how software may be used to meet student-scripted attempts at editing film noir. The feathered head of a dancer is overlaid by digital scenography that allows abstracted cave paintings to dance on his skin as he moves between temporal planes of the acutely present and the shadowy distant.

Against these backdrops, we recall the directions given by Latour (2005: 261) on understanding how to conduct social science relationally:

> Clear the path for the composition so that it can go through the complete loop and take it up again, making sure that the number, modes of existence, and recalcitrance of those that are thus assembled are not thwarted too early.

Fortunately, there has been little recalcitrance in the project groups and partnerships assembled here. However, there were many instances when our overall goals seemed likely to be thwarted by the pull of diverse interests and needs. Despite this, for readers we hope that our 'multimodal assemblages' may create several relational loops back to their own designing, teaching, and researching in the many domains of technology-enhanced communication. For us, this would be to have achieved, to echo Bateson (1979/2000: 7), 'the pattern that connects.'

ACKNOWLEDGMENTS

The contributors to this book made valuable suggestions for this chapter and enriched it with their individual texts. My thanks to Ola Erstad and Sten Ludvigsen for critical comments en route, and especially to Synne Skjulstad, Ole Smørdal, Even Westvang, Dagny Stuedahl, and Lars Lomell, without whom this chapter would be the poorer.

NOTES

1. For us, this is to stretch, not replace, linguistic formulations and foundations of multimodality within a wider frame of mediated meaning making. This extension demands to involve closer attention to matters of design that is anticipatory as much as it works out of given and assured experience and reflection. Here, as Carter (2004) argues, we need to not only understand but also give voice to the processes and positions of creativity in the arts that all too easily may be overridden by what he labels the algebraic formalism of some studies in social semiotics. The value of creativity from the arts may not always be visible in or connected to formalist empirical studies in multimodal discourse, design, and learning. It is through studies of rhetoric, poetics, and aesthetics that multimodality may also be extended to the speculative and the imaginative. This allows us to investigate processes of composing, that is, the giving of form and the multiple utterances and articulation that have always also been present in the ongoing negotiations and transformations of the meaning making. It also allows us to take a reflexive turn back to other types of inquiry and to contribute to them.

2. This reminds one of the work of Bateson (1979/2000: 134, original italics) and his concept of double description:

> For change to occur, a double requirement is imposed on the new thing. It must fit the organism's internal demands for coherence, and it must fit the external requirements of environment. . . . what I have called double description becomes double requirement or double specification. The possibilities for change are twice fractionated.

3. The concept of 'meaning potential' from Halliday lies behind much of recent work on multimodal discourse and the related field of social semiotics. Meaning potential refers to the potential for signification that words, sentences,and discourse may realize, that is drawn from earlier contexts and purposes of use and circulation, via and as use and not only as structure. This potential is then realised in situated activity as well as in our engagement with tools, technologies, discourse conventions and social formations and relations. Meaning potential is related to Halliday's (1985) conceptualization of four main meta-functions of language, referred to in terms of meaning, and influenced by Jacobsen and Hjelmslev (see also Chapter 15). Experiential meaning concerns our shaping of experience in the world, interpersonal meaning refers to social relations, textual meaning concerns the ways we arrange and convey messages as articulations, and logical meaning is to do with the framing of logical relations.

4. The image is of the start screen that here is oriented to Oslo and not to its many other locales across the country. In the site, at the top is a strip of images from contributors. Below is a map that is centered on the position of who sees the page (explicitly or from their IP). To the left, posts shown are marked pub-

lic. In the right-hand column (not all visible here), 'Zones' show those with the highest number of new members in the past week. 'People' signals the most recent log-ins, while 'Local zones' identifies examples of collaborations with local newspapers, and 'Events' refers to popular happenings. The map is marked to show how often items have been geolocated by users, while 'Identity and roles' points to members that are authenticated and the roles that may be used to sign posts. 'Conversations' list just that, with recent comments.

REFERENCES

Arnseth, Hans Christian & Ludvigsen, Sten. (2006). 'Approaching institutional contexts: systemic versus dialogical research in CSCL.' *International Journal of Computer-Supported Collaborative Learning*. Vol. 1, No. 2, 167-185.

Bakhtin, Mikhail. (1981). *The Dialogic Imagination: Four Essays by M.M Bakhtin*. Holquist, Michael (Ed.). Emerson, C. & Holquist, M. (Transl.). Austin: University of Texas Press.

Bakhtin, Mikhail. (1984). *Problems of Dostoevsky's Poetics*. Emerson, Caryl (Ed. & Transl.). Minneapolis: University of Minnesota Press.

Bakhtin, Mikhail. (1986). *Speech Genres and Other Late Essays*. Emerson, Caryl & Holquist, Michael (Eds.). McGee, Vern (Transl.). Austin: University of Texas Press.

Baldry, Anthony. (2004). 'Phase and transition, type and instance: patterns in media texts as seen through a multimodal concordancer.' In O'Halloran, Kay. (Ed.). *Multimodal Discourse Analysis*. London: Continuum. 83-108.

Baldry, Anthony & Thibault, Paul. (2006). *Multimodal Transcription and Text Analysis*. London: Equinox.

Bateman, John, Delin, Judy & Henschel, Renate. (2004). 'Multimodality and empiricism: preparing for a corpus-based approach to the study of multimodal meaning-making.' In Ventola, Eija, Charles, Cassily & Kaltenbacher, Martin. (Eds.). *Perspectives on Multimodality*. Amsterdam: John Benjamins. 65-87.

Bateman, John, Delin, Judy & Henschel, Renate. (2007). 'Mapping the multimodal genres of traditional and electronic newspapers.' In Royce, Terry & Bowcher, Wendy. (Eds.). *New Directions in the Analysis of Multimodal Discourse*. London: Routledge. 147-172.

Bateson, Gregory. (1979/2000). *Mind and Nature: A Necessary Unity*. Cresskill, NJ: Hampton Press & The Institute for Intercultural Studies.

Bereiter, Carl. (2002). *Education and Mind in the Knowledge Age*. Hillsdale, NJ: Lawrence Erlbaum Associates.

Bødker, Susannne & Bøgh Andersen, Peter. (2005). 'Complex mediation.' *Human-Computer Interaction*. Vol. 20, 353-402.

Bolter, Jay & Gromala, Diane. (2003). *Windows and Mirrors: Interaction Design, Digital Art, and the Myth of Transparency*. Cambridge, MA: The MIT Press.

boyd, d. (2004). 'Friendster and publicly articulated social networks.' In *Conference on Human Factors and Computing Systems* (CHI 2004). Vienna,

Austria. 24-29 April. ACM Press. 1279-1282. Available at http://www.danah.
org/papers/CHI2004Friendster.pdf

boyd, d. & Heer, J. (2006). 'Profiles as conversation: networked identity performance on Friendster.' In *Proceedings of the Hawai'i International Conference
on System Sciences (HICSS-39)*. Kauai, HI: IEEE Computer Society. 4-7 January
2006. Available at http://www.danah.org/papers/HICSS2006.pdf;
http://csdl2.computer.org/persagen/DLAbsToc.jsp?resourcePath = /dl/proceed-
ings/&toc = comp/proceedings/hicss/2006/2507/03/25073toc.xml&DOI = 10.1
109/HICSS.2006.394

Buckingham, David. (2003). *Media Education. Literacy, Learning and Contemporary
Culture*. Cambridge: Polity Press.

Buckingham, David, Grahame, Jenny & Sefton-Green, Julian. (1995). *Making
Media-Practical Production in Media Education*. London: The English and
Media Centre.

Burn, Andrew & Parker, David. (2001). 'Making your mark: digital inscription, animation and a new visual semiotic.' *Education, Communication and Information*.
Vol. 1, No. 2. Available at http://www.open.ac.uk/eci/burn/femo set.html

Butler, Judith. (1993). *Bodies That Matter: On the Discursive Limits of Sex*. London:
Routledge.

Carr, Tony, Morrison, Andrew, Cox, Glenda & Deacon, Andrew. (2007).
'Weathering wikis: net based learning meets Political Science in a South
African university.' *Computers and Composition*. Vol. 24, No. 3, 266-284.

Carter, Paul. (2004). *Material Thinking: The Theory and Practice of Creative
Research*. Melbourne: Melbourne University Press.

Czikszentmihalyi, Mihaly. (1996). *Creativity: Flow and the Psychology of Discovery
and Invention*. New York: Harper.

Deleuze, Gilles. (1993/1997). *Essays: Critical and Clinical*. Smith, Daniel & Greco,
Michael (Transl.). Minneapolis: University of Minnesota Press.

Deleuze, Gilles & Guattari, Félix. (1987). *A Thousand Plateaus: Capitalism and
Schizophrenia*. Minneapolis: University of Minnesota Press.

Dourish, Paul. (2001). *Embodied Interaction*. Cambridge, MA: The MIT Press.

Engeström, Yrjö. (1987). *Learning by Expanding: An Activity Theoretical Approach
to Developmental Research*. Helsinki: Orienta-Konsultit.

Engeström, Yrjö. (1999). 'Innovative learning in work teams: analysing cycles of
knowledge creation and practice.' In Engeström, Yrjö, Miettinen, Reijo &
Punamaki, Raija-Leena. (Eds.). *Perspectives on Activity Theory*. Cambridge:
Cambridge University Press. 377-404.

Engeström, Yrjö. (2001). 'Expansive learning at work: toward an activity theoretical
reconceptualization.' *Journal of Education and Work*. Vol. 14, No. 1, 133-156.

Engeström, Yrjö, Miettinen, Reijo & Punamaki, Raija-Leena. (1999). (Eds.).
Perspectives on Activity Theory. Cambridge: Cambridge University Press.

Engeström, Yjrö, Virkkunen, Jaakko, Helle, Merje, Pihlaja, Juha & Poikela, Ritva.
(1996). 'The change laboratory as a tool for transforming work.' *Lifelong
Learning in Europe*. Vol. 1, No. 2, 10-17.

Fagerjord, Anders. (2005). 'Prescripts: authoring with templates.' *Kairos*. Vol. 10,
No. 1. Available at http://english.ttu.edu/KAIROS/10.1/

Fairclough, Norman. (1992). *Discourse and Social Change*. Cambridge: Polity Press.

Fei, Victor. (2004a). 'Developing an integrative multi-semiotic model.' In O'Halloran, Kay. (Ed.). *Multimodal Discourse Analysis*. London: Continuum. 220-246.

Fei, Victor. (2004b). 'Problematising "semiotic resource."' In Ventola, Eija. (Ed.). *Perspectives on Multimodality*. Amsterdam: John Benjamins. 51-62.

Fei Victor. (2007). 'The visual semantic stratum: making meaning in sequential images.' In Royce, Terry & Bowcher, Wendy. (Eds.). *New Directions in the Analysis of Multimodal Discourse*. London: Routledge. 195-213.

Fishwick, Paul. (2006). (Ed.). *Aesthetic Computing*. Cambridge, MA: The MIT Press.

Gitelman, Lisa. (2006). *Always Already New: Media, History, and the Data of Culture*. Cambridge, MA: The MIT Press.

Greene, Maxine. (1995). *Releasing the Imagination: Essays on Education, the Arts and Social Change*. San Francisco, CA: Jossey-Bass.

Hall, Stuart. (1997). 'The work of representation.' In Hall, Stuart. (Ed.). *Representation: Cultural Representations and Signifying Practices*. London: Sage. 13-64.

Halliday, Michael. (1985/1994). *Functional Grammar*. 2nd edition. London: Edward Arnold.

Halliday, Michael & Hasan, Ruqaiya. (1976). *Cohesion in English*. Longman: Harlow.

Hanseth, Ole. (2007). 'Complexity and risk.' In Hanseth, Ole & Ciborra, Claudio. (Eds.). *Risk, Complexity and ICT*. Cheltenham: Edward Elgar. 75-93.

Iedema, Rick. (2003). 'Multimodality, resemiotization: extending the analysis of discourse as multi-semiotic practice.' *Visual Communication*. Vol. 2, No. 1, 29-57.

Ivarsson, Jonas & Saljö, Roger. (2005). 'Seeing through the screen: human reasoning and the development of representational technologies.' In Gärdenfors, Peter & Johansson, Petter. (Eds.). *Cognition, Education and Communication Technology*. Mahwah, NJ: Lawrence Erlbaum Associates. 203-222.

Jenkins, Henry. (2006). *Convergence Culture*. New York: New York University Press.

Jewitt, Carey & Kress, Gunther. (2003). *Multimodal Literacy*. New York: Peter Lang.

Kaptelinin, Victor & Nardi, Bonnie. (2006). *Acting With Technology. Activity, Theory and Interaction Design*. Cambridge: The MIT Press.

Kok, Arthur (2004). 'Multisemiotic mediation in hypertext.' In O'Halloran, K. (Ed.). *Multimodal Discourse Analysis: Systemic-Functional Perspectives*. London: Continuum. 131-159.

Kolb, David. (1996). 'Discourse across links.' In Ess, Charles. (Ed.). *Philosophical Perspectives on Computer-Mediated Communication*. Albany: State University of New York Press. 16-26.

Kress, Gunther. (1998). 'Visual and verbal modes of representation in electronically mediated communication: the potentials of new forms of text.' In Snyder, Ilana. (Ed.). *Page to Screen: Taking Literacy Into the Electronic Era*. New York: Routledge. 53-79.

Kress, Gunther. (1999). '"English" at the crossroads: rethinking curricula of communication in the context of the turn to the visual.' In Hawisher, Gail & Selfe, Cynthia. (Eds.). *Passions, Pedagogies and 21st Century Technologies*. Logan: Utah State University Press. 66-88.

Kress, Gunther. (2003). *Literacy in the New Media Age*. London: Routledge.

Kress, Gunther & van Leeuwen, Theo. (1996). *Reading Images: The Grammar of Visual Design*. London: Routledge.

Kress, Gunther & van Leeuwen, Theo. (2001). *Multimodal Discourse: The Modes and Media of Contemporary Communication*. London: Arnold.

Latour, Bruno. (1996). *Aramis or the Love of Technology*. Cambridge, MA: Harvard University Press.

Latour, Bruno. (1999). *Pandora's Hope: Essays on the Reality of Science Studies*. Cambridge, MA: Harvard University Press.

Latour, Bruno. (2005). *Reassembling the Social*. Oxford: Oxford University Press.

Lave, Jean & Wenger, Etienne. (1991). *Situated Learning: Legitimate Peripheral Participation*. Cambridge: Cambridge University Press.

Law, John. (1997). 'Topology and the naming of complexity.' Available at http://www.lancs.ac.uk/fss/sociology/papers/law-topology-and-complexity.pdf

Law, John & Hassard, John. (1999). (Eds.). *Actor Network Theory and After*. Oxford: Blackwell.

Lemke, Jay. (1995). *Textual Politics: Discourse and Social Dynamics*. London: Taylor & Francis.

Lemke, Jay. (1998). 'Metamedia literacy: transforming meanings and media.' In Reinking, David, McKenna, Michael, Labbo, Linda & Kieffer, Ronald. (Eds.). *Handbook of Literacy and Technology: Transformations in a Post-Typographic World*. Mahwah, NJ: Lawrence Erlbaum Associates. 283-301.

Lemke, Jay. (2005). 'Place, pace, and meaning: multimedia chronotopes.' In Norris, Sigrid & Jones, Rodney. (Eds.). *Discourse in Action: Introducing Mediated Discourse Analysis*. London: Routledge. 110-122.

Leont'ev, Alexei. (1978). *Activity, Consciousness, and Personality*. Englewood Cliffs, NJ: Prentice Hall.

Leont'ev, Alexei. (1981). *Problems of the Development of the Mind*. Moscow: Progress Publishers.

Löwgren, Jonas & Stolterman, Eric. (2004). *Thoughtful Interaction Design: A Design Perspective on Information Technology*. Cambridge, MA: The MIT Press.

Machin, David. (2007). *Introduction to Multimodal Analysis*. New York: Oxford University Press.

Manovich, Lev. (2001). *The Language of New Media*. Cambridge, MA: The MIT Press.

Martin, James. (1992). *English Text: System and Structure*. Amsterdam: John Benjamins.

Martin, James & Stenglin, Maree. (2007). 'Materialising reconciliation: negotiating difference in a transcolonial exhibition.' In Royce, Terry & Bowcher, Wendy. (Eds.). *New Directions in the Analysis of Multimodal Discourse*. London: Routledge. 215-238.

Matthiessen, Christian. (2007). 'The multimodal page: a systemic functional exploration.' In Royce, Terry & Bowcher, Wendy. (Eds.). *New Directions in the Analysis of Multimodal Discourse*. London: Routledge. 1-62.

Miettinen, Reijo. (1999). 'The riddle of things. Activity theory and actor network theory as approaches of studying innovations.' *Mind, Culture, and Activity*. Vol. 6, No. 3, 170-195.

Moran, Seana & John-Steiner, Vera. (2003). 'Creativity in the making: Vygotsky's contemporary contribution to the dialectic of development and creativity.' In Sawyer, Keith, John-Steiner, Vera, Moran, Seana, Sternberg, Robert, Feldman, David, Nakamura, Jeanne & Czikszentmihalyi, Mihaly. (Eds.). *Creativity and Development.* Oxford: Oxford University Press. 61-90.

Morley, David & Chen, Kuan-Hsing. (1996). (Eds.). *Stuart Hall: Critical Dialogues in Cultural Studies.* London: Routledge.

Morrison, Andrew. (2001). *Electracies: Investigating Transitions in Digital Discourses & Multimedia Pedagogies in Higher Education. Case Studies in Academic Communication from Zimbabwe.* Unpublished doctoral dissertation. Department of Media & Communication, University of Oslo. 450 pp & 2 CD-ROMs.

Morrison, Andrew. (2003). 'From oracy to electracies: hypernarrative, place and multimodal discourses in learning.' In Liestol, Gunnar, Morrison, Andrew & Rasmussen, Terje. (Eds.). *Digital Media Revisited.* Cambridge, MA: The MIT Press. 115–154.

Morrison, Andrew & Love, Alison. (1996). 'A discourse of disillusionment: letters to the editor in two Zimbabwean magazines 10 years after independence.' *Discourse & Society.* Vol. 7, No. 1, 39-75.

Morrison, Andrew & Skjulstad, Synne. (2007). 'Talking cleanly about convergence.' In Storsul, Tanja & Stuedahl, Dagny. (Eds.). *The Ambivalence of Convergence.* Göteborg: Nordicom. 217-335.

Morrison, Andrew, Skjulstad, Synne & Sevaldson, Birger. (2007). 'Waterfront development with Web mediation.' Paper presented at *Design Inquiries. 2nd Nordic Design Research Conference.* Konstfack, Stockholm, 27-30 May.

Morrison, Andrew, Skjulstad, Synne & Smørdal, Ole. (2004). 'Choreographing augmented space.' *Proceedings of Future Ground International Conference 2004.* Vol. 2 Proceedings. Design Research Society/Faculty of Art and Design, Monash University, Melbourne. CD-ROM.

Morrison, Andrew, Westvang, Even & Skogsrud, Simen. (in press). 'Whisperings in the undergrowth: collaborative design and performativity in online social networking.' In Wagner, Ina, Bratteteig, Tone, & Stuedahl, Dagny. (Eds.). *Exploring Digital Design.* Vienna: Springer.

Nardi, Bonnie. (1996). (Ed.). *Context and Consciousness: Activity Theory and Human-Computer Interaction.* Cambridge, MA: The MIT Press.

Norris, Sigrid & Jones, Rodney. (2005). (Eds.). *Discourse in Action: Introducing Mediated Discourse Analysis.* London: Routledge.

O'Halloran, Kay. (2004). (Ed.). *Multimodal Discourse Analysis.* London: Continuum.

O'Toole, Michael. (1994). *The Language of Displayed Art.* London: University of Leicester Press.

O'Toole, Michael. (2004). 'Opera ludentes: the Sydney Opera House at work and play.' In O'Halloran, K. (Ed.). *Multimodal Discourse Analysis: Systemic-Functional Perspectives.* London: Continuum. 11-27.

Pang, Alfred. (2004). 'Making history in *From Colony to Nation*: a multimodal analysis of a museum exhibition in Singapore.' In O'Halloran, K. (Ed.). *Multimodal Discourse Analysis: Systemic-Functional Perspectives.* London: Continuum. 28-54.

Prior, Paul, Solberg, Janine, Berry, Patrick, Bellwoar, Hannah, Chewning, Bill, Lunsford, Karen, Rohan, Liz, Roozen, Kevin, Sheridan-Rabideau, Mary,

Shipka, Jody, van Ittersum, Derek & Walker, Joyce. (2007). 'Re-situating and re-mediating the canons: a cultural-historical remapping of rhetorical activity.' *Kairos*. Vol. 11, No. 3. Available at http://kairos.technorhetoric.net/11.3/binder.html?topoi/prior-et-al/index.html

Ross, Heather. (2003). 'Digital video and composition: gauging the promise of a low-maintenance high-reward relationship.' *Kairos*. Vol. 8, No. 1. Available at http://kairos.technorhetoric.net/8.1/index.html

Royce, Terry. (2007). 'Intersemiotic complementarity: a framework for multimodal discourse analysis.' In Royce, Terry & Bowcher, Wendy. (Eds.). *New Directions in the Analysis of Multimodal Discourse*. London: Routledge. 63-109.

Royce, Terry & Bowcher, Wendy. (2007). (Eds.). *New Directions in the Analysis of Multimodal Discourse*. London: Routledge.

Sawyer, Keith. (2006). *Explaining Creativity: The Science of Human Innovation*. New York: Oxford University Press.

Scollon, Ron. (1998). *Mediated Discourse as Social Interaction: A Study of News Discourse*. New York: Addison Wesley.

Scollon, Ron. (2001). *Mediated Discourse: The Nexus of Practice*. London: Routledge.

Scollon, Ron & Wong Scollon, Susie. (2004). *Nexus Analysis: Discourse and the Emerging Internet*. London: Routledge.

Shaffer, David & Clinton, Katherine. (2006). 'Toolsforthoughts: reexamining thinking in the digital age.' *Mind, Culture & Activity*. Vol. 13, No. 4, 283-300.

Shotter, John. (2003). 'Cartesian change, chiasmic change: the power of living expression.' *Janus Head*. Vol. 6, No. 1, 6-29.

Shotter, John. (2006). 'Organising multi-voiced organisations: action-guiding anticipations and the continuous creation of novelty.' Paper presented at *Polyphony and Dialogism as Ways of Organising* Conference. University of Essex, Essex. 29-30 April.

Skjulstad, Synne. (2007). 'Communication design & motion graphics on the Web.' *Journal of Media Practice*. Vol. 8, No. 3, 359-378.

Stöckl, Helmut. (2004). 'In between modes: language and image in printed media.' In Ventola Eija, Charles, Cassily & Kaltenbacher Martin (Eds.). *Perspectives on Multimodality*. Amsterdam: John Benjamins. 9-30.

Star, Susan Leigh. (1989). 'The structure of ill-structured solutions: boundary objects and heterogeneous distributed problem solving.' In Gasser, Les & Huhns, Michael. (Eds.). *Distributed Artificial Intelligence*. Vol. 2. Pitman: London. 37-54.

Threadgold, Terry. (1997). *Feminist Poetics: Poiesis, Performance, Histories*. London: Routledge.

Turner, Victor. (1982). *From Ritual to Theatre: The Human Seriousness of Play*. New York: Performing Arts Journal Publications.

Ulmer, Gregory. (1994). *Heuretics*. Baltimore: The Johns Hopkins University Press.

Ulmer, Gregory. (2003). *Internet Invention: From Literacy to Electracy*. New York: Longman.

van Leeuwen, Theo. (1999). *Speech, Music, Sound*. Basingstoke: Macmillan.

van Leeuwen, Theo. (2003). 'A multimodal perspective on composition.' In Ensink, Titus & Sauer, Christoph. (Eds.). *Framing and Perspectivising in Discourse*. Amsterdam: John Benjamins. 23-61.

van Leeuwen, Theo. (2004). 'Ten reasons why linguists should pay attention to visual communication.' In Levine, Philip & Scollon, Ron. (Eds.). *Discourse and Technology: Multimodal Discourse Analysis.* Washington, DC: Georgetown University Press. 7-20.

van Leeuwen, Theo. (2005a). *Introducing Social Semiotics.* London: Routledge.

van Leeuwen, Theo. (2005b). 'Multimedia, genre and design.' In Norris, Sigrid & Jones, Rodney. (Eds.). *Discourse in Action: Introducing Mediated Discourse Analysis.* London: Routledge. 73-94.

van Leeuwen, Theo & Jewitt, Carey. (2001). (Eds.). *Handbook of Visual Analysis.* London: Sage.

Ventola Eija, Charles, Cassily & Kaltenbacher, Martin. (2004a). (Eds.). *Perspectives on Multimodality.* Amsterdam: John Benjamins Publishing Company.

Ventola Eija, Charles, Cassily & Kaltenbacher, Martin. (2004b). 'Introduction.' In Ventola Eija, Charles, Cassily & Kaltenbacher, Martin. (Eds.). *Perspectives on Multimodality.* Amsterdam: John Benjamins Publishing Company. 1-6.

Vygotsky, Lev. (1962). *Thought and Language.* Cambridge, MA: The MIT Press.

Vygotsky, Lev. (1978). *Mind in Society: The Development of Higher Psychological Processes.* Cambridge, MA: Harvard University Press.

Wartofsky, Marx. (1979). *Models: Representation in Scientific Understanding.* Dordrecht: D. Reidel Publishing Co.

Wells, Gordon. (1999). *Dialogic Inquiry: Toward a Sociocultural Practice and Theory of Education.* Cambridge, MA: Cambridge University Press.

Wenger, Etienne. (1998). *Communities of Practice: Learning, Meaning, and Identity.* Cambridge: Cambridge University Press.

Wenger, Etienne, McDermott, Richard, & Snyder, William. (2002). *Cultivating Communities of Practice: A Guide to Managing Knowledge.* Cambridge, MA: Harvard Business School Press.

Wertsch, James. (1991). *Voices of the Mind. A Sociocultural Approach to Mediated Action.* Cambridge, MA: Harvard University Press.

Wertsch, James. (1998). *Mind as Action.* Oxford: Oxford University Press.

Wertsch, James. (2002). *Voices of Collective Remembering.* Cambridge: Cambridge University Press.

Wertsch, James, Del Rio, Pablo & Alvarez, Amelia. (1995). *Sociocultural Studies of Mind.* Cambridge: Cambridge University Press.

Wittgenstein, Ludvig. (1953/2001). *Philosophical Investigations.* Oxford: Blackwell Publishing.

Wysocki, Anne, Johnson-Eilola, Johndan, Selfe, Cynthia & Sirc, Geoffrey. (2004). *Writing New Media.* Logan: Utah State University Press.

PART II

MEDIATING

PREFACE

CARETAKERS OF MULTIMODALITY

Cynthia Haynes

For me the noise of Time is not sad: I love bells, clocks, watches—and I recall that at first the photographic implements were related to techniques of cabinetmaking and the machinery of precision: cameras, in short, were clocks for seeing, and perhaps in me someone very old still hears in the photographic mechanism the living sound of the wood. (Barthes 1981: 15)

The rings of a tree tell a story. The insects burrowed inside it tell, by way of the trails of their feeding, a story. The nests of birds among the branches tell a story (their songs, another). A tree house nestled among its limbs, long ago crafted for some little girl, tells a story. Her initials, carved much later next to those of her sweetheart, tell a story. Pulp turned to paper tells an entire world history of stories. A tree is a multimodal composition—it is the apotheosis of hybrid communication, an amalgam of technology, interface, and 'meaningware' (cf. Liestøl Chapter 3). Gregory Ulmer (2005: xii) reminds us that 'an apparatus of literacy' is comprised of multiple modes of 'collective and individual identity,' and the 'lesson of history is that there will be a change in the fundamental realities of our lives associated with the transformation of the language apparatus.' Each author in Part II offers testimony to this claim, and the image of a tree is (perhaps) an emblem of such modes and transformations.

This pre-mediation, more of a meditation, takes as its cue the insights of polished wood, those compositions that bear the wear and tear of words over time, those texts that tarry in the late age of mechanical deconstruction. It is a 'relay' (cf. Fagerjord Chapter 4) situated in the 'synaptic' leaps (cf. Morrison & Skjulstad Chapter 5) between multimodal communication design and its rhetorical roots. Take *The Lawrence Tree* (see Fig. II.1), a painting by Georgia O'Keeffe (1929) of the tree outside D.H. Lawrence's cabin near Taos, New Mexico. Lawrence, writer and painter, is re-doubled beneath this truncated wood, made erotic in his not-so-pulp fiction (such as his *Women in Love* or *Lady Chatterly's Lover*).

I have seen the tree; it still exists, as does the pinecone I plucked from the ground beneath its ungainly canopy, which sheltered (along with the bench on which he, and O'Keeffe, sat gazing up at the New Mexico night sky) the enclosure for two wild coyotes, rescued (after their mother had been killed by an irresponsible hunter) by a retired professor, Al Bierce, the then caretaker for the D.H. Lawrence ranch and infamous shrine (made from adobe mud bricks, the composition of which contained Lawrence's ashes, much to the chagrin of Lawrence scholars and devotees). We, the caretaker and I, set the coyotes to howling as we fed them beneath the tree (beside the cabin, home to Lawrence's typewriter, hat, and other primitive technologies).

This mediated event, more of a remediation (the bench, the painting, the novels in progress), was capped off by coyote coffee, sweetened by the honey from a nearby Native American pueblo (the people who most likely nurtured this tree's original composition). That coffee, so strong you had to stand back and throw sugar at it (as my son-in-law's North Carolinian daddy would say), bound us together—the caretaker, Lawrence, O'Keeffe, the coyotes, and me. Ulmer (2003) has described such associations (my pinecone, Lawrence's tree, O'Keeffe's translation of it, the language of its

Figure II.1. Georgia O'Keefe (1887-1986). *The Lawrence Tree* 1929. Oil on canvas, 78,9 x 99,5 cm. Waldworth Antheneum, Hartford, Connecticut, USA.

multimodal organisms, this essay) as the elements (relays) of what he calls a 'mystory' (see his *Internet Invention*). It is a genre characterized by saturation, full of the granulated (cf. Morrison & Skjulstad) sugar I stir into this rhetorical energy (Kennedy 1992) concoction.

You see, I considered my rhetorical audience that day. Lawrence's cabin is off limits officially. But I had it in mind to see it, and that caretaker had it in mind to have some company, to share some coffee, to feed his coyotes, to sit beneath that tree with me on an otherwise uneventful winter day. I persuaded him to show me—the cabin, the typewriter, the tree. The rings of a coffee cup tell a story. They join the chain of relays conducting this text, these means of mediating me pretexting you.

Whereas the following caretakers enact and imbue multimodes in/of 'crossmedia designs' (cf. Morrison & Skjulstad), no rhetorical consecration of their collective contributions can sufficiently preface the experience of their mediating forces—a tribute to rhetoric's power to emerge in creative and figurative technoliteracies, portrayed (textually and visually) through straits, maelstroms, maps, wagon trails, and kinetic impulsing lights. A preface is 'unseemly': It delays an otherwise clockwork collection of computing technologies, flash animation, and hybrid auto/mobiles, each serving as pretexts for the more organic literacies involved. As with caretakers, these chapters should be experienced with a cup, or two, of strong coyote coffee.

REFERENCES

Barthes, Roland. (1981). *Camera Lucida*. New York: Hill & Wang.

Kennedy, George. (1992). 'A hoot in the dark: the evolution of general rhetoric.' *Philosophy and Rhetoric*. Vol. 25, No. 1, 1-21.

O'Keeffe, Georgia. (1929). *The Lawrence Tree*. Oil on canvas, 78,9x99,5 cm. Wadsworth Antheneum Museum, Hartford, CT. The Georgia O'Keeffe Online Gallery. Available at http://www.happyshadows.com/okeeffe/

Ulmer, Gregory. (2003). *Internet Invention: From Literacy to Electracy*. New York: Longman.

Ulmer, Gregory. (2005). *Electronic Monuments*. Minneapolis: University of Minnesota Press.

3

POWERPOINT

BEYOND HARDWARE AND SOFTWARE

Gunnar Liestøl

DIGITAL GENRES

Throughout history, education and research have fostered a multitude of oral and written genre systems, such as the lecture, talk, project presentation, seminar, colloquium, thesis, article, paper, and essay. There is a growing body of research and learning on genres and academic communication tracing the development from antiquity to the present and prescribing the rules for its conduct and practice. With the emergence of new information and communication technologies (ICTs) in general and digitalization in particular, great expectations have formed concerning the possible benefit for educational institutions and learning activities.

Early on, the hope for 'new media' was met by vast investment in hardware equipment, desktop PCs, and special classrooms dedicated to ICT work. However, it soon became evident that hardware accessories and infrastructure were only (necessary) parts of the puzzle. As a consequence, attention increasingly became directed toward software. Over the last decade, focus has been on developments including Computer-Supported Collaborative Learning, Learning Management Systems, Learning Objects, and attempted investments in the combination of computer gaming and learning applications. Most recently, the employments and success of constructive hypertext functionality (blogging, wiki) and other more complex and converged kinds of social network services

(*MySpace, FaceBook*) have gained increased attention from the education-al authorities and communities. Despite all the long-term expenditure and these more recent approaches, surprisingly few, if any, inventive or innovative genres have emerged and established themselves in digital learning.

Traditionally, and especially in literary criticism, genre has been defined in terms of formal patterns or types (Genette 1992). More current-ly, in the rhetorical and social semiotics tradition, genre is conceived of as related kinds of expressive responses that recur across space and over time in the social contexts of communicative actions (Miller 1984; Devitt 2004). Genres and their individual mono- or multimodal texts engage in dynamic relationships of change and remaking. Genre invention and radi-cal innovation is rare, but mutation happens, most often accidently, occa-sionally by design. Genres always include material markers, the matter that both constrains and makes them possible. Changes in hardware and software make room for changes in and among genres. In hardware/soft-ware evolution and development, however, there seems to be a cultural lag when it comes to corresponding digital genres. This is most obvious in the context of learning and education.

PowerPoint as Presentation and Critique

Meanwhile, the *PowerPoint* presentation is rapidly gaining ground and strengthening its position as the dominant digital form of presentation (and file format) in schools and universities. Fortunately, alongside the spread of *PowerPoint*, so too have the critical comments and discussions of its use and influences been growing (see Parker 2001; Tufte 2003a; Shworn & Keller 2003; Norvig 2003; Kjeldsen 2006; Yates & Orlikowski 2007).

Although *PowerPoint* principally has been a business tool, teachers and students around the globe make thousands and thousands of *PowerPoint* presentations every day. The *PowerPoint* presentation, per se, is perhaps the closest thing we have come to a pervasive digital genre in learning and education. Despite its pervasiveness among students and teachers, its reputation is not that impressive in critical discourse on media and communication.

In this chapter, I take the critical debate on *PowerPoint* as a starting point. My purpose is to use this discourse as a means to get inside some key characteristics of digital media and how they interact with the multi-modal employment of ICT in learning, particularly the relationship between hardware/software on the one side and genres of digital textuali-ty on the other. How may genre innovation (and invention) assimilate and benefit from the complexity of software functionality and multiple media applications that continue to emerge? I believe an understanding of digital media characteristics in terms of answers to this question is crucial and could prove decisive for further employments of multimodal technology in education. As a consequence, it is necessary to explore the terrain beyond the known strata and paradigms of hardware and software. Following the generation or invention of new communicative accomplishments from classical rhetoric, this corresponds to some degree with the 'logic of invention' proposed by Ulmer (1994) concerning digitally mediated communication.

POWERPOINT AND ITS CRITICS

Genesis and Generations

In 1987, *PowerPoint* was released by Forethought for the Apple Macintosh computer as an editing tool aimed at creating black-and-white text and graphics transparencies for overhead projection in business settings. The application had been in development under the name of *Presenter* since 1984. Shortly after its release, both the company and the software were acquired by Microsoft, and in 1990, *PowerPoint* was eventually made available for PCs and the Windows platform. Since then, it has been an integral part of Microsoft's popular Office package. Over the years, other similar presentation software has challenged *PowerPoint*: Aldus' *Persuasion* (later acquired by Adobe but discontinued in 1997), Apple's *Keynote* (released in 2003), and *Impress* from OpenOffice.org (originally released by Sun Microsystems as part of the StarOffice suite in 1999). So far, little success has been achieved in defying the dominant position of Microsoft's presentation software.

The current build of *PowerPoint* (version 2007) is designed to 'Create dynamic and high-impact presentations faster than ever' (www.microsoft.com). The *PowerPoint* application is now basically an editing tool for the composition of digital presentations combining writing, graphics, pictures, audio, and video. *PowerPoint* presentations (*PP* presentations) are primarily and traditionally used to accompany oral communication in some form, whether in business, training, or education. Throughout history, a series of technologies have been developed and deployed to support oral, real-space presentations—from plates, blackboards, and scrollable maps to slide shows, overhead projections, film, television, and video (Cuban 1986; King 2001). *PowerPoint* represents a digitalization and convergence of all these techniques, combining a multitude of media, traditions, text types, and conventions in one application for the purpose of multimodal text production (Liestøl 2007).

However, *PowerPoint* is not only a tool to visualize and support topics in an oral presentation with illustrations (charts, animations, pictures, video, etc.). Increasingly, *PowerPoint* has become an editor and a vehicle for a certain kind of language use and communication. In *PP* presentations, across the disciplines, we predominantly encounter information and knowledge that are broken down into short, incomplete sentences or statements divided by:

- bullet points

following the rule '6 words pr. bullet, 6 bullets pr. slide' and embellished with overloads of special digital effects. Often this reductionist structure and the superficial effects confuse rather than contribute to our understanding of the message to be conveyed. This fragmented and pitch-oriented style is heavily encouraged and supported by the software's many built-in templates and prescriptions.

Critical comments directed toward the *PP* presentation, as such, are as old as its popularity (Mahin 2004). One of the best known and acclaimed *PowerPoint* critiques is, in fact, a *PP* presentation. By using the *PowerPoint* 'Auto Content Wizzard', Peter Norvig turned Lincoln's Gettysburg Address of November 1863 into a six-slide *PP* presentation with statistical graphics (Norvig 1999). The effect is both parodic and precarious. Lincoln's eloquent and admired oratory is easily reduced to fragmented and bald statements accompanied by bullet points.

From Parker's (2001) famous article in *The New Yorker*, we learn how *PP* presentations have expanded beyond their initial stronghold of pecuniary and public seminar spaces and penetrated the private sphere of the nuclear family, where it has been utilized to repair derelict communication between parents and children. The article refers to a family where in despair a mother found it necessary to use *PowerPoint* to enforce her daughters to take part in elementary housework duties.

PowerPoint as 'Particularly Disturbing'

The harshest and most influential critic of *PP* presentations is graphics designer and theorist Edward Tufte, who has caused considerable discussion, in both professional settings and academic debates, concerning *PowerPoint*. Tufte (2003b: 1) states that, 'Particularly disturbing is the adoption of the PowerPoint's cognitive style in our schools. Rather than learning to write a report using sentences, children are being taught how to formulate client pitches and infomercials.' His criticism is further introduced in the now classic article, 'The Cognitive Style of PowerPoint:

Pitching Out Corrupts Within' (Tufte 2003a; revised and reprinted in 2006: 157-185). This article is only a part of his influential and intricately designed book series that depicts and analyzes both presentational and representational multimodal discourse in various media.

Tufte's critical comments are direct and to the point. As a presentation tool, *PowerPoint* reduces the analytical quality of serious presentations. Tufte (2006: 157) is particularly concerned with the superficial use of the ready-made templates that come with the software package, which 'weaken verbal and spatial thinking.' The serious trouble caused by this mode of expression is:

> . . . foreshortening of evidence and thought, low spatial resolution, an intensely hierarchical single-path structure as the model for organizing every type of content, breaking up narratives and data into slides and minimal fragments, rapid temporal sequencing of thin information rather than focused spatial analysis, conspicuous chartjunk and PP Phluff, branding of slides with logotypes, a preoccupation with format not content, incompetent designs for data graphics and tables, and a smirky commercialism that turns information into a sales pitch and presenters into marketeers. (Tufte 2006: 158)

After this triade, Tufte goes on to ground his criticism through a series of examples. The most grievous of these is the tragic case of the NASA space shuttle Columbia.

The Case of NASA, *PowerPoint*, and the Columbia Space Shuttle

In a video showing Columbia's takeoff in January 2003, a few frames displayed a piece of foam breaking loose from the liquid fuel thank and then disintegrating. It was unclear from the visual footage whether the object had hit and damaged the wing. To calculate the risk of dangers on reentry, NASA's engineers started extensive tests and calculations. In the process, their main tool of communication and exchange was the *PP* presentation. As the reports moved upward in the organization, *PP* presentations became the central documentation on which the responsible directors were to make their decisions. *PP* reports contained the information needed to execute further investigations and actions. However, vital information neither made it to the required level in the bullet point hierarchy of the *PP* slides nor was it formulated in a language clear enough to reach decision makers. The consequence, as we know, was catastrophic.

In the large organization of NASA, over time the *PP* presentation had come to be substituted for the technical paper as the main format of internal communication and documentation for decision making. Tufte and the review boards investigating the disaster partly blame *PowerPoint* and reject its excessive and uncritical use in the organization. They conclude that '(1) PowerPoint is an inappropriate tool for engineering report, presentations, documentation and (2) the technical report is superior to PP' (Tufte 2006: 168). At this point, it may be appropriate to note that one of *PowerPoint*'s most hated features, the bullet point, is not an invention that emerged with this particular piece of software. It is in fact as old as the ancient technology and conventions of the papyrus book rolls. In certain rolls, 'every tenth line is marked by a small bullet (•) . . . ' (Sider 2005: 35). This application of bullet points, however, is used for navigation and orientation in long successive texts. It does not reduce the original text to short fragments.

TUFTE AND HIS CRITICS

Communicative Countercurrents

Tufte's attack on *PowerPoint* and the *PP* presentation has been countered by both communication designers and information systems theorists. Shworn and Keller (2003: 4) argue that Tufte is wrong in casting *PowerPoint* as the villain in the story of the Columbia disaster:

> . . . PowerPoint did not cause such problems. Rather, the engineers apparently do not understand fundamental rhetorical principles. They don't ask themselves, 'What does my audience need to know? What point am I trying to make? How do I make that point clearly, thoroughly, transparently? And is the organization of information effective for making my point clear and understandable.'

Shworn and Keller do not locate the problem in the *PowerPoint* editing tool as such, but rather in the thinking of the people who use the application. In the case of NASA engineers, their failure was threefold: They lacked clear thinking, clear writing, and clear organization. Shworn and Keller go on to conduct a visual demonstration of their point. Through a series of self-designed slide layouts, they show that the crucial NASA *PP* slides could have been designed perfectly well otherwise, and in a way that would have limited the confusion and perhaps even have prevented the fatal misunderstandings and misjudgements. To further proclaim the potential of *PowerPoint*, Shworn and Keller also unveil how some of Tufte's exemplary designs for good visual statistics (Tufte 2006) may be easily reproduced using the layout capabilities of *PowerPoint* (Shworn &

Keller 2003). Such mediated evidence challenges Tufte's authoritative view represented via his beautiful and skillful books.

PowerPoint and Genre

Tufte's critique of *PowerPoint* has not only been attacked from a practical rhetorical perspective, but also from a theoretical point of view concerning genre. Information systems and genre theorists Yates and Orlikowski (2007) discuss how the *PP* presentation genre has been historically constituted and developed as an extension of the business presentation genre. They criticize Tufte because his argument

> . . . conflates the use of graphics in written documents such as articles and newspapers with the use of graphics as visual aids in oral presentations, failing to distinguish between fundamentally different genres (the article and the oral presentations) and the recurrent situations in which they are enacted. Moreover, as with all technologies, it is not the technology per se but how it is used that determines outcomes and consequences. (Yates & Orlikowski 2007: 76)

The genre perspective is important (and we return to it later). In Yates and Orlikowski's article, there is no argument or demonstration of how and why Tufte presumably confuses written and oral genres in his article. Tufte is clearly arguing from a genre perspective when he declares the need for the replacement of the *PP* presentation with the technical report in scientific documentation and communication. Yates and Orlikowski further repeat Shworn and Keller's critique that it is not the software one should blame, but the users who choose to apply it in certain ways.

There are obviously two distinct positions here concerning the reciprocal relationship between software applications, on the one hand, and the messages you create with them, on the other hand. Tufte is accused of giving all the responsibility to the software tool, whereas his critics claim that it is the user who is responsible for how a message is designed.

These opposing views raise the question of the relationship between *PowerPoint*, the software application (editing tool), and the *PP* presentation, as the individual messages and texts that people produce by means of the software. Tufte seems to imply that, as an application, *PowerPoint* deterministically conditions its textual production and that the solution not only lies in changing genre but also in changing software:

> Serious problems require a serious tool: written reports. For nearly all engineering and scientific communication, instead of PowerPoint, *the presentation and reporting software should be a word-processing pro-*

gram capable of capturing, editing, and publishing text, tables, data graphics, images, and scientific notation. Replacing PowerPoint with Microsoft Word (or, better, a tool with non-proprietary universal formats) will make presentations and their audiences smarter. (Tufte 2006: 168; italics original)

Again, Tufte argues that the problem is the particular software (*PowerPoint*), not the conventional uses of it. The solution, he postulates, is for students and teachers to switch to another software application more suitable for the job—namely, a word processor (with some multimodal capabilities)—and thus strengthen the practice of the cognitive style found in the tradition and genre of written reports. As with the earlier approach by Shworn and Keller (2003), this argument and its solution to the problem can also be tested by means of comparative visual evidence.

Parallel Presentations

The fact is that a deep and detailed written argumentative text, such as the technical report or a chapter in Tufte's last book, can (almost) as easily be made in *PowerPoint* as in *Word* or any other layout application (see Figure 3.1).

I have devised a parallel text that mimics Tufte's almost exactly. To be precise, there are a few minor differences. Tufte's text is printed in Etbembo, a typeface made by Dmitry Krasny and not available in the Office 2004 version for Mac OSX. As a substitute, I have used Adobe Garamond Pro. Given the drawing tools in *PowerPoint* and the size of my slide, it was difficult to reduce the arrowhead to the same size as in Tufte's illustration. With these minor differences in layout elements, it is obvious that the basic meaning potential stays the same in both versions, at least compared with the context of the technical report genre.

Compositionally, the converse also applies: The typical PowerPoint slide, with its fragmented bullet point presentation, can be written effortlessly in Word to look exactly like a *PowerPoint* presentation (see Figure 3.2).

This demonstration of the common capabilities of different software editing tools shows that Tufte's opponents might be right in their criticism that the user has more power over the software than Tufte is willing to admit. However, we need to ask: Can it be correct that software applications such as editors (for all text types, words, images, sound, and/or video) do not constrain the users nor do they, as Tufte (2006: 158) puts it, 'come with a big attitude'? To further understand these opposed positions and attempt an answer to the questions, we need to take a closer look at the relationships between levels in digital media and how they interact and influence each other.

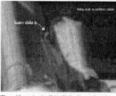
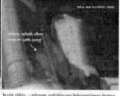

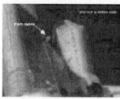
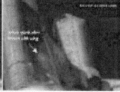

Figure 3.1. (Top) Page 8 from Edward Tufte's essay, 'The Cognitive Style of PowerPoint: Pitching Out Corrupts within' (Tufte 2003, 2nd edition) taken from the sample available at www.edwardtufte.com. (Bottom) My own reconstruction of the page done entirely in PowerPoint.

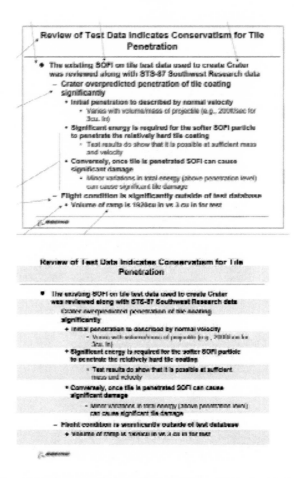

Figure 3.2. (Top) The crucial PowerPoint slide used in the NASA investigation concerning the damage to the Challenger air shuttle annotated by Tufte (see www.edwardtufte.com). (Bottom) My reconstruction of the same slide using Microsoft Word.

BEYOND HARDWARE AND SOFTWARE

Two Levels

The stratification in digital media has a long tradition in computer science, but the main levels are basically limited to two: hardware and software. *Hardware* is defined as the physical elements of a computer system, '. . . the computer equipment as opposed to the programs or information stored in the machine' (Downing et al. 1998: 211). The contrast is *software*, here indirectly defined as 'programs or information.' Software signifies the programs that tell a computer what to do. The hardware by itself is of little value without the software instructions. Software is then further defined and divided into *system software* (operating system) and *application software* (text editor, e-mail client, etc.).

This hardware–software dualism does not help us much in the differentiation between (a) *PowerPoint* the software application, and (b) the *PP* presentation, the individual slide series, and their textuality. In the vocabulary of computer science, there is no distinct software level designating the *PP* presentation. In this paradigm, the individual *PP* presentation would be described as a file and the file as a container filled with data. To understand the relationship between the *PowerPoint* software application and the *PP* presentation, and how it is shaped by and shapes the user's expressions, the informatics distinction between software and data does not seem adequate or helpful. Other perspectives and ways of differentiating digital media are needed.

In his book on the networked information economy, Benkler (2006) presents a model for how to distinguish among the layers of digital media networks or what he calls 'the institutional ecology of digital environments.' His model expands beyond the dualism of traditional computer science and consists of three levels: physical, logical, and content. Benkler (2006: 392) writes that:

> The physical layer refers to the material things used to connect human beings to each other. These include the computers, phones, handhelds, wires, wireless links, and the like. The content layer is the set of humanly meaningful statements that human beings utter to and with one another. It includes both the actual utterances and the mechanisms, to the extent that they are based on human communication rather than mechanical processing, for filtering, accreditation, and interpretation. The logical layer represents the algorithms, standards, ways of translating human meaning into something that machines can transmit, store, or compute, and something that machines process into communications meaningful to human beings. These include standards, protocols, and software—both general enabling platforms like operating systems, and more specific applications.

Because Benkler is a law scholar, the descriptions of his triple-layered paradigm do not go into much detail about the nature of the so-called content layer. Lessig (2001: 23), based on earlier work by Benkler (2000) and focused on the relationship between creativity and control in cultural production and innovation, describes and specifies the top layer as '. . . digital images, texts, on-line movies, and the like.'

My aim here is to shed some light on the interrelationship between software applications and texts created by a given software. With Benkler, we have a separate level for the individual *PP* presentation (content layer), distinct from *PowerPoint* the software application (logical layer). But how do these two layers relate, how do activities at the one layer influence activities and products at the other, and vice versa? Both Benkler and Lessig develop the three-layered model in the context of discussing copyright and commons. The layers are described as '. . . functioning together to define any particular communication system' (Lessig 2001: 23) and to represent '. . . the basic functions involved in mediated human communication' (Benkler 2006: 392). To learn more about the vertical relationships between the levels, we need to look elsewhere.

The Concept of Dependent Hierarchies

In his writings on context theory, Wilden (1981, 1982, 1987a, 1987b) presents the concept of dependent hierarchies. Dependent hierarchies are everywhere, in nature, society, and culture. The integrated relationship among nature, society, and culture can also be seen as a dependent hierarchy:

> In context theory the four major orders of complexity [inorganic nature, organic nature, society and culture] form a dependent hierarchy coded and constrained at each level by ever more diverse kinds of information. (Wilden 1987b: 32)

A dependent hierarchy is constituted by levels or orders, where each level serves as an environment for the system at the next level. To know whether we have a dependent hierarchy organized and oriented the right way, we must apply '*The extinction rule*: To test for the orientation of a dependent hierarchy, mentally abolish each level (or order) in turn, and note which other level(s) will necessarily become extinct if it becomes extinct' (Wilden 1981: 3; 1987a: 74).

Concerning the major orders of complexity, we know that society is dependent on nature for its long-range survival. As a consequence, we also know that the extinction of life-sustaining activities in nature (e.g., by pollution) by necessity entails the extinction of society. Yet if human society becomes extinct, nature continues to exist. The human individual must be conceived as a complex of all four orders.

The lower orders constrain and sustain but do not condition the higher ones. In a dependent hierarchy, such as the one from nature to culture, complexity increases at the higher levels, whereas the lower levels increase in generality and relative simplicity. At the higher levels, in culture, increased complexity and diversity also sustain increased constraints and emergent qualities.

Another example of dependent hierarchies is the relationship between quality and quantity. These are not at the same level of reality; they are not a binary opposition. When applying the extinction rule, we see that quality constrains quantity. According to Wilden (1987a: 126), 'Quantity is a kind of quality, but quality is not a kind of quantity.' Human language and discourse also form a dependent hierarchy: language universals, a particular language, the dominant discourse, and individual speech. Wilden (1987a: 133) notes that this schema ' . . . represents the general case: the dominant language and dominant discourse can be remade—are remade—by individuals and groups in history.'

Enter Meaningware

Benkler's triple-layered model of digitally mediated communication also forms a dependent hierarchy: The physical layer constrains the logical layer, which again constrains the content layer. In addition, there are sublayers and constraints inside each order of complexity in digital media: At the software level, for example, systems software constrain application software. Human beings, as users and producers, relate to and interact with all three layers when communicating by means of digital media.

As argued elsewhere, I am not completely satisfied with Benkler's nomenclature (Liestøl 2006: 262). The 'content layer' is a simplistic and reductionist term, and it is not suitable for the most complex and diverse of the media orders or levels. Extrapolating on the dualism of computer science, I have suggested digital media as a dependent hierarchy in the following terms (see Figure 3.3). A level of meaningware is added to that of hardware and software.

To test that we have the hierarchy correctly oriented, we apply the extinction rule: There will be no execution of code, no operating system handling individual applications, if we pull the plug and cut off the energy supply for the hardware layer. Neither is there going to be any communication of meaningware messages on the Web or the Internet if we do not have the proper protocols in place.

The *PP* presentation as a genre norm and an individual text resides at the level of meaningware. The relation between *PowerPoint* as an application/editing tool and the *PP* presentation as an individual file, discussed earlier, is also a relationship between software and meaningware. In the Tufte debate, his critics claim that software is not to blame for the way

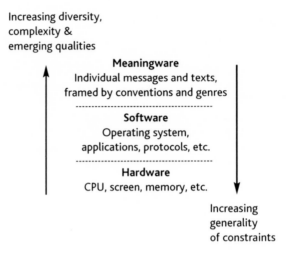

Figure 3.3. Digital media as a dependent hierarchy of constraining levels: Hardware, software, and meaningware.

that meaningware is composed or structured. I have further demonstrated that with current multifunctional and multimodal software packages (*PowerPoint* and *Word*), a certain type of meaningware textuality can be created by a number of different software applications.

Templates

As I see it, the discussion between Tufte and his critics is a pseudo debate. Tufte is not criticizing the application as such, but rather the style the templates constrain and render possible. According to Tufte, *PowerPoint's* ready-made guides may help some people to organize their presentations, but overall it is a curse in relation to both the content and the audience (Tufte 2006: 158). It is the cognitive *style* of the templates that is the problem. It is the way it reduces our ability to think and communicate our thoughts.

What is a template in this context? Templates come with software packages, particularly production tools, such as text editors, webpage editors, and editors for creating slide presentations, such as *PowerPoint* and the like. Templates or prescripts are often genre dependent (Fagerjord 2005). In Microsoft *Word*, you find templates for letters, business cards, memos, reports, biography, CVs, and much more. These templates come with layout examples, detailed descriptions of necessary ingredients, and so on. Many of the key criteria or aspects of the various genres are represented in the templates and their ready-mades. As such, the templates are manifestations of key genre features and help the user to produce/articulate texts within certain genre constraints and conventions. Traditionally, genre characteristics and criteria belong to the meaningware level of media and communication. They are the (often) unwritten conventions we must internalize and learn to master both constructively and interpretatively in praxis (Devitt 2004). In digital text editors, because of the complex and dynamic relationship between software and meaningware, the use and function of templates and guides have evolved into something different.

Templates are also rhetorical devices. In formal classical rhetorical theory, they belong to the operation of invention, the act of finding the argument and subject matter of a presentation, thus also called *topics*. According to Cicero, we may '. . . define topics as the region of an argument' or 'Pigeonholes in which arguments are stored' (Cicero 1948: ii.5; 1960: II.8; Barthes 1988). Templates are topics in the rhetorical sense. They are constructions that, when used in the proper way, produce elements of the final presentations. In Microsoft *Word,* the business card template, for example, constitutes a topic that needs to be consulted and filled in and/or altered by the user (see Figure 3.4).

Figure 3.4. Template for creating a business card. Some of the places (topoi) are filled in automatically.

Rules of Meaningware Coded in Software

In editing tools such as *PowerPoint* and *Word,* defining genre characteristics have been operationalized to form templates. These are rhetorical mechanisms or devices to help create texts of various kinds. In analogue media, genre conventions and their companion operations for production reside at the level of meaningware. The templates in *PowerPoint* and *Word*, however, are embedded in the software. In digital media, we thus see that some of the features or rules associated with the meaningware level may be coded in software. This is what has happened in the relationship between *PowerPoint* as an application and the operations of making a *PP* presentation. What used to be more or less unwritten generic norms following and guiding the ongoing production of individual texts have been converted to software as rules executed by computer code, a materialized norm. The problem, however, is that these templates of genre conventions operate in different ways and have not always been subject to critical evaluation. In addition, they are applied with excessive naiveté by most users. As a consequence, the application *PowerPoint* is not used according to its potential. Instead of being an open multimodal editor for innovative digital textuality, where every one of the text types is handled on 'equal' terms (in other words, that it has its own editing app.), *PP* is reduced to remediate genre constraints from analogue media and limit creativity and composition by means of badly designed layout, readymades, and overbearing effects.

This conversion from meaningware to software helps explain some of the confusion between the positions in the Tufte debate. When certain genre features (such as the bullet point list) are coded as a software template (including the 'auto content wizard', which is a dynamic template), and not just a practiced convention, they are associated with the software application. If the ready-made templates are not enactments of sound rhetorical principles and if, in addition, they are applied without critical judgement by the (prod)user, the resulting text will often turn out accordingly.

Aristotle defines rhetoric as finding the available means for effective communication. Digital textuality is constituted and constrained by a dynamic composite of hardware, software, and meaningware. To find the available means for digital and multimodal genre development, employing software applications such as *PowerPoint*, it is important to not let the crucial relationship between software and meaningware be obscured by templates and ready-mades, but experiment creatively and with less bias with the real potential of the software–meaningware interplay. In principle, *PowerPoint* has an abundant supply of multimodal functionality just waiting to be explored in inventive and innovative ways, both as standalone texts and as support for face-to-face oracy. Because presentation software has been met with so much criticism, it is important to also point to some of its rich tradition and good practice.

EXCURSION: TELLING AND SHOWING (PROPER POWERPOINT)

Augmentation

PowerPoint is a tool for creating digital display to support oral presentations. However, increasingly, *PP* presentations have become stand-alone files living a 'meaningful' life on their own detached from the accompanying oral context of description, commentary, and explanation. This is what happened in NASA. The *PP* presentations were communicated via e-mail and substituted for the technical report, which, contrary to the average bullet point-type *PP* presentation, is designed to be self-contained and meaningful.

PowerPoint can be seen as the digital convergence of a long tradition of the interaction between oral presentations and various visual displays. In *PowerPoint*, the blackboard, overhead projector, and slideshow converge to form a multifunctional and multimodal tool for the design of any thinkable kind of support and augmentation of the oral–verbal presentation.

Oracy has not always been open to this kind of augmentation. Let us return to ancient rhetoric. The Roman rhetorician Quintilian (2002) goes into detail describing and criticizing the use of theatrical effects and extraverbal elements as supplement to oratory, including pictures, wax tablets, busts, wounded or crying persons, and so on. In the lingocentric paradigm of ancient rhetorical discourse, only speech and writing were, according to Quintilian, considered dignified means of communication and persuasion (see Figure 3.5). He also refers to Cicero to support his position. In the speech *pro Rabirio*, Cicero (1927) attacks the use of pic-

Figure 3.5. **An illustration of an ancient Greek teacher displaying a papyrus scroll in front of the student.**

tures, as an accompanying nonverbal element, to improve the effect of rhetorical communication. However, this is not compatible with Cicero's own practice. In his famous case against Verres, he surprisingly skips the long opening speech and goes straight on to present (show) the witnesses and evidence in the case. The fourth part of the rhetorical machine, *actio*, is mainly a nonverbal operation and concerns the visual and auditive context of the speech to evoke the intended emotions in the audience: ' . . . the whole of a person's frame and every look on his face and utterance of the voice are keyed up like the strings of a harp, and sound according as they are struck by each successive emotion' (Cicero 1948: III. lvii. 216).

In more recent teaching, the use of extraverbal visual support has typically been an integral part of communication and exchange (see Figure 3.6). Over the centuries, the latest technology, from drawing and writing to slides and television, have supported and augmented oral presentations.

Within literary theory and analysis, one finds debates on the difference between telling and showing (Booth 1961; Genette 1980). Nowhere is this distinction more obvious, and at the same time intimately related, than in oral presentations supported by visual exhibition. *PowerPoint* is a most suitable software for such situations. Even Edward Tufte uses *PowerPoint* (or some alternative slideware) at his seminars, not as a means to verbally summarize the substance of his oral communication, but as a mode of illustration and display, in addition to showing and to the distribution of hand outs (see Figure 3.7).

Presentation software is not only limited to the display of static text types (writing and imagery). They support all modes of multimodal discourse, including audio, video, dynamic graphics, and 3D. In my next visual example (see Figure 3.8), Swedish professor of international health,

Figure 3.6. A lecture on archaeology given in a Danish worker's academy in the early 20th century. Note the illustrator to the left continually drawing the object about which the presenter is talking.

Hans Rosling, demonstrates how visually engaging a *PP* presentation can be. A modest use of *PP* functionality and a great deal of enthusiasm for teaching and scholarly mediation combines to create an impressive multi-modal orchestration, where the oral track interacts with the dynamic display of statistics in the most impressive way.

Figure 3.7. Edward Tufte at one of his seminars talking about and showing how Galileo in his book on astronomy used illustrations as a complement to his writing.

Figure 3.8. Swedish professor of international health, Hans Rosling, relating to his dynamic visualizations during a talk (see Rosling 2006).

The Importance of Timing

Creating and combining multimodal performances demand, above all, timing and complementarity. The various text types must not compete but interact with each other, and the interrelation between them must match precisely across the temporal axis. Apple's legendary chief executive officer, Steve Jobs, is a master of timing multiple modes for the purpose of suspense and publicity in his famous keynote addresses (see Figure 3.9).

Even more refined and advanced when it comes to timing and synchronization is law-professor Lawrence Lessig. Lessig uses presentation software to emphasize certain aspects and words, in the sentences of his speech by means of a minimalistic temporally constrained mode of discourse (see Figure 3.10).

Figure 3.9. Steve Jobs on the podium with his remote and the big screen of surprises.

Figure 3.10. Lawrence Lessig's minimalistic use of verbal elements to underline or accentuate parts of his own oracy (see Lessig 2005).

These are only a few examples of the creative ways in which employments of multimodality in contexts of presentation have evolved from antiquity and its pure but often reductionist refinements of speech and writing to current complex practices in digitally supported environments. Reductive and restricted monomediality once had their purpose but are now mostly long gone, particularly in communicational settings, such as education and learning. The relapse to monomodal reductionism and template naiveté found in the NASA case (and elsewhere) should be avoided and critiqued.

CONDUCTING CRITICAL INVENTION OF MEANINGWARE

Digital discourse is still an evolving and immature form of textuality, and genre systems are only beginning to materialize. The hardware and software constraints of emerging genres are thus continually changing. To release the potential of digital multimodality and genre innovation, we may explore multimodal discourse further by aiming more at conducting critical invention and construction at the meaningware level of digital media. Meanwhile, we must understand the constraining dynamics of digital media as a dependent hierarchy of complex relationships among levels. That, I believe, can only be achieved by critical and cross-disciplinary approaches to the design and practice of digital textuality and genre development.

REFERENCES

Barthes, Roland. (1988). 'The old rhetoric: an aide-mémoire.' In Barthes, Roland. (Ed.). *The Semiotic Challenge*. Oxford: Blackwell. 11-94.

Benkler, Yochai. (2000). 'From consumers to users: shifting the deeper structures of regulation.' *Federal Communications Law Journal*. Vol. 52, 561-563.

Benkler, Yochai. (2006). *The Wealth of Networks. How Social Production Transforms Markets and Freedom*. New Haven and London: Yale University Press.

Booth, Wayne. (1961). *The Rhetoric of Fiction*. Chicago: University of Chicago Press.

Cicero, Marcus Tullius. (1927). *Orations* (Loeb Classical Library No. 198). Grose Hodge (Transl.). Cambridge: Harvard University Press.

Cicero, Marcus Tullius. (1948). *Divisions of Oratory* (Loeb Classical Library No. 349). H. Rackham (Transl.). Cambridge: Harvard University Press.

Cicero, Marcus Tullius. (1960). *Topica* (Loeb Classical Library No. 386). H. Hubbell (Transl.). Cambridge: Harvard University Press.

Cuban, Larry. (1986). *Teachers and Machines: The Classroom Use of Technology Since 1920*. New York: Teachers College Press

Devitt, Amy J. (2004). *Writing Genres*. Carbondale: Southern Illinois University Press.

Downing, Douglas, Covington, Michael & Covington, Melody Mauldin. (1998). (Eds.). *Dictionary of Computer and Internet Terms*. 6th Edition. New York: Barrens' Educational Series.

Fagerjord, Anders. (2005). 'Prescripts: authoring with templates.' *Kairos*. Vol. 10, No. 1. Available at http://english.ttu.edu/kairos/10.1/coverweb/fagerjord/index.html

Genette, Gerard. (1980). *Narrative Discourse: An Essay on Method*. Jane Lewin (Transl.). Ithaca, NY: Cornell University Press.

Genette, Gerard. (1992). *The Architext. An Introduction*. Jane Lewin (Transl.). Foreword by Scholes, Robert. Berkeley: University of California Press.

King, Kenneth. (2001). *Technology, Science Teaching, and Literacy. A Century of Growth*. New York: Kluwer Academic/Plenum.

Kjeldsen, Jens E. (2006). 'The rhetoric of PowerPoint.' *Seminar.net–International Journal of Media, Technology and Lifelong Learning*. Vol. 2, No. 1.

Lessig, Lawrence. (2001). *The Future of Ideas. The Fate of the Commons in a Connected World*. New York: Random House.

Lessig, Lawrence. (2005). 'Creative commons.' Talk at Kopinor's 25th Anniversary International Symposium. 20 May 2005. Oslo, Norway. Video available at http://www.kopinor.org/hva_er_kopinor/kopinor_25_ar/kopinor_25th_anniversary_international_symposium

Liestøl, Gunnar. (2006). 'Conducting genre convergence for learning.' *International Journal for Continued Engineering Education and Lifelong Learning*. Vol. 16, Nos, 3/4, 255-270.

Liestøl, Gunnar. (2007). 'The dynamics of convergence and divergence in digital domains.' In Storsul, Tanja & Stuedahl, Dagny. (Eds.). *Ambivalence Towards Convergence. Digitalization and Media Change*. Göteborg: Nordicom. 165-178.

Mahin, Linda. (2004). 'PowerPoint pedagogy.' *Business Communication Quarterly*. Vol. 67, No. 1, 219-222.

Miller, Carolyn R. (1984). 'Genre as social action.' *Quarterly Journal of Speech*. Vol. 70, 151–167.

Norvig, Peter. (1999). 'The Gettysburg PowerPoint presentation.' January. Available at http://norvig.com/Gettysburg/.

Norvig, Peter. (2003). 'PowerPoint: shot with its own bullets.' *The Lanchet*. Vol. 362, No. 9381, 343-344.

Parker, Ian. (2001). 'Absolute PowerPoint. Can a software package edit our thoughts'? *The New Yorker*. 28 May, 76-87.

Quintilian, Marcus Fabius. (2002). *Institutio Oratoria I-XII*. (Donald A. Russell, Trans.). Cambridge, MA: Harvard University Press.

Rosling, Hans. (2006). TED-talk. Available at http://www.ted.com/tedtalks/tedtalksplayer.cfm?key = hans_rosling&flashEnabled = 1.

Shworn, Barbara & Keller, Karl. (2003). '"The great man has spoken. Now what do I do?" A response to Edward R. Tufte's "The Cognitive Style of Power

Point."' *Communication Insight*. Vol. 1, No. 1, 1-16. Available at http://www. communipartners.com/documents/ComInsV1._000.pdf

Sider, David. (2005). *The Library of the Villa dei Papiri at Herculanum*. Los Angeles: The J. Paul Getty Museum.

Tufte, Edward. (2003a). *The Cognitive Style of PowerPoint*. Cheshire, CT: Graphic Press.

Tufte, Edward. (2003b). 'PowerPoint is evil. Power corrupts. PowerPoint corrupts absolutely.' *WIRED Magazine*, September. Available at http://www.wired. com/wired/archive/11.09/ppt2.html

Tufte, Edward. (2006). *Beautiful Evidence*. Cheshire, CT: Graphic Press.

Ulmer, Gregory. (1994). *Heuretics*. Baltimore, MD: The Johns Hopkins University Press.

Wilden, Anthony. (1981). 'Semiotics as praxis: strategy and tactics.' *RSSI–Recherches Sémiotique/Semiotic Inquiry*. Vol. 1, No. 1, 1-34.

Wilden, Anthony. (1982). 'Postscript to "Semiotics as Praxis: Strategy and Tactics."' *RSSI–Recherches Sémiotique/Semiotic Inquiry*. Vol. 2, No. 2, 166-170.

Wilden, Anthony. (1987a). *The Rules Are No Game. The Strategy of Communication*. New York: Routledge & Kegan Paul.

Wilden, Anthony. (1987b). *Man and Woman, War and Peace. The Strategist's Companion*. New York: Routledge & Kegan Paul.

Yates, JoAnne, & Orlikowski, Wanda. (2001) Genre systems: chronos and kairos in communicative interaction. In Coe, Richard, Lindgard, Lorelei & Teslenko, Tatiana. (Eds.). *The Rhetoric and Ideology of Genre: Strategies for Stability and Change*. Cresskill, NJ: Hampton Press.

Yates, JoAnne, & Orlikowski, Wanda. (2007). 'The Power-Point presentation and its corollaries: how genres shape communicative action in organizations.' In Zachry, Mark & Thralls, Charlotte. (Eds.). *The Cultural Turn: Communicative Practices in Workplaces and the Professions*. Amityville, NY: Baywood Publishing.

4

MULTIMODAL POLYPHONY

ANALYSIS OF A FLASH DOCUMENTARY

Anders Fagerjord

A MULTIMODAL WEB

From Alphabet to Image?

In his 'Afterword' to the anthology *The Future of the Book* (1996), Umberto Eco revisits the age-old opposition between words and images to check its status in our computerized age. According to Eco, '[t]he main feature of a computer screen is that it hosts and displays more alphabetic letters than images. The new generation will be alphabetic and not image oriented' (297). Regardless of whether we believe Eco's diagnosis is right, it is hard not to notice the abundance of images on the World Wide Web. It is simply full of photos, music, and video. Never before has it been easier for anyone to distribute an amateur film; never before has anyone had access to such a large number of images as the Web surfer may access with a Web browser. We must realize that the Web is incredibly full of both writing and images.

We should probably also ask ourselves whether it is likely that the simple labels of 'alphabetic' and 'image oriented' will be sufficient to describe the communication practices of coming generations. Kress and van Leeuwen (1996) witnessed in *Reading Images* how Western culture over the last decades has become increasingly more visual. That does not mean that we are using images and not words, but rather that we more and more tend to combine writing and images. In fact, Eco's (2004) own novel, *The Mysterious Flame of Queen Loana*, is a case in point, the book being illustrated throughout with examples of visuals that the book's protagonist, Yambo, encountered in his youth. The computer revolution has of course accelerated this development, but, more important, it has given us media where we can combine the static modes of writing and still images with dynamic forms, such as recorded speech, music, sound effects, and moving images—what has become known as 'multimedia.'

With their later book, *Multimodal Discourse* (2001), Kress and van Leeuwen opened up the research into these new multimedia forms, yet their book focuses mostly on the many various modes we communicate through and offers little new understanding of combinations of modes. If we wish to understand multimedia, we need to understand how different modes are combined and which effects result from these combinations.[1]

Expressive Practice

In my view, to be competent in multimodal composition is to develop an understanding of which mode or modes will be effective for an author to express him or herself. Such a competence is normally acquired through practice and seems to be tacit (and described as 'experience,' 'instinct,' or 'gut feeling') for most skilled authors (or designers, as they usually call themselves). To get on the inside of these communicative practices, we need to develop a vocabulary to discuss composition in simultaneous modes and use this vocabulary to build theory. One obvious approach with long tradition in the arts and humanities is to develop such vocabularies and theories through close analysis of works.

I believe that multimodal works necessarily will have to draw on the long traditions of print, visual arts, film making, radio, and television. To be able to communicate, it is of no use to make up a new language no one knows; new genres and works may slowly expand on known vocabularies and genres, but the basis has to be a means of expression that the audience recognizes. I thus find it useful to view multimedia works as combinations of means of expression from earlier media, such as writing styles, rules of visual composition, and schools of film editing.

Rhetorical Convergence

The tradition of rhetorics has always identified effective communication techniques that may be isolated and used by others. In line with this tradition, I have earlier used the broad term *rhetorics* for the various means of expression, and I introduced the concept of *rhetorical convergence* to describe how rhetorics of different earlier media are combined in web-sites and other digital texts (Fagerjord 2003a, 2003b).

This chapter is a close analysis of a Web site to develop a vocabulary for describing and analyzing multimodal works. We are assisted by theories developed for different media and modes, such as visual culture, film studies, and musicology. My analysis is inspired by rhetorics, in that we identify 'figures,' that is, means of expression that may be isolated and given a name.

We examine National Geographic's *Flash* documentary *Sights and Sounds From the Way West*, and we find that it is made up of different modes, such as writing, speech, music, sound effects, photography, painting, and camera movement. I argue that the different modes form different voices that not only communicate on their own, but also work together in a melange that could be described meaningfully with musical terms such as 'homophony,' 'dissonance,' 'polyphony,' and 'accompaniment.'

FLASH DOCUMENTARIES

A Web Genre

I have tried to select a genre that is both quite typical of the Web and still a bit removed from the genres we know from print media. I have selected a genre that is a rhetorical convergence of television, photography, radio, and regular Web sites: the 'Flash documentary' is a true Web genre that became widespread in 2000 and 2001.

Using Macromedia's Flash software, Web authors were able to create documentary films of still images and voice-over commentary and distribute them as files small enough for Web download. These are narrated, timed slide shows, where still images are 'made moving' by moving the frame in what cinematographers know as panning (a horizontal move), tilting (a vertical move), or zooming over the image.[2] This technique is known from documentary film and television (most notably in Ken Burn's historical documentaries). Liv Hausken (1998) calls this technique 'slide-motion film,' a term we adopt here.

Combinations of Modes

Flash documentaries are one example of how the dynamic modes of speech, music, and sound effects may be combined with the still modes of photography and painting. Furthermore, such documentaries are inserted ('embedded') into written Web pages. They stand firmly in the middle among television, still photography, and print, using rhetorical means of all three.

Viewed from one perspective, this is little different from the combinations of image and language we know from print: A slide-motion film is a story in language and a collection of photos put together into a text.

From another perspective, it is very different, at least in three important ways: Language is read aloud so we can listen and look at the same time; language is dynamic, and the photos projected one after another, so time and rhythm becomes a factor; and the frame moves, so new rhetorical possibilities arise, and we identify a few of them.

When I describe this kind of multimodality as *rhetorical convergence*, it is to stress that it is not sufficient to note that, for instance, images and sound are combined. We need to see what kinds of images and sounds are combined to what effect. Images, speech, music, and sound effects all have been used in many different ways throughout the years. If we agree to call these historical uses different 'rhetorics,' we could also see that what is combined is not merely different media or modes, but different rhetorics.

SLIDE-MOTION FILM: THE WAY WEST

National Geographic

The Flash documentary we are going to examine in this chapter is made by the National Geographic Society using photos taken on an assignment for the *National Geographic Magazine*.

The Society's publications have been famous for their high-quality photography ever since the publishing in 1905 of 11 pages with photos from Tibet (Lutz and Collins 1993). Always embracing new technologies, the Society has maintained an extensive Web presence since 1996. Every month from September 2000 to February 2008, *Nationalgeographic.com* has published a new slide-motion film under the title 'Sights and Sounds,' all made following a rather strict template. Born out of bandwidth concerns, the 'Sights and Sounds' series is a true Web compromise, using still images (to save bandwidth), but presenting them in a television format (borrowing television rhetoric). It is also typical of how Web media are used as supplements to traditional media: Because the Web has virtually no limits to the amount of material that may be published, Web sites of magazines or broadcasting stations routinely offer material that did not fit into the pages or minutes available. In its 'Sights and Sounds' series, the National Geographic Society makes use of some of the thousands of photos taken on each assignment but not included in the magazine.

Selected 'Webumentary'

Our example is the first film in the 'Sights and Sounds' series: 'Sights and Sounds of The Way West' from September 2000 (see Figure 4.1). This film is not only the first, but also was longer and experimented with a larger number of effects than most of the later films. It is an online addition to the article "The Way West" in the September 2000 issue of *National Geographic Magazine*, commemorating the more than 200,000 people who traveled in covered wagons the perilous 4-month journey from the Missouri River to California in the middle of the 19th century.

In the film, photographer Jim Richardson explains in voice-over the route the settlers followed. Combined with Richardson's narration are many quotes from diaries of the emigrants themselves, read by other voices. These excerpts from the diaries are combined into a description of the whole trail in what Gérard Genette (1980) called the *iterative*, recounting once in discourse what happened many times in (hi)story. Thirty-five photos and five watercolours are timed to the narration. The film is divided into five sections that can be accessed out of order by the reader from the links under the picture pane, each of the five beginning with a section of a map of the journey. If the reader does not interrupt the playback, the film runs for some 20 minutes (or longer if narrow bandwidth causes pauses while a part downloads).

Figure 4.1. Screenshot of the Flash documentary 'Sights and Sounds of the Way West.' http://www.nationalgeographic.com/ngm/0009/feature2/

The Interplay of Modes

We analyze 'The Way West' to see how different modes interplay into a multimodal text. Which modes are used in this film, then? Writing, images (photography and watercolor), speech, music, and sound effects. In addition, I argue that the moving frame and the timed projection also add meaning and might be considered as separate modes in this film.

Writing

There is not much alphabetic writing in 'The Way West,' but it serves important functions: The film begins with a written introduction, and the links to different chapters are written below the film pane on the page.

'The Way West' requires that a fairly large Flash file be downloaded before one can start watching. To cover the download time, the authors have taken advantage of the fact that writing loads faster than recorded sound and color photographs. While data are downloading, an animated title sequence appears first, and then a written introduction to the film fades in, three lines at a time. This 'splash sequence,' as it is called in industry lingo, cleverly fills the download time with interest; at the same time, the animated writing makes a smooth transition from static text to the moving images that are to follow.

Static writing is also chosen for the links to the film's five chapters for obvious reasons. Because the links are always present, the static mode of writing is more effective than a sound loop would be. (Static images could have been used but might clash visually with the photographs. It is also generally more difficult to explain links with images than with words.)

Making the Still Move

Photographs and narration carries most of the message in 'The Way West.' The photographs follow an aesthetic we might call 'beautiful nature,' influenced by the tradition of realistic painting. In framing and composition, the photographs tend to follow the examples set up by Western art. Among the practices followed are dividing the image in three equal horizontal and vertical bands (or using the golden section), taking care of the balance of the volumes, and letting lines (planes) have a harmonious and balanced flow. Important in achieving this is to avoid clutter in the photo by framing out elements that do not fit the composition. A sense of depth is achieved by showing recognizable elements separated and at different distances from the spectator or by showing continuous lines disappearing in the horizon.

Along with the modern photographs, five watercolors made by one settler, William Henry Jackson, are included as documents of the time. A few maps are also used.

In a slide-motion film, still images are given dynamic qualities and turned into something resembling video. I argue that the moving frame adds more levels of meaning to the images because it changes the composition of each image, directs the reader's eye in reading, and gives the still images.

When the frame begins to move, it changes the composition of the images. The 35 mm film has a format of 3:2, and most of the pictures in *National Geographic Magazine* are printed in this format. In the online slide-motion film, the movie pane is a fixed 9:5 format, which all the images have to fit in, including Jackson's watercolors (which most likely have other formats originally). To fit, the images are either cropped or the frame moves over the image, always blocking out a part. Thus, the original composition is dissolved, and a series of new ones are put in its place. Thirteen of the 35 photographs are never shown in full frame because the moving frame always frames part of the image out.

The autumn river scene in Figure 4.2, for example, is presented with a tilt motion, first showing the trees, then the river, and finally revealing the white water in the foreground.

In Figure 4.3, I have reassembled the image from screenshots to indicate its original composition. The more complete image gives a different impact as a more balanced whole, establishing the rocks, the trees, and

Figure 4.2. Camera movement over a still image.

Figure 4.3. The still image reassembled.

the background at three distinct distances, given a third of the frame each. This unity is lost under a moving frame; the tilting instead causes the image to be perceived as assembled of parts.

The frame moves in most of the images, either as a slow pan or tilt, zooming in or out, or in a combination by first panning in one direction and then changing the direction and zooming out while panning. These movements direct our gaze and give the image a preferred reading. We can identify the four figures *examining, revealing, pointing, and contextualizing.*

Examining is when the frame moves slowly over the image. The movement shows the detail of the image to the reader, as in the autumn river scene in Figure 4.2.

Revealing is when an examining move reveals something important that was hidden at first. In this panoramic image in Figure 4.4 (presumably of the South Pass), for example, a panning frame leads us to examine the horizon in a certain direction. When this suddenly reveals deep trails in the grass plain to the right of the panorama, our understanding of the scene is simultaneously altered. Although the possibility to view the trails as part of the whole scene is blocked (or left to our memory), a proto-narrative[3] quality of surprise is inserted instead. The revealed item makes us rethink the whole scene in retrospect.

Pointing is to zoom in on a detail in an image, literally pointing it out to the reader. It is a rare figure in 'The Way West,' most typically used in two of the watercolors, where a large canvas is shown at first and then the frame zooms in on a detail, pointing it out to us: a settler chiselling his name into a rock in one picture, gold diggers by the river in another (see Figure 4.5).

Figure 4.4. As the camera moves right, tracks are revealed.

Figure 4.5. Pointing: The camera points out a detail in the image.

At the beginning of each part of 'The Way West,' a map with animated features is shown to help the reader orient him or herself. Instead of zooming, these maps use animation to lead the eye in a pointing manner. All names of places appear large and then shrink while they move to their proper position on the map, giving an impression of hovering over the map and then flying down to land where they belong. Note how the names 'Courthouse Rock' and 'Chimney Rock' are lowered onto the map (see Figure 4.6). The effect is similar to a zoom: As we follow the 'descending' words, we focus on a certain detail in the map (not unlike the iris used in cinema before zoom lenses became available).

These devices are effective for pointing to the illustrative features of the map, but at the same time, one of the main functions of maps is taken away. Maps are most powerful when they provide both detail and overview in one image—what Edward Tufte (1990) calls a micro/macro view in his treatment of maps. Micro/macro views allow the reader to see how details relate to a whole. This requires some time, as the eye scans the image back and forth in a criss-crossing manner. When a map is put under the dynamic movement of a television sequence, this way of reading is hindered, and with the panning and demonstrative animation, it is almost completely blocked. What is easy to see in the case of maps is what happens in all the images. Normally, we read still images by moving

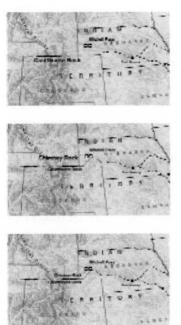

Figure 4.6. Names 'fall down' onto the map.

our gaze in several directions over the image, back and forth, led both by the motive and the composition, relating details to the whole (Gandelman 1991; Kress and van Leeuwen 1996, 2001; Tufte 1990). As the moving frame (or moving detail in the case of maps) catches and leads the eye, certain details and their relations to the whole are pointed out at the expense of others. Thus, all the figures—examining, revealing, and pointing—are demonstrative figures, as is the fourth, *contextualizing.*

Contextualizing is the opposite of pointing: to zoom out from a detail in a picture to the whole scene, thus relating the detail to the whole of which it is a part. Like pointing, it is the use of one image to illustrate two aspects after each other: both overview and detail.

These four figures could probably be combined in many ways, but in 'The Way West,' there is one combination that is dominating: examining the image in a horizontal pan, then tilting the camera diagonally while zooming out, and making the frame drawing a figure-Z over the image (see Figure 4.7). In other words, one first examines the interior of the image before stepping back to view the interior in the context of the whole. It seems to be more effective in images where there isn't one telling detail to be contextualized.[4]

I have presented these figures as figures of the moving frame only. In 'The Way West,' they are paired with sound, music, and voice-over narra-

Figure 4.7. Figure-Z camera movement.

tion, and it stands to reason that the demonstrative devices often will harmonize with the narration, thus pointing out or revealing something that is described in language. Even without language, however, the movement figures would impose a certain preferred reading on an image, which is why I have presented them as figures of movement alone. In addition, we should consider a couple of quite specific combinations of moving frame and voice-over narration causing specific effects, which we call *directing* and *projection*.

In Figure 4.8, the moving frame reveals the deep wagon trail in the rock only after the voice-over has told about it, which gives the effect of the language commanding or *directing* the frame's movement.

The directing figure is also used in a more poetic manner. The story of a company of settlers crossing a desert is illustrated with a photograph of a flat desert land under a blazing sun. As the voice-over says what a young mother wrote in her diary about crossing the desert, the frame zooms in on the sun, thus illustrating the feelings and perils of the family, inviting us to empathize with the settlers. We may call this *projection*—when a person's inner feelings are projected onto a landscape photograph (see Figure 4.9).

Directing and *projection* are about the combination of sound and vision, language and image. These combinations give many other effects, which we discuss more systematically later. Before that, we should note the effects of time and rhythm in the film.

Voiceover: *At Guernsey, Wyoming, the wheels were cutting deep...*

Voiceover: *...into the rock, just as the experience was cutting deep into the personalities of the pioneers.*

Figure 4.8. Voice directing the image.

(Male voiceover:) [. . .] *but most disastrously, they followed the 'Hastings Cutoff' onto the Salt Lake Desert.*
(Female voiceover:) *'Mother knelt down . . .*

. . . and began thoughtfully fitting the ragged edges of paper together. The writing was that of Hastings and her patchwork brought out following . . .

. . . words: 'Two days. Two nights. Hard driving. Across desert. Reached water.' Eliza Donner'

Figure 4.9. Projection of thoughts and emotions onto a landscape.

Time

A sound track is dynamic and moves in time, so adding a sound track also lends dynamic qualities to the presentation. Coordinated with the rhythm of the image projection, it heightens the sense of images existing in a dynamic time, a time that is running. We become aware of the span of each image. To read an illustrated essay is to let the eye go back and forth between image and text because one cannot read the text and view the image at the same time. When sound is added to an image collection, we move into the rhetoric of film and broadcast media—not just because it is sound, but also because language becomes timed. No longer is the reader free to pause from the text and dwell at the details of the photograph. The reader doesn't have to move back and forth between image and text, and cannot either.

When image projection is tied to a verbal commentary, the images tend to become subordinate to language. To see an image for as long as we like, to dwell at details, we would have to pause the soundtrack, which is to destroy it (this can't be done in the first 'Sights and Sounds' installments, including 'The Way West'). When we start the narration again, it most likely begins mid-sentence, and the flow is interrupted.

More important, the use of sound effects adds a sense of reality. The sound of hoofs and wooden wheels are paired with the image of old wagon trails or old paintings of covered wagons. Images of snow-covered mountains are accompanied by the sound of wind. Together with an image of a waterfall, we hear the sound of one. In the photograph, the water is airily frozen as a soft veil using a long exposure. When the sound is added, the water becomes alive and moving again to my imagination. Hausken (1998) noted the same in her study of a selection of fiction slide-motion films—that the addition of sound to freeze frames made the viewer perceive the images less as frozen slices of a time past and more as a section of the dynamic space 'behind the image,' the space we can hear the sounds from, with its own, continuous diegetic time. Sound effects may also anchor both the image and the language, serving as a bridge or mediator between the two. In one place, a landscape with majestic rock formations in fog is paired with the sound of rain while the narrator reads a description of the landscape formed 'by wind and rain.' Without the rain sound, both the wetness of the landscape and the mentioning of rain erosion might have passed unnoticed to me when watching the film.

In addition to sound effects, language, of course, makes complex relations with the images, which we return to later.

Projecting images one after another adds rhythm to a collection of pictures. There is no pause button in 'The Way West,' so the reader has no alternative but to follow the pace of the projection. When we encounter the extremes in pace of 'The Way West,' rhythm becomes noticeable as a device of its own. At the end of the introduction of 'The Way West,' the photographs shift too fast for us to study each one of them; they are instead taken together as a montage whole. This fits the narration nicely as the photographer-narrator here speaks about his travels across half of the United States and the diversity of landscapes he saw. In the fast-paced rhythm of the projection, the images become a summary of the travel route across half of America. (The same figure is mirrored at the end of the slide-motion film, again acting as a summary.)

The other extreme is when the frame pans over certain images and then pauses for a noticeable period of time. At these moments, the viewer is taken out of the flow of television documentary rhetoric and allowed to view a photograph more like in a print magazine or a gallery. The viewer is invited to become more active in reading the image and, at the same time, more contemplative. At one point, the pause also gives an almost musical effect. The story is about the death of one settler; when the narrator then pauses respectfully, so does the images, underscoring the thoughtfulness the scene invites. Such pauses establish 'The Way West' as placed in a middle position between still photography and television.

PUTTING IT TOGETHER: LANGUAGE AND IMAGE

Two Levels

We noted earlier the ability of the voice-over narration to direct frame movement. This is, of course, not the only relation between image and language in a slide-motion film. To understand this relationship in 'The Way West' and other films in National Geographic's 'Sights and Sounds' series, we need to look at this at two levels: (a) each separate image's relation to the narration, and (b) the syntagma of images and sentences: the textual level. We begin at the textual level.

Illustrated Radio

'The Way West' may perhaps best be described as 'illustrated radio.' Without the images, the story told by the narrator would still seem complete, while the sequence of images, although still pretty, would lose its coherence without the narration. Natural languages have grammars that ensure flow within sentences. Linguist and social semiotics theorist M.A.K. Halliday (1985) explains the *coherence* in language 'texts' of several clauses as caused by the clauses containing the same subjects and objects (*reference*) or common words (*lexical organization*), words that are implied (*ellipsis*), or words that bind clauses together (*conjunction*). Narration in 'The Way West' not only has this kind of cohesion, but it also tells a story where codes such as chronology and characters ensure cohesion, flow, and direction of the text (as Roland Barthes [1993] noticed in *S/Z*). Thus, there are many codes that bind the narration together, whereas there are few such cohesive devices in the image sequence.

Certainly, an image sequence may be coherent, using many of the same cohesive codes as language (shared characters, places, activities, etc.). Many books for small children tell stories in images only. In 'The Way West,' however, this is not the case.

Because the language is coherent and the images less so, the resulting appearance to the reader is that the language orders the images, which are there to illustrate and embellish the story.

Image and Writing

According to Roland Barthes (1977b/1964) in 'The Rhetoric of the Image,' there will always be words inside or next to an image that assists us in our interpretation. Barthes lists several kinds of possible relations between words and images; in 'The Rhetoric of the Image,' he discerns between *anchorage* and *relay*. Images are always polysemous, and anchorage is to use language to:

> fix the floating chain of signifieds in such a way as to counter the terror of uncertain signs. [. . .] At the level of the literal message, the text replies—in a more or less direct, more or less partial manner—to the question: what is it? (Barthes 1977b/1964: 39; italics original)

Relay is when:

> text (most often a snatch of dialogue) and image stand in a complementary relationship; the words, in the same way as the images, are fragments of a more general syntagm and the unity of the message is realized at a higher level, that of the story, the anecdote, the diegesis. (Barthes 1977b/1964: 41)

I have already used the word *illustration* twice in describing 'The Way West.' How is illustration related to Barthes' concept of *anchoring*, which we discussed earlier? Barthes (1977b/1964) defined *anchoring* in 'The Rhetoric of the Image.' In the earlier essay, 'The Photographic Message' (Barthes 1977a/1961), however, Barthes also speaks of *illustration*, a language/image relationship that has disappeared in 'The Rhetoric of the Image.' Illustration runs in the opposite direction of anchorage: 'the image function[s] as an episodic return to denotation from a principal message (the text) which was experienced as connoted since, precisely, it needed an illustration [. . .]' (Barthes 1977a/1961: 25). Why is this left out in 'Rhetoric'? Perhaps Barthes came to the conclusion that the image always is polysemous and thus cannot limit or reduce the possible meanings of language. But is language in principle more denoted? Is there in this world a sentence that only has one possible meaning and no connotation? It seems to me (and the reading of 'The Way West' will soon support this) that image and language are always in relay, each limiting each other's polysemy by giving priority to the field of possible meanings that is common to both messages. This balance may lean toward the meanings in the linguistic message, in which case we could call it *anchorage*, or it may lean toward the meanings of the image, deserving the name *illustration*.[5]

At the same time, it appears to me that the reading sequence most of the time will go in the opposite direction: from the polysemous message to the limiting, assisting message. In the case of illustration, the sequence is from a text to an image that assists the text and then back again to the text. Anchorage moves opposite: from an image to its caption, then back again to the image. Relay would then be the middle position between the two, when image and words are interdependent, and there is no privileged reading sequence, but instead images and words are taken in together.

As a whole, 'The Way West' is a text told mostly in words, images added, together with sound effects and occasional music. Its relation between language and image is best described as illustration. If we are to classify each single image, however, we find a variety of forms.

LOCAL RELATIONS

Matters of Sequence

In 'The Way West,' it is often impossible to decide whether the image illustrates the narration or the narration anchors the image. In many cases, it seems to be merely a matter of sequence. If a new subject first is mentioned in the narration before the image appears, it functions as an illustration. A field of meanings is opened and then the image shows it and limits my visual imagination. Instead of wondering what something looks like, I can see it. When the image appears first, it often produces exactly the question in me that Barthes told was what anchorage answered: 'What is it'? So it appears that anchorage and illustration, most of all, are about sequence. Still, when an image appears after the linguistic message, often the reason that I do not wonder what it is of is the fact that it is preanchored in the announcement of the theme. Further, most of the images in 'The Way West' (31 of 45) are landscape photographs, paired with a voice-over story about a journey. Landscape photography always raises an implicit question: 'Where is it?,' whereas a travelogue will make one wonder, 'What does it look like'? It is a circular relation: The image illustrates the linguistic images that anchor it.

Homophonic

Rather than trying to pinpoint which is denoting, language or image, we may look to music theory for inspiration. Musicology has a well-developed terminology for multiple voices unfolding simultaneously over time, and we will apply some of its terms. When image and language have much of the same message (and, in the first case, also the sound track), they reinforce each other, illustrating and anchoring, and we call it *homophonic*. Two examples are given in Figure 4.10.

(Rain sound)
Voiceover: *The action of the wind and the rain upon the soft marley formation of the country presents some of the most curious and interesting objects, which seen in the distance are remarkable imitations of magnificent works of art, partially in ruins. J. Quinthorne, 1846.*

Voiceover: *At the end of the 40-mile desert, they ran into sand dunes.*
"The heat of the day increased, and the road became heavy with deep sand.
The dead animals seemed to become at every step of the way more numerous.
They lay so thick on the ground, that their carcasses, if placed together,
would have reached across many miles of that desert. The stench arising
was continuous and terrible." Margaret Frank, August 1850.

Figure 4.10. Two examples of homophonic word-image relationship.

Polyphonic Relay

In our vocabulary, the relationship that Barthes called *relay* would be a *polyphonic* relationship; when image and language each contributes with something not in the other. There are no examples of polyphonic combinations of language and image in 'The Way West.' Barthes' own example may be used, however—that of narrative movies, where the dialogue refers to something that is shown in images but not mentioned specifically by any of the characters. Thus, image and language are equal parts of the message.

Some of the stranger alignments of image and language in the 'Sights and Sounds' slide-motion films can be attributed to another figure of television rhetoric: what we could call an 'image imperative.' On television, there always has to be images. A blank screen is a sign of failure, an error in the broadcasting system. Even when no program is on, then, many television stations broadcast an image just to show that everything is in order. The demand for images is perhaps most obviously revealed in traditional news broadcasts, in which the studio host is shown reading much of the time. This form is inherited from radio, where it is proven through the years to work very well without any pictures. Modern newscasts, of course, also broadcast a large amount of news footage, but it is rare that all the images shown can be said to have any extra information beyond what is spoken. Most financial news stories, for example, are illustrated with exterior shots of office buildings and interior shots from factory lines, often working without any other relation to the story than a visible company logo. Stories have to be illustrated—that is the demand put on television rhetoric—so journalists and photographers always have to search for suitable imagery.

Accompaniment

The same demand arises in narrated slideshows. When the story is written independently of a prior selection of images, images are sought to accompany the words. As soon as shifting images are introduced, a blank screen is not an option. This often makes the relationship we might call *accompaniment*. In several places in 'The Way West,' the image contributes little more than filling the pane. It does not contrast with the linguistic message, but it is hard to find any illustration or anchoring either. The image is a mere embellishment, an *accompaniment* to the leading (in this case, linguistic) voice (see Figure 4.11).

Voiceover: *South pass was the continental divide, the highest part of the Rockies . . .*

Voiceover: '. . . *Passed the South Pass, the back bone of North America. I got out the Star Spangled banner, and planted it on the south pass . . .*

Voiceover: . . . *A breeze waved it. Our folks came around it, and passed a cheerful evening, fiddling, singing and dancing.' Peter Decker, June 1849.*

Figure 4.11. Image as accompaniment.

We may well ask how likely it is that language will play a soft accompaniment to a leading image. It would have to be a strong image with just a fleeting, casual comment ('Oh, that's a nice one'!). It does not happen in any slide-motion film I have seen on the Web.

Consonant and Dissonant Relations

All three relations we have sketched—homophony, polyphony, and accompaniment—are what we could call harmonious or *consonant*; language and image do not contradict each other.

When they do contradict each other, we will call it *dissonant,* as in the following example from 'The Way West' (Figure 4.12). In the figure, three

Voiceover: *There is in Wyoming a place called 'The Parting of the Ways,' but there were many such partings as pioneer parties split up to take different trails depending on their condition and on the year. We're going to take you on three of them . . .*

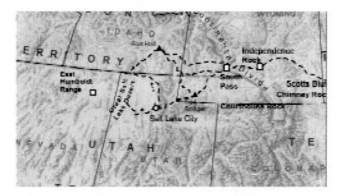

*One called the Hastings Cutoff down across the Salt Lake Desert, another
called the Applegate trail across the Black Rock Desert in Northwest Nevada.*

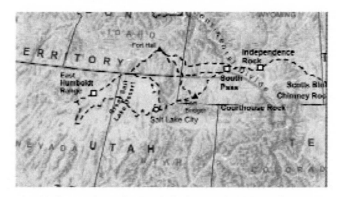

. . . And a third route down the Humbolt river to the Forty-Mile Desert. [. . .]

**Figure 4.12. Image and words do not make sense together, so the image
becomes accompaniment.**

routes are listed in the narration while five are drawn on the map. The
narrator speaks of an 'Applegate trail,' which is not among the five
drawn, and all five run down to the Forty-Mile Desert, the only name that
is found both on the map and in the narration.

The map is drawn too quickly to assist anyone not familiar with the
geography and history, so I guess most readers just forget about the map
and listen to the narrator.

To find an example of dissonance with a photograph, I had to turn to
another installment in the 'Sights and Sounds' series, 'Sights and Sounds
from the New Europe' of January 2002. In 'The New Europe,' many pictures illustrate the narration, but some form strange contrasts (Figure
4.13).

Voiceover: *Hi. I'm Tom Reed. Last spring . . .*

. . . the great photographer Stuart Franklin and I travelled all over Europe . . .

. . . in a huge black BMW we had, looking at a phenomenon . . .

Voiceover: *. . . we are calling 'the new Europe.'*

Figure 4.13. Dissonance between word and image in 'Sights and Sounds of the New Europe'; http://magma.nationalgeographic.com/ ngm/data/ 2002/01/01/sights_n_sounds/media.1.1.html

Dissonance occurs when the narrator tells how he and a photograph-er drove a 'huge black BMW' and a photo of factory workers assembling a small sports car is shown, and especially when 'the great photographer Stuart Franklin' is paired with a shot of a woman feeding goats. So obvi-ously do the two tracks not match that we become aware of it. In the first frame, narrator Tom Reed's portrait is pasted in the corner and thus avoids the danger of identifying one of the men in the background photo of a church with him. The church has little to do with Mr. Reed, howev-er—as little as the fourth picture is an image of the 'new Europe' rather than an anonymous city street. Where pictures two and four are disso-nant to the narration, images one and four are too anonymous to be noticed, they become what we called *accompaniment* previously. I have to select what to focus my attention on because there are two competing messages. Invariably, I choose the language, most of all because it is the coherent, dominating story, but also because the images are so quickly paced that I never get to dwell at them in my own rhythm.

What is considered dissonant is probably a matter of culture and con-vention. For instance, some might immediately recognize the photo of the elderly woman as a great photograph, thus being totally consonant with the narration. Connotations—to language and image alike—are never universally shared, and the consonance or dissonance occurs between the two messages' connotational fields. It is still in line with (con-sonant with) the musical metaphor because dissonance and consonance also are historically and culturally situated. What is a beautiful chord to a jazz fan may not be beautiful to a country and western devotee, and while parallel thirds were considered ugly in the Middle Ages, they are a roman-tic cliché today.

MULTIMODAL POLYPHONY

Continuity Alliance

'The Way West' is a multimodal text, a mix of several modes working together to create meaning for the audience. We have seen how writing only plays a minor part in this Web site. Instead, the message is brought across mainly by spoken language and photography. Sound effects, music, watercolor paintings, and maps also contribute, but their shares in the final message are much smaller. I have also argued that the moving frame and the timed projection add meaning to the text, and thus should be seen as additional modes present in the text. A slide-motion film requires more constant attention to its text than static texts do, but at the same time offers more to attend to. It caters for hearing as well as sight, language as well as iconic images and sounds. The language, the narrative, and the camera movement, and dissolves and fades between images and sound that continue across image shifts all function as cohesive in bringing the text together as a unified, engaging flow—what Hausken (1998) has called the 'continuity alliance.'

We have studied how the relations between the messages in the different modes vary throughout the text, resulting in many different local relations. Still, the overall effect is that one mode, speech, is the most important, and the other modes either support this voice or, at least, are relatively neutral.

I have called this neutral, noninterfering role 'accompaniment,' and I found that this and other musical concepts such as homphony, polyphony, consonance, and dissonance were useful to describe 'The Way West.' Hopefully, this vocabulary can also be helpful in describing other multimodal texts—texts made up of many simultaneous 'tracks' of meaning.

Consonant Combinations

Word and image are still competing for our attention in the digital age. However, if current Web sites are in any way similar to popular genres in the future, it does not seem that coming generations will be alphabetic or image oriented. Almost every day, authors of blogs, journals, Web sites, newsletters, or invitations find it natural to use both writing and images, and many will probably incorporate sound and movement too.

I believe this simple analysis of a Web site with few artistic ambitions has shown that in multimodality one plus one is often much more than two. Complex meanings and conflicting voices frequently occur when several modes are combined in a dynamic text. The skills needed in a multimodal age are probably not just the ability to select one mode or the other, but also to combine modes in a consonant manner, so music does not drown out the words, the words do not contradict the images, and the 'look and feel' of the design harmonizes with the message.

NOTES

1. In fact, it is hard to think of any kind of communication that does not use several modes at once. Even when talking, we make gestures and face expressions, and we add layers of meaning through speech melody. As long as man has written, he has also drawn images on the same surface. Paradoxically, it might be that communication through relatively modern media such as printed

novels, telephone conversations, and recorded instrumental music are the best examples of monomodal communication.

2. Technically speaking, these are not pans or tilts, but shots where the camera moves horizontally or vertically ('tracking' and 'crane' shots) over the still image. In true pans and tilts, the camera is mounted on a fixed point, so the perspective changes as the camera moves. In this chapter, I use the imprecise but shorter terms *pan* and *tilt* for horizontal and vertical movements of the frame.

3. Compare with how Edward Branigan (1992) believes we comprehend narrative. For Branigan, a narrative is held together by a causal logic—a logic the reader constantly is trying to reveal. New developments will make the reader understand the meaning and importance of earlier events. Revealing could thus often be called a *narrativizing* or a *narration* of an image.

4. A watercolor was chosen here as the most extreme, and thus illustrative, example. The figure is also used on many photographs in the feature.

5. Scott McCloud (1994) voices a similar position in *Understanding Comics* when he discusses different relations of words and image in comic strips.

REFERENCES

Barthes, Roland. (1977a/1961). 'The photographic message.' *Image Music Text* Stephen Heath (Transl.). London: Fontana. 15–31. Trans. of 'Le message photgraphique.' *Communications, 1*.

Barthes, Roland. (1977b/1964). 'The rhetoric of the image.' *Image Music Text* Stephen Heath (Transl.). London: Fontana. 32–51. Trans. of 'Rhétorique de l'image.' *Communications, 4*.

Barthes, Roland. (1993). *S/Z*. Richard Miller (Transl.) Oxford: Blackwell.

Branigan, Edward. (1992). *Narrative Comprehension and Film*. London: Routledge.

Eco, Umberto. (1996). 'Afterword.' In Nunberg, Geoffry. (Ed.). *The Future of the Book*. Berkeley: University of California Press. 295–306.

Eco, Umberto. (2004). *The Mysterious Flame of Queen Loana*. Geoffry Brack (Transl.). San Diego, CA: Harcourt.

Fagerjord, Anders. (2003a). 'Rhetorical convergence: studying web media.' In Liestøl, Gunnar, Morrison, Andrew & Rasmussen, Terje. (Eds.). *Digital Media Revisited: Theoretical and Conceptual Innovation in Digital Domains*. Cambridge, MA: The MIT Press. 225–293.

Fagerjord, Anders. (2003b). 'Four Axes of Rhetorical Convergence.' *Dichtung Digital* (4/2003). Available at http://www.dichtung-digital.org/2003/4-fagerjord.htm

Gandelman, Claude. (1991). *Reading Pictures, Viewing Text*. Bloomington: Indiana University Press.

Genette, Gérard. (1980). *Narrative Discourse*. Jane E. Lewin (Transl.). Ithaca: Cornell University Press. Trans. of 'Discourd du récit.' *Figures III*. Paris: Seuil, 1972.

Halliday, Michael. (1985). *An Introduction to Functional Grammar.* London: Arnold.

Hausken, Liv. (1998). *Om det utidige: Medieanalytiske undersøkelser av fotografi, fortelling og stillbildefilm* [Of the Untimely: Media Analytical Investigations of Photography, Narrative, and Slide-motion Film]. Unpublished doctoral dissertation, Department of Media Studies, University of Bergen.

Kress, Gunther & van Leeuwen, Theo. (1996). *Reading Images: The Grammar of Visual Design.* London: Routledge.

Kress, Gunther & van Leeuwen, Theo. (2001). *Multimodal Discourse: The Modes and Media and Contemporary Communication.* London: Arnold.

Lutz, Catherine & Collins, Jane. (1993). *Reading National Geographic.* Chicago: University of Chicago Press.

McCloud, Scott. (1994). *Understanding Comics: The Invisible Art.* New York: Harper Perennial.

Tufte, Edward. (1990). *Envisioning Information.* Cheshire, CT: Graphics.

5

MEDIATING HYBRID DESIGN

IMAGINATIVE RENDERINGS OF AUTOMOTIVE INNOVATION ON THE WEB

Andrew Morrison

Synne Skjulstad

CONTEXT

The Web and Communication Design

The World Wide Web has now been a part of popular and commercial culture for over a decade, and it has spawned and cross-hatched a medley of design disciplines and practices. In particular, earlier approaches to graphic design have been transformed on the Web via the application of digital tools and systems.

In contrast to many publications about the Web in the field of Human–Computer Interaction (HCI; e.g., Nielsen 1999), we approach Web design from a mediated communication design perspective (see also Skjulstad, Chapter 11). This refers to the connections and combinations of content, media, information, and style that constitute a blended discourse that has communication as its overarching intent. Our interest in this chapter is on how effective communication design in the domain of Web advertising is achieved through the use of visual media and references to digital imaging technologies as part of the semiosis of a digital aesthetic. We relate media types, modes of visualization, and layers of content in one Web site to the branding of a product—a luxury hybrid-powered sports utility vehicle (SUV)—that is marketed as a design innovation in its own right (see Figure 5.1; Heffner et al. 2006).

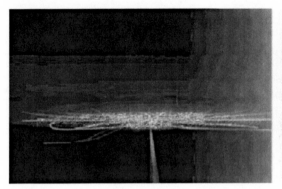

Figure 5.1. Screengrab from Flash movie inside Toyota's Web site for their hybrid SUV.

Goals of the Chapter

Our main goal in the chapter is to account for how visual communication strategies are employed in a Web site that markets innovation in one of the leading commercial areas of product design—namely, the automotive industry. In contrast to the analysis of earlier print-based graphic design and advertising discourse, we focus on the Web-based mediation that draws on a medley of media types and their connotations within digital media aesthetics (e.g., Cubitt 1998; Morrison et al. 2007). Through close textual analysis, we explain how visually oriented communication design is used to build a persuasive, coherent conceptualization of a hybrid, yet luxury, vehicle. Online, this luxury vehicle is projected as both a techno-logically advanced product for purchase and as a visionary conceptualiza-tion of a sustainable future made possible through design. In this sense, the overall Web site, and one video in particular, embodies principles of design innovation, together with sustainable and ecologically motivated design (e.g., Fry 2004).

These principles are inscribed within a digital aesthetic (e.g., Manovich 2001) that is achieved by way of reference to developments in digital imaging technologies and their connotations. Scanning, neural net-working, animation, and x-ray-like tracings are used to inscribe the tech-nologically insightful as part of a scopic domain. Here innovations travel from minute sparks of creativity in the brain and mind across hemi-spheres to hybrid mechanical and electrical systems. In turn, these gener-ate ideas and experiences that move physically and conceptually, across networks of roads and communication channels as ideas, memes, and experiences. We show, too, that recent writings on experience design (e.g., McCarthy & Wright 2004) may be extended to the detailed analysis of the articulation of persuasive discourse on the Web. Intertextual references may also be invoked from popular science fiction texts such as the film *Minority Report*.[1]

We present a microanalysis (e.g., Fagerjord 2003) of one Web site of a global automotive corporation that projects their market leadership and technological advantage in hybrid fuel technologies. This analysis functions as a means of also addressing issues of the uses of visual media and visualization techniques as part of advertising socially responsible appetite at a time of diminishing oil reserves and conflicts related to them. We argue that attention to a social semiotics and rhetorics of the visual adds to an understanding of Web design as a complex of communication with and through digital technologies in which digital representations are part of the texturing of online branding and mediated persuasion.

In zooming in on one Web site—and a video that is a main part of it and the relationships between the site and a video in *Flash*—we show how this car maker uses design superiority and confidence as content in its Web promotion. We reveal how a digitally inflected aesthetics is achieved through visualizations of scanning technologies (e.g., Dumit 2004) and microlevel neurosystems and their electrical activity. We demonstrate how hybrid design is projected through metaphors of networking and transmission centered on neurological imaging technologies and the movement of ideas between the individual and the collective.

Between Page and Screen

Hybrid design is often used to refer to the convergence of digital media types and online communication strategies. We argue that the close study of a Web site can inform our understanding of how design innovation is mediated metaphorically where visual references to digital technologies are a part of branding. At this early point in the chapter (as part of our goal in linking analysis to its textual referent), we encourage readers to depart from this print document and to access the Web site to which we refer. We are keen that readers experience how this site is designed and how the video therein functions. The specific vehicle in focus is the Lexus RX400h from Toyota.[2]

ISSUES

In this section, we cover a range of interlinked issues that help contextualize the manner in which the hybrid SUV is represented as a design idea, object, and innovation. These areas are: Web design as a diffuse field, languages of advertising, branding and advertising on the Web, automotive design, and hybrid car design.

Web Design: A Diffuse Field

Web design is a field where researchers, practitioners, developers, software designers, and graphic designers all center around Web sites but from somehow different viewpoints (e.g., Skjulstad 2007a). Differences in how Web design is conceptualized are deeply rooted in the history of Web development, where engineers saw the medium as an arena for exchange of documents. Researchers and developers tended to see the Web as providing users with freedom to customize the presentation of content to their own needs. As the Web took a more visual turn, graphic designers began to explore the possibilities of this new medium. The variety of professional approaches to Web site design has created both problems and challenges for finding adequate research strategies to a medium that is considered as both a transparent 'window' (following Bolter & Gromala 2003) for uncluttered flow of information and a 'mirror' where the mediated interface is considered as an integral part of the communication (Bolter & Gromala 2003; Engholm 2003; Munster 2003; Strain & VanHoosier-Carey 2003).

This chapter approaches Web design as something in between the window and the mirror. Choices made in the selected *Lexus* site a part of a prefigured information strategy, where notions of usability and a focus on ambient audio visual experience are successfully paired. We refer to the focal point of this analysis as communication design.

Media, Advertising, and the Web

Issues of representation and relationships between visual and verbal text have been widely studied in advertising and in media and communication. Researchers have concentrated on how intertextuality has been employed to create overall persuasive texts, whether in magazines or on billboards. Much of this research has arisen from a critical social semiotic perspective (Dyer 1982; Vestergaard & Schrøder 1985; Williamson 1978/1994; Goddard 1998; Cook 1992). Relations between visual and verbal language have been central to these approaches, drawing on semiotics and rhetorical analysis, and also relations between art and advertising (Gibbons, 2005). This has extended to work on the branding of cars (e.g., see Kilbourne 2000).

However, this tradition of close mediated commercial and cultural analysis of advertising seems not to have permeated much into the study of ads on the Web. There appears not to be much close analysis of how Web ads communicate and how various approaches to the study of digital texts might be applied in their uses of digital tools and mediation (see e.g., Goggin 2000). Web-specific design issues for mediating and communicating content are not prominent. Our chapter is concerned with studying Web text as product and less its process-oriented uses.[3] This has been the approach we have taken to other analyses of Web-based advertising, where we focus on mediating artifacts and artifacts of mediation in relation to the online marketing of waterfront development (Morrison & Skjulstad 2007) and the use of hyperrealist visualizations in mediating and selling as yet to be built residential properties (Morrison & Skjulstad 2007, 2010). These publications may be seen as close textual analyses of innovations in digitally mediated branding and advertising in 'new media' (Stafford & Farber 2005). There are few studies that look into the multimodal and multimediational articulations of online advertising. Although it is not our direction here, elsewhere we look at how advertisers are making use of a variety of techniques to motivate and indeed circulate consumers' own production of messages on brands (Morrison & Skjulstad 2007).

Interest in branding has grown in recent years (e.g., Arvidsson 2006) in part popularized by the work of Naomi Klein (2001). Online advertising is now a huge part of the commercial structure of the Web, as well as our daily experience as consumers of digitally mediated goods and services. As the design of communication aimed to persuade, advertising on the Web is often not researched from a visual design perspective. It is predominantly analyzed in terms of customer behavior and revenue systems (e.g., John et al. 1998; Lin & Yang 2004; Sundar & Kim 2005). To date, there is little close analysis of how Web sites function as symbolic and communicative constructs in which static and dynamic elements of mediated design coexist.

Much of this research has been on business models, marketing strategies, and consumer behaviour and little on rhetorically related analysis, even in online journals. However, the Web has been used as a site for marketing car design and brands in ways not easily achieved in print and in earlier electronic media. A strong example of this is the BMW short film competition on the Web.

Automotive Design

Car design is a growing field within research on product design, and it is increasingly being aestheticized commercially (e.g., Welsch 1997). Norman (1992), for example, referring to car signals, argues that feedback will need to be developed as part of human-device relations, arguing more recently that 'There's an automobile in HCI's future' (Norman

2005). This is taken up in a growing literature on satellite navigation, vehicle sensing technologies, and hybrid fuel systems. In addition, the design process in the automotive industry has incorporated computer-aided design software and research into the uses of digital tools in the design process that has been studied, in terms of engineering and body design (e.g., Lin & Yan 2004). Gender-focused design and development, as well as gendered market orientation, has been taken up at Volvo (Styhre et al. 2005). Hay and Packer (2004: 230) remind us that automotive design, especially in the United States, has to do with regimes of mobility (after Foucault) that are about emerging arrangements of people and resources but also contracts about their management. They ask, for example, in relation to the 'smart car' and its sensing apparatus, how the self may be conducted through technologies and their assemblages. These writers link the 'intelligent' car with mediation, although their attention is primarily on the negotiation and regulation of freedom with respect to 'automobility.' Few studies examine the articulation via persuasive discourse of such 'intelligent automotive design.'

Digital tools are now widely employed in the design and implementation of robotic construction of cars. This has been most apparent in Toyota's approach to transforming modes of production from the earlier assembly line of Henry Ford to machinically automated ones. It is thus no surprise that digital imaging technologies and an overall digital design ethos and aesthetic are prevalent in Toyota's Web site for their luxury brand *Lexus* hybrid SUV. This is in marked contrast to critical and analytical discourses about the emergence of SUVs in popular culture (e.g., Andersen 2000) as multipurpose vehicles, and their contribution to increased fuel consumption and emissions.

Hybrid Car Design

Intensive and competitive research is now underway into alternative fuel sources for automotive transportation (e.g., Motavalli 2001; Westbrook 2001).[4] It is part of a changing landscape of 'automobility' (Urry 2004). In contrast to most automakers, other than perhaps Honda, Toyota invested early in hybrid fuel technologies, linking petrol engines with electric motor systems. The development of electric motors has a long design history of its own (Anderson & Anderson 2004). Hybrid vehicles have also now entered popular consumer culture; researchers now investigate the wider cultural acceptability and self-image construction of hybrid vehicle owners (Heffner et al. 2005).

Toyota's investment and vision to transform the nature of powered transportation is in marked contrast to the strategies of other world leaders, especially those original brand leaders in North America, Ford and

General Motors. In the last decade in the North American market, automakers have centered on the sales of SUVs, which have until recently powered revenues. Strong environmental lobbying and changes in legislation on emissions and the taxing of SUVs, together with escalating oil prices, have challenged this growth avenue. Toyota has been able to literally drive its way into the SUV market with the launch of its luxury hybrid model. Once considered imitators, Japanese car manufacturers, including Honda and Nissan-Renault, are now world leaders in both technology and environmental positioning vis-à-vis the automotive industry.

It is a bitter irony for Ford[5] that it has had to licence hybrid fuel cell technology from Toyota. However, Ford has committed to hybrid technologies (e.g., having bought *THiNK*[6] from its Norwegian owners) and continues to do so. A range of hybrid alternatives is also being researched across the industry, including fuel sources other than electric. Toyota is in a rather unique position to brand its hybrid SUV online.[7] It is able to use its design innovation and its hybrid character as content and as a point of reference for articulating this in an explicitly digital aesthetic. To understand this more fully, we next turn to a more granulated outline of communication design relating to the Web.

APPROACH

On Communication Design

A formal vocabulary for analyzing visually oriented Web design is not fully developed. In contrast, there are numerous books on how to design for the Web, many of which provide excellent guidance built on designers' experience. However, despite the enormous variety of Web site designs, sites are often just referred to as Web 'pages' without any further specifications. We propose that Web media, and indeed other digital media, may be usefully viewed from a communication design perspective.

Communication design may be conceptualized as an overarching analytical framework within which the communicative intent, texturing, and design for engagement of users may be considered, at times also along with users' views. In such a view, Web design is considered as more than the sum of the parts over time (Löwgren & Stolterman 2004). These researchers from informatics refer to such a holistic conceptualization of software design as 'the dynamic gestalt' (Löwgren & Stolterman 2004: 137). This is important in our analysis because we are primarily concerned with investigating how a Web site is designed for communicating a certain image/idea about a product or a company, that is, as online advertising and branding. However, in our socioculturally framed view of communication design, how the content is worded and what is actually communicated and through what patternings of media are central.

Layers of Meaning Making

An analytical communication design approach sees the design of possible and intended communication as working through several layers of semiosis (Kress & van Leeuwen 1996). First, there is the matter of technically oriented design of the site as framework (e.g., single-screen interface in *Flash* or html sites with interlinked 'documents,' and taking into consideration whether there is movement in the interface in the form of moving menus, and whether the transitions between sections of the site are visualized as moving elements or more like 'jumps' between sections of the site). Second, there is the interplay of digital graphic design elements, such as the use of colors, fonts, images, animations, white space, and graphical density in realizing mise-en-scéne in the site (Skjulstad 2004). Third, the written/spoken messages in the site are realized through choices of voice, modes of articulation, and media types. These levels are all considered as equally important in a communication design-oriented analysis of a Web site and the interplay between the design choices made therein. Here we may speak of cross-media design.

CONTEXT

Background

Our analysis is informed by our own extensive use of the Web since its popular inception, together with experience as codesigners in several Web-based projects concerned with the online mediation of multimedia content (e.g., Skjulstad & Morrison 2005). This research has been conducted through combinations of developmental research projects and analytical approaches. The framework has been interdisciplinary, but the main focus has mostly been on experimental media and communication design. Our wide use and study of art and design sites—as users, designers, teachers, and researchers of digital media (Skjulstad 2007b)—has also made us aware of how commercial online advertising tends to be designed by professionals who are fluent in designing web sites that reflect and mirror the values that the producers of commercial products want users to associate with their product.

Neural Imaging Technologies and Research

Focus on this Web site and its uses of digital imaging technologies was in part prompted by interest in technologies of visualization. In particular, the Blue Brain research project on the building of a simulated large cortical neural network drew our attention to the visualizations of neural activity and their representations.[8] In this project, still images and their contextualization as part of mediating the kinds of microactivity of electrically mediated messages inside our heads and throughout the network of the body's nervous system provided identifiable visual synonymy with several of the images appearing in the *Lexus* advert.

ANALYSIS

We now move to examine aspects of hybrid semiosis embedded in this Web site. These aspects are: hybrid visual discourses, the construction of ambient aesthetics, micro- and macrorelations between elements of the site, visual metaphors, and visualization and visual layering. We cover each of these en route to a main point of focus—that is, the analysis of the 60-second animated sequence that is central to the site.

A Hybrid of Discourses

One interesting feature with the *Lexus* advert is that it successfully combines three different visual discourses. Through this merging of visual styles, multiple meanings are articulated, and in the last instance, the *Lexus* hybrid SUV is communicated as the result of cutting-edge technology and innovation in several ways. The three visual discourses that are intertwined are: (a) science fiction, (b) neurology in the form of microprocesses and brain signals, and (c) advanced technological visualization techniques related to scanning technologies. Through the blend of these visual discourses in the ad, a medley of connotations is created. This medley may be read separately or as a set of possible interpretations and connotations.

   These visual components are also further inscribed through verbalization (e.g., Kress & van Leeuwen 1996; Kress 1998). The start screen, as with all others, includes verbal text that is closely pared down and paired with the visual material. At the level of main menus, this verbal text is accompanied by still images, at times with delicate cycles of organic images. Further in, and especially relating to the technical specifications of the vehicle, small animated features are included. These trace the references to medical imaging and functional MRI capacities related to movement, visibility, and intensity. In these more specific layers, we also see zoom-ins, animations, and uses of block color that are part of an integrated digital aesthetic. This contrasts with the earlier 'muscular,' outdoor adventure representation of SUVs (Andersen 2000).

An Overall Communication Design Aesthetic

As critical discourse analysis has shown (e.g., Morrison 2005), intimate linkages and layers of discourse exist between verbal and visual text, here encapsulated by reflexive wording of the design qualities in the site and the positioning of the vehicle as a superior design product.

The *Lexus* site (see Figure 5.2) makes explicit its own design aesthetic in a subsection on design. It is important to refer to this first because it sets the tone for the whole site, including the *Flash*-based material analyzed later. This aesthetic is framed with reference to simplicity and precision, although this is clearly phrased as being achieved through more than the design of surface attributes. The site states that:

> Japanese design seeks to achieve simplicity through masterful use of materials. It strives for the purest possible expression using minimum resources. There is a word for this, muda, meaning 'to avoid needless waste.'

The overall site maintains an ambient and minimalist aesthetic. The designed material of the car is presented alongside natural materials such as a stone and leaves. In an animated sequence, organic close-ups of a leaf are included, together with zooms in on a speedometer and roving shots of car body lines.

The ambient aesthetic is maintained across a variety of features presented in a Web site that, despite its positioning as innovation for hybrid technology and the economy of design, is still concerned to market a large vehicle made of steel. In contrast, white space and natural lines are included. As part of this mixed and cross-media site, a design booklet may be downloaded alongside stories of cars on the road, such as the RX 400 in Iceland. A further section employs a horizontal menu bar and layout conventions from film editing software (see Skjulstad & Morrison 2005).

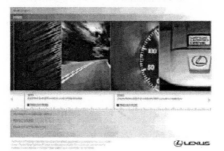

Figure 5.2. (Top two images) Design principles articulated, verbally and visually with automotive and organic materials shown; (Middle) *Lexus* downloadable magazine with featured stories; (Left) 'Timeline,' with hybrid selected, showing film software conventions.

Aestheticizing the Technical

The site extends its ambient aesthetic and mediation of precision further to other genres of technical mediation. Alluding to technical manuals and a variety of visualizations, core features of the hybrid SUV are annotated in the genre of a showcase (Figure 5.3), which blends the realist photographic with the cutaway illustration. A gallery is also included.

In addition, a pop-up menu leads to 'The Technology Explorer.' This section allows one to scroll through and select from a diversity of features in a verbal menu. Each item leads to a visually illustrated feature. Here a

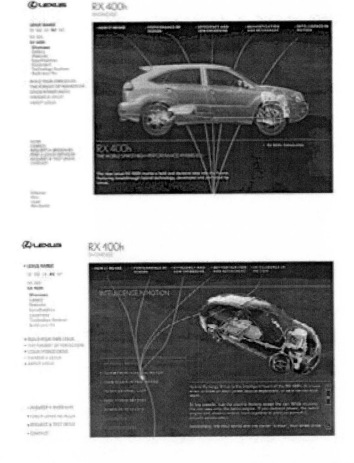

Figure 5.3. (Top) Dynamic menu for showcase. (Bottom) Item selected from dynamic menu leads to visual cutaway with accompanying verbal explanation.

variety of visualizations is included that connects to the specific technical feature being presented. In Figure 5.4, we see the photographic realism of an item in the steering wheel—namely voice command in two European languages that allows control of satellite navigation, air quality, and the audio system. In visual contrast, a number of features are depicted through multitone line drawings, such as that illustrating the added feature of knee airbags.

Ambient Aesthetics and an Animated Film

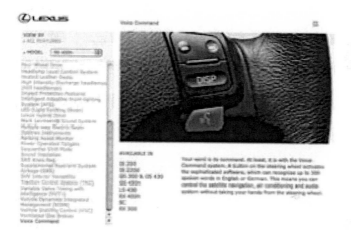

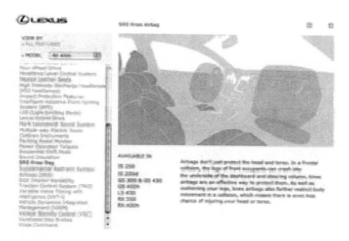

Figure 5.4. Selected features from Technology Explorer section. (Top) Voice command on steering wheel interface. (Bottom) Knee airbags.

The Web site contains an animated sequence made in Macromedia *Flash*, where still images are juxtaposed.[9] There is also the option to see these elements of the animation in a video. This video is the primary visual object in the site and it provides a strong dynamic, aesthetic, and conceptual frame for the overall site. The video is broadcast on TV, too. In this section, we refer to the *Flash* animation because this has some other features than the video. In general, this may be framed as part of a 'widescreen aesthetic' applied to online advertising (Cossar 2005).

Below, we do not use captions for the images. As is visible in the first of the selected still images in the series shown in Figure 5.5, the animation space is split in two by a white line. In the animation, this line moves back and forth from the right to the left and back as the images in both spaces are replaced by other images. The white line moves steadily and slowly, at the same vertical angle, demarcating something that may be seen as a Web-related distant relative of the cutting between movie clips or mediation via a scanner.

The scanner-like features included in this advert serve as a device for the replacement of the images in the *Flash* file. It also adds an extra layer of science, science fiction, and neurology discourse to the animation. The simple white moving stripe with its fades between images is reminiscent of those of MRIs, although these do not represent strictly the actual medical imaging. The white in the moving stripe is also the same color as the background of the rest of the Web site.

There are two different images visible in the animation at all times. This signals the overall concept of linking two domains that runs through the video as well as the broader marriage of different fuel technologies in this vehicle. The surrounding Web site supports this visual rhetoric with

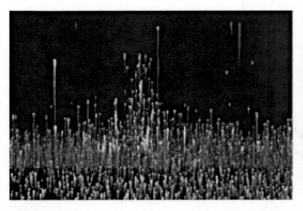

Figure 5.5. A series of stills in sequence from the video advert for the Toyota hybrid SUV.

an open and spare design, as already mentioned, that evinces an economy of verbal expression, mirroring the statement in the submenu on *Lexus* design.

Clicking on the video option launches the *Flash* animated movie. The

movie picks up the blue-grey tonal range of the overall site. Particles rise from a base, accompanied by piano music. This leads to the particle burst (left), connoting both micro and macro representations from both physics and galactical space.

The overall dynamic computer-generated aesthetic is established. This overhead shot is replaced by movement into a weave of fibre-like elements, dense and then entangled.

There is a sense of an organic quality in this emerging kinesis, along with one of complexity. From this sequence, one strand shoots upward and then reappears in a new frame.

These small impulse-like visualizations are encased in a complexity of fibers, Ganglia-like, and are all active and moving. Strands shoot up and then appear in the background.

These impulses filled with energy, light, and motion then burst upward and cascade against a ceiling.

One lone beam of energized motion makes it through this membrane, reaches beyond its boundary, and moves out into a deep dark space. Only at this point does the voice over commence: 'Some ideas evolve. Some ideas break through and change everything'

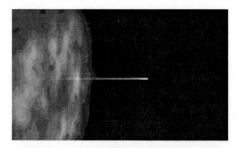

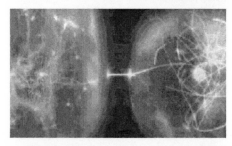

The animation has been leading up to this trajectory of an idea, a meme, that crosses a boundary, a hemisphere, and finds new ground. This single impulse then reaches a second hemisphere, the synaptic jump signalled and the electricity of the hybrid activity visualized.

Intelligent thought has traveled within the mind and across spheres. The voice over announces, 'Introducing the world's first performance hybrid SUV.' The 'intelligent' car is born, conceptually, visually, and via media.

The synaptic jump moves from the brain to the wider network through a radiant line that becomes the car. This shifts through a pull-back shot of the two hemispheres, which morphs into a pixelated image, revealing the grill and logo of a *Lexus*. This becomes the 'blueprint' line drawing of the hybrid vehicle, in motion, its motor apparent, but driverless. Movement is symbolized by an underlying dynamic image in *Flash*. The point of view then shifts to an overview with the second power system also visible at the rear. This is accompanied by the voice over saying, 'The RX400h. Breakthrough thinking, from *Lexus*.' The car then transforms back into an idea impulse, somewhat like an illuminated match head. It becomes a line of moving light that connects to a larger network. This network is illuminated, electrified as if it were now in wide shot, synapti-

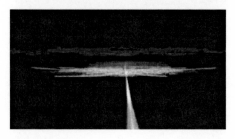

cally spread to form a night cityscape. The screen then fades to black with a logo for *Lexus* and the buyline 'The pursuit of excellence.'

Micro/Macro

The *Lexus* ad brings together different scales. One is concerned with visualizing microprocesses that cannot be seen by the human eye—the other macroprocesses that cannot always be seen without a crane or special apparatus. In the ad, the perfection of the superior, hybrid product is achieved through this blending of micro- and macrophenomena made universal and encompassing everything from the smallest detail to the more general qualities of the car. The use of visualizations of microphenomena in the ad brings forward connotations to the detailed microtechnology in the car. It creates a notion of the car as being perfected down to the smallest high-tech detail, to the craftsmanship and innovation that has paved the way for details in the car that is not visible to the human eye, but that are the building blocks—the molecules of the hybrid *Lexus*. The visualization of macrophenomena (i.e., the universe) is part of visually branding this car as something also immense and undeniably novel.

Visual Metaphors Metaphors and Layering

The blending of similar visual expressions though differences in scale suggests that this hybrid car is innovative from the smallest particle to the whole galaxy of parts. Advances in space technology are a related reference. For the ad to move even further away from the greasy motorized mechanics of the industrial age, a visual 'techno' discourse is introduced that is strongly cinematic (Manovich 2001). This visual discourse may be found in graphic design, films, research books on new media, as well as other popular cultural phenomena. A certain technoaesthetic that has appeared alongside the popularizations of computers has been explored within the now well-established field of electronic art (e.g., Paul 2003). This, too, is a strong point of reference.

FINDINGS AND CONCLUSIONS

To Be Persuaded?

Despite the overall ambient design of this Web site and its connotative persuasion, the body text asserts that, '. . . the parameters of perfection shift and expand.' Further, Toyota '. . . acknowledges that this pursuit involves a continuing and evolving journey, rather than a destination.' The *Flash* animations in the form of scanned material, the video file, and the related animated features in the specifications sections all work to create layers of persuasive discourse not possible in print advertising.

The visual conceptualizations of the *Lexus* hybrid SUV departs from the mechanical, rusty, and greasy assemblies of machine parts so far important in motorized culture. Digital technology and fine-tuned electronics have replaced this conceptualization through the application of contemporary brain imaging technology specifically in online car advertising. Following McQuarrie and Phillips (2005), increased use of images in advertising strengthens branders' indirect and inferential mediation of a product.

Collaboration between humans and machines has been theorized extensively within technology studies and HCI. In this advert, the car is not only visualized as a computer, but as a brain, and as an intelligent, independent agent. Humans are not portrayed as interacting with an advanced machine; rather, they are absent from the entire Web site. The human agent is portrayed as pure brain power interacting with another intelligence embedded into the nervous center of the car. The *Lexus* is thereby represented as offering a sophisticated version of postembodied interaction, reaching beyond the body into the immateriality of communication via thought. Earlier study of SUV cultures and advertising (Andersen 2000) concentrated on vehicles adaptable to varied needs and their symbolic naturalization as part of the rough outdoors. These representations camouflaged their negative effects on the environment. In contrast, this advert of the Lexus hybrid SUV erases earlier discourses of SUVs and the outdoors and their contradictory consumption of scarce resources. Instead, we experience a wholly digital simulated immateriality within which a superior hybrid fuel technology offers added value. It provides drive power that is greater than that of petrol models. It also rides above natural landscapes and steers consumers toward reading automotive activity on the 'infobahn.'

In such a reading, the car and the human are represented as equal parts in electrically laden communication. The sparks in the human brain match fully the sparks in the intelligently designed 'mind' of the *Lexus* because artificial intelligence is directly linked to the driver's brain. This somehow makes the car more than a machine: It is now projected as an intelligent entity, the result of the cumulative technology research. The car becomes part of human consciousness; we are persuaded that it now lodges in our cortex, part of a network of associations and references, a designed product beyond many of our pockets but a Web-mediated instance of hybrid design that resonates in its innovativeness.

In researching communication design and explorative digital design in various forms, we have found that there appears to be a gap between the volume of specialized Web designs for advertising and branding purposes and a scarcity of humanistic communication design-centered research. It is important to investigate how selected examples of commercial Web sites apply various communicative resources available for Web communication in designing persuasive online discourse. Web design and advertising are connected fields because the majority of businesses have a Web presence. Businesses that are preoccupied with innovation tend to also market themselves through innovative Web design and, through this, position themselves as innovators in this domain as well (see Skjulstad 2007b). Innovative examples of advertising are often collected into glossy coffee table books, such as a recent collection of adverts by the fashion company Deisel (Klanten 2006), which, although visually strong, rarely accompanying analytical text.

Driving Ahead

Our focus on one Web site and its intricate blend of media types, intertextual references, and connotations shows how detailed the persuasive moves may be in Web-based advertising. The inscription of cerebral imaging, and by association clearer thinking, amplifies the need for clear ecologically situated choices in the future design of the automotive industry. Toyota employs its own rhetoric of design success to mediate its design innovation.

The analysis of the selected Web site indicates that branding online may be understood as a complex of associations and connotation through which the popular, symbolic, technological, and digital may be seen as coaxially constructed and mediated, persuasively. The complexity of this and other carefully shaped online dynamic mediations may be appreciated through repeated viewing and attention to their granularity. A communication design approach, which draws on media studies perspectives alongside others in Web design, may be further grounded in social semiotics and critical discourse studies that are framed in a wider sociocultural view of mediated communication.

Multimodal Multiliteracies

As online mediation changes over time, reflecting changing practices in the relations between tools and signs, students of media and communication will continue to need to examine the multiple modes of persuasion. There is clearly room already for closer analysis of Web-based advertising at a textual level. This is needed to supplement the study of online advertising as mediated marketing based on user-driven models with click through rates and the tracking of customer loyalty.

Toyota released a hybrid version of its luxury flagship, the Lexus sedan, ahead of other luxury automakers, such as Mercedes, BMW, and Cadillac. In terms of product design, the auto industry now has several hybrid manufacturers that also need to articulate their innovations to a public that has seen hikes in oil prices, most aggressively outside North America. Yet in 2010 we have seen the mass recall of Toyota's most popular hybrid cars and the tarnishing of their earlier near seamless marketing.

A range of fuel technologies continue to be researched. Drawing on experience in Brazil in ethanol-based fuel production from sugar (and applied as far afield as Zimbabwe), in the United States farms have begun to diversify into ethanol production from a variety of materials. Conflicts in the Middle East, the closure of an oil pipeline in Alaska, and the ongoing war in Iraq have together again raised oil prices. Not since the oil crisis of the 1970s have consumers been faced with the production politics that lie behind their own motoring and have been forced to examine the 'costs' of car makers advertise. There is also the demise of the U.S. car industry following the recent financial crisis and a corresponding range of new stimulus measures. In the advert for the *Lexus* hybrid SUV, it is the ambient articulation of innovation and the online building of persuasion that mark this advert as a mediated innovation.

Students of media and communication, as well as those in business and art and design schools, will continue to need to deconstruct mediated persuasion, to study its texturings and layers of meaning making, and its intertextual and intermediated construction. Branding a luxury vehicle is a far cry from intertextually marketing and supporting a popular 'economy' model. Do we need much persuasion? Hydrogen is now the new allegedly zero emissions fuel of the future and Honda is one of the market leaders, already taking concept car mediation into online video of commercial sedans.

NOTES

1. http://www.lexus-europe.com/lexus_cars/rx/rx400h/index.asp
2. We hope to be able to take this up in a later publication.

3. See a film with Madonna: http://www.metacafe.com/watch/76518/ bmw_vs_madonna/

4. http://www.ingentaconnect.com/search/article?title = henry + ford&title_type = tka&year_from = 1998&year_to = 2005&database = 1&pageSize = 20&index = 8

5. See http://www.ford.com/en/innovation/technology/puttingHybridsOnThe Road.htm

6. On 'ThiNK,' see http://www.aftenposten.no/english/business/article401371.ece http://news.bbc.co.uk/2/hi/uk_news/2309397.stm

7. On the potential for negative effects of the extension of branding and flagship models, see John et al. (1998).

8. The Blue Brain Project is developed by the Brain Mind Institute, EPFL, Switzerland, in conjunction with IBM. For details, see http://bluebrain project. epfl.ch/Blue%20Brain%20Project.htm. Specifically on the neocortical column, see http://bluebrainproject.epfl.ch/brain%20images1.htm. See also a related journalistic article in New Scientist called 'Mission to build a simulated brain begins': http://www.newscientist.com/article.ns?id = dn7470

9. Please follow the link for video under the main image midscreen: http://www. lexus-europe.com/lexus_cars/rx/rx400h/index.asp

ACKNOWLEDGMENTS

An earlier version of this chapter was presented at the WonderGround design research conference, October 1-4, 2006 (http://www.iade. pt/drs2006/). Our thanks to Gunnar Leistøl for his critical reading and to conference participants for their suggestions. All images and text used with permission from the Toyota Motor Corporation. This research, however, was not funded by Toyota.

REFERENCES

Andersen, Robin. (2000). 'Road to ruin: the cultural mythology of SUVs.' In Andersen, Robin & Strate, Lance. (Eds.). *Critical Studies in Media Commercialism*. New York: Oxford University Press. 158-172.

Anderson, Curtis & Anderson, Judy. (2004). *Electric and Hybrid Cars*. Jefferson, NC: McFarland.

Arvidsson, Arild. (2006). *Brands: Meaning and Value in Media Culture*. London: Routledge.

Bolter, Jay. (2003). 'Critical theory and the challenge of new media.' In Hocks, Mary & Kendrick, Michelle. (Eds.). *Eloquent Images*. Cambridge, MA: The MIT Press. 19-36.

Bolter, Jay & Gromala, Diane. (2003). *Windows and Mirrors*. Cambridge, MA: The MIT Press.

Cook, Guy. (1992). *The Discourse of Advertising*. 2nd Edition. London: Routledge.

Cossar, Harper. (2005). 'Taking a wider view: the widescreen aesthetic in online advertising.' *The Journal of New Media Culture*. Vol. 3, No. 1. Available at http://www.ibiblio.org/nmediac/winter2004/cossar.html

Cubitt, Sean. (1998). *Digital Aesthetics*. London: Sage.

Dumit, Joseph. (2004). *Picturing Personhood. Brainscans and Biomedical Identity*. Princeton, NJ: Princeton University Press.

Dyer, Gillian. (1982). *Advertising as Communication*. London: Methuen.

Engholm, Ida. (2003). *WWW's designhistorie: websiteutviklingen i et genre- og stilhistorisk perspektiv* [WWW's design history: Website development in a genre and style historical perspective]. Unpublished doctoral dissertation, Copenhagen IT University, Denmark.

Fagerjord, Anders. (2003). 'Rhetorical convergence: studying Web media.' In Liestøl, Gunnar, Morrison, Andrew & Rasmussen Terje. (Eds.). *Digital Media Revisited*. Cambridge: The MIT Press. 293-225.

Fry, Tony. (2004). 'The sustainment and its dialectic.' In Willis, Anne Marie. (Ed.). *Design Philosophy Papers. Collection One*. Ravensbourne: Team D/E/S. 33-45.

Gibbons, Joan. (2005). *Art & Advertising*. London: I.B. Taurus.

Goddard, Angela. (1998). *The Language of Advertising: Written Texts*. London: Routledge.

Goggin, Gerard. (2000). 'Pay per browse? The web's commercial future.' In Gauntlett, David. (Ed.). *Web.Studies: Rewiring Media Studies for the Digital Age*. London: Hodder Arnold. 103-112.

Hay, James & Packer, Jeremy. (2004). 'Crossing the media (-n): automobility, the transported self and technologies of freedom.' In Chouldry, Nick & McCarthy, Anna. (Eds.). *Mediaspace: Place, Scale and Culture in a Media Age*. London: Routledge. 209-232.

Heffner, Reid, Kurani, Kenneth & Turrentine, Thomas. (2005). 'Effects of vehicle image in gasoline-hybrid electric vehicles.' *ITS-Davis*. April. UCD-ITS-RR-05-08. Retrieved April 5, 2006, from http//www.its.ucdavis.edu/publications/2005/

Heffner, Reid, Turrentine, Thomas & Kurani, Kenneth. (2006). 'A primer on automobile semiotics.' *ITS-Davis*. February. UCD-ITS-RR-06-01. Retrieved April 5, 2006, from http://www.its.ucdavis.edu/publications/2006/.

John, Deborah, Loken, Barbara & Joiner, Christopher. (1998). 'The negative impact of extensions: can flagship products be diluted'? *The Journal of Product Innovation Management*. Vol. 15, No. 5, 470-471. Retrieved April 5, 2006, from http://www.ingentaconnect.com/content/els/07376782/1998/00000015/00000005/art00018

Kilbourne, Jean. (2000). *Can't Buy My Love: How Advertising Changes the Way We Think and Feel*. New York: Touchstone.

Klanten, Robert. (2006). *Fifty*. Berlin: Die Gestalten.

Klein, Naomi. (2001). *No Logo*. London: Flamingo.

Kress, Gunther. (1998). 'Visual and verbal modes of representation in electronically mediated communication: the potentials of new forms of text.' In Snyder, Ilana. (Ed.). *Page to Screen*. New York: Routledge. 53-79.

Kress, Gunther & van Leeuwen, Theo. (1996). *Reading Images: The Grammar of Visual Design*. London: Routledge.

Lin, Ming-Chyuan & Yan, Ing-Horng. (2004). 'Development of a computer-assisted procedure for car style design.' *International Journal of Vehicle Design.* Vol. 35, No. 4, 289-306. Retrieved April 5, 2006, from http://www.inderscience. com/browse/index.php?journalID = 31&year = 2004&vol = 35&issue = 4

Löwgren, Jonas & Stolterman, Erik. (2004). *Thoughtful Interaction Design.* Cambridge, MA: The MIT Press.

Manovich, Lev. (2001). *The Language of New Media.* Cambridge, MA: The MIT Press.

McCarthy, John & Wright, Peter. (2004). *Technology as Experience.* Cambridge, MA: The MIT Press.

McQuarrie, Edward & Phillips, Barbara. (2005). 'Indirect persuasion in advertising: how customers process metaphors presented in pictures and words.' *Journal of Advertising.* Summer 2005. Retrieved April 5, 2006, from http://findarticles.com/p/articles/mi_qa3694/is_200507/ai_n14716358

Minority Report. (2002). Director Spielberg, Stephen. 145 mins.

Morrison, Andrew. (2005). 'Inside the rings of Saturn.' *Computers & Composition.* Vol. 22, No. 1, 87-100.

Morrison, Andrew & Skjulstad, Synne. (2007). 'Talking cleanly about convergence.' In Storsul, Tanja & Stuedahl, Dagny. (Eds.). *The Ambivalence of Convergence.* Göteborg: Nordicom. 217-335.

Morrison, Andrew & Skjulstad, Synne (2010). 'Unreal estate: digital design and mediation in marketing urban residency.' In Wagner, Ina, Stuedahl, Dagny & Bratteteig, Tone. (Eds.). *Exploring Digital Design.* Vienna: Springer.

Morrison, Andrew, Skjulstad, Synne & Sevaldson, Birger. (2007). 'From waterfront development to web mediation: the co-ordination of digital design in promoting new residence.' *Design Issues.* Nordes 2007: Second Nordic Design Research Conference. Stockholm, Konstfack. 27-30 May. Retrieved April 5, 2006, from http://www.nordes.org

Motavalli, Jim. (2001). *Forward Drive: The Race to Build 'Clean' Cars for the Future.* Sierra Club Book.

Munster, Anna. (2003). 'Compression and the intensification of visual information in Flash aesthetics.' In *Proceedings of DAC 2003* conference. 135–142. Retrieved April 5, 2006, from http://hypertext.rmit.edu.au/dac/papers/

Nielsen, Jacob. (1999). *Designing Web Usability.* Indianapolis: The New Riders Press.

Norman, Donald. (1992). *Turn Signals are the Facial Expressions of Automobiles.* Cambridge, MA: Perseus Publishing. Retrieved April 5, 2006, from http://www.jnd.org/dn.mss/turn_signals_ar.html

Norman, Donald. (2005). There's an automobile in HCI's future. *Interactions.* Vol. 12, No. 6. Retrieved April 5, 2006, from http://portal.acm.org/ toc.cfm?id = 1096554&type = issue&coll = portal&dl = ACM&CFID = 72075212 &CFTOKEN = 8335836

Paul, Christianne. (2003). 'Public Cultural Production Art(software).' In Stocker, Gerhard & Schöpf, Christine. (Eds.). *CODE: The Language of Our Time.* Osterfildern-Ruit: Hatje Cantz Verlag. 129-135.

Skjulstad, Synne. (2004). '"Flashback": tracing developments from electronic paper to dynamic digital environments in the software Flash.' CD-ROM

Proceedings of FutureGround, Design Research Society, Melbourne, Australia. 17–21 November.

Skjulstad, Synne. (2007a). 'Clashing constructs in Web design.' In Melberg, Arne. (Ed.). *Aesthetics at Work*. Oslo: UniPub. 81-103.

Skjulstad, Synne. (2007b). 'Communication design & motion graphics on the Web.' *Journal of Media Practice*. Vol. 8, No. 3, 359-378.

Skjulstad, Synne & Morrison, Andrew (2005). 'Movement in the interface.' *Computers and Composition*. Vol. 22, No. 4, 413-433.

Stafford, Marla & Faber, Ronald. (2005). (Eds.). *Advertising, promotion, and new media*. Armonk, NY: M.E. Sharpe.

Strain, Ellen & VanHoosier-Carey, Gregory. (2003). 'Eloquent interfaces: humanities-based analysis in the age of hypermedia.' In Hocks, Mary & Kendrick, Michelle. (Eds.). *Eloquent Images*. Cambridge, MA: The MIT Press. 257-281.

Styhre, Alexander, Backman, Maria & Börjesson, Sofia. (2005). 'YCC: a gendered carnival? Project work at Volvo cars.' *Women in Management Review*. Vol. 20, No. 2, 96-106. Retrieved April 5, 2006, from http://www.emerald insight.com/10.1108/09649420510584436

Sundar, Shyam & Kim, Jinhee. (2005). 'Interactivity and persuasion: influencing attitudes with information and involvement.' *Journal of Interactive Advertising*. Spring. Retrieved April 5, 2006, from http://www.jiad.org/ vol5/no2/sundar/index.htm#sundar.

Urry, John. (2004). 'The "system" of automobility.' *Theory, Culture & Society*. Vol. 21, Nos. 4/5, 25-39.

Vestergaard, Torben & Schrøder, Kim. (1985). *The Language of Advertising*. Oxford: Blackwell.

Welsch, Wolfgang. (1997). *Undoing Aesthetics*. London: Sage.

Westbrook, Michael. (2001). *The Electric Car*. London: Institute of Electrical Engineers.

Williamson, Judith. (1978/1994). *Decoding Advertisements: Ideology and Meaning in Advertising*. London: Marion Boyars.

PART III

MAKING

PREFACE

TRIGGERS ARE FOR GUNS; REALITY IS CONTINUOUS

Maja Kuzmanovic

PRACTICE-BASED RESEARCH IN MULTIMODAL DESIGN

Multimodal design can be applied in manifold interdisciplinary fields, from developing Web sites to planning dinner parties. This part of the book focuses on applying multimodal design within the context of "new" media education and practice, from the perspectives of both the design process and the users' engagement with the works. The particular field into which the chapters delve is design for digital media, as applied in artistic works, including film, multimedia, and mixed-reality (MR) situations. The writers are a diverse group, including people creating new media works, developers of authoring tools, and researchers involved in the analysis of the field. Although their perspectives on experimental (or new) media may vary, the makers and researchers confront similar questions. What are the design principles that can guide multimodal creative processes? How do we move toward making attractive multimodal designs for responsive digital media? How do we design synaesthetic experiences where learning and languaging (Maturana, 1995) can occur through and between multimodal sensory perceptions?

The chapters connect this volume to a wider field of practice-based research in multimodal design, conducted by several technoartistic collectives in Europe, North America, Australia, and Japan. The artist researchers are exploring these questions by producing MR situations and environments for learning, creativity, or play. The works are usually conceived as full-scale productions, exposed to a wide spectrum of audiences, including both novice users and experts (media designers, performance artists, scientists, engineers, etc.). These works are rewarding case studies for those investigating multimodal literacy because they are often designed to be used by thousands of people in real-life situations. As such, they deal with issues of multiculturalism, robustness, (un)predictability, and (im)permanence that cannot be explored in technological demonstrations or controlled usability studies. The most prominent feature of these works is their ability to intertwine physical reality with digital media. They are worlds in continuous transition between actual and virtual, inside and outside, personal and social, and so on. People involved in making such responsive spaces often refer to them as complete realities or imaginary universes, where the continuity between different sensory stimuli (in their range of modalities) is an important measure of success.

A Continuum of Sensory Experience

There are various approaches to designing for a continuum of sensory experience (e.g., simulating large collections of discrete objects [or events] that work together as flocks or swarms, or treating data, media, and materials as continuous streams). Both approaches question closed modalities and offer designs based on a promiscuous entanglement between disparate carriers of information. One of the more successful examples of works integrating both approaches are those by the collective *Time's Up*. Over a period of several years, *Time's Up* developed the *Sensory Circus*, a series of playful situations in which direct, local interactions influence global changes of atmospheric 'mood,' expressed in sound, graphics, and haptic stimuli. *Sensory Circus* can be described as a protoscientific installation, translating concepts from digital physics into the design and construction of a complete MR world. The players in *Sensory Circus* tend to intuitively grasp the workings of this world by physically manipulating mechanical and digital interfaces that are embedded in custom-built props and architecture. *Sensory Circus* engages the players on two distinct levels: Localized games act as 'discrete interactions' allowing the players to experience an immediate response to their actions, whereas the slowly changing atmosphere adds an underlying continuity to the experience, revealing the collective influence that players have on the environment as a whole. The interplay of a range of digital media and physical interfaces makes the modalities of the *Sensory Circus* strongly entangled so that meaning becomes constructed through the process of active engagement with all elements of the installation, directly and indirectly (see Figure III.1).

Similarly inspired by physics, Seiko Mikami and Sota Ichikawa designed *Gravicells*, a responsive space where visitors navigate through an audiovisual translation of two opposing physical forces (gravitation and

Figure III.1. Players in the Sensory Circus (Photo by Time's Up).

resistance). Guided by a 'hypothetical dynamics,' influenced by the specific GPS location of the installation and the presence of people in the space, the visual and sonic patterns of *Gravicells* are continuous expressions of forces exerted by the earth's uncontrollable magnetic field, punctuated by the discrete actions of participants—distinct physical pebbles plunging into a flow of continuous digital data.

'MAKING' MR

When experiencing multimodal works, the participants usually perceive the event synaesthetically, as a continuous reality (Merleau Ponty, 1962). The strongest synaesthesia often occurs in MR spaces, which wrap the visitors' bodies in immersive situations (see Figure III.2). By weaving a media membrane around the participants' physiological and kinetic actions, the media systems generate their responses in real time, increasing the participants' awareness of their own presence and influence on the events unfolding around them. An interesting example of such immersive, intimate works is *Trajets*, a 'movement-based installation' (directed by Susan Kozel and Gretchen Schiller). The artists examine human responses to the simulated movement of digital images and the mechanical motion of projection screens. Audiovisual media and physical

Figure III.2. Illustration for an MR environment (Drawing by Theun Karelse).

architecture both respond to participants' movements, as well as encouraging various patterns of navigation through the space. Multimodal composition in *Trajets* becomes a continuous choreography of multiple modalities extending through media, materials, and (human, architectural, and digital) bodies.

Making MR works implies designing for a total experience, working with interconnected objects or modalities, or possibly going a step further and abandoning objects altogether and working with media as fields of mutual influence (Sha, 2003). Although the instances of media (e.g., a CG mesh, a dynamics algorithm, a costume) are often made separately, they tend to be treated as 'spimes' (Sterling, 2005), or open objects, whose boundaries are fuzzy and semipermeable, allowing them to remain adaptive and dynamic, able to change their function, behaviour, or even substance while evolving through interactions with other 'actors' in the continuum. Actors in this context may include human participants, along with media, procedures, physical phenomena, and so on.

Cultivating Responsive Environments

This type of production tends to require designers to work akin to gardeners, who gather, plant, and cultivate their seeds, gently encouraging growth, while steering away from decay and allowing the ecosystem to gradually find its balance. Since 2000, FoAM has been engaged in 'cultivating' a series of responsive environments (t* series: *TGarden, txOom,* and *trg*), which look at different approaches to embodied interaction and mixing realities (see Figure III.3).

In *TGarden*, FoAM (in collaboration with sponge; http://sponge.org) designed a space where human bodies could become calligraphic instruments and bodily movement became an act of writing or scrying. The participants molded visual forms projected beneath their feet and modu-

Figure III.3. Players in trg environment in Kibla, Slovenia (Photo by FoAM).

lated sonic grains of an abstract soundscape. In *txOom*, the human participants became symbionts of a hypothetical ecology. Their movement was 'recycled' to influence the morphology of a myriad of discrete digital forms, sprayed continuously over the physical architecture, of which the participants' bodies were a structural component. *Trg*, the most recent in the series of FoAM's environments, was a poetic interpretation of contemporary 'Theories of Everything.' Within *trg's* soft physical shell, the participants could individually unfold, curve, and sculpt the physical and digital environments by moving, jumping, or rolling through it, stretching and deforming its architecture, while collectively energizing its visual and sonic fields.

Transmodal Realities

In all these works the continuity of experience is an important design principle, guiding continuity of sensory stimuli, physical and digital media, as well as individual and collective actions (see Figure III.4). The works move away from being discrete objects, which can be 'triggered' to follow predefined links, and toward synaesthetic, pliant media spaces that can 'sense' human presence, offering rich and emergent responses. To describe the design of these works, we can label them as multimodal, in the sense of a unifying multiplicity of modes, rather than a collection of multiple linked, yet separated modalities.

Figure III.4. **Continuity between physical architecture and digital media in trg (photo by FoAM).**

With these works, multimodal design becomes 'intermodal' or 'transmodal,' placing a stronger accent on the transitions, on the spaces that open up new potential meanings, forms, and functions. If such a design process is followed, it can lead beyond collections of interconnected, fragmented multimodal media systems and toward smooth and coherent, transmodal realities.

Links to artistic works mentioned in the text:
  Sensory Circus: http://timesup.org/sc/
  Gravity and Resistance: http://www.g—r.com/
  Trajets: http://www.trajets.net/
  t* series: http://fo.am/tgarden/, http://fo.am/txoom/, http://fo.am/trg/

REFERENCES

Maturana, Humberto. (1995). *The Nature of Time*. Available at http://www.inteco.cl/biology/nature.htm

Merleau Ponty, Maurice. (1962). *Phenomenology of Perception*. London: Routledge.

Sha, Xin Wei. (2003). 'Resistance is fertile: gesture and agency in the field of responsive media.' *Configurations*. Vol. 10, No. 3, 439-472.

Sterling, Bruce. (2005). *Shaping Things*. Cambridge, MA: The MIT Press.

6

REACTIVE AND RESPONSIVE ARTIFACTS IN DISCOURSES OF MULTIMODAL EMBODIMENT

Andrew Morrison

Even Westvang

FROM TEXT TO EMBODIMENT

Multimodal Mappings

In the 1990s, the body, as opposed to orthographic and written text, received considerable attention in the humanities and social sciences, in both the visual and performing arts. Simultaneously, through the expansion of digital technologies and research in the field of Human–Computer Interaction (HCI), we experienced a shift from the desktop and graphical user interface (GUI) and attention to design for direct manipulation (Shneiderman, 1983) to encounters with digitally enhanced communication in tangible, haptic, and kinetic environments (e.g., Ishii et al. 1994; see Figure 6.1). These latter environments have been designed to engage us in using our fuller corporeal senses, not separations between mind and body (Clark 1997; Ihde 2001) but intersections between the corporeal and the conceptual in experiencing technologically mediated communication (e.g., Wood 1998). In a more humanistic skein, Hayles (1999), for example, has argued that we have entered into a posthumanist phase in which our meaning making is now increasingly technologically mediated to the extent that it is often prosthetically enacted. In our daily world of work and leisure, digital tools and technologies now also move as we move, the mobile phone reaching far from urban spaces into rural areas. The shift from the interfaces of desktops to mobile screens, and to those that

Figure 6.1. The vice-rector of the University of Oslo, Anne-Brit Kolstø, experimenting with her own shadow at InterMedia, 2005.

include and demand our embodied engagement beyond the drag, scroll, or click of a mouse, have been made possible due to developments in what go under the various names of tangible, ubiquitous, pervasive, and even intelligent computing. As Martin and Stenglin (2007: 235) observe, concerning a transcolonial exhibition design and multimodality, space envelops us: '. . . we feel space. It surrounds us absolutely. It's not just something we make part of us (by hearing, reading, observing, and thus consuming it); it makes us part of it.'

Developments in technologically enhanced exhibition and installation spaces, and their design and enactment, have made it possible to connect place and space, person and community across media and communication platforms. In this chapter, we focus on the term 'tangible computing' because it reflects a concern with the relationships between computational systems and our senses. More important, tangible computing has advanced earlier approaches to HCI with their focus on software and information systems design toward making links between people and computational artifacts. In their work on the 'graspable' in interface design, Ullmer and Ishii (2000), for example, argued that tangible interfaces allow us to integrate representation and control in interaction. One of the concerns has been to design and run seamless interfaces between the bits of the information system and the unfolding human interaction with them in physical environments (Ishii & Ullmer 1997). In the field of HCI, the focus has also shifted away from earlier functional use-driven perspectives to ones that are concerned with experience (Hallnäs & Redström 2002). Fairly recently, researchers have further talked of emerging frameworks for tangible user interfaces (Ullmer & Ishii 2000). In this chapter, we refer to this body of work and to that in embodied inter-action as championed by Dourish (2001). At the same time, there has been an increase in artistic experimentation that has been constructed through intersections of programming, poetics, design, and aesthetics (e.g., Mignonneau & Sommerer 2003; Manovich 2003; Festwick et al. 2005; Bertelsen 2006). These interlaced interests are evidence of a shift toward the importance of embodied interaction (Hanson 2004) in which we engage with the computational through our wider sensorial and pro-prioceptive selves, sometimes alone, but also collaboratively.

We take up the notion of tangible interfaces, where there is an ele-ment of direct manipulation of the environment, or reactivity, for the user. Further, the resulting mediated artifact is one that is continually built through the participant's responses to it. A way of looking at the working of such systems is as a feedback loop. The user acts and the system responds. The user then probes the system by finding actions that will further reveal its function. This creates a feedback loop driven by the user's expectation and the system's adherence or deviation from this expectation (see Chapter 7). Given this process, it becomes clear that such systems cannot be designed without an understanding of how user expec-tation is anticipated, built, and maintained. Schiller (2005: 182) discusses movement-based installations as having the potential to provide more than one-to-one feedback. They may also open out for '. . . multimodal crossed-body-to-environment-mappings. These mappings introduce multi-modal feedback variations to choreomedia applications in movement-based interactive art.'

The case presented next concerns the making of an installation work called *Karakuri*. The name *Karakuri* is borrowed from the Japanese for mechanism; it also refers more specifically to the wind-up dolls of the Edo period and intricate wooden boxes with complex opening mechanisms. The name thereby also carries connotations of constructions that bring the inanimate to life and the workings of a hidden apparatus that creates what appears to be magical. In our piece, the human participant never touches the interface directly. The interaction takes place through sen-sors, and embodied interaction is materialized as a mimetic reproduction of the user's visual or kinetic self. The user, or more aptly the player-like participant, encounters a shadowy or penumbral realization of their actions and less the 'graspable' correspondence of action and embodi-ment. In *Karakuri*, as Edmonds (2007: 3), one of the early proponents of interactive art in the 1970s, writing today reminds us, 'Interaction is not material. It is experienced, perceived, understood but we cannot touch it.' As composition, we investigate how system, sensors, and participant are intertwined and how visual and gestural relations are designed to allow for embodied actionable interpretation (see also Thibault 2004).

Practice and Interdisciplinary Composition

We are interested in how links may be made between necessarily reactive interactional elements in a mixed-reality (MR) arts environment and more responsive ones that are connected to notions of presence, to an ambient setting, and to participants' sense of unfolding performance. We discuss these in terms of the design of the environment and its tangible interface, as well as the notion of a causative, yet embodied, mode of activity.

Work is now being carried out into mobile technologies, identities, and kinetics influenced by phenomenological approaches to embodied interaction (e.g., Dourish 2001). We do not present our investigation into understanding responsive artifacts in terms of phenomenology and the recent assertion on experience and its design in digitally mediated environments (McCarthy & Wright 2004). What we are interested in is to connect a practice-based route of inquiry to the intersection of software and embodied engagement with theoretical frameworks across these previously mentioned domains so as to hopefully approach a richer understanding of the roles of designers and users in shaping causation in digitally mediated interfaces. Our aim is to use this process of interdisciplinary composition as a foil to the discussion of causation and reactive and responsive interpretation. In several senses, our overall approach is similar to that proposed by Kozel (2005: 34), who discusses the notion of techne from Heidegger in relation to performance in responsive systems as a bringing forth, a revealing, or an unfolding. This is a bringing forth of what is concealed in the ecosystems of electronic installation-performance works (Kozel 2005: 37). In this approach, dualisms (mind-body, machine-human) are side stepped in a move that is motivated toward the uncoverings of layers of physical, conceptual, and social knowledge through movement and reflection (Kozel 2005: 35).

We outline the process of framing, designing, and building such a digital mediatized installation work. The installation allows the user to enter a space and use his or her captured silhouette to affect changes in a simulated landscape of physically acting objects. In blending the physical space of the installation with a mediated representation, the work may be described as an MR space (Milgram & Kishino 1994). The installation may seem somewhat obtuse when described in language. In practice, it has proved to be straightforward to understand. Overall, we argue that it is by way of the participant's engagement in the work that he or she may develop a sense of actionable interpretation, albeit broadly.

In the following, we address issues of incorporating not only the modes that define digital media as semiotic resources, which are realized through our engagement with them as is argued in social semiotics, but also the implications of user action in realizing nonverbal multimodal discourse. Our focus is on building a reactive computational artifact and the ways in which processes of composition inform our understanding of causation as a mode in engaging with nonverbal, digital discourses and the interfaces through which we access and enact them. We examine a category of digital media artifacts that are not only embedded in software, but that embed software as a communicative strategy. It is this, in terms of multimodality, that we approach as a causative mode. This involves us in a discussion of the interplay between digital media and information systems design and embodied interaction in computationally composed and mediated environments.

In the next section, we discuss the concept and practice of responsivity. In Section 3, we cover issues of mode and multimodality, followed in Section 4 with issues relating to designing for actionable interpretation. Section 5 gives details of the work developed, while Section 6 concludes with the suggestion that the notion of a causative mode be added to our understanding of multimodality within and beyond the types of embodied interactional environments mentioned across the chapter.

TOWARD RESPONSIVITY

User Actions in Nonverbal Domains

In recent years, the polymorphic nature of digital media has provided an impetus to a widening out of theoretical and methodological approaches in discourse analysis to the study of multimodality (Kress & van Leeuwen 2001; O'Halloran 2004; Scollon & Scollon 2004; Ventola et al. 2004; Baldry & Thibault 2006). However, this literature—originating in applied linguistics—rarely strays into the large body of research into digital media, electronic art, and HCI and the interplay of theory and practice that characterizes much of the work in these emerging fields in which construction and experimentation with multimodality are central.

In this chapter, we inquire into links between multimodality and movement-based installation arts, in which in/tangible interfaces and responsivity on the part of participants are central. We draw together two main views and argue that they may inform a wider understanding of nonverbal and kinetic multimodality. The first relates to responsivity as a key concept and its links to activity in electronic performing arts (Kozel, 2005), in which movement awareness methods may be linked with the practices of 'interactive' art (Schiller 2005). 'Responsivity is about relinquishing control and letting something else emerge' (Kozel 2005: 40). Movement-based installations have the potential to provide more than one-to-one feedback. They may also open out for '. . . multimodal crossed-body-to-environment-mappings. These mappings introduce multi-modal feedback variations to choreomedia applications in movement-based interactive art' (Schiller 2005: 182).

The second view arises from HCI and the design of intangible interfaces in which nonverbal kinetics are part of a perceptual and computational loop between the reactive and the responsive. The system responds to manipulation by the user, and the user reacts to system-driven events and to those generated by their own actions. Such interfaces may be composed for artistic environments that involve bodily kinetic interplay with a computer system in contexts that are aesthetically ambient. These expressive yet movement-inflected environments have an emergent and ecological character that invites the participant to co-compose the texture and narrative of the work (Zuniga Shaw & Lewis 2006). Intangible interfaces may differ considerably from ones that feature in nonartistic domains (to which they are often well suited), where responses are effected by clicking on a mouse or other 'hard haptic' actions that result in direct manipulations.

Emphasis on Continuous Interaction and Ranges of Expression

Reactive installations, as found in technological prototypes and electronic artworks, have received some attention from media studies (Manovich 2002), although the modes of mediation in such works are not related to writings elsewhere on multimodality. These prototypes and art environments employ media technologies such as video projections along with sensors to react to the actions of the audience. Such environments may be studied in terms of the ways in which they may employ media, but in addition the behavior they display may be studied. In their ability to concretize interaction by integrating sensing technologies, which allow input directly through bodily movement, these environments may offer a general insight into the nature of reactive and responsive artifacts, much like the computer systems we encounter in everyday usage.

When encountering reactive computational artifacts, one incorporates interpretations of the artifact's internal workings into subsequent action. Software reacts by producing signs programmatically according to rules and inner state. One then attempts to incorporate these signs into a pattern that one again uses to assess the validity of the pattern. It is through action that one is able to assess this validity. This involves the user in responsive loops. This process of trying out, sensing and acting, works toward stabilizing these interpretations. In discourse terms, one is engaged in a heuristic interplay between software as discoursed and the nonverbal discourses of embodied human action. Schiller (2005: 183) writes that 'These mapping techniques create a feedback loop between movement and the imagination.' We therefore see designing for reactive and responsive systems as needing to provide multimodal stimulus for a self-reflexive quality in installation arts so that participants are given enough material and adequate space to explore their sense of self in relation to the intangibly mediated 'object.' In movement-based interactive art installations, Schiller (2006: 185-186) observes that:

> The public does not learn a new bodily 'movement expressive technique' which they can repeat in other situations (like dance technique gestures) in the installations. Instead they experience movement sensations which are mapped to their kinaesthetic memory. Such modalities of multi-modal feedback in movement-based interactive installations invite the participants to become kinaesthetically aware of their moving body with the environment and experience variations of 'haptic touch.'

Composition and Spatial Semiotics

In *Multimodal Discourse*, Kress and van Leeuwen (2001) extend their earlier work with image and text (Kress & van Leeuwen 1996) by directing it toward the interplay of various modes in meaning making. Through a generalization of Halliday's (1985) meta-functional categories (ideational, interpersonal, functional), they propose a general theory to assess and analyze assemblages of any permutation of modes.[1] Along with their attention to modes, Kress and van Leeuwen establish an analytical vocabulary with which to address how design, distribution, and production of media all contribute to semiosis. This offers a coherent means with which to regard many features of multimodal discourse. For instance, it offers an explanation for how the texture of film grain resulting from an aspect of the distribution process of film becomes an aesthetic abstract, which, by digital means, for example, may become a part of any designed assemblage.

For the graphic designer of print communication or words on the page for the writer, the ability of the reader to comprehend or be affected by the message is paramount. For the designer of interaction (or the reactive artifact), the ability of the user to interact with or perceive some pattern by which to start unravelling the internal working of the machine will always be the primary concern. In such environments, other facets of the communication will be overridden by the frustration of the user in encountering apparently incomprehensible and autistic machinery. A causative mode in this sense exposes what may be implied when Web sites and MR environments are referred to as 'intuitive.' It offers a more situated alternative to the imperative 'mental models' that characterized much of earlier HCI research.

In computational systems with discrete, bounded state sets, such as those found in software constructed according to prescriptive HCI methodology, the stabilization of common code may be trivial as the sign sets are overdetermined by genre tropes (and convention). The modes and their associated blendings in this context may be seen to follow established multimodal theory for reading image and text, such as that proposed by Kress and van Leeuwen (1996, 2001), with an added dimension for discourse. The notion of discourse as a dialogical construction is central here. Dialogical implies more than a face-to-face exchange event because the participant in a digitally mediated installation-like environment may engage proxemically and kinetically with an apparently reactive system. This is important because causative discourse moves lie in the somewhat shadowy domain between reading text and carrying out conversation: You may test your 'interpretation,' but the system won't ever improvise around your shortcomings.

Research on discourse analysis within domain of interaction and computational systems has been carried out, such as that of Suchman (1987/1999). However, it is possible to imagine other underdetermined systems that attempt the opposite: an active destabilization of fixed interpretations and, by implication, the profusion of open sites for interpretation. Examples of this may be found within media arts, lacking in most contemporary multimodal discourse studies, although present in the formalist semiotic approach of O'Toole (1994) in relation to displayed art and Muntigl (2004) on gesture (see Chapter 14). What is challenging is how to understand interactive media artworks that are designed to resist trivial decoding by way of play on the communication breakdowns encountered in HCI. In embodied interaction environments, the ludic elements that are designed to address the character of digitally mediated communication provide us with compositional material for discussion of the constraints of 'conversation' that appear to be surrendered to a technological imperative. As Kozel (2005: 38) writes, 'A deep physical understanding of how a system is likely to respond arrives through "dwelling" within the system.'

More interestingly, however, concerning mechanisms of interpretation and action are systems that accept continuous inputs and that modify their internal states and external representations smoothly. By removing the fixed codes of iconic representation known from GUIs, such systems may afford the user an expressive space in which to explore the rules of the system. In a sense, this stretches earlier attention to social semiotic to a spatial semiotic (Cheville 2006). The rules exposed to the user through the 'surface' also may be further manipulated by other rule sets to change their behavior and thereby prolong or prevent closure. This is not to argue for cycles of inescapable and pointless causation but rather to engage us as active participants who see such environments as realized through our own gestural performativity (see also Chapter 7).

By distancing an interactive system from the familiar mappings of mouse, keyboard, and screen and moving it into the physical domain of unencumbered gestural expression, our expectations from the everyday use of limited GUIs may be extended to a space for new interpretation. In this respect, a number of interesting challenges arise for multimodal discourse theory. If one considers the behavioral qualities of reactive artifacts and our responses to them, what happens to the concept of mode? What is the role of the behavior of such systems with respect to other concurrent modes (color, composition, kinetics) and their interpretation as assemblages?

MODE AND MULTIMODALITY

Embedding Software Communicatively

Outside of a specifically systemic functional linguistic approach to multimodal discourse, multimodal composition may be conceptualized as also entailing nonverbal, creative, artistic, and expressive utterances. Approaches to these nonverbal modes are now well established in electronic arts and to some extent in digital media studies. They appear only in a limited way in the major recent approaches to multimodal discourse (e.g., O'Halloran 2004; Levine & Scollon 2004; Ventola et al. 2004).

Uncited in these interesting collections is research drawn from media and informatics that goes into production relationships and processes in digital domains that include art, design, and performance (e.g., Halskov Madsen 2003). For example, Kjølner and Szatkowski (2003) describe processes of collaborative design in the production of a multimodal performance. They detail the activity of devising as a means of understanding creative composition involving the combination of media elements. They define a devised performance as the composition of material by the production team. This material is generated from the shared competencies of the development group. This relates to '. . . how actions can be created and composed for performances, installations or exhibitions' (Kjølner & Szatkowski 2003: 127).

Linguistically inflected theories of multimodal discourse have been successfully put to use in analyzing a wide range of assemblages of modes (e.g., Kress & van Leeuwen 1996; Fei 2004). However, there would seem to be a piece missing from these frameworks. Although much discourse through digital media may be effectively analyzed through this theoretical lens, a significant category would appear to be made invisible by it.

Reactive Interfaces as Artifacts

What interests us is how software design is part of designing a communicative strategy. As we mentioned earlier, digital media artifacts are embedded in software, but, communicatively, they also embed software. Such artifacts surround us to such a degree that they are nearly invisible. Most familiarly, these artifacts are the GUIs known from daily computer usage. The GUI is a common mode with shared historical roots and may be experienced as articulated through either Apple's OSX, Microsoft's incarnations of Windows, or various instantiations of Linux projects such as KDE or Gnome.

Further afield we find Web pages that are no longer necessarily 'solid' documents, but rather embed Macromedia Flash or Javascript libraries such as Prototype and Scriptaculous. Such interfaces may be explorative in their aesthetic discourse. They may be imaginative, kinetic, and counterintuitive (as regards textual norms and user expectations), but they may also be firmly aligned with the logic of task efficiency that has inspired the widget sets and controls of the fully fledged applications surrounding them on the desktop. Additionally, physical objects that embed computation and nontrivial reactions to user input also belong to this category.

The ways in which the software underlying these interfaces constitutes a communicative practice is not apparent in much of the literature on digital mediations. Often curtailing their investigations of the literacies needed in multimodal digital assemblages, they leave invisible the practices involved in the making of software, not necessarily line by line, as well as hopping over the compositional activities of coding potential causative modes and moves.

With regards to composition through digital media, two critical points are therefore left unaddressed. First, what inflections on creative expression and style does software have? Second, and perhaps more opaquely, how may software be seen as composition? Where the first question tends to how immanent structures in software influence and shape design, the second question more importantly addresses how software design is a communicative strategy. It is the second question we address here. Our direction, however, is not to present a close study of the scripting of an installation work but rather to relate that process to designing for causative as well as responsive interpretation. This connects embodied interaction to multimodal discourse.

Composing with Vernaculars

Visual literacies and multiple media in online communication have now received considerable attention in research literatures. Digitally mediated literacies, however, are often discussed outside of the domains of programming and interface design, referring to individual competences in applying readymade software tools. In recent years, developments in software have resulted in situations in which tools are rapidly moving into becoming vernaculars. They allow users to become designers who may make or modify their own tools.

Previously, software and interface design professionals set the boundaries of how multimodal discourse may be enacted through software tools. In contrast, in many settings, an emergent vernacular of software design is taking shape. This is a result of broadening electronic literacies, but it is also due to the properties and functionalities now ensconced within software applications. This is an important point in our discussion of how conceptualizing a causative mode may contribute to understanding how we may design reactive and responsive artifacts.

DESIGNING FOR ACTIONABLE INTERPRETATION

Designing Design

In a sociocultural approach to communication, argued in many chapters in this book, we learn to move and to 'sign' in contexts of shared meaning making. This places greater emphasis on participation in the cultural and contextual unfolding of mediated activity. It avoids essentializing experience in technologically enhanced environments as recent phenomenologically centered work on experience design may tend toward (McCarthy & Wright, 2004).[2]

In a sociocultural approach to design (Morrison et al. 2010, see also Chapter 2), the design of any communication must be based on commonly held frames of reference that a designer may assume. When examining ranges of reactive artifacts, it becomes apparent that the commonly held frame in play with regards to causative mode may vary widely. To overly simplify, one could perhaps construct a continuum running from tools to toys. At these extremities, one finds different strategies and demands for designs. Toys (and experiments) need offer neither immediate closure nor a great degree of specificity in their interactions. The assumed common ground between designer and user may therefore be gathered from farther afield than in the case of tools, which often have task-oriented designs and specificity as their objective.

Ross and Keyson (2007: 69) identify two main trends in the design of tangible interfaces. The first is a shift from use to presence, and the second moves from task-oriented to experience-driven design. Their interest is in the design of tangible expressive interaction, as opposed to the functionalist and work-related studies in this field (van den Hoven et al. 2007: 110). This too is our concern, although in contrast to their interest in product design, our expressive-oriented interaction is in the domain of art and movement.

Following an outline of the current state of research into tangible interaction, Hornecker and Buur (2006: 439) offer a nontaxonomic framework structured around the following four interrelated themes: (a) tangible manipulation, or material representations that are manipulated; (b) spatial interaction, where interaction occurs via movement in space; (c) embodied facilitation, where material objects and space impact on emerging group actions; and (d) expressive representation, or ' the material and digital representations employed by tangible interaction systems, their expressivity and legibility.' In different configurations, these four themes have a bearing on MR environments. MR is a current term that is connected with tangible user interfaces in artistic as well as more task-oriented settings. Bolter et al. (2006: 23) see that the MR '. . . application re-presents the world to the user, by enhancing (distorting in a creative way) the user's physical and social space.'

From GUI to MR

At one end one of the scale, one finds the complex (segmented, hierarchical) graphical environments of operating systems. These environments have seen 20 years of gradual refinement, technology, and language, moving in lock step with user literacies of usage. For the designer, the complexity of handling the causative mode of the GUI is lowered by the spread of custom tools for building interfaces and sets of guidelines and a common set of graphically expressed communication tools.

At the other end of this continuum, there are artifacts that have no demands made as to their efficiency, but that attempt to instill a feeling in, or convey an experience to, their users. In terms of their causative mode, such reactive artifacts may be said to employ behavioral aesthetics (Penny 2004) of connotative meaning where causation is situated and locally developed. As long as there is a feedback loop and the user may continue to develop a local ontology of the apparatus they are faced with, such artifacts may prolong closure of a system working indefinitely. One example of this we have actively engaged with as users is *Trash Mirror* by

Daniel Rozin (2003), which was set up in the large entrance hall to the Ars Electronica festival. This mimetic work allows participants to see their movements outlined in a physically responsive surface made of discarded material. The kinetic and moving human form is dynamically transformed into physically aestheticized ripples of rubbish.

Designing for Tangible Interfaces

For interaction designers, one of the main challenges is to design for how users find their way in patterns of causation. Approaches to interaction design, which accentuate visual and graphic elements (see Bolter & Gromala 2003), may well buttress the claims by Kress that the visual has replaced the verbal as the dominant mode in contemporary communication with the screen superceding the book as our primary site of mediated communication. Recent work in visual corpus analysis extends earlier studies of intertextuality and cross-genre effects, for example, in print advertising. Kress and van Leeuwen (2001) go as far as to argue that, with screen-based media, communication designers now offer users 'available designs:' At the surface level of texts, these function as options for engagement in what may be complex multimodal environments.

However, these leading writers on multimodality do not discuss in any depth that these are incarnations of designers' own (often emerging) digital competencies that need to transverse and interconnect a variety of media types and their histories. Their work does not extend to discussion of the underlying systems designs and coded texts that, through information architectures and software languages and tools, enable these choices to be enacted via a mouse or through tangible interfaces such as the one we present later.

As suggested in the opening image of *Karakuri* in use, in between the layers of information systems design and the semiotic arrangement of content through the categories and tables of content at the level of the interface, there lies causation. It is here that users need to be able to identify that there is a structural design and that this recognition is part of their affordances for effecting activity via the interface. In short, users need to be able to get at what it is they are doing. This is taken up by Liu and Davenport (2005). They investigate the notion of the self-reflexive performer who engages with the intersections of system and self in the processes of these being realized through flows and patternings of cultural symbols and information. In their piece called *Identity Mirror*, Liu and Davenport (2005: 241) present the opportunity for the participant to be immersed in abstract cultural flows of identity and to respond to them at different levels of delicacy through a gestural interface. Although this is an ambient work, it is strongly based on the streaming and selection of concepts that are rendered as typographic words. In contrast, our interest was to involve users in a setting in which the nonverbal would be primary. We were interested to create a specifically ambient visual environment that would paralinguistically transform the participant's sense of his or her mirrored self.

In much information systems design work today, visual design follows attention to structure and architecture in the computing. How then are we to design for the provision of a means to causative and responsive engagement? How too might we design for active participation when users encounter dynamic, nonverbal spatial MR environments that demand engagement in intangible interfaces? To answer this question, we now turn to *Karakuri* (see Figure 6.2). We give an account of the detailed processes of conceptualizing and realizing *Karakuri* as a means for heuristically exploring the causative mode in an embodied sense. The MR installation attempts to find a shared point of causal reference between the designer and the user through the experience of the behavior of physical objects simulated in a digital realm.

Figure 6.2. The designer at play in *Karakuri* (Frames 1-4).

DESIGNING A REACTIVE
AND RESPONSIVE ARTIFACT

Description of *Karakuri*

In *Karakuri*, participants could interact with a simulation using their silhouettes. The simulation system is presented to the user as a back projection and portrays objects that clearly obey physical rules, yet have no physical presence or reality. In this context, the process of discovering system rules through moves, motions, and interpretation becomes a rediscovery of rules tacitly known to the users through their embodied knowledge of physical reality, but in a new domain and with new parameters.

When audiences are brought into augmented interactive performances as active participants, an inversion of roles and relationships occurs (e.g., Melrose 2006). In this inversion, from the artist-author to the audience-as-generator, a number of issues arise. Chiefly, these concern both the role of the performer in his or her ability to control and use his or her surroundings expressively, the role of the developer as choreographer in designing such a system, and the resulting work as an artifact of this interplay. The relationships between these processes become clearer when looking at systems where the performer is not in possession of a script for the performance and where contextual understanding has to be built incrementally through processes of interaction (Kozel 2005).

Karakuri: Shadows Working on the World

In *Karakuri*, interaction is unencumbered by devices worn to facilitate interaction. In this installation, the user interacts with the system through continuous gestural movement. The system reads the entire silhouette of the user's body through a computer vision system and feeds it to a simulation. Compared with a virtual reality (VR) system, the degrees of freedom are fewer in the spatial domain. However, the granularity with which you can interact with the space is greater than a VR environment because you have the entire outline of your body to interact with, not just the wand of a cave or the mouse of screen. This also affects the ease with which users can enter the stage. In employing unencumbered interaction, there need be no assistants to help you don the gear required for interaction or explain what button carries out what command. The 'performer' is simply free to walk on stage and begin to move and experiment, as is shown in Figure 6.1. The user's mediatized and abstractly rendered shadow is looped back to his or her embodied actions in 'the world.'

Anticipation of Action

In *Karakuri*, the user builds a domain-specific ontology of system function through his or her interaction with that system. As the system grows more available to the user through knowledge, his or her facility for making accurate assumptions about the system's response also grows. Ideally, the design of interactive performances should allow the user to plan a series of actions that he or she wants to perform. To ease planning and make it sufficiently effortless, the system may work within domains in which users have prior knowledge. If the system makes the execution of these plans nontrivial through being sufficiently challenging, but not impossible, they may become interesting and enticing for the user to effect. The question then becomes, what domains allow this kind of planning behavior to take place?

Embodying *Karakuri*

In *Karakuri* (see Figure 6.2), the user faces a back projection surface. In periods without interaction, the piece displays an empty stage of shifting light in shades of electric blue and metallic grey. As the performer steps into the space, he or she is gently enveloped by a life-size border representation of their silhouette, extruded into a three-dimensional space. A series of discrete volumes mark the border of the participant. The volumes are kept semitransparent, alluding to the perceptual position of the performer, split between the real space of his or her body and the mimicry of his or her projected shadow. The user acts within a space of continuous gestural interaction and the border mimics the performer's movement faithfully. The volumes representing the shadow also participate in a rigid body dynamics system. After a short period of acclimatization, the space is populated with abstract shapes, such as boxes (see Figure 6.2), allowing the user to engage with them as she would physical objects. The objects react according to users' expectations of physical objects in the world, such as mass, friction, and restitution.

No behavior is enforced or explicitly encouraged by the system; it is simply a set of mappings. All mappings between user action and system response in *Karakuri* are purposely kept direct and familiar. However, the level of abstraction in the two-dimensional representation renders existing skills directly inapplicable. For the user, it forces a relearning of causal links between behavior and effect. By design, *Karakuri* presents a clearly defined subdomain of interaction, that is, one in which a user bases interaction on a rich repository of his or her already embodied knowledge, specifically that of physical objects.

On Mapping

It is through the programmed mappings of the system that the gestural actions of the user are realized within the system. The history of unencumbered gestural interactive installations dates back to Myron Krueger's (1969) seminal work with *Videoplace* and has been revisited many times. One reason for this is the granularity of input it provides for interaction and the directness it affords.

These embodied systems fall into two main categories of either being conceptualized as generative tools for performance or experiential artworks that allow users to affect a situation by body movement (see Chapter 7). For the former, the degree of causality in the mappings imposed between the gestural space and the computationally generated result varies according to purpose and aesthetics. Some systems, such as David Rokeby's (1982-1990) *Very Nervous System*, demand the user learn an exact set of discrete motions in order to 'play' the system (and where the interface is not visible). Others, like that by Golan Levin (2000), try to find more direct strategies for clear and visible of mappings in performative use.

In *Karakuri*, mappings are kept direct. The visuals may present you with an abstraction, but there is no question as to how your motions affect your silhouette. When you move, the silhouette moves with you. This is somewhat different from works where figuring out the causal relationship between movement and system reaction is a central feature. In *Karakuri*, this directness of mapping was a strategic decision. Any obscuration of causality in the interface would reduce the effectiveness of the work.

Technical Details

In its implementation, *Karakuri* combined a minimum of custom written software and off-the-shelf software for rapid development. This allowed it to be developed in a relatively short period of time by a single person, Even Westvang. This allowed him freedom in terms of giving more time to explore the potential of the system, but it also created an open design process where the system did not need to be specified at an early stage to other parties, but rather could be iteratively and experimentally developed.

To turn to more technical matters, the isolation of the user's silhouette is facilitated by lighting the projection surface evenly with near-infrared (NIR) light. An IR-sensitive consumer video camera is fitted with an IR pass filter that blocks wavelengths below 720 nm, only passing the NIR. This allows capture of relatively clear silhouettes of objects in front of the back projection surface, irrespective of what is shown in the visible spectrum. A custom application running under OSX uses Apple's accelerated imaging architecture for processing the capture. After gaussing and thresholding of the frame, the silhouette is found by a chain code algorithm and presented as a fixed set of two-dimensional Cartesian coordinates roughly describing the shape of the object.

These data are then made available as an XML stream on a socket, where it is retrieved by another machine running Macromedia's *Director* software. Since version 8.5 (2001), this software has allowed the generation of OpenGL and Direct3D accelerated graphics and has as an integrated component the Havok rigid body dynamics library for physics simulation. A system has been developed within *Director* for constructing graphs of objects with physical interrelations. The objects can also contain behaviors for reaction and animation.

Implementing *Karakuri*

Following this description of its design, the practical details of the implementation of *Karakuri* are now given in Figure 6.3. The space in which the installation was to be built is a windowless, partially underground stu-

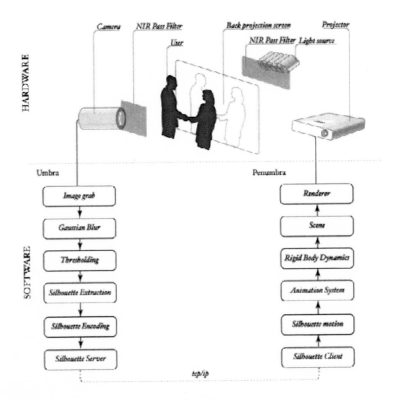

Figure 6.3. *Karakuri* components and data flow.

dio location at the research center InterMedia. The space was originally set up to act as a TV studio and therefore has a ceiling-mounted lighting grid and light mixer. The installation of *Karakuri* filled 16 m by 3 m by 3 m of studio space. Mirrors were not used to short the throw distance for the projector and camera.

As Simon Penny intimated (in e-mail correspondence with Even Westvang), the heat buildup in the NIR lighting rig was substantial, and the filters quickly became heat hardened and crispy in their holders. After testing other settings, the lighting was therefore never run at more than 50% capacity so as to avoid burning through the filters.

A back projection screen was acquired, and a stiff metal beam was threaded into it along a fold sewn into it along one edge. The beam was hung with clamps along from the ceiling grid, along with the lighting. The Umbra image recognition system ran off a 1 Ghz G4 Alu Apple Powerbook, while the Penumbra renderer ran off a more powerful dual processor Apple G5.

A Technical Critique

Karakuri has a few technical shortcomings that affect the experience in various ways. One issue lies with the translation of the captured silhouette into the discrete volumes that represent the shadow of the user. The number of volumes are fixed and distributed evenly along the line representing the performer's boundary. This creates a problem when the topology of the recorded shape significantly changes, such as when an arm moves in to join the body. This creates a discontinuity in the representation and causes the shape to quake briefly, thereby creating a flaw in the representation and giving the user a sense of loss of control. Additionally, if the user is currently balancing objects on her arms or legs, this glitch in the representation may cause the objects to suddenly accelerate and jump off the silhouette.

Given its origin in modified off-the-shelf software, there are also some latency issues in *Karakuri* in terms of lag between user and shadow response. The latency is approximately 200 to 300 ms. However, augmented spaces differ from VR, where so much latency would be perceived as a shattering of illusion and a generator of motion sickness. In our context, the lag merely adds a temporal layer to the abstraction of your representation and acts as a reminder of mediation and the '. . . continued productive implication of the body in the phenomenal world' (Ryan 2001: 72).

Discussion

Karakuri tried to furnish a space with clearly communicated affordances in terms of a straightforward, yet abstract, representation of the user's motion. However, for this to be effected, the user is first struck by the discontinuity between their embodied knowledge of their own movement and that presented to them by the system. This discontinuity works in terms of abstraction of visual representation from that of three dimensions into two, the slight lag in representation, and the presentation of the border in a new three-dimensional space. The latter produces a sense of wonder in some of the experimental testers of the installation, who were media students, fellow digital arts and design researchers, informatics researchers, and developers and digital artists.

Karakuri also provides the user with a domain grounded in everyday knowledge—that of interacting with physical objects. This is clear with all those who have engaged with it as performers. Having grown accustomed to their representation in the space, none of the performers have had to be prompted to try to see how their shadow would work on the objects provided for interaction. The performers reach out to stabilize their anticipations with regards to how their shadow would work on the world around them. As Kozel (2005: 40-41) observed in her performing the work *immanence*, the user engages in cycles of 'reception-assimilation-response' in which the visual material is the impetus for emotional and physical spatial shifts.

The effectiveness and immediacy of this aspect of the installation can be judged by the feeling of unease that occurs in the space among visual feedback, kinesthetics of motion, and the missing haptic feedback of physical interaction. An immediate feeling of strangeness occurs in the situation where 'I can see that I am moving these seemingly heavy boxes with my arm, but why aren't they heavy?,' as one of the performers put it. However, again as Kozel (2005: 43) observes in relation to our sensibility in engaging with responsive systems, in this work we too managed to preserve '. . .a set of qualities often eradicated from computational environments: the invisible, the interior, or immanent, qualities of a rapport.' As stated earlier, the performer's anticipation of system reaction can be seen as a simulation extending from the current point and into the manifold space of eventualities that his or her interactions can produce. This creates a feedback system in the exchange between two simulation systems.

At one end of the simulation, one finds the human engaged in constructing a world through processing of semantics of perceived events; on the other end, a machine parses a set of syntactic rules in response to user action and internal state change. On the part of the user, the intensity of the simulation and the amount of attention it captures is based on

the management of the gap of possible outcomes, the continuous conflation of possibility into fact, and his or her ability to chart and make
assumptions about this process.

CONCLUSIONS

Inside Actionable Interpretation

In the work *Karakuri*, dancing with one's shadow becomes a form of self-
reflexive performance (Liu & Davenport 2005: 245). At a wide performative level, our interest was to help turn spectators into visitors
(Courchesne 2002). These visitors cast their shadows onto their own stage
such that '. . . shadows foment a dramatic nimbus of potentialities about
the performer' (Liu & Davenport 2005: 246).

In a multimodal perspective, we might argue that *Karakuri* may be
seen as parallel to a continuous and largely nonspecific gestural mode. In
contrast, the GUI paradigm we mentioned earlier would appear to be
derived from a linguistic-semiotic mode. Kress and van Leeuwen (2001:
113) suggest that:

> Once a mode has become grammaticalised, it will acquire some other
> powerful and highly valued facilities, such as the ability to produce
> meta-signs, to comment on representations in that same mode, and
> to produce theoretical statements. In the case of the visual, the post-
> modern stress on visual irony, pastiche, parody, etc. can be seen as a
> forerunner of visual meta-language. Computer interfaces now develop
> it further.

However, these leading authors do not venture into digital interfaces or
the variety of interface designs and modes, in addition to those traditionally found on the web, as, for example, Squier (2005) demonstrates
through the enactment of an online visual rhetoric. In a time of expanding
mobile communications and pervasive computing, with attention to tactile and also ubiquitous but adaptable interfaces, attention to a multiplicity
of modes is important. It is therefore necessary to go beyond what Kress
calls available designs, which is content and modes of representation on
screen, and acknowledge that tighter links need to be made between
signs, tools, representations, and their articulations in nonverbal as well
as auditory modes.

Drawing on Finnemann (1997), it is tempting to assert that computational artifacts are essentially different from other artifacts. He writes that
'The computer is not an artifact on a par with other artifacts, since it can

only function as an artifact (i.e., simulate artifacts) with the help of symbolic representations' (Finnemann 1997: 2). If we follow this logic, the mappings between the internal state of the machine, therefore, must be explicitly mapped by the designer to the external representation. Yet as Edmonds (2007: 5) reminds us, it is the interaction between the computational and the humanly compositional that matters. Here he suggests we might turn to terms such as influence, stimulus and interchange, cooperation, or conversation to account for the interactions between artwork and audience. In a related move, Liu and Davenport (2005) also position their self-reflexive cultural 'mirroring' approach in performance and technology as part of a wider dialogical mode of the dynamic interchange between human and machinic, software, and cultural symbolic. We have suggested how this might be connected to theories of multimodality, as well as to developments in the stagings and enactments of interfaces and experiences of 'virtual' embodiment.

Design Matters and Movement

Designers assembling such mediations of embodied and gestural meaning making must, in addition to utilizing semiotic resources pertaining to traditional modes (visual, aural, tactile), take into account the reactive nature of such artifacts. However different these objects may seem, they share certain key characteristics, in that they are designed for actionable interpretation. Users of such artifacts need to be able to approach them and generate sufficient understanding as to start acting with intent on them, whereby the artifact must respond with causal patterns in order to stabilize interpretations of the artifacts' function ascertained through action.

Hasan (1985: 57) views modes as consisting of three dimensions: language role, medium, and channel. If we follow her distinction, it would seem that what qualifies the modes employed in designs for reactive-to-responsive artifacts are neither channel nor language role. Rather, mode is to be found in the affordances for feedback in the medium. In the spoken medium, for instance, text is co-created by speakers, and misunderstandings and breakdowns may be corrected in an ad-hoc, real-time fashion. The mode of textual discourse is characterized by the inflexible yet interpretable written text. Reactive, but responsive, artifacts may perhaps be said to occupy a middle ground between these modes in terms of their potential for providing feedback. They may not improvise to account for breakdowns in communication, yet they may be designed to support and scaffold the process of discovery by which the user through action exposes the rules governing the reactions of the artifact. Some of these artifacts are tools, and their value is defined by their efficiency. This efficiency may be significantly impaired if the user does not understand how to use the tool.

Therefore, the need for stable interpretations of causation may give rise to designs that bind and orchestrate other attendant modes such as image, text, and sound to this prerogative of efficiency. It would therefore seem that one could postulate a *causative mode* employed in the design of reactive-responsive artifacts. This causative mode forms a temporal lexico-grammar of possible behaviors that may be displayed by interfaces and that are a necessity in the formation of stable interpretations of user interfaces. However, as Kozel (2005: 40) has argued, installation arts and systems engage us in modes of responsivity that are realized in our active participation in the unfolding of these computationally designed and mediated works:

> For a system to be responsive, there needs to be a feedback loop whereby both the systems and the participants respond to each other. What this means is that we, as the participants, need to allow ourselves to be interrupted and to integrate or assimilate what we receive from the system into our bodies and thoughts; equally, the system needs to be designed to generate meaningful responses.

We suggest, then, that the notion of a causative mode be extended and linked to one that may be labeled a *responsive mode*.

Composition and 'Pervasive' Computing

Despite the many rich and layered approaches and cases of engaging with digital tools and processes of use in formal and informal educational settings, in writings on multimodal literacies, little attention is given to gestural, kinetic, and embodied interaction. Much formal education is still conducted in pictorial and orthographic modes, even in more elaborate learning environments (LEs) that demand collaboration and a considerable degree of acumen with spatial processing. As the spaces for interaction and engaged participation become more mobile and tactile, such as in the recent *Wii* by Nintendo and Apple's *iPhone*, designers and educators will need to identify and integrate proxemic and kinetic aspects into multimodal design and understand its place expressively.

Nonprofessional developers and designers are now in a position to shape interfaces and related environments by way of the compositional features provided in software. They are no longer wholly dependent on the elaborately tuned skills of Web and system developers. For example, they are able to compose sites and settings in which attention to the GUI may be reduced to a minimum, as, for example, with blog software. High school-going programmers may download, configure, install, and rewrite open source software to enable online social interaction with their friends.

In such circumstances, the ability to write software and design interfaces is social currency, a strong incentive to learn the nuts and bolts of these systems from the bottom up. What is interesting, then, is how to provide a set of discourse modes to enable users to enact embodied discourse moves themselves. Compositionally, the context and the implicit causative discourse potential have to have been designed.

Currently, the changes enacted through open source software, along with licensing strategies such as the Creative Commons, further leverage software literacies. As bricolage reaches the layer of the immaterial software, we foresee that the gap between the expressive potential of reactive artifacts and the explanatory force of multimodal discourse as a theoretical frame will become increasingly unbridgeable unless causative and responsive modes are explicitly addressed.

Toward Relational Dynamics in Composition

In conclusion, we argue that a theory of multimodal discourse that does not attend to software and its design falls short of the full explanatory potential its analytical vocabulary may embody. However, such design needs to consider that all technically mediated action is embodied (Schiller, 2006: 109). This embodiment is more and more connected to the interplay of the humanly corporeal and the technologically mediatized.

This chapter has attempted to show how different interface discourses with completely different prerogatives and organization may follow causative to responsive modes in designs for actionable interpretation. Causative modes do not entirely script either our actions or our interpretations. They provide, in a sense, a stance for mediated movement that may then cross into a variety of gestural actions and dynamic relations and, as we repeatedly found, the expression of verbal commentaries in and around the spaces of movement. As a consequence, and reaching from causative to responsive, as Schiller (2006: 109) says, 'Whether apprehended passively or actively, these experiences contribute to the range of one's movement repertoire and kinaesthetic condition.'

Our kinaesthetic compositions are already being extended in performance and popular cultural spaces. *Karakuri* sought to bring the loop of composition closer to the self while mediatizing the meta-proximinal as part of embodied interaction and engagement within a tangible interface. Again, Schiller (2006: 109; original italics) phrases this aptly:

> If we accept this entanglement between human-created techniques and movement as a dynamic structural and relational event, then we replace discussions of the *body and space* or *body and machine* with the fluid surprises of relational dynamics.

Nonverbal interfaces are becoming a part of an expanding digitally mediated experience, whether in 'swipeable' public transport travel cards via near field technologies in the form of RFID tags or the haptic qualities of upgraded multimodal mobile devices (as already emblazoned via Apple's *iPhone*). The intersections of such tangible and gestural interfaces and their implied responsive affordances contribute to an extended stage or space for multimodal and kinaesthetic composition. Students are likely to continue to meet such movement in the interface and in their own peripatetic engagement as part of building fluid exchanges of media and information types across devices and platforms, and via a variety of nonverbal modes of communicating together with more familiar formal learning.

Emerging communicative repertoires need to be understood from within such a dynamics of relational composition as much as through the affordances of given products and the communicative commercialization of shared platforms. Acts of reflexive and iterative design, such as the case we present here, show how software and shadows may be co-configured as compositions. In these co-configurations, our own embodied interaction becomes part of the fluid and oscillating choreographies of the hermeneutic via causative, collaborative, and responsive design between human and machine. We suggest, too, that this may be extended in not only artistic contexts to conceptualizing and examining more than the gestural but its contextualisation in a *performative* mode.

ACKNOWLEDGMENTS

Thanks to our colleagues at InterMedia, University of Oslo, for comments and to InterMedia for supporting Even Westvang in an electronic artist/designer-in-residence as part of the MULTIMO project. This chapter is an extension of an earlier conference paper (Westvang 2004) from the project.

NOTES

1. Three language functions—tenor, field, and mode—are central to understanding linguistic meaning making as socially situated in Halliday's (1978) framework. These functions are also cross-hatched, respectively, with Halliday's meta-functions: interpersonal, ideational, and functional. The functions have been extended to paralinguistic and nonverbal communication, for example, gestural and proxemic aspects of communicating multimodally, music and gesture (van Leeuwen 1999), and gesture and speech (e.g., Muntigl, 2004). In this

perspective, modes are semiotic resources that allow the simultaneous realization of discourses and types of (inter)action (Kress & van Leeuwen 2001: 21). They serve to ground the given process-participant configuration with reference to the addresser's evaluation, in the case of declarative propositions, and the addressee's evaluation in the case of interrogatives, as to how likely, certain, possible, usual, obligatory, and necessary this may be.

2. The concept of affordances and that of embodied interaction are two routes to understanding how users may comprehend and intuitively make sense of the range of expressions in augmented spaces (Westvang 2004). Both approaches help us to explain the interplay of processes of perception and the sensitivity to situation and surroundings. Affordances, following the ideas of James Gibson (1979) and widely taken up in HCI, are counterweighted by constraints, both of which refer to qualities or a certain torque imbued in objects in the world that have bearing on how we can relate to them. Embodied interaction (Dourish 2001), deriving from the phenomenology of Merleau-Ponty (1962/2002), argues that the mind's knowledge of body is realized in physical action, where this knowledge is often tacit.

REFERENCES

Baldry, Anthony, & Thibault, Paul. (2006). *Multimodal Transcription and Text Analysis.* London: Equinox.

Bertelsen, Olav. (2006). 'Tertiary artefactness at the interface.' In Fishwick, Paul. (Ed.). *Aesthetic Computing.* Cambridge MA: The MIT Press. 357.368.

Bolter, Jay, & Gromala, Diane. (2003). *Windows and Mirrors: Interaction Design, Digital Art, and the Myth of Transparency.* Cambridge, MA: The MIT Press.

Bolter, Jay David, MacIntyre, Blair, Gandy, Maribeth, & Schweitzer, Petra. (2006). 'New media and the permanent crisis of aura.' *Convergence.* Vol. 12, No. 1, 21-39.

Cheville, Julie. (2006). 'The bias of materiality in sociocultural research: reconceiving embodiment.' *Mind, Culture, & Activity.* Vol. 13, No. 1, 25–37.

Clark, Andy. (1997). *Being There.* Cambridge, MA: The MIT Press.

Courchesne, Luc. (2002). 'The construction of experience: turning spectators into visitors.' In Resier, Martin, & Zapp, Andrea. (Eds.). *New Screen Media.* London: BFI. 256-267.

Dourish, Paul. (2001). *Where the Action Is: The Foundations of Embodied Interaction.* Cambridge, MA: The MIT Press.

Edmonds, Ernest. (2007). 'Reflections on the nature of interaction.' *CoDesign.* Vol. 3, No. 3, 1-5.

Fei, Victor. (2004). 'Developing an integrative multi-semiotic model.' In O'Halloran, Kay. (Ed.). *Multimodal Discourse Analysis.* London: Continuum. 220-246.

Festwick, Paul, Diehl, Stephan, Prophet, Jane, & Löwgren, Jonas. (2005). 'Perspectives on aesthetic computing.' *Leonardo.* Vol. 38, No. 2, 133-141.

Finnemann, Niels Ole. (1997). *Modernity Modernised: The Cultural Impact of Computerisation.* Available at http://www.hum.au.dk/ckulturf/pages/publications/nof/modernity.htm

Gibson, James. (1979). *The Ecological Approach to Visual Perception.* Boston: Houghton Mifflin.

Halliday, Michael. (1978). *Language as Social Semiotic.* London: Edward Arnold.

Halliday. Michael. (1985). *An Introduction to Functional Grammar.* London: Arnold.

Hallnäs, Lars, & Redström. Johan. (1992). 'From use to presence: on the expressions and aesthetics of everyday computational things.' *ACM Transactions on Computer-Human Interaction.* Vol. 9, No. 2, 106-124.

Halskov Madsen, Kim. (Ed.). (2003). *Production Methods: Behind the Scenes of Virtual Inhabited 3D Worlds.* London: Springer.

Hansen, Mark. (2004). *New Philosophy for New Media.* Cambridge, MA: The MIT Press.

Hasan, Ruquiya. (1985). *The Structure of a Text.* In Halliday, Michael, & Hasan, Ruquiya. (Eds.). *Language, Context, and Text: Aspects of Language in a Social-Semiotic Perspective.* Geelong, Victoria: Deakin University Press. 52-69.

Hayles, N. Katherine. (1999). *How We Became Posthuman: Virtual Bodies in Cybernetics, Literature, and Informatics.* Chicago: University of Chicago Press.

Hornecker, Eva, & Buur, Jacob. (2006). 'Getting a grip on tangible interaction: a framework on physical space and social interaction.' In *CHI 2006 Proceedings Designing for Tangible Interactions.* Montreal, Canada. 22-27 April. 437-446.

Ihde, Don. (2001). *Bodies in Technology.* Minneapolis: University of Minnesota Press.

Ishii, Hiroshi, Kobayashi, Minori, & Arita. Kazuho. (1994). 'Iterative design of seamless collaboration media.' *Communications of the ACM.* Vol. 37, No. 8, 83-97.

Ishii, Hiroshi, & Ullmer, Brygg. (1997). 'Tangible bits: towards seamless interfaces between people, bits and atoms. *Proceedings of CHI '97.* Atlanta, Georgia. 22-27 March. 234-231.

Kjølner, Torunn, & Szatkowski, Janek. (2003). 'Dramaturgy in building multimedia performances: devising and analysing.' In Halskov Madsen, Kim. (Ed.). *Production Methods: Behind the Scenes of Virtual Inhabited 3D Worlds.* London: Springer. 125-148.

Kozel, Susan. (2005). 'Revealing embodiment: Heidegger's techne interpreted through performance processes in interactive systems.' *Performance Research.* Vol. 10, No. 4, 33-34.

Kress, Gunther, & van Leeuwen, Theo. (2001a). *Multimodal Discourse: The Modes and Media of Contemporary Communication* London: Arnold.

Kress, Gunther, & van Leeuwen, Theo. (1996). *Reading Images: The Grammar of Visual Design.* London and New York: Routledge.

Krueger, Myron. (1969). 'VIDEOPLACE an artificial reality.' In *SIGCHI 85 Proceedings.* New York: ACM. 35-40.

Levin, Golan. (2000). *Painterly Interfaces For Audiovisual Performance.* MSc. Thesis. Art and Design, Massachusetts Institute of Technology. Available at http://acg.media.mit.edu/people/golan/thesis/.

Levine, Philip, & Scollon, Ron. (2004). *Discourse & Technology: Multimodal Discourse Analysis.* Washington, DC: Georgetown University Press.

Liu, Hugo, & Davenport, Glorianna. (2005). 'Self-reflexive performance: dancing with the computed audience of culture.' *International Journal of Performance Arts and Digital Media*. Vol. 1, No. 3, 237-247.

Manovich, Lev. (2002). *The Language of New Media*. Cambridge, MA: The MIT Press.

Manovich, Lev. (2003). 'The poetics of augmented space.' In Everett, Anna, & Caldwell, John. (Eds.). *New Media: Theories and Practices of Digital Textuality*. New York: Routledge. 75-92.

Martin, James, & Stenglin, Maree. (2007). 'Materialising reconciliation: negotiating difference in a transcolonial exhibition.' In Royce, Terry, & Bowcher, Wendy. (Eds.). *New Directions in the Analysis of Multimodal Discourse*. London: Routledge. 215-238.

McCarthy, John, & Wright, Peter. (2004). *Technology as Experience*. Cambridge, MA: The MIT Press.

Melrose, Susan. (2006). 'Bodies without bodies.' In Broadhurst, Susan, & Machon, Josephine. (Eds.). *Performance and Technology: Practices of Verbal Embodiment and Interactivity*. Basingstoke: Palgrave Macmillan. 1-17.

Merleau-Ponty, Maurice. (1962/2002). *Phenomenology of Perception*. New York: Routledge.

Mignonneau, Laurent, & Sommerer, Christa. (2003). 'From the poesy of programming to research as an art form.' In Stocker, Gerfried, & Schöpf, Christine. (Eds.). *CODE: The Language of Our Time*. Osterfildern-Ruit: Hatje Cantz Verlag. 242-249.

Milgram, Paul, & Kishino, Fumio. (1994). *A Taxonomy of Mixed Reality Displays*. IEICE Transactions on Information Systems. Vol E77-D, No. 12. December. Available at http://vered.rose.utoronto.ca/people/paul_dir/IEICE94/ieice.html

Morrison, Andrew, Stuedahl, Dagny, Mörtberg, Christina, Wagner, Ina, Liestøl, Gunnar & Bratteteig, Tone. (2010). 'Analytical perspectives.' In Wagner, Ina, Stuedahl, Dagny & Bratteteig, Tone. (Eds.). *Exploring Digital Design*. Vienna: Springer.

Muntigl, Paul. (2004). 'Modelling multiple semiotic systems: the case of gesture and speech.' In Ventola, Eija, Charles, Cassily, & Kaltenbacher, Martin. (Eds.). *Perspectives on Multimodality*. Amsterdam: John Benjamins Publishing Company. 31-50.

O'Halloran, Kay. (Ed.). (2004). *Multimodal Discourse Analysis*. London: Continuum.

O'Toole, Michael. (1994). *The Language of Displayed Art*. London: Leicester University Press.

Penny, Simon. (2004). *After Interdisciplinarity*. ISEA 2004, Presentation given in Tallinn.

Ricardo, Francisco. (2009). 'Reading the discursive spaces of *Text Rain*, transmodally.' In Ricardo, Francisco. (Ed.). *Literary Art in Digital Performance*. London: Continuum. 52-67.

Rokeby, D. (1982-1990). *Very Nervous System* (VNS). Available at http://homepage.mac.com/davidrokeby/

Ross, Philip, & Keyson, David. (2007). 'The case of sculpting atmospheres: towards design principles for expressive tangible interaction in control of ambient systems.' *Personal Ubiquitous Computing*. Vol. 11, No. 2, 69-79.

Rozin, Danile. (2003). Trash mirror. *CODE—The Language of Our Time*. ars electronica 2003. 6-11 September. Linz, Austria. Available at http://www.aec.at/de/festival2003/programm/project.asp?area = 11&iProjectID = 12222

Ryan, Marie-Laure. (2001). *Narrative as Virtual Reality: Immersion and Interactivity in Literature and Electronic Media*. Baltimore: The Johns Hopkins University Press.

Schiller, Gretchen. (2005). 'Awakening the "dynamic index of the body": linking movement awareness methods with interactive art practice.' *International Journal of Performance Arts and Digital Media*. Vol. 1, No. 3, 179-188.

Schiller, Gretchen. (2006). 'Kinaesthetic traces across material forms: stretching the screen's stage.' In Broadhurst, Susan, & Machon, Josephine. (Eds.). *Performance and Technology: Practices of Verbal Embodiment and Interactivity*. Basingstoke: Palgrave Macmillan. 100-111.

Scollon, Ron, & Scollon, Susie. (2004). *Nexus Analysis: Discourse and the Emerging internet*. London: Routledge.

Shneiderman, Ben. (1983). 'Direct manipulation: a step beyond programming languages.' *IEEE Computer*. Vol. 16, No. 8, 57-69.

Squier, Joseph. (2005). 'The 3-dimensional web.' *Kairos*. Vol. 9, No. 2. Available at http://kairos.technorhetoric.net/9.2/binder2.html?coverweb/squier/index.htm

Suchman, Lucy. (1987/1999). *Plans and Situated Actions: The Problem of Human Machine Communication*. Cambridge: Cambridge University Press.

Thibault, Paul. (2004). *Brain, Mind, and the Signifying Body: An Ecosocial Semiotic Theory*. London: Continuum.

Ullmer, Brygg, & Ishii, Hiroshi. (2000). 'Emerging frameworks for tangible user interfaces.' *IBM Systems Journal*. Vol. 39, Nos. 3-4, 915-931.

van den Hoven, Elise, Frens, Joep, Aliakseyeu, Dima, Martens, Jean-Bernard, Overbeeke, Kees, & Peters, Peter. (2007). 'Design research and tangible interaction.' *TEI '07, First International Conference on Tangible and Embedded Interaction*. Baton Rouge, Louisiana. 15-17 February. 109-115.

van Leeuwen, Theo. (1999). *Speech, Music, Sound*. London: Macmillan.

Ventola, Eija, Charles, Cassily, & Kaltenbacher, Martin. (2004). (Eds.). *Perspectives on Multimodality*. Amsterdam: John Benjamins Publishing Company.

Westvang, Even. (2004). 'Karakuri: shadows working on the world.' In *Proceedings of VSMM 2004 Conference Hybrid Realities, Digital Partners*. Ogaki, Japan. 17-19 November. 1106-1115.

Wood, John. (1998). *The Virtual Embodied. Practice, Presence, Technology*. London: Routledge.

Zuniga Shaw, Norah, & Lewis, Matthew. (2006). 'Inflecting particles: locating generative indexes for performance in the interstices of dance and computer science.' *Performance Research*. Vol. 11, No. 2, 75-86.

7

BEHIND THE WALLPAPER

MULTIMODAL PERFORMATIVITY
IN MIXED-REALITY ARTS

Andrew Morrison

Idunn Sem

Martin Havnør

SURFACES AND BACKGROUNDS

Dynamics of Production and Reflection

Figure 7.1 shows an early design of the back wall for a mixed-reality (MR) installation artwork called *Tapet,* meaning wallpaper in Norwegian. We developed *Tapet* to investigate multimodality in the context of MR arts. In MR arts, 'The emphasis has shifted from the object of representation to the emergent situation, the performative current, and the materialisation of technology itself' (Birringer 2003). This emphasis was realized in *Tapet* through collaborative and interdisciplinary production-based inquiry. In this chapter, we show how multimodality may be extended to hybrid-made and experienced environments, while these may also be understood as being made of different media along with modes of engagement and enactment. We use the metaphor of peeling back the wallpaper in this enactment to trace modes of engagement in the making of the work. Geared to highlight concepts involved in designing MR installation arts, in *Tapet* the main concept we developed was *multimodal performativity.* Briefly, this term refers to ways in which participants in digital environments enact multilayered, mixed modes of mediated engagement with underlying computational designs, thereby realizing a larger communicatively artistic event (see also Chapter 6).

Figure 7.1. Pasting the wallpaper onto board in devising the set for *Tapet*.

Outline of the Chapter

Section 2 provides background to *Tapet* and coverage of production-based research. In Section 3, we present and discuss the main features of MR arts and the concept of performativity. In Section 4, we peel back *Tapet* through four layers, each of which has a description and an analysis. The technical design and systems behind *Tapet* are given in Section 5. Finally, in Section 6, we discuss performativity in relation to digitally mediated and multimodally expressive artistic discourse and the role of production-based inquiry therein.

On *Tapet*

We had previously collaborated with a young Norwegian choreographer, Inger-Reidunn Olsen, in developing an experimental dance work that included digital scenography in its design and performance (Sem 2006). In designing *Tapet*, we asked Olsen to abandon her traditional live stage space and move with us into constructing a mixed media one that would include elements of interactive and generative composition. The related set we developed consists of a physical back wall covered with wallpaper of a forest landscape and a facing 3 x 3-meter canvas onto which is back-projected a video recording of the same wallpaper. On entering the space, the participant sees four marked spaces at the bottom of the wall between which they may move. Onto the canvas (the space facing the participants that mirrors their surroundings) appears a dancing figure (Olsen herself) who entices the participant to move. As a result, printed scenic wallpaper and back-projection of it are blended together with prerecorded material in an interplay between a mediatized dancer and a live participant within a digital landscape. Depending on the video-tracking input of audiences' movements and the composed performance, the participants may see their own image and physical presence in the displayed space and a blurring of the boundary between 'real' and 'virtual.'

In summary, this is a theatrical, performative installation. We therefore take up the relationship of the performance and relations of front stage and back stage (Goffman 1959) derived from theatre. By way of experimental design and development, we explore the dynamics of embodied interaction in which technology and layers of mediated performance place the participant as a co-performer. Ours is a design for performativity. The participant is engaged as both actor and audience in partnerings with a mediatized dancer with whom they may interact through the projections of their own moving figure and a generative computer system. Coherence in this 'staged' environment is ultimately built through iterative performative moves that ask the participants to reflect on their activity and that which responds to it from within the work.

IN THE MIX

Nonsequential, Nonverbal Modes

Our interest in designing and developing *Tapet* was to move from writings on verbal-visual semiosis and studies of meaning making in spoken interaction to the dynamics of a nonverbal and kinetic environment. Due to their generative kinetics, many MR works are 'unstable,' yet they are also realized through audience participation and have been discussed in respect to presence (Murphie 2003; Murphie & Potts 2003). According to Galanter (2003), generative (or MR) art refers to '. . . any art practice where the artist uses a system, such as a set of natural language rules, a computer program, a machine, or other procedural intervention, which is set into motion with some degree of autonomy contributing to or resulting in a completed work of art.' Much of the research on MR arts focuses on intersections between software and aesthetics.

In the design, development, and trialing of *Tapet*, mixed media, programming, sensors, a choreographed figure, and, more important, the audience as co-performer (Wilson 2002; De Oliveira, Nicolas, & Oxley 2004) were joined together in designing for performativity. We aimed to devise a visual, kinetic, and, indeed, ludic artifact and articulation. These would be not only responsive and interactive, but also generative in a mode of performative engagement with participants (e.g., Raley 2009: 32). In interdisciplinary design terms, the computational and mediational were assembled via intersections between elements drawn from choreography, installation arts, and informatics (e.g., ESG 2004). It was these interdisciplinary intersections that enabled us to further devise four interrelated multimodal states or layers: embodied, mediated, interactive, and generative. For audience participants, potentially multilevel enactment with the work was designed to allow them to reflexively face their own enacted *multimodal performativity* and engage with it.

Production-Based Inquiry

Referring to the field of software art, Brouwer et al. (2005: 7) argue that, 'Artistic research is distinguished from scientific and technological research by the fact that it is not a means of reflection and theory formation nor of problem-solving and product development, but is itself a form of reflection.' We argue for a less schematic split than these authors; however, we do argue that *Tapet* was a form of reflection (Skjulstad et al. 2003), both in its making and in its potential for the enactment of multimodal performativity through reiterative engagement. As a complex of media, software, and performance, *Tapet* functions as an heuristic for investigating multimodal performativity by way of collaborative design and enactment and shared analysis.

In a multimodal, practice-based art research frame, we were concerned with processes and relations of making and analyzing. Leggett (2006) discusses production-based research in digital domains. With software and system as material, choices are made that also place boundaries on the realization of a work. Digital documents, information sets, and elements within an environment may be shifted and exported, thus adding to the malleability of a work. In developing *Tapet*, as we show later, we needed to find a fit between artistic and communicative expression and the functionalities and stability of information systems design. This too is a matter of multimodal composition. For example, besides the computational, the historical and commercial dimensions of wallpaper (Idealdecor 2000; Kosuda-Warner & Johnson 2001) were considered in developing the metaphor of 'Tapet' and the scenographic layerings involved in it (e.g., Cheesmond 1999).

In relating production to critique, we were motivated to stretch Schön's (1983, 1987) notion of the active, reflective practitioner into creative, interdisciplinary, and digital domains. In the development of the work, this involved intensive specialist design activity but also a convergence of skills and competencies in shaping a shared work. We also drew on our experience as participants and audiences in a variety of MR pieces over several years at events and artistic venues, such as *ars electronica* and *Transmediale*. The design of *Tapet* was also enriched by observing test users and videotaping participants engaging with the near-completed design.

We occupy an intermediary space of linking making and analyzing in changing humanistic inquiry and approaches to production-based research from informatics as well as the 'new media arts.' As digital media increasingly move off the desktop, the diversity of digital media involved necessitates a corresponding diverse and interdisciplinary approach to analysis (Bolter 2003a, 2003b). At a broad level of documenting and analyzing practice-based arts research, Haseman (2006) proposes that the performative may be seen a mode of research alongside the quantitative and the qualitative. We explore what this may mean, analytically, by referring to research into the performative from multiple disciplines: performance studies, anthropology, sociology, electronic arts, digital design domains, media studies, and informatics. In particular, we draw on elements from activity theory, which provides a sociocultural frame for understanding situated semiosis and our use of the concept of multimodal performativity. In a close textual analysis of *Tapet*, we do this by including two strands, one descriptive and one analytical. These stands are further related to the four main concepts of enactment and engagement we identify: embodied, mediated, interactive, and generative. At a descriptive level, we include a series of still images from the development of the work and link these to the activities of an idealized character engaging with the work. This is done to offer readers a sense of the nonsequential layers of potential engagement.

CONCEPTUAL FRAMES

From Mixed Media to Multimediation

Hybrid or MR is the term used to refer to blends of art and technology (Grau 2003). MR works engage participants in embodied interaction, in which they are asked to piece together different sensory and analytical capacities in spaces that blend live and mediated components. The dynamic, fleeting, and processual qualities of much electronic art and its participativeness have challenged earlier notions of art. As Brouwer et al. (2005: 6) argue, 'Electronic art proved troublesome to existing art institutions, because the artistic experiences it generates are difficult to place within existing aesthetic categories, which mainly concern art made with stable media, such as painting and sculpture.'

MR arts, then, refer to works in which digital technologies augment the experience of space and time and the role of participants in expressive enactments (e.g., deLahunta 2002). Often developed collaboratively, contemporary MR artworks are characterized by their flexibility of relations between human embodiment and machinic mediation (Hansen 2005). Previously, argues Hansen, we thought digital technologies might help us escape some of the constraints of materiality and our cultural embodiment. In many respects, MR arts have drawn attention to embodied interaction. For Dourish (2001: 126), 'Embodied interaction is the creation, manipulation, and sharing of meaning through engaged interaction with artifacts.' This attention to engaged meaning making, according to Dourish (2001: 160), is a phenomenological matter in which users have increased control over the management of a work. In the process, interaction involves an assemblage of steps through which the immediate circumstances of a work are made visible. Dourish (2001: 161ff) suggests several principles for understanding embodied interaction: computation needs to be seen as a medium, meaning occurs on multiple levels, users create meaning from and on the designed, embodied technologies participate in world they represent, and embodied interaction moves action into meaning.

For each of the disciplines and fields that intersect in MR arts (i.e. media studies, art, performance, informatics), this presents questions about relationships between practice and theory, between making and analyzing. Digitally augmented performative spaces may extend traditional settings, genres, and conventions of artistic display and enactment (see Figure 7.2; Manovich 2002). They may involve projections of computer-generated images and dispersed sound. They may also include computer agents, avatars, and 'masked' characters. These MR works are curated and made available in public spaces. In such environments, conventionalized dance and theatre performance may move beyond the stage and time of enactment to multimodal intersections of digital scenography, dramaturgy, and kinetics (e.g., Sparacino et al. 2000; Schiller 2001, 2006; Dinka 2002; Evert 2002; Ballectro 2002). Here as Nolan (2009) argues, attention is needed to the role of agency in kinaesthetic performance and our understanding of embodied, gestural expression.

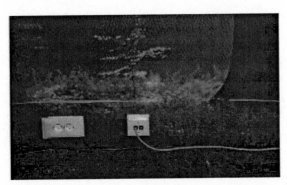

Figure 7.2. **Down at floor level the wallpaper and the ethernet link coexist.**

We see that four key components are crucial for the analysis of aspects of MR. First, regarding space, materiality is mediated, and our sense of embodiment is realized through both the physical or material and the mediatized. Here, too, we find shifts in place and time. Second, attention is often on responsiveness over formalist, visual aesthetics. As a result, process overshadows product as the work of art and consequently performativity, not representation, is of concern. Third, interaction is relational. Birringer (2003), writing on digitally mediated dance, sees that this is to move beyond spectacle and body discourse:

> To work with the designing of digital interfaces in dance means to organize a sensory and intelligent space for communicative acts that are inherently changeable and unpredictable. The space is not 'set' for a fixed choreography, but programmed for potential interactions and movements in which partners behave within a network of relays and responses, and in which technologies and media generate realities and perceptions. Interaction thus involves the whole environment, and it maps its 'world' through the continuous biofeedback it receives via direct sensory stimuli which are also technically mediated. . . .

Birringer goes on to say that the work is unstable and needs to be seen in relation to a processural digital aesthetic. This results in a move from previous preoccupation with an object of representation to that of the emergent situation. Fourth, in addition, reflexive relations come into play between the work, observer, and generative character of the system. We argue that these insights need to be highlighted further to mark a shift from earlier writings on responsivity and electronic arts to the enactment and engagement of performativity (Sha & Kuzmanovic 2000; Paul 2005). The four main modes or layers we have devised—embodied, mediated, interactive, and generative—correspond to these broad components of MR arts in general. They are embedded in the work *Tapet*, and we use them in our descriptions and analysis of it.

Performativity Across the Disciplines

Focusing on performativity allows us to place attention on intersections of human, machine, and mediational actors in the digital environment. We now cover some of the main approaches to the performative and performativity. Our point of convergence is on multimodal performativity, which we unpack with reference to activity theory and the terms 'performative artifacts' and 'artifacts of performativity.'

A performative turn, as it were, took place in the Social Sciences in linguistics, sociology (Goffman 1959), and anthropology (Turner 1987). In discourse terms, the performative has origins in speech act theory (e.g., Austin 1962) that accounted for how words are used to enact specific events and situated meanings. This approach, which centers on the utterance as a performative act, has been taken up in applied linguistics in the fields of discourse analysis and pragmatics and in written hypertextual rhetoric and pedagogy (e.g., Thomas 2003). Poststructuralist approaches to performativity in iterative textual domains were addressed by Derrida in several contexts and publications, but perhaps most often the work of Butler is associated with performativity in this vein. Butler (1993) drew attention to the gendered performativity in which citation and iteration are addressed as aspects of enactment, diverging from the work of Austin (Butler 1995). She also extended this to specific analyses of hate speech and discrimination (Butler 1999) and refers to discursive performativity (see Morrison et al. 2007, 2010).

For Turner (1982), performativity is connected to changing modes of understanding human behaviors and their patternings. He sees the liminal as referring to premodern societies and their ritual actions and collective activities. In contrast, the liminoid refers to a performativity concerned with the open-ended and exploratory engagements in often marginal settings. Elsewhere, performativity has featured in social science and technology studies. For example, Mol (1998: 145) argues that what people do may be traced through observation and reconstructive narratives that attribute meaning to participants. The discursive handling of a particular medical condition is performative, in that it may also act on and transform the way the condition is constructed (Mol 1998).

In the performing arts and in the emerging field of performance studies, performativity has been developed as a concept (Parker & Kosofsky Sedgwick 1995) that has also extended within and across the humanities (e.g., Hughes-Freeland 1998). However, considerable differences may be discerned between uses in theatre studies and the concept of theatricality, often approached in Europe, and uses in performance studies that have emerged in North America (Reinelt 2002). Saltz (2003) sees a confluence between contemporary interactive computer arts and the participatory environmental theatre of the 1960s, which aimed to engage audiences in the activity of making artworks collaboratively. However, he sees that the former has two advantages. The first is that the computer is always a 'fresh' actor, less sentient and consistently 'natural' when compared with human actors. Second, he sees that, in participatory theatre, the acts of audiences joining in the realization of the work may lead to their becoming self-conscious, while the actors become the observers of the audience on whose actions their own success depends. Given these distinctions, Saltz (2003) labels interactive computer art that is participatory *performative* and not performance art. We take this up, but move behind this distinction into designing for this performativity. In our case, participants may know that the computer is an artifice, yet they cannot avoid experiencing a self-reflexive view of their own mediatized performativity.

Mediatized Performativity

It is through the intersections of computation and performance that new modes of performativity and reconfigurations of earlier notions of performance, such as in theatre (Schieffelin 1999), may be realized. 'Mediated performance' is a term investigated in detail with reference to dance (Birringer 1998, 2002). It may also refer to the potential for performance to be in real time, stored or a hybrid mediation of these (Auslander 1997). Further, MR space may be related to performance in the ways in which software has been applied as part of the process of creating choreography, such as by Merce Cunningham (e.g., Dils 2002; see also deLahunta 1998, 2003). In MR artworks, there is often a blend of art domains, such as installation arts, choreography, and performance. In the field of conceptual installation arts, the use of electronic media and computing may be extended into new spatial relations, in which audiences move and may influence the configuration of artworks. This is not typically what is possible in traditional performance approaches to dance. It is the interrelation among media, art, and technology in experimental, creative, yet research-driven initiatives that is needed to further our expectations of what constitute multimodal utterances, expressions, and genres and our understanding of them and by way of performing them.

In addition, performativity may be used to refer to the ways in which media may be characterized as 'actors' in augmented spaces in which digital media is prominent in artistic expression (e.g., Denard 2002). Although digital media elements do not bear agency in the way we usually refer to it in more sociological or psychological senses concerning human behavior, machine–human interaction now challenges this considerably. A media-as-actors approach (Sparacino et al. 1999) refers to the scripted movement and the blending of material and immaterial communication and media types, largely through computerized routines.

In the design of interactive systems, Iacucci et al. (2002) propose three concepts: the creation of a fictional space, the role of imagination, and interactional creativity. Looking inside the space and outward from it provides some means to developing a critical view on the performance and the design. Performances are thus interpreted by the participants, and it is through their emergence that 'interactional creativity' is built (Iacucci et al. 2002: 174), influenced also by their roles (whether designerly, as improvisational actors, or related to their daily activities).

Performance is useful in helping the designer engage with the contingent to arrive at the development of a sustainable design (Iacucci et al. 2002). This has led these researchers (Jacucci et al. 2005) to develop a manifesto for performativity that includes these features.

Performative Artifacts, Artifacts of Performativity

These approaches to performance and performativity in digital design, inflected by theatre, anthropology, gender studies, computing, and design research methods, may be further extended to the relations between tools, signs, and mediation in MR environments. In particular, a focus on the mediating artifact from activity theory helps frame further the notion of performativity and embodied interaction in MR environments. Artifacts are often referred to as tools and signs (Leont'ev 1978, 1981; Wartofsky 1979). They are embedded in and realized through the intersections of activities. These too are socioculturally situated. In addition to the arte-fact, they include the subject, rules and norms, community, division of labor, and the object (or goal) of the activity.

Activity theory has seldom been applied in artistic domains. Diaz-Kommonen (2004), however, has argued that in art there is a dynamic between artifacts of expression and expressive artifacts. Artifacts of expression are the materials, tools, and sign systems that together enable mediation or expression. Expressive artifacts, in contrast, are 'texts' designed to communicate as autonomous wholes. We extend this from mediated articulation to mediated performativity. Artifacts of perfor-mance are the materials, tools, and sign systems that together enable enactment. Performative artifacts are the enacted 'texts' that as a whole constitute communication but where the processural is present. The dynamic between these two enables multimodal performativity. In the case of a MR installation work, the computer-based system and its stored mediatized performance components are reconfigured as expressions through the activity of participants and the intersections of their actions and those generated by them. These multimodal activities take the form of performative artifacts. They involve us in the translations of different modes of meaning making by the activity of our engagement.

They may be seen to embody theory in their articulations without mapping it directly. However, our interest is in moving beyond attention to the expressive and experiential. We are interested in seeing how what we might label performative artifacts may be enacted where the relations between tools and signs are realized through participants' active involve-ment in their embodied meaning making. This refers to both relating process and product in a multimodal composition.

Toward the Expressive, Experiential, and Embodied

We see that the concept of performativity also helps us to understand the ways in which our active involvement with MR works becomes part of their artistic form. Often this occurs through reference to our corporeality and position—spatial, physical, and conceptual—in relation to the work. At the level of culture, focusing on performativity accentuates the role of these data-devised, computer-mediated, and electronically distributed works as socially constructed events in which our participation is necessary for their enactment. They are sites in which implicit and explicit conventions may be teased out (Diamond, 1996). However, Hansen (2005: 153) declares that 'New media art parts company with its processural forebears to the precise extent that it sheds their narrowly aesthetic aim—to operate a critical deconstruction of the discourse of Western art —in favour of a broadly experiential one—to trigger new sensations of life.' This expressive, experiential, and embodied sense of being in an MR world may heighten our sense of performativity.

However, to replace critical deconstruction with the experiential is to erase the potential for interplay between them. *Tapet* included both of these aims. In *Tapet*, we inscribed the possibility of reiterations so as to offer participants some means of developing their own deconstructions, in and through their embodied engagement alongside their unfolding and refolding expressions realized through an experiential but performative mode of proprioceptive discourse.

Performativity and Relational-Responsive Understanding

In several senses, this stance and discourse in action view is congruent with the approach to 'posthumanist performativity' advocated by Barad (2003). She sees 'Practices of knowing and being as not isolatable, but rather they are mutually implicated. We do not obtain knowledge by standing outside of the world; we know because "we" are *of* the world. We are part of the world in its differential becoming' (Barad 2003: 829; emphasis original). It is the intra-active becoming that concerns Barad. In a work such as *Tapet*, then, we argue that it is necessary to engage with our being in the technically and corporally mediated environment, and in its unfoldings that are performed through our activities that are coaxially intertwined with the ways in which that 'system' is designed and the defined, potential, and dynamic scriptings it allows us to enact. This implies we work toward building relational-response understanding instead of representational-referential ones, as Shotter and Billig (1998) propose (see also Chapter 9).

In anthropology, Turner (1982) conceived of the liminoid to refer to social critiques present in complex, industrial societies that present ongoing, multiply framed alternatives and challenges to the status quo. *Tapet* accentuates the multimodal liminoid rather than the declarative and denotative. *Tapet* accentuates—within one MR environment—shifts between artifacts of performance and performative artifacts that allow participants to experience and interrelate a complex of relations. Further, in our view, multimodal, multimediational performativity may be explored through a participatory and exploratory design process. Where much focus on mixed electronic arts concerns selection for art festivals and academic publications address matters of aesthetic computing (e.g., Fishwick 2006) and 'software art' (e.g., Goriunova & Shulgin 2004), we return to the design studio and write about the experimental, collaborative, and interdisciplinary making or devising of multimodal design for performativity built there (see also Christensen & Lamm 2003).

TAPET: LAYERS OF LINKED ENGAGEMENT AND ENACTMENT

Four Broad Intersecting Layers

Giving an account of aspects of multimodal production-based research in mediatized, generative performance is not only a matter of conveying spatial/temporal expressions in writing (see Figure 7.3). It is also a matter of mediating the interactive and generative artefacts. Installations are plastic: Some participants may experience a mediated performance, whereas some experience an interactive installation and others a generative work.

We have demarcated four broad, schematic 'layers' or scenarios, not necessarily sequential ones, that apply to the design and embodied use of *Tapet*. Similar categories were developed by Candy and Edmonds (2002) to refer to relationships between the artist, work, spectator, and contextual environment (Edmonds et al. 2006). Those categories are: static, dynamic-passive, dynamic-interactive, and dynamic-interactive (varying). Our categories or layers have been built with reference to these and to wider writings on electronic arts. We have been 'joining the wallpaper' across modes of performativity as a means to understand the multiple activities possible in such a work. In distinction to other analyses, our heuristic focuses on a work in which spatial performative relations, and

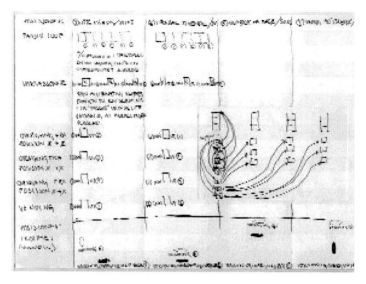

Figure 7.3. Sketching and choreographing recursive architecture and choreography. (In Norwegian)

not so much tactile media, are the focus. Our four layers referring to modes of enactment and engagement are: (1) embodied, (2) mediated, (3) interactive, and (4) generative.

In our approach, scenarios form the basis of performance; they can assist in pitching a script or providing an account or a synopsis of an action or event. In 'new' media, computing, and digital design research, scenarios are widely used to project potential articulations and their contexts of use. Although the scenarios shown here overlap, we have needed to provide an explanatory frame to account for shifts in design, potential for use, and perception in enactment. Each of these layers is marked by the extension of the traditional immobile spectator role, as well as the exploration of the performative interplay between participant and system, including the materialization of technology (Birringer 2003; see Figure 7.3).

Layer 1, 'Embodied,' refers to the physical installation work and the participants' entrance into it and sense of their own embodiment in an MR space in which media is used to visualize and sonify a forest exterior. In Layer 2, 'Mediated,' the participants experience the digitally mediated presence of a dancer and observe the activity of dance. Moving inside this performance as an active participant is what occurs in Layer 3, 'Interactive,' with the participant now able to have some direct effect on the sequencing of dance material and its location. Finally, in Layer 4, 'Generative,' the participants move from affecting the nature of the performance to being 'actors' in the mediated stage and staging, moving with the dancer inside the work and shaping the interplay between computer-generated patternings and the participants' own mediated presence.

In the following, we use these layers to describe modes of engagement embedded in the work. We do this by reference to a fictional visitor, Terje (although *Tapet* can be experienced by more than one person at a time). His 'experiences,' which we place under 'Description,' are followed by more formal 'Analysis' on the activity. The descriptions aim to give readers a sense of the installation environment and how it works from the point of view of a participant. The more analytical and conceptual reflection that follows allows us to relate *Tapet* to other studies and works and thereby to place its composition and performative use in a wider view.

Layer 1: Embodied

Description

> Terje approaches the artspace which is set up in a large studio suited to television production and experimental design events. To his left, a large semitransparent screen is suspended and reaches right down to the floor. A desk with computers sits some distance behind this screen. To his right is a back wall onto which has been wallpapered a forest scene. Terje follows the visual directions to a small strip of plastic lawn grass that runs along the base of the wallpapered image of the forest.

> As he walks toward the grass and its gaudy green texture, Terje looks at the wallpapered landscape scene. The wallpaper image is clearly a mass-produced image. It's an archetypal forest of tall spruce it seems. A still image, almost a glen, with a sense of calm, perhaps the sound of a small stream, a feeling of quiet, of being in the middle of an enveloping world. The size of the image and the glow of sunlight between the large trees invite him to another world far removed from the physical room in which he stands.

> Terje moves onto the grass where spots are clearly marked. It's a space designed for use. He turns toward the projected screen space opposite the wallpaper, a replica of the glen opposite. A gentle bird-song replaces the lack of sound, supplementing the represented forest. The sense of an audiovisual immersiveness is slightly out of sync. Terje feels his own body physically present in the room but senses his presence in a mediated space that surrounds him. He sees that under the studio lights there's a network cable running across the floor from the wallpaper to a desk with computers behind the projected screen.

Analysis

Hybrid or MR artworks are concerned with building imaginative participation between the context or environment of staging and users' embodied activity in effecting the overall performance of the work. The point of entry and the manner in which the work is staged as a set largely frames the ways in which the expectations of the participant are primed (see Figure 7.4). Specific paths to active engagement need to be signalled while cues to participation need to be underdetermined so that the participants are engaged in finding their logic. MR arts often play off expectations of time and space, and our initial entry into such spaces needs to alert us to some of the features that will be in flux. Participants typically see that the spaces are not windows onto the world but are instead self-reflexive uses of mediated technologies that involve us in productive engagements with modes of representation and participation.

How then may we design for participation between the environment of staging and users embodied activity in and by a physical set and space? How may we embody and evoke expectations of participation by the physical environment? A key concept and a key design in *Tapet* was the creation of a multimodally represented exterior. This is achieved by virtue of its being both, on the one hand, immersive or transparent and, on the other hand, by being hypermediated and enabling the embodied, self-reflexive use of mediated technologies. In Layer 1 of *Tapet* (physical installation, participants' entrance, embodiment), we aimed to clearly materialize technology in the form of an ambient, self-reflexive environment composed by print media, digital projection, and sound (see Section 4 for further details of the technical set). The self-reflexive use of mediated technologies places *Tapet* in relation to works that problematize

Figure 7.4. **Back projection view of dancer on digital wallpaper (in the foreground), with print wallpaper in the background.**

phenomenologically the viewer's perspective and invite the participant to partly leave the passive spectator role and participate in the actual space rather than consume the represented or, rather, consume by participation.

The design was informed by the cross-disciplinary and poststructural-ist view of looking through and looking at mediating artifacts, expressions, and texts. Bolter and Grusin (1999) propose a double logic of immediacy and hypermediacy derived from their discussion of the tendency of reme-diation in screen-based media. Immediacy and hypermediacy are oppo-site manifestations of the same desire. This is to move beyond the limits of representation and to achieve the 'real,' that is, a sense of the authentic in the viewer's response. It is the denial of mediation, that is, transparen-cy, that marks the immediacy in digital media. For Bolter and Grusin (1999: 81), hypermediacy is an '. . . immediacy that grows out of the frank acknowledgment of the medium and is not based on the perfect visual re-creation of the world. In such cases, we do not look through the medium in linear perspective; rather, we look at the medium.' The multi-modal environment of *Tapet*, engaging strategies of immediacy and hypermediacy, is in many senses a reflexive design that embeds potential for interaction. The interactive and generative computational aspects of the work are as yet concealed in the layer outlined earlier (installation space, participants' entrance and embodiment, media). The participants need to enter into a believable context where there are adequate referents to connect to and through which expectations may be awoken.

The occasional ambient sound and plastic grass strip both build and break the seeming realism just as the difference in the high-resolution print backdrop and the more diffuse projected image point to the mediat-ed nature of the projection. That the participants are led to a narrow band of grass right next to the wallpaper presses them to face the front and look into the digitally mediated representation. Their own position is sug-gested as an embodied one in relation to the mediated space. In contrast to many electronic artworks, which have a direct haptic interface, here distance and depth of field are shown by the separation of this space for action and the large screen beyond reach. It is clear that this is not an immersive work. The interface is spread over the four spots; it also includes the participants' own bodies and is ultimately enacted via medi-ated material and prompts in the screen space.

Layer 2: Mediated

Description

Standing on the fake grass, Terje looks across the space to the large screen. The screen shows a woman in a matching florescent orange top and short skirt. Her arms and legs are bare as she stands in the delicate light. She is visible in the mirrored image of the forest behind Terje. Her skirt and t-shirt are slightly ruffled, but the skirt seems to have been starched or strangely stitched so that it points outward and slightly upward. Terje is not sure about her location, however. She wasn't behind the screen when he entered the artspace. She might be in another room nearby, or perhaps telepresent, beamed in live from a remote setting.

The woman begins to bounce up and down a little before returning to her passive mode–looking straight ahead. There seems to be no symbolic meaning in this movement.

After a short while, she begins to look toward Terje, as if sensing that he is present, and then moves across the forest space where Terje is standing and faces him. Knowingly playful, she lines up with Terje on a specific spot. It seems now that she can see him and that she is toying with his presence.

She makes sure she stands in the right position opposite him, still playful, before suddenly altering her facial expressions into a mock smile. She begins bouncing again but now in a slightly different posture, introducing a short performance of movements.

Terje isn't sure whether the figure can see him. The dancer seems to follow well-rehearsed and pre-prepared material, so it must have been choreographed beforehand. But the attention she is giving him seems live.

Analysis

The following analysis of *Tapet*, Layer 2, 'Mediated,' addresses how the interplay between expectations of participation and the reflexive toying with representation and constructions of artefacts are developed and explored further via the mediated performance (see Figure 7.5). Whereas multimodality was emphasized in the reflections on the previous layer, another type of multimodality is clear here, namely, mediatized.

The choreographed dance performed in *Tapet* is not a live performance as 'performance' has been defined since the 1960s (Goldberg, 1998) but a mediated one. Ours is not 'representation without reproduction and distribution' (Auslander 1997) but a hypermediated one that explores other and sometimes contradictory strategies of authentication and presence than being live in a shared physical space.

The notion of presence needs further discussion because it is closely tied to notions of performance and performance art. In the 1960s, there was focus on relations between the performer and spectator in shared events not staged spectacles. In the 1980s, the focus shifted to the

Figure 7.5. Inger-Reidun Olsen poises between movements in keying in the bluescreen.

absence of presence and thus emphasis on the absence of presence (Copeland 1990). 'Presence,' then, may be defined as a way of performing that generates an impression of the work as authentic in the perceiving audience, that is, authentic in the sense that the performance reveals its own performativeness (Sem 2006), resonating Auslander's (1997) prior observation above. Similar to how the hypermediated exterior with its sporadic audio draws attention from the constructed hypothetical space to its own mediatedness, so the performance too draws attention from representation to the mediatized signifier. There is a mediatized presence in the same conceptual space as the physical audience space, that is, in an interactive installation context.

By challenging aesthetic notions of mimesis and representation, the non-narrative and nonrepresentational piece might be experienced rather than interpreted. When the participant selects one of the four spots (each referring to a different choreography and theme), the dancer colocates herself with the participant. A nonreferential internal dynamic begins in which, as Tronstad (2004) argues, referring to Austin, the moves '. . . do not refer to some external reality but constitute themselves as acts.' The hybridization of real and virtual in *Tapet* aligns too with '. . . contemporary performance and dance which use digital processes and are affected, in particular, by the transformations of audio-visual space and bodily perceptions within interactive and streaming media environments' (Birringer 2003). These acts are a blend of live and mediatized (Auslander 1997). Yet they are not simply distinguishable as either live or mediatized: the participant is encouraged to discern the links and differences between these in building understanding of how the piece works. The participant senses the figure and his own body as being in the same mixed space, as well as the links that cross the physical distance of the flow between the belt of grass and the suspended screen.

These moves draw attention to the ways in which, in MR artworks, there is an interplay between reflexivity and performativity. Here we see this extended to the pastiche of a previous medium, wallpaper being embodied as a mediatized landscape. These relations of ironic mirroring and differentiation draw attention to technology as mediating artifact and an artifact of mediation. Irony travels from the screen to the wallpaper and vice versa. For the participant, as we elaborate in the next layers, there remains the move from spectator to co-creator.

Layer 3: Interactive

Description

Terje has watched the dancer complete a sequence and then line up with him again. The dancer seems to be waiting for something to happen. She is bouncing up and down again as if giving him his cue to move. Leaving the comfort of his spectator role, he moves to another spot on the grass.

Again the dancer follows him and he laughs. It is a playful move, almost commenting on his actions. Terje realizes that he is the one who is now having an effect on her position in the forest. Again she begins to dance. It's a different dance to the one she did the first time when she was performing using the whole space. Now she performs in one place moving the upper part of her body only. Her feet are still.

Terje suddenly decides to shift position and moves to another spot on the grass and stops. The dancer completes the choreographed piece she was doing, bounces a little, and then follows him to the spot. She faces him again and starts to bounce up and down, introducing a new choreography. This time the dancer moves slowly toward him on unstable legs and closer than any of the other positions. Terje stands still observing her movements, thinking about the feel of the moss on her bare feet. He remains motionless. The dancer completes her sequence and comes to rest opposite him once again with another bounce. Terje isn't sure whether the bounce marks an ending or the start of something.

Terje stands there thinking about how he is actually shaping and editing the components in a dance work. Something is definitely happening behind that screen! A real live dancer can't be there, can she? This is still interactivity, though. But it's a different kind of interaction to the one he knows from the Web and from computer games. And it's not like traditional dance either because the stage is altered, yet the performer is very much present.

Analysis

Many MR works attempt to involve participants in elaborate games and self-conscious involvement in understanding how the work functions. In Layer 3 of *Tapet*, the participant moves from playing the interactive relations between the dancer and the positions to one of having an effect on a mediated choreography. A twofold setting is in place: that of an interactive installation work and a performance.

In contrast to a more literal sense of interaction, concerning responsive environments, Douglas and Hargadon (2001) make the important distinction between 'immersive' affective experience and 'engaged' affective experience, where the participant becomes performer, engaging himself in dynamic moves and feels a sense of being in the same performance space. In 'Aesthetic Paradigms of Media Art,' Giannetti (n.d.) discusses the role of the viewer or participant as a meta-author of mediated pieces. In addition in terms of reflexivity, for Dinka et al. (2002: 26), 'In place of the conventional enjoyment of art there arises a state between perception and action, analogous to the oscillating state of the dancers and leading ultimately to self-recognition.'

In *Tapet*, there is also a move into engagement as the participants' moves are part of choreographing the activity and stretch previous notions of embodied interaction. This is in keeping with the pliability of such works, in which their unfolding and malleable 'materiality' is part of their enactment and aesthetics. Referring to the work of the artist Kruger, Cameron (2005: 15) conceptualizes this as a matter of an 'enlarging repertoire.' This points to changing relationships between art as object and viewer, here dance-like participant and installation MR space. We may ask, then, how might the new forms of engagement in MR works change the nature of the art object? This has a direct bearing on the tension and synergy between the responsiveness of the work and the realization in the time of enactment of a visual aesthetic. There is still the artistic struggle with the 'canvas' and the role of the conceptual, of movement, and of chance, as Rush (1999) mentions in the development of much modern art in the past century.

How, then, did we stretch previous notions of embodied interaction in *Tapet*? How did we evoke expectations for interactive participation? What propelled this potential interaction? Designing for interaction by multiple 'participants,' where delay is applied both conceptually and aesthetically and the physical body in the actual physical space is the interface, is not easy. *Tapet* does not overcome all these difficulties. Although *Tapet* might overcome the lack of embodied and collaborative constraints much present in tangible interaction, the more spatial interaction (Hornecker & Buur 2006) of this work with temporally locked video entities may not make a clear and immediate link between what participants do and what happens. *Tapet*, however, is a device for exploring important factors of interactivity, such as homogeneity, linearity, complexity, and longevity (Havnør 2006). Key aspects of the design that became important in our effort to propel expectations and longevity for interactive participation and ease the mentioned contradicting factors for interaction in *Tapet* were the inclusion of clearly differentiated choreographed material and the feature of intermittent bouncing.

Apart from being a technically generated feature designed to smooth the transition between two clips, the recurring, monotone bouncing begins to bear aesthetic qualities. Perhaps most important, the dancer's evocative qualities (see Figure 7.6) introduced shifts in material in the form of choreographed performing sections, improvised reflexive sections where the performer addressed the spectator in playful ways, or passive sections when no input was given.

The choreographed material was then further differentiated according to four positions in the performance space. These correlated with the positions in the physical participation space so as to drive the interaction and co-composition by changing activity and its various outputs. As a participant, one is not fully aware of the relationships between the positions, the space, and the dance until these have been enacted: The four different positions in a sense comment on the movement in the bounded space of the forest setting. Position 1 is connected to a lateral movement across the screen; the movements attached to the second position are tied to one stance–the performer working with details of movements in her upper body only. At Position 3, the performer moves from deeper into the space and face on, now keeping her upper body still while balancing slowly on uncertain feet. Finally, Position 4 repeats Position 2, but this

Figure 7.6. **The dancer appears in the forest. Her image is backprojected onto the suspended screenspace. The image of the forest is a projection from the back wall of the installation.**

time the dancer moves side on so that the participant develops a different point of view to the otherwise face-to-face mediation. In a sense, these perspectives comment on one another in retrospect: You develop a realization of how the dancer's movements are playing with your expectations of responsivity and interaction and that the stances, angles, and depth are being offered as a marking of how mediatized activity is limited by, yet can be varied in, space.

Responsivity is, in part, linked to the ways in which the video material presents the work as comprised of readymades, following Duchamp (see e.g., Qvortrup 2003) or Auslander's 'reproduction without representation,' that are compiled and presented. However, these mediatized, prerecorded videos are also ready-to-be-made again through the embodied poetics of the moving participant as a choreographer of an MR work. In addition, the participant now needs to shift from a level of composition to that of reflection and interpretation as the potential choreographic patterning demands a mixture of trial and error and considered forethought.

The technologically driven travesty of the spectator interacting with the artistic work, and her co-composing the actual output/artefact, is explored further in the next layer. The layer elaborates how the spectator interacts with the piece as the performer becomes part of the emerging work.

Layer 4: Generative

Description

> *Terje has been standing quite still for some time now thinking about this installation space. The mediated performance shifts from knowing playful interaction with him to pre-prepared material performed for him. He shapes and edits the choreography, using his own body, moving here and then there across the grass to get the dancing figure to move and dance inside the forest.*
>
> *He looks up and realizes that she has been waiting for him again. She's bouncing up and down once more, but seems to have changed her attention to him this time.*
>
> *Suddenly he sees a difference. It's him in the forest with her! But it's a recording of him standing thinking. It must be from a little while back. And the image does not correspond with his position. He moves his arm, but his arm does not move in the forest. So it is his earlier self relocated. He sees himself standing there before in the role of a spectator. There's movement again: The dancer crosses right in front of him as if she is now the one in control. Looking at Terje first before she moves toward him in the forest, she knows both are watching her.*

She is standing very close to him, almost touching him. This is so different from before.

There he is beside her in the forest, with its dappled sunlight and tall trees. He now imagines himself in the space, sensing her beside him, but he's looking down, if only he would look up! He notices what he is wearing; he sees he is the taller of the two. He laughs out loud, seeing himself in a mirror-like view that isn't showing his immediate reflected image. There is contrast between her active performance and his passive response as a spectator.

The dancer repeats her material performed just seconds earlier, but faces towards the other side and a rather blank-looking Terje, who watches her as she moves through the forest. He isn't moving much though in the version of him in the forest, but now he sees he is shifting his feet and scratching his head. Then Terje appears to change his attention now, lifting his arm as he did 10 seconds ago.

Things have definitely changed in this forest! What is he going to do now? Dance as well? He tries a few movements, feeling a little self-conscious that they aren't particularly elegant. His dancing self then again appears in the forest. He sees there is a duet that, in some unsynchronized but inevitable way, creates a whole. He laughs again, and he begins to move much more actively, using his arms and bouncing up and down as he moves across the strip of grass. Now he is repeating the dancer's movements as if he is part of the choreography, yet also in an unintended parody of modern dance.

The woman has stopped dancing. She rests in the position where she began. Again, she starts to bounce. Terje sees his image disappear from the screen. What's going on now? He wants to get back into the picture and feel the sense of visual and almost tactile responsiveness when she stands next to him. So he moves into another position and the cross-cycle of performativity begins again.

Analysis

Tapet clarifies that there may not always be a sharp division between the interactive and generative. The relation between these two is complex and may be understood as a gradual engagement of chance from interactive to generative, where multiple variations of nongenerative output sit somewhere in between as a matter of co-composition.

In the final layer of this MR work, the features and functionalities of earlier layers are connected to generative qualities and actions. The participant in the work engages in an interplay between what the participant effects and what is generated computationally (see Figure 7.7). We may conceive of this as a dynamic environment in which the participant comes to understand the agency that lies inside the system behind the screen and how to work this in relation to his own movement. This draws us into how we perceive and act on, as is mentioned in the context of the immersive work *Promenade*, '. . . the ambiguous relationship between the three-dimensional space and its two-dimensional representation as perceived from a dynamic moving viewpoint' (Szegedy-Maszák & Fernezelyi 2005: 60).

Tapet is both interactive and generative. The actions of the participant have resulted in related responses from the system. The system co-choreographs generatively via the code. The participant generates action via the generation of video of the participant. This is placed inside the screen, where the dancer then registers this new 'immediate' placement and moves toward this embedded representation. The participant is in a sense simultaneously redundant and embodied. The participant's '. . . sense of self is turned and displaced from the body to the representation of the body on the screen' (Brouwer et al. 2005: 17). The live-mediatized relation is now seemingly reversed, with the irony being that the recently moving participant is now mediatized material with which the dancer may play. The dancer appears to choose where she can move and moves to the virtual participant rather than the physically embodied one. She moves in our physical time but leaves it; she is co-present in both. However, she performs in a delayed, mediated time; we are confronted with both of these. What we meet as a consequence is a multimodality that is not only visually but temporally hybrid.

Figure 7.7. **Two participants against the print wallpaper background see themselves projected into the performance space, generative participants in a mixed reality installation.**

Here the spatial merger and temporal displacement highlight the activity of producing an augmented space and its performativity. Just as earlier the dancer seemed to stare out at the participant, now the participant seems to have adopted this role and by proxy suggests that the participant should move. The dancer's moving over towards the participant and her appearing to touch him also introduces a strange sense of augmented haptics: The contact occurs in screen space, and the participant senses this in his own (mirrored self). The work now shifts from having a performer move in a mediated space and as a mediatised performer to there being a sense of both co-option and collaboration in a dance of MR.

The participant is now challenged to reinterpret his earlier perceptions and activities. For Qvortrup (2003: 257), 'It is an important consequence of the way in which interactive artworks function that one has to reinterpret the interpretation process.' The participant sees his own recent actions as mediatized ones. He then sees that the dancer has recognized his mediated embodiment within the screen space as if acknowledging that he has now joined her in a level of augmented performativity that she already recognizes. Again, he may engage as a viewer repeating the stage-staged view from earlier. However, he may further devise movements of his own and stretch this augmented space one level further, thereby moving his own moving self into the image space. The result is, then, that the referent swings not in real human time or in the time of the machine, but as and in their interactive continuity.

This multitemporality challenges participants to review their involvement in their own processes of nonverbal meaning making. Unlike many other generative electronic artworks, the participant now has to begin to think choreographically in terms of the overall functionalities that have been discovered and then move within the environment in which they are now a third party. At this level, aesthetic qualities are overridden by the quality of interaction, not as responsivity but as performativity. The material in these layers is achieved through the intersection of artistic and information systems design. It is to the latter that we now turn.

BEHIND THE SCREEN: LAYERINGS IN SYSTEMS DESIGN

Tapet: The Set

At the core of the systems design process in *Tapet* were software engineering principles such as reusability, modability, and maintainability. Although not a typical treat in the art world, this approach allowed a fairly advanced technological problem to be solved using a minimum of resources. Dourish (2001: 207) reminds us that the design and analysis of tangible interaction systems need '. . . to encompass more than simply their "tangible" characteristics, and to understand how they are caught up in larger systems of meaning that connect the physical to the symbolic rather than separating them.'

Physically, the *Tapet* installation consists of a wallpapered surface, two cameras, a projector with corresponding canvas, two speakers, two Macintosh computers, two Windows computers, and a patch of artificial grass indicating where the audience members are invited to stand (see Havnør 2006 for details; see Figure 7.8). Each computer has a specific task in the installation, ranging from playing simple ambient background sounds to performing live chroma keying (van den Bergh & Lalioti 1999).

The two main computers involved in running the *Tapet* system were a server and a client. Although the base architecture of the application is built along the lines of the Model View Controller (MVC) principle, the choice of HTTP as control protocol gives a server/client aspect. The server component is a servlet acting as the controller component of the MVC pattern. It instantiates a model component containing a state machine representing the interaction logic. The client is essentially the view component, communicating with the controller over the HTTP protocol.

Video Material: The Dance

The actual dance performance is stored as a set of 40 mpeg-4 simple format video files, varying from 9 to 90 seconds. The dance is carefully choreographed to fit this pattern so that every possible transition between

Figure 7.8. A view from the system control desk.

two clips can run smoothly. That is, the position of the dancer at the end of the clip that starts has to match her position at the start of the ending clip. This is achieved by having her move around four base positions.

Server and Client Architecture

The business logic of the *Tapet* set is realized by a servlet. This Web application contains four interconnected classes and the specification of a state machine in 'scene.xml.' The scene descriptor format used in scene.xml provides an easy way to the narrative structure of the installation without changing code or recompiling the system. Through numerous user tests, the advantage of this approach became apparent because the representation of the state machine had to be updated frequently. The client part of *Tapet* is a Java application based on the Java Media Framework (JMF). In the basic structure of client, an input stream of encoded video is read through a VideoStreamer object, and two ClipPlayer objects are instantiated for the current and the next video clip to render.

Business Logic

Tapet can be split into two main parts with regards to logic: the background and the foreground. The background can be one of two states: a static image taken from the start of the video feed or the actual video feed, which is a slightly delayed live video stream of the audience. The delay may be adjusted. We decided after trials to use a 10-second one, on aesthetic grounds, and to avoid the immediate interaction in much works, thereby emphasizing the reflection on the spectator role, but not to the extent that the physical memory of moving in certain ways was hampered.

The foreground is split into four major positions. For the dancer, these are four different physical locations she can occupy on the canvas. For the audience, the positions follow the same pattern, making it possible to determine whether the dancer and the audience are located opposite each other. Through the (structured) feedback of the test participants in *Tapet*, a set of interactivity patterns were identified while attempting to expand Lee's (2000) definition of interactivity to the field of interactive art. By applying these patterns to the different forms of interaction offered by *Tapet*, some aspects of the user experience could, to some extent, be predicted. The level of impact a user has on the installation and its narrative structure, and the possible mismatch between actual and expected responses, were among the main aspects covered (see Havnør 2005).

PRACTICE AND PERFORMATIVITY
PRACTICE-BASED RESEARCH

We have devised and applied four modes or layers–embodied, mediated, interactive, and generative–in the context of MR arts. Through the interplay of these layers, we have shown how multimodal performativity comes into being. To recap, the tools, materials, and sign systems that together enable enactment are artifacts of performance. Performative artifacts are the enacted and processural works that make up a communicative sum. Together these create intimate knowledge of the overall computational and mediated activity and its performative aspects. This interplay is both fed by practice-based design and feeds back into it conceptually.

The resulting MR piece *Tapet* is responsive; it is multilinear and hypertextual in its implicit linkings. It includes real-time transmission of data using the viewer's body movement as part of the interface/input device that is tracked by a video application. *Tapet* collapses the distinction between recorded content and the physical, mediated environment. Further, it can be customized and relocated to different contexts and public spaces in an adaptive design frame. The materiality of the work is realized through scripted language and video recordings of its environment. This allows one to shift the piece, and thereby the participant's role, from a mediated dance performance to a responsive installation (and back).

Developments in digital technologies have impacted on artistic production and expression, and research processes have refined the knowledge of such 'canvases' (e.g., Sem 2006). A recursive series of translations between different modes of engagement-between creation, experience, and reflection on experience–may help build an understanding of the interplay between digital technology and artistic, expressive innovations. As digital technology evolves and diverges at a rapid pace, such intimate, production-based understanding might be particularly crucial to reduce the distance and risk of misrepresentation between object and concepts of the humanities. Production-based methods may represent a third path to conceptual knowledge or a '(re)source' for the analytical purpose of humanities (Liestøl 2001) when secondary mediated knowledge ends, such as theoretical adaptation from neighboring disciplines or the potential of a general semiotic approach. Multimodal, multilinear, and spatial expressions may motivate us further to question the potential of language-based theories of communication and meaning. Production-based methods allow us to explore multimodality by constructing MR creative artifacts that inhabit or embody theories and their unfolding aesthetics.

In studies of digital media, Liestøl (1999) argues that we need to investigate synthetic-analytic relations among media types, changing forms, and their incorporation of earlier media types in new 'compositions.' He argues that traditional humanistic reflections on texts as completed activities, studied in hindsight, are now challenged by the intersections of media and technologies (see also Drucker 2009). Drawing on approaches from the natural sciences and increasingly from computer science, we may reconfigure hermeneutical approaches typical of the humanities to meet and account for rapid, emerging, and developmental design changes in digitally mediated communication. This is not to say that there is no given or preexisting knowledge or histories of media and art, but rather that our roles as makers and analyzers of digital narratives, artworks, and environments draw us into new knowledge practices and understandings that influence one another. The turns between contradiction and innovation are a part of struggling with the collaborative context of reflexivity and the emerging multimodal 'canvas.'

How a practice-based method may be a part of a process of exploring, challenging, and refining theory has also been covered. We have designed a work that challenges tools; through the processes and the product of the piece, we have explored performativity theoretically and practically; reflexively refining our understanding of the work has involved reflection on both the processes of making and the interdisciplinary intersections that have continued into postproduction analysis. We have conceptualized this dynamic through the interplay between the concepts of artifacts of expression and expressive artifacts (Diaz-Kommonen 2004), so that there is a bidirectional relationship between theory and practice (see Figure 7.9).

Figure 7.9. Observing the work side on; this was used while also filming ways in which the work was used by participants (not show here).

Performativity and MR Arts

In conclusion, we see that notions and realizations of performativity may be included in a wider conceptualization of mediated articulation in digital domains. We argue that composition may be understood as more than experimentation with hypertextual, written, and expository modes of digital discourse, interesting and important as these are in finding forms and functionalities of digital communication.

In augmented, MR settings, this requires that software and systems remain flexible and function dynamically and aesthetically (e.g., Fishwick 2006). Such coded responsive and performative electronic art may augment reality at the same time as it may try to mimic the open-ended and emergent character of 'reality.' Here, the interface is central to our engagement and to the enactment of human-computer performance. Hansen (2005: 154) writes that:

> It is important to underscore the dual structure of the interface: the interface encompasses computer-mediated rendering of data coupled with motorically triggered human response. In contradistinction to the apparatus of cinema, video and photography, where the framing of information is pre-inscribed in the technology itself the spectator-participant of digital media environments and interfaces must contribute to the process of framing by actively selecting data in conjunction with the computer. . . .

The interface may thus become reflexive; it is connected to software agents but also to our actions and behaviors as participants within digitally mediated, multidimensional environments. These are interfaces in which spatial representations, navigation, and information design challenge us to devise and analyze communication in which we as artists, users, and interpreters may be present and 'perform.' On digital art, Bolter and Gromala (2003: 147) write that:

> As users, we enter into a performative relationship with a digital design: we perform the design, as we would a musical instrument. Digital artists and designers create instruments that the user will play. . . . At their best, however, digital designs will enable their users to produce results unforeseen by their designers.

In designing for performativity in interactive environments, the aim is to 'provide contexts within which actions are performed' (Saltz 2003: 405). These contexts are intended to be spaces for participants and the performers to adapt to one another, although computationally software does not bear the same ontological knowledge of multiple contexts in the world that participants carry and to which they may refer. It is in the participants' partnering with a generative system that the sense of performativity is accentuated. Often in generative art, performativity is nonverbal; this has received little conceptual analysis in terms of acts of performing. Ours is not an interaction analysis of participation in an MR work, but as a design experiment, *Tapet* was built collaboratively and tested by a variety of users who were observed and, in several cases, videotaped. These observations centered on what participants do in this digital installation piece as active, dynamic, and moving performers, themselves crossing the boundaries between choreography and performance, and informing the iterative design activity.

In this chapter, however, we have tried to move inside multimodal composition and communicate how we have tried to design *for* performativity, that is, to conceptualize and affect a technology-enhanced environment that makes and leaves room in its 'scripting' for the performativity of the 'player.' In a discussion of the concepts of theatricality and performance, Reinelt (2002: 213) concludes that:

> Performance makes visible the micro-processes of iteration and the non-commensurability of repetition, in the context of historically sedimented and yet contingent practices, in order that we might stage theatricality, and render palpable possibilities for unanticipated signification.

We have shown how multimodal composition in MR arts may be investigated via conceptual analysis in processes of making and experimental use, as well as in postproduction. We have argued that it is at the level of articulation, or the giving of mediated form with content in and via use, that it is possible to explore ways in which experimental, kinetic, and interdisciplinary MR arts may be understood through a dynamic of practice and theory. We argue that it is possible to move beyond a separation of works that accentuate either a deconstructive aesthetics or an experiential phenomenology of participation. Although intertwined, in a liminoid stance, these approaches give the participant room to maneuver.

Multimodal Performativity

New media arts are moving out of galleries and museum spaces into other public domains, such as piazzas, and from domestic desktops to living rooms (Edmonds et al. 2006). We suggest that, in tandem, our digital literacies may be extended to include mobile, kinetic, and expressive aspects of multimodality. In these domains, meaning making may be conceptualized through situated, embodied, nonverbal performativity in an interplay between human and machinic participants. This is to move from grammars of visual design (Kress & van Leeuwen 1996) to performative discourse, above the level of the syntagma, beyond sign, to mediated semiosis in MR. Works such as *Tapet* may also be understood through closer social semiotic readings than the one we offer here.

What we have tried to show is that it is possible to design MR works as a blend of media and space, time and live and mediatized distribution that make for multiple modes of participation in which the participant experiences a self-reflexive sense of performativity. Artistic expressions are being extended from defined canvases to 'unstable' contexts with the potential for chance patternings, in which perception shifts from observation to participative co-creation. In this light, the concept of *multimodal performativity* is a potentially useful one for going behind the surfaces of embodied encounters and the complexity of layered expressive, experiential, and performatively enacted discourses of MR arts.

ACKNOWLEDGMENTS

We are indebted to Inger-Reidun Olsen (choreographer, dancer) and InterMediaLab (Ole Smørdal, Per Christian Larsen) for helping *Tapet* happen. Thanks also to colleagues and visitors for their comments. This chapter draws on our two master's theses in MR arts (Havnør 2006; Sem 2006) related to the *MULTIMO* and *Designing Design* projects at InterMedia, University of Oslo. It is also an outcome of an EU Culture 2000 program project, *gRIG: Guild for Reality Integrators and Generators*. Our thanks to our colleagues in the guild for their input.

REFERENCES

Auslander, Philip. (1997). 'Ontology vs. history. Making distinctions between the live and mediatised.' *1997 Performance Studies Conference*. Available at http://webcast.gatech.edu/papers/arch/Auslander.html
Auslander, Philip. (1999). *Liveness*. London: Routledge.
Austin, John. (1962). *How to Do Things With Words*. Cambridge, MA: Harvard University Press.
Ballectro. (2002). *Ballectroweb*. Research project website. InterMedia, University of Oslo. Available at http://www.intermedia.uio.no/ballectro/
Barad, Karen. (2003). Posthumanist performativity: toward an understanding of how matter comes to matter.' *Signs: Journal of Women in Culture and Society*. Vol. 28, No. 3, 801-831.

Birringer, Johannes. (1998). *Media & Performance*. Baltimore: Johns Hopkins University Press.

Birringer, Johannes. (2002). 'Dance and media technologies.' *Performing Arts Journal*. Vol. 70, 84-93.

Birringer, Johannes. (2003). 'Dance, the body and the internet.' *Design and Performance Lab*. Brunel University, London. Available at http://people.brunel. ac.uk/dap/bodynet.html

Bolter, Jay. (2003a). 'Critical theory and the challenges of new media.' In Hocks, Mary, & Kendrick, Michelle. (Eds.). *Eloquent Images*. Cambridge, MA: The MIT Press. 19-36.

Bolter, Jay. (2003b). 'Theory and practice in new media studies.' In Liestøl, Gunnar, Morrison, Andrew, & Rasmussen, Terje. (Eds.). *Digital Media Revisited*. Cambridge, MA: The MIT Press. 15-33.

Bolter, Jay, & Gromala, Diane. (2003). *Windows and Mirrors*. Cambridge, MA: The MIT Press.

Bolter, Jay, & Grusin, David. (1999). *Remediation*. Cambridge, MA: The MIT Press.

Brouwer, Joke, Fauconnier, Sandra, Mulder, Arjen, & Nigten, Anne. (2005). 'Introduction and manual.' In Brouwer, Joke, Fauconnier, Sandra, Mulder, Arjen, & Nigten, Anne. (Eds.). *aRt&D: Research and Development in Art*. Rotterdam: V2_Publishing/NAI Publishers. 4-9.

Butler, Judith. (1993). *Bodies That Matter*. London: Routledge.

Butler, Judith. (1995). 'Burning acts: injurious speech.' In Parker, Andrew, & Kosofsky Sedwick, Eve. (Eds.). *Performativity and Performance*. London: Routledge. 197-227.

Butler, Judith. (1999). *Excitable Speech*. London: Routledge. 10-26.

Cameron, Andy. (2005). 'Dinner with Myron. Or: rereading artificial reality 2: Reflections on interface and art.' In Brouwer, Joke, Fauconnier, Sandra, Mulder, Arjen, & Nigten, Anne. (Eds.). *aRt&D: Research and Development in Art*. Rotterdam: V2_Publishing/NAI Publishers. 10-26.

Candy, Linda, & Edmonds, Ernest. (2002). *Explorations in Art and Technology*. London: Springer.

Cheesmond, Robert. (1999). 'To behold the swelling scene, the emergence of "scenography" in twentieth century theatre.' *Scenography International*. No. 3. Available at http://www.scenography-international.com/

Christensen, Maria, & Lamm, Bettina. (2003). 'Morgana: grom vision to visualisation.' In Halskov Madsen, Kim. (Ed.). *Production Methods: Behind the Scenes of Virtual Inhabited 3D Worlds*. London: Springer. 249-269.

Copeland, Roger. (1990). 'The presence of mediation.' *The Drama Review: The Journal of Performance Studies*. Vol. 34, No. 4, 28-44.

deLahunta, Scott. (1998). 'Sampling . . . convergences between dance and technology.' Paper presented at the *Art Crash Symposium*, Aarhus, Denmark. 2-4 April. Available at http://www.art.net/ ~ dtz/scott2.html

deLahunta, Scott. (2002). 'Virtual reality and performance.' *PAJ*. Vol. 70, 105-114.

deLahunta, Scott. (2003). 'Open source choreography?' In Stocker, Gerfried, & Schöpf, Christine. (Eds.). *CODE: The Language of Our Time*. Proceedings of Ars Electronica 2003. Osterfildern-Ruit: Hatje Cantz Forlag. 304-311.

De Oliveira, Nicolas, & Oxley, Nicola. (2004). *Installation Art in the New Millennium*. London: Thames & Hudson.

Denard, Hugh. (2002). 'Virtuality and performativity: recreating Rome's theatre of Pompey.' *Performing Arts Journal*. Vol. 70, 25-43.

Diamond, Elin. (Ed.). (1996). *Performance and Cultural Politics*. London: Routledge.

Diaz-Kommonen, Lily. (2004). 'Expressive artifacts and artifacts of expression.' *Working Papers into Art and Design*. Vol. 3. Available at http://www. herts.ac.uk/artdes1/research/papers/wpades/vol3/ldkabs.html

Dils, A. (2002). 'The ghost in the machine: Merce Cunningham & Bill Jones.' *Performing Arts Journal*. Vol. 70, 94-104.

Dinka. Söke. (2002). 'Towards a rhetoric and didactics of digital dance.' In Dinka, Söke, & Leeker, Martin. (Eds.). *Dance and Technology*. Berlin: Alexander Verlag. 14-29.

Douglas, J. Yellowlees & Hargadon, Andrew. (2001). 'The pleasures of immersion and engagement: schemas, scripts and the fifth business.' *Digital Creativity*. Vol. 12, No. 3, 153–166.

Dourish, Paul. (2001). *Where the Action Is*. Cambridge, MA: The MIT Press.

Drucker, Johanna. (2009). *SPECLAB: Digital Aesthetics and Projects in Speculative Computing*. Chicago: University of Chicago Press.

Edmonds, Ernest, Muller, Lizzie, & Connell, Matthew. (2006). 'On creative engagement.' *Visual Communication*. Vol. 5, No. 3, 307-322.

ESG (Extended Stage Group). (2004). 'Interactive generative stage and dynamic costumes for Andre Werner's "Marlowe: The Jew of Malta" .' In Leopoldseder, Hannes, Schopf, Christine, & Stocker, Gerfried. (Eds.). *Cyberarts 2004*. Linz: Ars Electronica/Hatje Cantz. 130-132.

Evert, Kirsten. (2002). 'Dance and technology at the turn of the last and present centuries.' In Dinka, Söke, & Leeker, Martin. (Eds.). *Dance and Technology*. Berlin: Alexander Verlag. 30-65.

Fishwick, P. (Ed.). (2006). *Aesthetic Computing*. Cambridge, MA: The MIT Press.

Galanter, Philip. (2003). 'What is generative art? complexity theory as a context for art theory.' In *Proceedings of Generative Art 2003*. Milan, Italy. 9-13 December. Available at http://www.generativeart.com

Giannetti, Claudia. (n.d.). 'Aesthetic paradigms of media art.' *Aesthetics of the Digital at Media Art Net*. Available at http://www.medienkunstnetz.de/themes/ aesthetics_of_the_digital/aesthetic_paradigms/

Goffman, Erving. (1959). *The Presentation of Self in Everyday Life*. Garden City, NY: Anchor.

Goldberg, Rosalee. (1998). *Performance: Live Art Since 1960*. New York: Harry Abrams.

Goriunova, Olga & Shulgin, Alexei. (Eds.). (2004). *Software Art & Cultures*. Digital Aesthetics Research Centre, University of Århus, Denmark.

Grau, Oliver. (2003). *Virtual Art: From Illusion to Immersion*. Cambridge, MA: The MIT Press.

Hansen, Mark. (2005). 'Embodiment: the machinic and the human.' In Brouwer, Joke, Fauconnier, Sandra, Mulder, Arjen, & Nigten, Anne. (Eds). *aRt&D: Research and Development in Art*. Rotterdam: V2Publishing/NAi Publishers. 150-165.

Haseman, Brad. (2006). 'A manifesto for performative research.' *Media International Australia* (incorporating Culture and Policy). Theme issue 'Practice-led research.' No. 118, February, 98-106.

Havnør, Martin. (2006). *A Conceptual Framework for Development Iterations of Digital, Interactive Art; System Response Patterns and Multi-Narrative Temporal Data Based Presentation.* Unpublished master's thesis. Department of Informatics, University of Oslo.

Hornecker, Eva, & Buur, Jacob. (2006). 'Getting a grip on tangible interaction: a framework on physical space and social interaction.' *CHI 2006 Proceedings. Designing for Tangible Interaction.* Montreal. 22-27 April. 437-446.

Hughes-Freeland, F. (1998). (Ed.). *Ritual, Performance, Media.* London: Routledge.

Iacucci, Guilio, Iacucci, Carlo, & Kuutti, Kari. (2002). 'Imagining and experiencing in design: the role of performances.' In *Proceedings of the Second Nordic Conference on Human-Computer Interaction.* Århus, Denmark. 19-23 October. 167-176.

Idealdecor. (2000). *Wall Murals.* Switzerland: Wizard & Genuis-Idealdecor AG.

Jacucci, Carlo, Jacucci, Guilio, & Wagner, Ina. (2005). 'A manifesto for the performative development of ubiquitous media.' In *Proceedings of the 4th Decennial Conference on Critical Computing: Between Sense and Sensibility.* Århus, Denmark. 20–24 August. 19-28.

Kosuda-Warner, Joanne, with Johnson, Elisabeth. (Eds.). (2001). *Landscape Wallcoverings.* London: Scala.

Kress, Gunther, & van Leeuwen, Theo. (1996). *Reading Images.* London: Routledge.

Lee, Jae-Shin. (2000). 'Interactivity: A new approach.' *Convention for the Association for Education in Journalism and Mass Media Communication (AEJMC).* Phoenix, Arizona. 9-12 August. Available at http://list.msu.edu/cgi-bin/wa?A2 = ind0101a&L = aejmc&T = 0&F = &S = &P = 14105

Leggett, Mike. (2006). 'Interdisciplinary collaboration and practice-based research.' *Convergence.* Vol. 12, No. 3, 263-269.

Leont'ev, Alexei. (1978). *Activity, Consciousness, and Personality.* Englewood Cliffs, NJ: Prentice-Hall.

Leont'ev, Alexei. (1981). *Problems of the Development of the Mind.* Moscow: Progress Publishers.

Liestøl, Gunnar. (1999). *Essays in Hypermedia Rhetorics.* Unpublished doctoral thesis. Department of Media and Communication, University of Oslo.

Liestøl, Gunnar. (2001). 'Research into the development of digital media as an interdisciplinary field based in the sciences and the humanities.' In Liestøl, Gunnar, & Morrison, Andrew. (Eds.). *Tverrfaglighet og digitale medier* [Interdisciplinarity and Digital Media]. Oslo: UniPub/InterMedia. 41-55.

Manovich, Lev. (2002). 'The poetics of augmented space: learning from Prada.' Available at http://www.manovich.net/

Mol, Annemarie. (1998). 'Missing links, making links: the performance of some aetheroscleroses.' In Berg, Mark, & Mole, Annemarie. (Eds.). *Differences in Medicine.* Durham, NC: Duke University Press. 144-165.

Morrison, Andrew, Westvang, Even, & Skogsrud, Simen. (2010). 'Whisperings in the undergrowth: collaborative design and discursive performativity in online social networking.' In Wagner, Ina, Stuedahl, Dagny, & Bratteteig, Tone. (Eds.). *Exploring Digital Design.* Vienna: Springer.

Murphie, Andrew. (2003). 'Negotiating presence: performance and new technologies.' In Auslander, Philip. (Ed.). *Performance: Critical Concepts in Literary and Cultural Studies*. Vol. 4. London: Routledge. 351-364.

Murphie, Andrew, & Potts, John. (2003). *Culture and Technology*. London: Palgrave Macmillan.

Nolan, Carrie. (2009). *Agency and Embodiment*. Cambridge MA: Harvard University Press.

Qvortrup, Lars (2003): 'Digital poetics: the poetical potentials of projection and interaction.' In Liestøl, Gunnar, Morrison, Andrew & Rasmussen, Terje. (Eds.). *Digital Media Revisited: New Media Methods and Theories*. Cambridge, MA: The MIT Press. 239–261.

Parker, Andrew, & Kosofsky Sedwick, Eve. (Eds.). (1995). *Performativity and Performance*. London: Routledge.

Paul, Christiane. (2005). 'Public cultural production art(software){...}.' In Stocker, Gerfried, & Schöpf, Christine. (Éds.). *CODE: The Language of Our Time*. Proceedings of Ars Electronica 2003. Osterfildern-Ruit: Hatje Cantz Forlag. 129-136.

Raley, Rita. (2009). 'List(en)ing post.' In Ricardo, Francisco. (Ed.). *Literary Art in Digital Performance*. London: Continuum. 22-34.

Reinelt, Janelle. (2002). 'The politics of discourse: performativity meets theatricality.' *SubStance*. Vol. 31, Nos. 1&2, 201-215.

Rush, Michael. (1999). *New Media in Late 20th Century Art*. London: Thames & Hudson.

Saltz, David. 2003. 'The art of interaction: interactivity, performativity and computers.' In Auslander, Philip. (Ed.). *Performance: Critical Concepts in Literary and Cultural Studies*. Vol. IV. London: Routledge. 395-410. (Originally published in *The Journal of Aesthetics and Art Criticism*. Vol. 55, No. 2, 117-127.)

Schieffelin, Edward. (1999). 'Problematising performance.' In Hughes-Freeland, Felicia. (Ed.). *Ritual, Performance, Media*. London: Routledge. 194-207.

Schiller, Gretchen. (2001). 'Kinesfields: transfiguring movement perceptions.' CAiiA-STAR Symposium: *Extreme Parameters. New Dimensions of Interactivity*. 11-12 July. Available at http://www.uoc.edu/caiia-star-2001/eng/articles/gschiller/schiller.html

Schiller, Gretchen. (2006). 'Body scenographies, jumping back to leap forward.' *Body, Space and Technology Journal*. Vol. 5. Available at http://people.brunel.ac.uk/bst/vol05/index.html

Schön, Donald. (1983). *The Reflective Practitioner*. New York: Basic Books.

Schön, Donald. (1987). *Educating the Reflective Practitioner*. San Francisco: Jossey-Bass.

Sem, Idunn. (2006). *Practice-Based Method. Exploring Digital Media Through the Dynamics of Practice, Theory, and Collaborative, Multimedia Performance*. Oslo: Department of Media and Communication, University of Oslo. Available at http://folk.uio.no/idunnsem/practice-based_method/

Sha, Xin Wei, & Kuzmanovic, Maja. (2000). 'From representation to performance: responsive public space.' *DIAC 2000*. Available at http://www.f0.am/publications/2000_diac/index.htm

Shotter, John, & Billig, Michael. (1998). 'A Bakhtinian psychology: from out of the heads of individuals and into the dialogues between them.' In Mayerfield Bell, Michael, & Gardiner, Michael. (Eds.). *Bakhtin and the Human Sciences*. London: Sage. 13-29.

Skjulstad, Synne, Morrison, Andrew, & Aaberge, Albertine. (2002). 'Researching performance, performing research.' In Morrison, Andrew. (Ed.). *Researching ICTs in Context*. Oslo: InterMedia/UniPub, University of Oslo. 211-248. Available at http://www.intermedia.uio.no/konferanser/skikt-02/skikt-research-conference.html.

Sparacino, Flavia, Wren, Christopher, Davenport, Glorianna, & Pentland, Alex. (1999). 'Augmented performance in dance and theatre.' *International Dance and Technology 99* (IDAT99). Tempe: Arizona State University. 25-28 February.

Sparacino, Flavia, Davenport, Glorianna, & Pentland, Alex. (2000). 'Media in performance: interactive spaces for dance, theater, circus, and museum exhibits.' *Systems Journal*. Vol. 39, Nos. 3&4. Available at http://www.research.ibm.com/journal/sj/393/part1/sparacino.html

Szegedy-Maszák, Zoltán, & Fernezelyi, Márton. (2005). 'Promenade.' In Brouwer, Joke, Fauconnier, Sandra, Mulder, Arjen, & Nigten, Anne. (Eds.). *aRt&D: Research and Development in Art*. Rotterdam: V2_Publishing/NAI Publishers. 58-65.

Thomas, Harun. (2003). 'Do "whatever" in three assignments.' *Computers & Composition Online*. Available at http://www.bgsu.edu/cconline/Thomas/sequencedassignments.html

Tronstad, Ragnhild. (2004). *Interpretation, Performance, Play, & Seduction: Textual Adventures in Tubmud*. PhD thesis. Department of Media and Communication, University of Oslo. Oslo: UniPub.

Turner, Victor. (1982). *From Ritual to Theatre*. New York: Performing Arts Journal Publications.

Turner, Victor. (1987). *The Anthropology of Performance*. New York: Performing Arts Journal Publications.

van den Bergh, Frans, & Lalioti, Vali. (1999). 'Software chroma keying in an immersive virtual environment.' *South African Computer Journal*. No. 24, November. 87-93.

Wartofsky, Marx. (1979). *Models: Representation in Scientific Understanding*. Dordrecht: D. Reidel Publishing Co.

Wilson, Steven. (2002). *Information Arts*. Cambridge, MA: The MIT Press.

8

MULTIMODAL PRODUCTION AND SEMIOTIC RESOURCES FOR LEARNING ABOUT FILM NARRATIVE

Andrew Deacon

Andrew Morrison

Jane Stadler

DESIGNS FOR LEARNING

The images in this chapter are from *Director's Cut*, a computer-based exercise designed to support university students' learning in a large introductory film theory course. The exercise considers how a student's decisions, acting out the role of director or editor of *film noir*, impact on film narrative and spectatorship. From our experience, students in these introductory courses display a limited appreciation of film production processes, having only ever been in the audience. This hints at why many students might be struggling with many concepts presented in lectures and readings that presuppose a broader understanding of film production.

It was such observations about how we might develop students' understandings of filmic conventions and theory, including affording additional modalities to express themselves, that initiated the discussions resulting in developing *Director's Cut*. For us as educators, this has interesting crossover between the disciplines of film and media studies and learning through media production. This chapter focuses on how such designs for learning emerge and how these design-based research processes can be understood and supported.

Production Skills

Students' limited appreciation of production processes is not surprising. Although most audiences watching television and films understand the messages being communicated through editing, they tend to be unaware of the specific conventions and techniques involved in their production. One of the objectives of introductory film courses is explaining such conventions, their relevance, and their impact on the audience (Stadler & McWilliam 2009). However, the majority of students studying film criticism for the first time have little or no practical experience in screen production. The teaching methodologies in film theory and analysis courses are traditionally lecture and text based.

One of our underlying premises is that the capacity of a film critic to recognize and assess the skill of a filmmaker is enhanced if he or she has a sense of the film production process rather than just the end product. Production-based learning approaches can support students' learning of film theory by enabling the analyst to do the cinematic equivalent of 'reading between the lines,' thereby appreciating decisions made by the director, the editor, and others involved in the filmmaking.

Director's Cut invites film analysis students to apply their understandings of theory in the process of editing a short sequence of their own. This is one component of an undergraduate film narrative course about film spectatorship, genres, and modes of composition, as well as editing practices and conventions. The exercise integrates other teaching and assessment components complementing the traditional essay assignments, seminars, and lectures.

LEARNING IN THE MAKING

Production-Based Learning

Analogous to how most viewers are unaware of film editing conventions, designs for learning are generally opaque even to colleagues involved in teaching other courses. Fostering designs for learning involves engaging academics who have shared interests in designing and developing contextually appropriate resources for students' own production-based learning. This includes students and academics alike in understanding and generating intersections of media types and modes of expressive communication. Finding ways to assist and improve students' learning in and through production is a rich area to investigate using information and communication technologies (ICTs). We see ICTs as providing flexible tools and communication sets for deconstructing film 'languages' and for reading and composing multimodal discourse (e.g., Kress & van Leeuwen, 2001; Rabinowitz, 2002). These theoretical frames focus on the design negotiations and evolution, rather than the final product or outcome, as we see these as the most valuable and adaptable in supporting emerging understanding among staff and students.

Following on from early writings on digital media and literacies in production-based learning in media education (e.g., Buckingham & Sefton-Green, 1995), in terms of social software and student-generated material in multiple contexts of communication, Erstad et al. (2007: 185) locate expressive experimentation with tools and cultural, semiotic resources as occurring in a 'transactional learning space.' This is a site for mediated semiosis that involves learners in meaning making that is achieved through not only locating cultural resources but also through their remixing (Erstad et al., 2007). As these authors argue, digital and cultural tools are co-present in the articulation of user-developed content. This is what concerned us in the development of *Director's Cut*, albeit with the necessary provision of selected video material to enable a large class of students to actually take part productively.

Director's Cut was collaboratively designed by the film lecturer (Jane Stadler) and the learning designer (Andrew Deacon). This drew on earlier work between lecturers in the Centre for Film and Media Studies (CFMS) and the Centre for Educational Technology (CET) at the University of Cape Town (UCT) in South Africa. Developmentally and analytically, this work is linked to a wider research project between the University of Oslo (Andrew Morrison) and UCT called ICT-UCT. The project investigates how humanities staff might further their competencies in using ICTs at UCT in their teaching and research (Morrison et al., 2005) and how a small and robust community of practice might be fostered (Wenger, 1998; Carr et al., 2005) through participation between subject lecturers and learning designers.

Situated Activity and Learning About Film

Through the *Director's Cut* design for learning, we explore links between exposing students to film theory using a mediated activity as practice and as a mode of hypermediated design (Murray, 1998). This can be viewed as an example of learning about compositional concepts and tools in film editing as learning through design in the making. We pursue these aims geared toward providing situated learning resources for students (Lave & Wenger, 1991).

This design for learning may be viewed as an example not only of collaborative design and redesign through use but also as a resource—as both process and product—for other educators whose participation might have been on the periphery but who are motivated to develop and deploy ICTs in their teaching and related research.

EXPANSIVE LEARNING

Reaching for Transformation

The Finnish educational researcher Yrjö Engeström has developed a model of expansive learning built on staged cycles of transformation (Engeström, 1987, 1999a, 1999b, 2001). These are framed in a sociocultural approach to learning via activity theory after Bakhtin and Vygotsky. In an activity system, a number of elements interact with one another to produce outcomes that then meet those from other systems and so on. The core elements of an activity system are: tools and signs, a subject and rules, community, division of labor, and mediating artifacts. These highlight the significant activities and relationships between them found in most work-related environments.

For Engeström, learning concerns 'processes of becoming' that are not necessarily set in stone or fully known ahead of their shaping. Emergence is therefore central to ways in which new cultural forms of activity are generated. This approach asserts that intersecting activity systems may result in additional outcomes and realizations. Awareness and analyses of these depend on attention to historicity, contradictions in the systems, deviations, and negotiations between them. Multiple intersecting activity systems complicate but also may enrich outcomes. The concept of the mediating artifact is especially useful in placing focus on the role in our case of a specifically designed digital learning 'tool.' We refer to these core concepts in the following sections.

Engeström's model of expansive learning (Engeström, 1999a, 1999b) is based on cycles of transformation that may be summarized as: (a) questioning practices; (b) analyzing existing practices; (c) jointly building new models, concepts, and artifacts for new practices; (d) analyzing and discussing models, concepts, and artifacts; (e) implementing these; (f) reflecting on and evaluating process; and (g) consolidating new practices. The overall outcome is the genesis of new modes of activity that transcend prior ones. This expansive learning model captures the work-related learning of academics and learning designers, building on an analysis of the historical development of their practices. New insights of learning emerge as work is transformed from traditional strategies toward conceiving more student-centric learning activities.

OUTLINE

Relations Between Activity and Development

Casting the *Director's Cut* design process in an expansive learning frame enables us to highlight what we see as important relationships within the activity system and development cycle. We draw on Engeström's first two stages, which involve questioning and analyzing existing practices, in the section titled 'Splicing Conceptual Scripts.' Stage (c) considers building new approaches that begin to address issues with current practices identified earlier, which involves the development of a learning activity described in the 'Editing Room.' Stages (d) and (e) are raised in 'Interface and Visual Sequencing' and 'Voiceover and Looping.' describing how the mediating artifacts both supported us as designers of learning and supported students as learners. The tools included linguistics-inspired concepts such as those from semiotics that have infiltrated film theory, software designs, and learning designs.

Reshaping Practice

Assessment, issues of understanding multimodal discourse, students' comments, and overall reflections and redesign processes are covered in the section titled 'Wideshot,' which corresponds to Stage (f) on reflection. The final section, called 'Rewind,' refers to consolidating new practices under Engeström's Stage (g). Here rewinding suggests shaping and reshaping the actual learning activity and drawing on new insights from participants as part of an ongoing, iterative, and participatory design process.

We see our research rhetoric as needing to reflect how we might influence teaching and learning through the use of multimodal production. The annotated illustrations in this chapter are a means of communicating the research text. Later we show the actual screenshots of the interface. The annotations are an instance of communicating multimodal pedagogies and analysis that depicts aspects of the learning experience that cannot be included on paper.

SPLICING CONCEPTUAL SCRIPTS

Teaching Film and Media

Taken together with expansive learning, production-based learning and learning design provide conceptual 'scripts' for tracing an educational and mediated design process and the roles that learning designers, subject lecturers, and students may have in shaping learning, which is emergent and exploratory in character.

Earlier separations of visual and verbal text have been quashed in calls for the study of intersecting multimodal discourse, particularly in learning contexts (Kress, 1998, 2003). Learning through production in media studies (Buckingham & Sefton-Green, 1995) has been heralded as part of an emerging new multiliteracy in schools in the past decade. Film and media studies provides a key site for the careful, creative uptake of digital tools in learning in higher education, where the focus is on mediation and not simply skills mastery. Learning about film and its conventions may now be built through short productions that draw on features of new digital tools as Manovich has argued (Manovich, 2002). Learning how to 'read' and 'write' film through digital tools (Buckingham & Sefton-Green, 1997) provides 'methods and metaphors,' Coyne (1997) argues, for understanding a range of textual and intersubjective designs in 'a digital age.' These contribute to a conceptual design framework that allows the lecturers to develop, change, and situate their teaching activities within wider, emerging, and participatory approaches to learning as socioculturally constructed. This requires 'multimodal' tools that are sufficiently flexible to scaffold learning tasks, hide potentially confusing aspects, and provide intrinsic feedback.

The rapid and expanding adoption of ICTs and consumer electronics has resulted in an expanding 'cross-media' domain in which a variety of media types and modes of communication may be related, combined, composed, and distributed. These changing relations between media theory and practice at universities raises expectations for a different balance in which theory and practice are intertwined and spliced together to complement one another. Jane Stadler, being aware of the opportunities and challenges, had for some years wanted to develop an exercise exposing her students to the film editing processes she saw as valuable in mediating their understandings of the film theory concepts. The needs assessment phase of the curriculum design process (Flowers, 2001) identified the importance of bridging the digital divide and enhancing multimodal connections between thinking and doing, as well as among image, sound, text, and abstract theoretical concepts.

While discussing possible exercises, we were reminded of the many apparent contradictions. The film culture that students are exposed to outside the university is inherently multimodal, which is in stark contrast to their experiences in a conventional film theory course. The traditional division between theory and practice as oppositional activity systems and modes of producing, with 'texts' on the one hand and analysis the other hand, has been asserted with craft separated from analysis by scholars. Additionally, there is a fine balance between learning activities inspired by production-based and situated learning achieving their goals and over-whelming the capacity of educators to support them. Although pedagogi-cally and epistemologically learning through production is rich in possibili-ties, developing a learning activity for a specific context involves making many design choices. As the first two expansive learning stages imply, these problems need to be questioned, analyzed, and negotiated. We had begun by considering the constraints on the learning activity design of assessment in a large class and wanting students to complete their task with the minimum of technical support.

Collaborative Learning Designs

The roles of support staff at universities tend to be shaped by activities that teaching staff consider to be outside their required competencies, as might expertise with software development, multilingualism, or teaching academic writing. If software developers become primarily responsible for ICT-based developments and there is no meaningful engagement with educators or students, the designs will tend toward reflecting developers' concerns; in the extreme cases, these developers might be the only ones learning anything. There is considerable interest in how more collabora-tive, co-configuration, and participatory designs emerge and succeed, where people with different backgrounds are jointly involved in designs for learning (e.g., Bratteteig, 2003; Kuhn & Winograd, 1996; Fleischmann 2006). There are links to be made between such design approaches and 'designs for learning,' as opposed to learning designs as templates for compliance.

At this level of work, the collaboration between lecturer and learning designer is a process of constant negotiation and redefinition, at times resulting in close adherence and agreement and at other times divergent views or understandings of one another's perspectives or direction. Links are increasingly being made about participatory relations among mediat-ing tools, participation, practice, and information systems design. However, seldom do film or media researchers appear in these domains; where learning design research often stays in educational conferences, learning about media through production is not an established part of film or media studies research. Here we make links between these approaches and also place weight on designing a mediating artifact relating to princi-ples of digital film editing. In various learning arenas, the views, uptake, and reflections of students are included as important components in the evaluation and redesign of ICTs.

Effective activity systems develop over several years, and in relation to Engeström's term 'historicity.' There is also motivation to relate knowl-edge, some components, and a mode of development from earlier collaborations in the frame of adaptive design. We benefited from having been involved in developing and using a number of production-based learning activities at UCT, centered on learning about media and popular culture, for several years (see also Buckingham, 1998). A first-year film course has a storyboarding exercise to develop understandings of screen aesthetics. Although different in nature, this can be seen as building toward the *Director's Cut* exercise. Another assignment, *NewsFrames* focuses on the major components of a newspaper's front-page layout and discovering how semiotic choices 'frame' both subeditors' construction of news and readers' interpretations (Deacon, 2002). A third multimodal exercise, *NewsBreaks* is concerned with the manufacturing of television news (van der Vliet & Deacon, 2004). Students research a news story, select and order video clips, and then write the accompanying voiceover script.

EDITING ROOM

A Collaborative Venture

Director's Cut began in discussions between the film program and Andrew Deacon about a collaborative venture. The primary organizational need was to be able to collaboratively develop an activity that could be used by a large class with many tutors. The activity would also need to function with a minimum of technical support. Educationally, the activity would need to provide enough room for creative uptake of digital editing tools and principles by students while also asking them to relate concepts taught in the course to their own production.

Film Narrative

Jane Stadler's second-year Film Narrative course investigates the process of film narration from screenwriting through to an 'auteur' approach to film studies that considers film authorship in terms of a director's 'signature style.' It examines the relationship among meaning, form, ideology, and narrative structure and explores the influence of the sociocultural context and the conditions of production and reception on storytelling and meaning making. Students are introduced to a range of theories of narration and spectatorship and are required to develop critical skills that enable them to analyze genre, national cinemas, and character engagement. Learning about how the audience is positioned within screen space by means of techniques such as camera angle, point of view, subjective imagery, and voiceover narration is fundamental to understanding how character engagement is facilitated.

Semiotics and Film Language

If we are to offer students an experience of the challenges and choices involved in positioning a film character in the screen space, we need various ways of mediating their engagement with the material. Wanting a short activity for a large class suggested a software design in which students can position a limited number of digital objects representing their characters in different ways. Linguistic concepts offer useful tools to model interactions in learning designs even if they do not fully describe all aspects. Christian Metz's (1974/1991) original and carefully conducted research into questions about the semiotics and language of film provides a starting point. He observes that film has two levels of signification: cultural codes, which are naturalized representations of objects and behaviors on screen; and specialized codes, the organization of film techniques such as editing and cinematography, optical effects, and sound. The objects and characters appearing on screen carry with them a host of culturally and contextually specific connotations that Metz terms the signifying organization of cinematic language.

Breaking film down into signifying units, such as frames, shots, sequences, and scenes, means that 'at any given moment in the making of his (*sic*) film, the filmmaker must choose from a limited series of syntagmatic ordering' (Metz, 1974/1991: 137). A film sequence can then be loosely understood as a coherent syntagma within which the 'shots' react to each other as words do with others in a sentence (Metz, 1974/1991: 115). The different shots from which filmmakers choose make 'different statements' because variations in shot scale, camera angle, and movement carry different connotations. For example, cinematic convention suggests that a low-angle closeup of a face will privilege the character in screen space, tending to enhance the impact and convey a sense of intimacy or power, whereas a mid-shot of the same character filmed from over the shoulder of another character will have a diluted influence on spectatorial identification. We draw on this organization of semiotic elements in getting students to intentionally manage the spectator's relationship with characters by selecting from a range of shots.

Film Noir Points of View

Students in an introductory course generally do not relate to these debates on film and language. As Bill Nichols (1976: 609) observes, 'a film is stylistic before it is grammatical.' Because it is the visual more than the symbolic relationships that will engage students, the interface needs to acknowledge this notion. The idea of selecting shots from a paradigm of possibilities influenced us in deciding on the type of story and shots we needed so we could later draw on the film language aspects. As described later, students are expected to draw on symbolic relationships, but this is not the only approach in constructing their narrative.

The storyline we developed describes a *film noir* style interrogation scene in which the detective questions the *femme fatale* about her where-abouts and actions on the night a crime was committed. The *film noir* genre—with its murky murders, rough-talking detectives, and mysterious *femme fatales*—was chosen for its established film narrative conventions. Rather than locating the story in the original *film noir* of the 1950s, we were also inspired by more recent *noir* films that incorporate modern styl-istic elements. Students were introduced to *film noir* and other genres in lectures, tutorials, and through film screenings in covering a variety of critical, cultural, feminist, and contemporary criticism relating to it.

We employed past students of the course to act in, film, and edit the footage we developed in the shot list (see Figures 8.1 and 8.2). This encouraged students to identify, both personally and narratively, with the material and their own edit. Some shots were filmed from both the detec-tive's and the *femme fatale's* points of view, as well as from multiple cam-era angles and different shot scales such as long shot, medium closeup, and big closeup. Several shots with cut-away imagery, including a gun, a glass breaking, and a champagne cork popping, were filmed to offer scope for a variety of explanations for a loud noise, which the *femme fatale* and detective might then use in describing the events concerning the murder. These shot choices are the building blocks for 'directors' to tell their own story, deciding whether the detective is suspicious about the *femme fatale* having an affair or that he suspects that she killed a man, among other possibilities. This footage enables students to choose whether to tell the story from her point of view, from his, or by alternat-ing between the two.

Figure 8.1. *Direct >r's Cut*—One of several video clips, shot from different points of view.

Figure 8.2. Same scene shot from different points of view.

INTERFACE AND VISUAL SEQUENCING

Preprofessional Tools

Although software for text and image editing are familiar to most students, surprisingly few had edited video to tell a story at the time *Director's Cut* was developed. Software applications for hobbyists tend to emphasize exotic transitions and other effects that professionals dismiss as gimmicks. There is little support for scriptwriting or even including detailed shot descriptions.

Typically, professional video editing tools are feature-rich but present stark interfaces with complex menus of options that already assume the user knows what to do. These are not well suited to large classes of novice film students. At UCT, it was not financially, pedagogically, or technically feasible to repurpose such software for large classes. Multiple-user site licences are expensive and demand high-end machines with training and support for students.

Interface Design

We of course wanted students to demonstrate fluency with conventions familiar to film theory but without expending time telling them about other possibly confusing conventions they would need to know to use a particular video editing application. The interface we developed had to communicate the affordances of our film editing tool through establishing the relations among cinematographic conventions, film narrative, and tool functionality. Interface design can be analyzed by considering the semiotic relations between students as users and the software tools (de

Oliveira & Baranaukas, 2000). Here the terms 'semiosis' and 'sign emission' are applied to describe the relations between how students interpret the interface and then understand how to communicate their intentions using the restricted set of tools the interface makes available.

This attention to the designing of underlying information architectures and related systems is essential to the formation of structures and processes that allow for activities of learning to be realized on screen and by students. However, this is only possible because of the development of the mediating artifact of the interface (Engeström et al., 1999), which enables 'thoughtful interaction' through design (Löwgren & Stolterman, 2004). Interfaces may appear simple or seem to be unimportant when they facilitate the remediation of content and a variety of user activities. However, effective interfaces are often pared down from more elaborate choices and positionings. Typically, they are patterned and spatialized so as to build and allow for layers of relations and transversals by users with various needs. In recent years, through software such as Flash, many user interfaces have come to include dynamic elements (Skjulstad & Morrison, 2005) in one environment.

Sequencing

We introduce *Director's Cut* to students in a computer laboratory. This allows us to briefly demonstrate and explain how to use the tool without having to provide exhaustive online help. Additionally, we can easily answer any conceptual problems which students experience that cannot be anticipated. One of the first things students need to do is familiarize themselves with the clips and try out various plot lines. There are 26 clips denoted by icons on a pallet (Figure 8.3). Clicking on a clip icon selects it. Once selected, the clip's caption is displayed; it can be played or a voiceover dialogue can be added in the textbox. Clips are arranged into a sequence by dragging them onto the timeline. In reality, there are a very large number of feasible permutations. Although there were popular combinations of clips, no two students, of the more than 800 who created sequences in the first 5 years, had more than five clips in the same order. The majority had at most two or three sequential clips in common. We saw the success of the exercise depending on there being many creative opportunities for students while constraining what was possible. Thus, students are prevented from investing time on, say, fine edits, such as choosing edit transitions or mixing sound effects, which we considered less important in this activity.

We justified limiting the range of options for sequencing clips by telling students they were producing a rough edit. They could indicate any additional editing information, such as suggested in- and out-point or transitions, as notes in their script as a director might do. We asked students to imagine that the reason that their film had many alternative shots was to keep the climax of their film a 'secret' from the 'press.' The students' task was to edit the footage to tell the story, adding explanatory voiceover narration and applying what they knew of film narrative, editing, spectatorship, and genre. They thus need to draw on established conventions and sign systems in film production and to specify what needs to happen in postproduction so that their tutors could understand their intentions and assess the project.

From a learning design perspective, such scenarios are important in offering a concise and convincing explanation of both the expectations for and limitations of the tool while not unnecessarily stifling creativity or individuality. During the design negotiations, devising the location of our editing process in the broader film-making process was valuable because it helped define the interface functionality and film language we used.

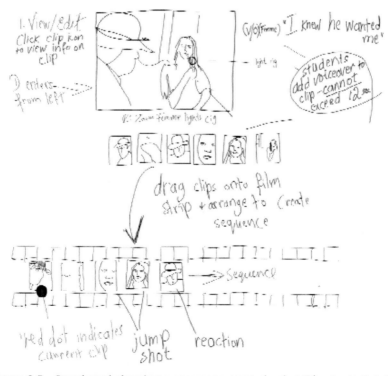

Figure 8.3. Storyboard showing a sequence created using *Director's Cut*. The jump cut (shot 4–5) will cause *Director's Cut* to remind the student about editing conventions.

Additionally, this offers an explanation of why we were expecting students to engage with the organization of semiotic elements we presented. The idea was to invite students to intentionally manage the spectator's relationship with characters by selecting from a range of shots: 'It suffices to vary one of these elements by a perceptible quantity to obtain another image. The shot is therefore not comparable to the word in a lexicon; rather it resembles a complex statement (of one or more sentences)' (Metz, 1974/1991:100).

Although the comparison between film and language has its limitations, it does highlight the enduring influence of linguistics on contemporary applications of semiotics to multimodal texts. For our purposes, it also foregrounds the emphasis placed in *Director's Cut* on engaging students in the process of constructing a meaningful narrative by selecting shots from a paradigm of possibilities and organizing them into a sequence while reflecting on and applying cinematic codes and conventions. Recent work centered on virtual gaming environments investigates cinematic conventions to create the look of television sports broadcasts while playing a motor racing game or soap opera genre games with big closeups of characters' faces as tensions rise.

Information System Design

Director's Cut was developed using Macromedia's Authorware. Using this or similar development tools, it is comparatively straightforward to write code for reordering clips. This represents a basic edit. At the time of development, it was difficult to include transitions or add music that faded during dialogue because these tools were not standard in readily available software libraries. As noted earlier, we restricted ourselves to the simple reordering of clips cast as a rough edit. Allowing students to set in- and out-points, although feasible, tended to be slow and cause jumpy effects on slower computers. This is an enhancement we plan to add in the future.

From an informatics perspective, good design encompasses the choice of appropriate data structures (Engeström, 2001). There needs to be a correspondence between functions that a user performs and operations on the underlying data structures. The drag-and-drop editing operations for adding, deleting, or moving a clip correspond to adding and deleting corresponding clip identifiers from an ordered list. Having access to these underlying data structures that represent a student's sequence allows us to check for 'violations' of cinematographic conventions by inspecting which clips were used and in what order they were placed. It is feasible to develop such rules because, in our case, the length and content of clips are known in advance. The rules trigger automated feedback that is displayed on the interface when a condition is met. We used this to remind students about jump cuts, crossing the line of action, and when the scripted dialogue was too long based on the length of the clip (the rule of thumb is one cannot speak more than three words per second).

This provides much more relevant and appropriate feedback than general-purpose editing applications could conceivably offer. Essentially, this exploits the 'Eliza effect' that depends on students believing that the feedback is actually intelligent, although the mechanism is simply an automated response (Hofstadter, 1995). Triggered rules make students aware of potential contradictions in their work, and this expects a response. To develop the rules and feedback, we had to imagine what students might do and what kind of responses would help them understand the underlying concepts and overcome the misunderstanding they might have. We had looked at the cinematographic conventions and semiotic relations discussed earlier as tools to open up these debates. Not all are easy to recognize using simple automated rules. We did not consider developing automated responses for any of the more complex or subtle relations. The responsibility of discussing these with students was delegated to tutors who expressed a preference for discussing 'interesting' cases over the routine ones.

Many students commented on the influence that feedback had on identifying issues they would not otherwise have considered but did not completely eliminate the types of mistakes students make. Collectively, these modes of feedback and their sign emission opened up learning conversations between students and tutors, including offering a basic film editing language that was adopted in preference to vague questions such as 'Is my thing ok'? This provided students with a sense of the voicedness that Engeström includes in his approach to expansive learning, here about contradictions and breaks in the student's own production, which needed to be described and discussed so that their own 'mark' could be inscribed in their sequence. Students were told that they could break cinematic conventions that the feedback informs them of to create a specific effect. The assessment does not directly reward compliance, although violations would need to be justified.

VOICEOVER AND LOOPING

Scaffolding

In addition to the rule-driven feedback, there is a detailed glossary, a set of readings, and further instructions on the conventions and concepts used by filmmakers. It was important that the feedback and instructions have an appropriate 'voice.' This voice could not be that of a frustrated educator but rather ended up something akin to a fastidious assistant film editor. In addition to sequencing clips, students write the accompanying script and must offer an explanation for their editing approach by drawing on film language.

Recording Sound

Having created a sequence, the next challenging aspect is writing voiceovers and imagining how audiences would respond. The voiceover text is entered into a textbox (Figure 8.3) for the associated clip and displayed again when the full sequence is played. Many students were uncertain about the application of scriptwriting conventions, such as indicating in their script who was speaking and whether it is a voiceover or off-screen dialogue (e.g., [v/o Femme] to indicate the *femme fatale*'s voiceover). The interface includes illustrative examples of the abbreviations used with voiceovers (Figure 8.4), whereas the automated feedback reminded students to include notes if no square brackets appeared in their script. Reflecting on experiences in 2004, we found that few students had understood that they could include more detailed explanatory notes in the scripts, such as indicating sounds effects, editing effects, or music. Changes were made to encourage students to add these details that many were discussing with us but not always including in their scripts. Three music clips were provided that could be played while viewing a sequence. Additional instructions and glossary entries were added,

Figure 8.4. Screengrab for the interface shown in Figure 8.3, with instructions on how clips are viewed, voiceover narration is added and feedback is generated.

suggesting how notes on postproduction effects could be added. These changes resulted in many more students adding appropriate editing notes and communicating their intentions.

Editing Moves

Creating the sequence and writing a script accounts for half of the total assessment of the overall task. The remainder requires students to explain their intentions and demonstrate understandings of film theory terms by using these appropriately. Students name their film, outline the back story to their sequence, identify the dominant point of view of the clips chosen, and draw on terms from their film theory reading in providing an explanation of the editing choices in their own sequence. Additionally, there are five multiple-choice questions that require students to play a clip randomly assigned to them and identify how particular film theorists would have characterized this clip. The articles discussing the film theorists' ideas are included in the course reader. Essentially, this quiz assesses whether students have done their readings and can understand and apply the theoretical terminology used in the academic articles to clips in the exercise. Students found this exercise challenging.

WIDESHOT

Making Prints

When closing *Director's Cut*, all work is saved in a central database, which allows students to return to where they left off, even when working from a different computer. From past experience, we knew that it was important to have a printout of each student's sequence, voiceover script, and responses to questions. The printout makes it easier for tutors in writing feedback, provides a record of completion, can be made available to the external examiner to review, and can be used in students' portfolios.

A 'Storyboard Loader'

Once all the tasks are complete, students open the 'Storyboard Loader.' a *Microsoft Word* document that retrieves their saved work from the database. The 'Storyboard Loader' tallies the number of correct quiz responses and formats the script in a storyboard layout, with frames from the sequence alongside their script and a formatted paragraph with all the written responses (see Figure 8.5). This process allows students to make final text edits, such as correcting spelling, before printing and handing in for assessment. Script changes are saved back to the database so students could return to change their sequence in the *Director's Cut* program.

The mode used in assessment differs slightly from that of the production, and we wanted students to be aware of this transformation and changing media. In the beginning, some tutors found their assessment role difficult because they had not become as familiar with the clips as students had in creating their own sequences and thus were not sufficiently confident in interpreting the students' intentions in the paper copy. Tutors needed to watch a number of students' sequences and understand the affordances of the *Director's Cut* interface before they could read a sequence on paper, recognize the reasons for some more subtle choices, or understand how the voiceover would sound in relation to the images. We had created a version of the *Director's Cut* program that allowed tutors to easily retrieve different students' sequences and play them while writing comments on the paper copies.

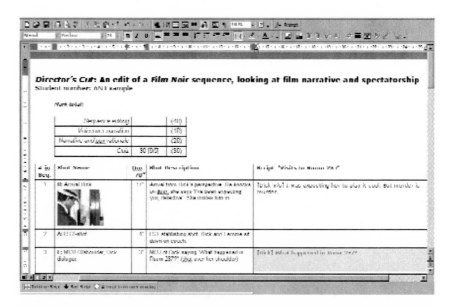

Figure 8.5. Screengrab of the Storyboard Loader showing a formatted sequence that tutors mark and add comments to. Independently, tutors can call-up and view the video sequence.

'Dolls and Diamonds' Closeup

One of the first students to finish their *Director's Cut* exercise titled his film 'Dolls and Diamonds.' Through creating a story of a jewelry heist being investigated by the detective, his understandings of the codes and conventions of the *film noir* genre are clearly demonstrated. The voiceover narrative establishes the woman being interviewed as a murder suspect and a classic *femme fatale*: 'She was playing with me . . . this doll's performance was a class act.' This is spoken over an image that sexualizes the female character and positions the spectator in a masculine, heterosexual viewing position by showing a medium closeup shot over the detective's shoulder as the *femme fatale* first displays and then covers her legs with her gown.

Subsequent shots within the dialogue sequence of 'Dolls and Diamonds' follow the shot-reverse-shot convention. Shots 3 and 4 alternate between the detective saying 'What happened in Room 237'? and the *femme fatale* saying 'What do you think'? as filmed from one side of the axis of action. The student did not select alternative shots filmed from behind the sofa because this would have involved crossing the line of action, as if the characters abruptly swapped positions on the sofa mid-conversation. Similarly, the student alternated shots of the protagonists rather than sequencing two consecutive clips of the *femme fatale* because this would have produced a jump-cut effect.

Shot transitions can function as cinematic punctuation—for instance, a dissolve joining two distinct sequences can signify 'a spatio-temporal break with the establishing of an underlying transitive link.' whereas a fade indicates 'a straightforward spatio-temporal break' (Metz, 1974/1991:99). Hence, the dissolve included in one of our clips is used to signal the flashback, a 'grammatically appropriate' editing technique that indicates the transition to a subjective insert which serves as imagery 'conveying not the present instance, but an absent moment experienced by the hero of the film' (Metz, 1974/1991: 125). The script intentionally aligns the spectator with the detective from the opening shot, which is filmed from his perspective outside the room, rather than selecting a shot from the woman's point of view as she answers the door. Warren Buckland (2000:59) points out that 'the spectator as decoder is an implicit premise of film semiotics.' Through these shot selections, the student demonstrates an ability to understand theories of film reception and analysis through applying the conventions of continuity editing and spectatorship consistently.

Given the emphasis in film theory on the relationship between text and audience, *Director's Cut* asks students to reflect on the 'pronoun effect' that arises from the selection of camera positions and the corresponding manipulation of the spectator's position. This relationship is integral to the production of a film text, as argued by film theorists such as Christian Metz (1974/1991), Thomas Elsaesser and Warren Buckland (2002), David Bordwell and Kristen Thompson (2004), and Murray Smith (1997). Students must draw on these theorists and their concepts of focalization, subjectivity, allegiance, and alignment to articulate how the spectator is positioned in relation to the camera and characters.

The student 'director' of 'Dolls and Diamonds' does this adeptly, stating that:

> Four of the mechanisms of cinematic identification that I have used are point of view editing (the view of the woman's legs), off screen sound (Dick's subjective monologue), shot scale (the Big Close-Up on Dick's face and eyes in shot 5T Dick's flashback; the woman is considerably smaller in screen space), and narrative placement of the sequence (the audience is encouraged to follow the detective's story).

The student astutely notes that

> the camera aligns the audience with Dick (the detective) by showing his reactions in Big Close-up. The audience experiences Dick's mental subjectivity in visuals and voice-over narration. In *noir* fashion, the audience is clearly aligned with him. We know only the extent of his knowledge. Very little room for allegiance with the woman is offered.

This extract suggests that the practical process of applying cognitive semiotic film theory has honed the student's analytic skills and helped to develop a sophisticated awareness of how cinematic codes and genre conventions create one narrow version of events that the spectator is encouraged to accept as the whole story, thereby privileging particular forms of subjectivity and social power.

User Perspectives

Since this exercise is very different in its modes of expression and forms of assessment when compared to other tasks in the course, students seemed keen to talk about what they liked and disliked. Many students remarked that the exercise provided a stimulating alternative to essays:

> I think this was a really creative exercise. Essays get very boring as the only means of assessment and this exercise was both practical and analytical. I think the time and effort spent making this programme is appreciated, and shows a sense of innovation.

At a more macrolevel, one student wrote:

> I really enjoyed completing this exercise; it was both interesting and challenging. It certainly teaches us as students the importance [of] film editors. I found the questions at the end were particularly useful in helping me justify my shot choices.

As this student implies, editing requires intimate knowledge of the material and processes. Several students expressed frustration over being constrained by the choice and length of clips. They felt that this restricted the dialogue they wished to write. Some of these constraints were deliberate on our part, whereas others were not always intentional. This dichotomy is reflected in their comments:

> I think that some of the close up shots could have been a little longer so that more v/o narration could be used in those sequences. Thank you for this opportunity.

In many cases, these students also had difficulty deciding on what is important and articulating their narratives dramatically. Seen across the class, most students evolved sensible ways to use short and clever dialogue voiceovers.

The Film Narrative course includes mainstream Film Studies students who mainly study film theory and analysis, as well as 24 students who are enrolled in quota-restricted screen production courses. At the time they did the *Director's Cut* exercise, the screen Production students were using professional editing software, and some expressed frustration with the constraints imposed on composing and editing their sequences:

> I did enjoy the exercise. However, I suppose because I am in Production, I was frustrated by the lack of freedom. I would have liked to chop some of the clips, add some sound and really get the feel and timing right.

This frustration reflects the difficulty we had in balancing the interests of all students because there is variation in students' own meta-media literacy (Lemke, 1998). The contradictions seem obvious to those with more skills and higher expectations but cannot always be resolved in large classes where we want everyone to engage in the same activity. Interestingly, several tutors remarked that these Production students were not the ones producing the best work in applying the theoretical understandings to tell a dramatic story. In 2005, we invested more effort in framing the task to these students to avoid some of these misunderstandings about the purpose of the exercise and why we had emphasized spectatorship and scriptwriting over producing a fine edit.

Most students accepted the boundaries on the task. Many remarked on the impact the feedback had on their work. A representative comment is:

> I thought that this was a very fun exercise, especially for those of us who are not doing the production skills program. It was the first time that I have ever edited anything and the program is helpful and informative. I especially appreciated the comments from the computer with regards to our clip choices—it made me think about what I was trying to say and how best to say it.

This perspective reflects a broad curiosity with how we designed the exercise, making it challenging yet rewarding for anyone participating. There was an interesting statistical correlation among the marks awarded for *Director's Cut,* the essays, and the final exam. Although this correlation was significant, suggesting that good students generally did well in all assessed tasks, it was slightly weaker in those involving *Director's Cut* in both years, suggesting that different types of understandings were being assessed to those in exam and essays.

REWIND

Design Choices

The designs for learning stages we describe capture the constraints and choices in developing learning experiences in a course. As David Wiley (2003) reminds us, design is always about choice under constraint. In addition to supporting student learning, from the start we saw a staff development role for *Director's Cut*; it can be a mediating artifact in showing other academics examples of the products of collaborative design and learning designs that otherwise might not be recognized. This has proved valuable even in cases where an academic might reach clarity that all they want is a course management system Web site. After describing *Director's Cut* to an architecture lecturer, we collaboratively designed a comparatively simple tutorial with a similar learning design. This involved positioning and changing the capacity of PhotoShop layers to communicate changes in the architectural space of a streetscape over time. Different questions were generated depending on the semiotic choices the students had made.

Although assessing learning outcomes is important to us, it is not our goal to present those results here. Our intention has thus not been to set up an experiment to measure the impact of *Director's Cut* on student learning; as in any real course, there are far too many variables that cannot be controlled. In these environments, such experimental designs tend to offer fewer insights into tutorial-style activities, such as *Director's Cut*, and contribute little that can be shared with other educators to change their teaching practice (e.g., Reeves, 2000; Sandoval & Bell, 2004). The more pragmatic view is to develop understandings of how to balance situated and production-based learning type activities with the more conventional modes of teaching and learning.

This section is arranged in four parts that draw together issues raised earlier; they are ordered loosely in how they link to the staged cycle of expansive learning: (a) film theory and creative praxis as focus for initiating our emerging designs for learning; (b) observations on collaborative designs for learning, abstracted from the case presented; (c) mediating the activity online, with suggestions on how student sequences, reflections, and evaluations might be linked; and (d) redirecting design, covering changes to the collaborative activity, and reflection on the practices we developed.

Questioning Practices: Theory and Praxis

The challenge we began thinking about concerned how theory and praxis can be linked within an activity. Many educators have similar questions, and production-based learning activities can address these queries directly (Buckingham & Sefton-Green, 1995, 1997). There are many other issues in developing practical learning designs. Asking the 'wrong' questions of pedagogy strategies can easily lead us to flounder in seemingly unsolvable teaching and learning challenges. What has stimulated us, in asking questions about what connects seemingly unrelated concepts, has been following the links that others have developed using social linguistic-inspired theories, such as Metz's 'film language,' Kress' multimodal discourse, and the opportunities that various people have recognized in using these in computer-based learning activities.

A central concern regarding the application of technology in educational activities (McGettrick et al., 2005) is whether we are succeeding in making ICT pedagogy a credible and viable complement to face-to-face education. Unpacking this enquiry highlights questions as to whether educators are being empowered to develop appropriate learning materials and whether there is broader adoption of languages and tools supporting these development processes and the assessment of student learning. Staff development processes tend to achieve effective transfer to practice when they integrate conceptual scaffolding and experiential learning (Wenger, 1998; Wenger et al., 2002). The model being piloted at UCT

includes both online and face-to-face interaction within and beyond labo-
ratory-based sessions.

We have been particularly interested in how to work around the constraints inherent in professional software tools to address the interests of
teaching large introductory classes specific skills. Designing these more
focusing, production-based learning activities is challenging, as we have
shown, although this effort is rewarded where we can achieve what would
otherwise be viewed as feasible. Students look for the lecturer's voice in
these designs and are willing to tolerate some aspects that are not fully
functional, as they are aware that they do not yet have the skills to use
high-end applications.

Collaborative Designs for Learning

Learning design, like film making, appears simple and obvious having seen
what others have accomplished. In practice, these designs do not simply
emerge but represent cumulative experiences and collaboration.
Engeström asks about processes and participants in learning in his model
of expansive learning. The stages are akin to iterative and emergent design
processes, in which negotiations between partners evolve and need to be
worked out as contradictions and potentials are or must be made apparent
for new plateaus to be arrived at. This is to cast collaboration between subject and learning specialists as an ongoing dialogue that needs awareness
of one another's disciplinary and interdisciplinary backgrounds and
approaches.

ICT-based learning activities in universities demand that we work in
flexible ways. They run for short stretches of time, typically over a few
days on an annual basis. Yet they are rich in adaptation to establish and
respond to emerging needs and demands. We cannot afford to overengi-
neer our software nor can we design away system failures without sacri-
ficing valued aspects of the learning design. There is a fragility inherent
in the ICT infrastructure of UCT that often requires fixes to work around
problems. Yet this can equally well be applied to limits in our understandings of student learning needs, which also demand managing what
cannot be anticipated.

The process of designing *Director's Cut* was a risky undertaking
because we could not be sure how the learning activity would be received.
The collaborative design was more manageable because we could learn
from experiences in earlier projects where such issues arose. Additionally,
focusing on praxis activities in a theory course seems to have resulted in
fewer contractions than if the activity aimed to teach the core theory, for
example. Expansive learning and collaborative design capture many familiar aspects of our learning design that have not always been foregrounded

in how educators work together. In a university context, focusing on theory and processes makes designs easier to negotiate than if the focus had been the equivalent of a textbook presenting content and with many dependencies on prior content. It is important to identify appropriate mediating artifacts that do not depend on content being transferred but rather focus on learning design as a workflow that technology facilitates while educators continue to play an active, face-to-face role.

Encouraging Creativity

We wanted each student in a large class to create a unique film sequence but also be able to recognize and share common ideas and appreciate how others have used the identical building blocks differently. The affordances of the interface and automated feedback remind students of the conventions and constraints that we imposed. In addition, tutors were initially available to discuss deeper questions and provide students with opportunities to voice their individual concerns. We were curious about the outcome but also keen to limit the permutations so that assessment might be easier to manage than in an earlier collaborative multimodal exercise at UCT, the open-ended EduSoap task (van der Vliet & Deacon, 2004). Having sufficient creativity in the learning design means we effectively avoided plagiarism. The storyboards students produced demonstrated a surprisingly wide range of interpretations and storylines, which suggests we have provided most students with a sense of the voicedness that Engeström includes in his approach to expansive learning. Some of this can be seen in the contradictions and breaks in the students' own production, which needed to be described and discussed to that their own 'mark' could be inscribed in their sequence.

Designing Adaptively: Multimodal Design

In reflecting on the value of *Director's Cut* as a project, we have been interested in understanding its role in encouraging educators to move beyond just analysis of film, emphasizing the importance of creative production as the most valuable way for students to develop the critical thinking so central to production learning (Buckingham & Sefton-Green, 1995). *Director's Cut* immediately became an influential demonstration to others, probably because filmmaking is so appealing, of what can be accomplished through collaborative design and student production activities.

Ultimately, the most stimulating aspect of the project for us as educational codesigners has been in the making of designs for learning that succeeded beyond our expectations and stimulated many fruitful debates among students. This stimulates theorizing around designs for learning as design-based research designs suggest (Reeves, 2000), as we illustrated in the intersections of film theory, learning design, and expansive learning.

REFERENCES

Bordwell, David, & Thompson, Kristen. (2004). 'Depth of story information.' In Bordwell, David, & Thompson, Kristin. (Eds.). *Film Art*. New York: McGraw Hill. 85-86.

Bratteteig, Tone. (2003). *Making Change. Dealing With Relations Between Design and Use*. Unpublished doctoral dissertation, Department of Informatics, University of Oslo. Available at http://heim.ifi.uio.no/ ~ tone/Publications/

Buckingham, David. (1998). 'Introduction: Fantasies of empowerment? Radical pedagogy and popular culture.' In Buckingham, David. (Ed.). *Teaching Popular Culture: Beyond radical pedagogy*. London: UCL Press. 1-17.

Buckingham, David, & Sefton-Green, Julian. (1995). *Making Media: Practical Production in Media Education*. London: English & Media Centre.

Buckingham, David, & Sefton-Green, Julian. (1997). 'Multimedia education: Media literacy in the age of digital culture.' In Kubey, Robert. (Ed.). *Media Literacy in the Information Age*. New Brunswick: Transaction Publishers. 285-305.

Buckland, Warren. (2000). *The Cognitive Semiotics of Film*. Cambridge, UK: Cambridge University Press.

Carr, Tony, Brown, Cheryl, Czerniewicz, Laura, Deacon, Andrew, & Morrison, Andrew. (2005, August 29-31). Communities of practice in staff development: Learning to teach with technology. In van Brakel, Pieter. (Eds.). *Proceedings of the 7th Annual Conference on World Wide Web Applications*, Cape Town, South Africa.

Coyne, Richard. (1997). *Designing Information Technology in the Postmodern Age: From Method to Metaphor*. Cambridge, MA: The MIT Press.

de Oliveira, Osvaldo Luiz, & Baranauskas, Maria Cecília Calani. (2000). 'Semiotics as a basis for educational software design.' *British Journal of Educational Technology*. Vol. 31, No. 2, 153-161.

Deacon, Andrew. (2002). 'NewsFrames: Engaging students in framing and debating news.' In *Proceedings of the Multimedia Education Group Colloquium*. MEG: University of Cape Town. 536-557.

Elsaesser, Thomas, & Buckland, Warren. (2002). 'Cognitive theories of narration: *Lost highway*.' In Elsaesser, Thomas, & Buckland, Warren. (Eds.). *Studying Contemporary American Film*. London: Arnold. 168-194.

Engeström, Yrjö. (1987). *Learning by Expanding: An Activity Theoretical Approach to Developmental Research*. Helsinki: Orienta-Konsultit.

Engeström, Yrjö. (1999a). 'Activity theory and individual and social transformation.' In Engeström, Yrjö, Miettinen, Reijo, & Punamaki, Raija-Leena. (Eds.). *Perspectives on Activity Theory*. Cambridge: Cambridge University Press. 19-38.

Engeström, Yrjö. (1999b). 'Innovative learning in work teams: Analysing cycles of knowledge creation and practice.' In Engeström, Yrjö, Miettinen, Reijo, & Punamaki, Raija-Leena. (Eds.). *Perspectives on Activity Theory.* Cambridge: Cambridge University Press. 377-404.

Engeström, Yrjö. (2001). 'Expansive learning at work: Toward an activity theoretical reconceptualization.' *Journal of Education and Work.* Vol. 14, No. 1, 133-156.

Engeström, Yrjö, Miettinen, Reijo, & Punamaki, Raija-Leena. (Eds.). (1999). *Perspectives on Activity Theory.* Cambridge: Cambridge University Press.

Erstad, Ola, Gilje, Øystein, & de Lange, Thomas. (2007). 'Re-mixing multimodal resources: Multiliteracies and digital production in Norwegian media education.' *Learning, Media & Technology.* Vol. 32, No. 2, 183-198.

Fleischmann, Kenneth. (2006). 'Do-it-yourself information technology: Role hybridization and the design-use interface.' *Journal of the American Society for Information Science and Technology.* Vol. 57, No. 1, 87-95.

Flowers, Jim. (2001). 'Online learning needs in technology education.' *Journal of Technology Education.* Vol. 13, No. 1.

Hofstadter, Douglas. (1995). *Fluid Concepts and Creative Analogies: Computer Models of the Fundamental Mechanisms of Thought.* New York: Basic Books.

Kress, Gunther. (1998). 'Visual and verbal modes of representation in electronically mediated communication: The potentials of new forms of text.' In Snyder, Ilana. (Ed.). *Page to Screen: Taking Literacy into the Electronic Era.* London: Routledge. 53-79.

Kress, Gunther. (2003). *Literacy in the New Media Age.* London: Routledge.

Kress, Gunther, & van Leeuwen, Theo. (2001). *Multimodal Discourse: The Modes and Media of Contemporary Communication.* London: Arnold.

Kuhn, Sara, & Winograd, Terry. (1996). 'Profile: Participatory design.' In Winograd, Terry. (Ed.). *Bringing Design to Software.* New York: ACM Press/Addison-Wesley. 290-294.

Lave, Jean, & Wenger, Etienne. (1991). *Situated Learning: Legitimate Peripheral Participation.* Cambridge: Cambridge University Press.

Lemke, Jay. (1998). 'Metamedia literacy: Transforming meanings and media.' In Reinking, David, McKenna, Michael, Labbo, Linda, & Kieffer, Ronald. (Eds.). *Handbook of Literacy and Technology: Transformations in a Post-Typographic World.* Mahwah, NJ: Lawrence Erlbaum Associates. 283-301.

Löwgren, Jonas, & Stolterman, Erik. (2004). *Thoughtful Interaction Design: A Design Perspective on Information Technology.* Cambridge, MA: The MIT Press.

Manovich, Lev. (2002). *The Language of New Media.* Cambridge, MA: The MIT Press.

McGettrick, Andrew, Boyle, Roger, Ibbett, Ronald, Lloyd, John, Lovegrove, Gillian, & Mander, Keith. (2005). 'Grand challenges in computing: Education—a summary.' *The Computer Journal.* Vol. 48, No. 1, 42-48.

Metz, Christian. (1974/1991). *Film Language: A Semiotics of the Cinema.* Chicago: University of Chicago Press.

Morrison, Andrew, Deacon, Andrew, & Stadler, Jane. (2005). 'Designs for learning about film genre.' *Proceedings of In-The-Making.* First Nordic Design Research Conference Copenhagen. Available at www.nordes.org

Murray, Janet. (1998, September 26). 'The god in the machine: design principles for digital resources in the humanities.' Plenary address at the Conference on the Future of the Humanities in the Digital Age, University of Bergen, Norway (via teleconference). Slides available at http://web.mit.edu/jhmurray/www/futHum/sld001.htm

Nichols, Bill. (1976). 'Style, grammar, and the movies.' In Nichols, Bill. (Ed.). *Movies and Methods*. Berkeley, CA: University of California Press. 607-628.

Rabinowitz. Paula. (2002). *Black & White & Noir: America's Pulp Modernism*. New York: Columbia University Press.

Reeves, Thomas. (2000, April 24-28). 'Enhancing the Worth of Instructional Technology Research Through "Design Experiments" and Other Development Research Strategies.' Paper presented at the annual meeting of the American Educational Research Association, New Orleans.

Sandoval, William, & Bell, Philip. (2004). 'Design-based research methods for studying learning in context: Introduction.' *Educational Psychologist*. Vol. 39, No. 4, 199-201.

Skjulstad, Synne, & Morrison, Andrew. (2005). 'Movement in the interface.' *Computers and Composition*. Vol. 22, No. 4, 413-433.

Smith, Murray. (1997). 'Imagining from the inside.' In Smith, Murray, & Allen, Richard. (Eds.). *Film Theory and Philosophy*. Oxford, UK: Clarendon Press. 412-430.

Stadler, Jane and McWilliam, Kelly. (2009). Screen Media: An introduction to film and television analysis. Crow's Nest, NSW, Australia: Allen and Unwin.

van der Vliet, Emma, & Deacon, Andrew. (2004). 'Media rich, resource poor: Practical work in an impractical environment.' *British Journal of Educational Technology*. Vol. 35, No. 2, 213-222.

Wenger, Etienne. (1998). *Communities of Practice: Learning, Meaning, and Identity*. Cambridge: Cambridge University Press.

Wenger, Etienne, McDermott, Richard, & Snyder, William. (2002). *Cultivating Communities of Practice: A Guide to Managing Knowledge*. Cambridge, MA: Harvard Business School Press.

Wiley, David. (2003). 'The coming collision between automated instruction and social constructivism.' In Gynn, Catherine, & Acker, Stephen. (Eds.). *Learning Objects: Contexts and Connections*. Columbus: The Ohio State University Press. 17-28.

PART IV

DOCUMENTING

PREFACE

TO CHOREOGRAPH

Adrian Miles

THE OVERBEARING AUTHORITY
OF PRINT

Flash is a good starting point because, like Synne Skjulstad in her contribution here, we find ourselves in a postliterate, remediated age where media objects no longer even grant us the security of being touched. Through their screens, these artifacts are now constituted by flows and vectors where any semblance to writing dissolves in the choreography that constitutes new media 'writing.' As Skjulstad (Chapter 11) points out, it is no longer just a question of choosing verbal or visual expression:I In the practice of multilinear and multitemporal composition, the artful (a rich word) becomes paramount. This recognition allows us to realize some of the possibilities of 'multimodalities' as a mode of criticism and develop a critique of it as a mode of practice. Perhaps its usefulness, and its failure, as each of the contributors begin to indicate through their particular, situated, practice-based investigations, is that the discourse of multimodality offers a language for analysis but perhaps less so for practice.

It is reasonable to identity that the theoretical work around multimodalities has developed within the traditional concerns of print and language literacy, and its premises work from the recognition that print is no longer the dominant discursive mode. The problem with such a beginning is that print retains its authority as origin and center, the moment from which Other modalities are then determined by or through.

A Discursive Other

It is clear that it is a discursive Other with its capitalized 'O.' For example, Morrison and Thorsnes, in 'Blogging the Ephemeral' (Chapter 10), astutely search for the intersection between choreography and multimodal practice, recognizing that the key question that such mixed modes of composition ask of us is much less what sort of object we might produce but rather how we make sensible what are otherwise the invisible aporias between modes. For example, when I include sound inside the 'space' of my writing, video, or even something as banal as a painting, what we celebrate is not the erasure of distance between modes, but their irreconcilable differences. This fact is particularly evident when other modes are used as discourses in their own right—that is, when I include music as music, film as film, or a painting as painting in the common space of my writing—then these Other media bear witness to my writing and to each other, and by their presence within the field of writing will always indicate the inadequacy of writing to meet, accommodate, or otherwise enter into conversation with Other media. This bearing witness is a posthermeneutic moment that shies away from interpretation as the necessary end moment of recapture (which so easily slides into the appropriation of one form into the monolingual norms of another) and offers the possibility of a dialogism internal to the forms being used. This notion is quite removed from many of the examples and even practices offered under sophisticated catchalls such as 'multimodalities', where it is common to find nontextual media relegated to the role of illustration, rendered mute servant to the written word. This is the value of Stuedahl and Smørdal's (Chapter 9) examination of a museum-based historical reconstruction, where they are able to identify, largely via actor network theory and multimodal discourse, a range of 'interested' discourses that affect their various practices. In this context, a potentially robust preliminary methodology is sketched that does not become compromised by an effort to consolidate all into a single or specific aggregate text so that it can retain its multiple discursive and interpretive modes.

The Importance of Design Practice

This has much in common with design, where there is recognition that there is no single modality to practice and that that which binds is the medium of realization, rather than the media used. As Morrison and Thorsnes (Chapter 10) indicate, the benefits of design practice to thinking within (rather than about) multimodalities is not to mistake design as an instrumental doing but to appropriate those aspects of design practice that describe, legitimate, and recognize design as a thinking 'in' and 'through' media. This particularly materialist thinking (Carter, 2004) does not treat writing or any other creative intellectual activity as first a conceptualizing and then a doing. Indeed, even where we attempt to conceive of such an activity, it never happens in practice (e.g., to write well is to remain open to the exterior of your ideas and to the materiality of language within the act of writing, which is why the 'good' use of puns, alliteration, and other devices is of value; after all these have nothing to do with clarity of argument and everything to do with the pleasure of the material, the written equivalent of dance). It is the same process in architecture, except the palette is now physical materials, space, and ideas, and it is a brief traverse from here to the genuinely multimodal practices that are evidenced in the collaboration that the authors undertake.

Emergent Material Practice as the Work

To work otherwise in new media is to maintain an old school distinction between 'thinking then doing', which is the last hurrah of a Cartesian dualism that insists, or more generously struggles with, distinctions between mind and body. This distinction is reified in the idealism of the idea and its imagined purity, which is then (and only then) given flesh in the material form of black text on the white page. The pleasures of a more designerly practice—that is to say a mode of work that recognizes that in our doing there is an experimental, exploratory, and experiential mode of material practice, where we recognize that our tools (a banal term) and media have material qualities and affordances that exist in a dialogical relation to the self and ideas—are often the object of deep suspicion, but as Morrison and Thorsnes discover, what emerges in doing constitutes the work itself.

How to Dance

This is the realm of affect, of an excess that lies somewhere beyond the recovery of meaning, which is precisely why it inserts itself so firmly as an Other mode of practice to our protestant academic traditions. It is not the imposition of my will onto the medium but between what I think I want to do and what the medium thinks—in there is the dialogical event (which is always plural) where each writes the other. In these moments, ideas are not 'mine' but form a part of this dialogue, and in the same manner what I do with media is less my choice than a conversation that emerges within the materiality of the medium.

How to dance, as perhaps Morrison and Thorsnes realize, is the crux of the problem that multimodal analysis seeks to answer. As the chapters gathered here indicate, multimodal theory goes some way toward providing us with a methodology of analysis but struggles to account for activity itself, of composing or performing multimodality. We could call this activity choreography, and this is what it is to be inside of multimodal composition.

REFERENCE

Carter, Paul. (2004). *Material Thinking: The theory and practice of creative research.* Carlton: Melbourne University Publishing.

9

BLOGGING THE EPHEMERAL

Andrew Morrison

Per Roar Thorsnes

STRETCHING

Emergences

Overleaf is an entry in the weblog *Docudancing* posted by Per Roar, a research fellow in choreography, on March 11, 2005 (Figure 9.1). It is from preparation of his work, 'A Rehearsal for Mortals,' part 2 in the trilogy *Life and Death: Choreography in Context*. The still images show rehearsal with a simple wooden coffin. Plain pine. Solid enough to endure handling and light enough to be pushed, tilted, and lifted. The coffin is a reminder of the absent body: death itself. In the spatial dynamics, created by the definite choices of the performers and the choreographer, a fifth body emerged, the choreography. As rhizome. Structured movement patterns and bodily awareness directed and set in space. Stretching performance as interstitial, between life and death. Performance as an ephemeral act. An act of disappearance, as Peggy Phelan (1993) writes. Movement and choreography always a display in space of a disappearance in time. In this act of disappearance lies the ontology of performance and its resemblance with the human body, our being.

Kristianne Mo's arms are outstretched, the work a medley of movements the dancers have come to sense and shape alongside their own writing and picturing. Stored photos and the dynamic pulses of live visuals. The dancers' bodies always in movement toward death. Peder standing

the day after - the 5th body emerges

11.3/2005

yesterday after our second showing, I had a day-off after the last weeks intense work. The relief I was experiencing, made me more receptive to the bodily insight absorbed the last two days from showing our movement material to an audience. While I was doing my yoga practice in the morning a rush of ideas came to me. Or to be more precise, from the pool of ideas I have got about the final version of the performance, a more articulated voice surfaced.

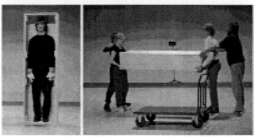

I realized that we were not any longer just 3 dancers and the choreographer, but a 5th body was emerging. A body without organs, as Deleuze and Guattari writes about in their *a thousand plateaus* (London, 1980). The performance itself started to talk back, it reyed, suggested, indicated and pushed me to engage in a dialogue. A most fascinating situation. (photo taken 9. March by Synne Skjulstad)

By Per Roar

Comments (0)

Filed under : Per Roar [choreographer] | Part 2: A Rehearsal for Mortals | on research kl. 14.59

Figure 9.1. 'A Rehearsal for Mortals,' part 2 in the trilogy *Life and Death: Choreography in Context.* (From Per Roar, *Docudancing* weblog entry March 11, 2005) stock still in the coffin. The audience in the position of all-seeing eye. The missing body stretched out in the coffin. The onlooker as existential participant. To the right, Per Roar stands in for one of the funeral attendants who will play himself in the performance, the red trolley to be replaced by their formal, extendable one. Stretching the performance space from the artistic stage space back into our memories of loss and funerals, into our own lives, merged with dance, rippling us back into the present. The dance work a hybrid performance, with stored and live documentary-like video feed, a blend of abstract and contextual photographs and the gritty textures of medical imagery.

.Drawn from the *Docudancing* blog, these images and texts are part of a dynamic unfolding of a creative collaborative process of meaning making based on design for performance (e.g., Skjulstad et al. 2002). They are multimodally shaped, yet their dynamic character also positions them through and across time as the blog becomes a lattice of polyvocal articulations. It is through the individual and collective entries, in a variety of modes, that meaning making is realized, in progress, but importantly through processes of mediated reflection and recollection (Lemke 2001). Socio-genesis from sociocultural approaches to meaning making and learning meet the choreography of research mediation.

Scope of Chapter

In this chapter, our main focus is on how a blog may be used as a tool and a site for multimodal, multimediational composition about processes of creative construction in the performing arts. Choreography is the disciplinary domain, and our main theoretical concepts are drawn from Bakhtin (1981, 1984, 1986). These concepts are related to the overall framework of mediated action and its relations to activity theory. Engeström and Miettinen (1999: 7), two of the leading authorities on activity theory, write that:

> In recent years, an increasing number of activity-theoretical studies have focused on issues of discourse and signification, often drawing on Wittgenstein and on the work of the Russian literary theorist and philosopher Michail Bakhtin. . . . However, the integration of discourse into the theory of activity has only begun.

This chapter aims to show how this blogging as *discourse in activity* (e.g., Norris & Jones 2005) may be taken up in the practice study of blogs as mediated activity. Unlike most other studies to date on blogs, our focus is on creative, developmental processes of collaborative construction. In print, and definitely online, few records exist of the choreographic unfoldings and emergent discourse processes in designing dance works for performance. As an unfolding, shared activity of meaning making, we position blogging within a sociocultural approach to mediated communication and learning. This allows us to get to how mediated meaning making (Wertsch 1991) is multiply made online, that is, sociogenetically.

The chapter includes a case drawn from the *Docudancing* blog. This blog contains processural reflections on the making of three experimental dance works by Per Roar Thorsnes as part of an emergent inquiry into art practice and practice-based artistic research. The case refers to the piece 'A Rehearsal for Mortals' that incorporates investigations into movements of the internal body visible through imaging technologies and finds ways to embody these not only in the choreographer's compositional design but in the dancers' own senses of movement. Such investigations have also been presented and discussed in the blog as part of the process of reflecting on and selecting from these movements artistically. *Docudancing* is a multiply voiced and mediated blog about processes of shaping this work, of its movement, a matter of being in-the-making and reflecting on it. In the *Docudancing* blog, we have broadly taken up the notion of the change laboratory (Engeström et al. 1996) not just a space for enacting change over time, but also for recording it and mediating it beyond the boundaries of the internally shared event of dance making. We show how our perspectives have accumulated and been modified over time, and we express this in a multimodal ethnographic style of online discourse.

Research has also been a part of this collaboration: The blog is a multimodal account of a process of making a context-driven performing art work, and it is written in the voice of a shared multimodal ethnography. Building the performance and developing the blog have been part of one another. Media have been present in both of these components. We merge elements from digital media arts, choreography, performance studies, and ethnographic discourse as part of an expanded multimodal research rhetoric. The focus in the blog is on mediated action, that is, what the participants do; how they reflect on their experiences and dialogical engagements verbally, visually, and proxemically; and how these are situated in terms of categories and internal and external linkages as environment. This situatedness is built through the agency of the participants and not an ethnographer external to the creative process

Figure 9.2. Reviewing a sequence in iMovie in the rehearsal room.

(Engeström 1995). The blog also reveals the appearances and concatenation of inner contradictions, tensions, and breakdowns, indicative, too, of the workings, gains, and frustrations in a complex process.

The chapter accesses styles and modes of writing from performance studies, as well as from experimental, reflexive rhetoric (Latour 1996; Heaton 2002), composition and ethnography (Kirklighter et al. 1997; van Maanen 1995), visual anthropology (Grimshaw & Ravetz 2005), virtual ethnography (Hine 2000) and autoethnography (e.g., Jackson 1998; Taft-Kaufman 2000; Bochner & Ellis 2002). Rhetorically, our text takes deliberate poetic and performative turns, similar to other accounts of academic reflection as an heuretic or 'invention' (Ulmer 1994). We include photographs from *Docudancing*, as well as screen shots of blog entries that function as a bridge between modes of reporting and analysis.

Research Questions

We address several interrelated research questions related to blogging as mediated meaning making. One demand is how to connect, multimodally, processes of making, rehearsing, redesigning, and performing. How might the mediating artifact of the blog be used to provide some means of the documenting aspects of dance making? In what ways might different media be used to communicate this? How, too, might a blog be developed as a collaborative object, drawing together a variety of voices and genres across the duration of its development? Might the attention to process have some bearing on how we approach blogs as both mediated action and mediating action?

Outline of Chapter

In the next section, we cover relations between choreography and composition, looking at utterance, multimodal discourse, and composing via blogs as instances of socially mediated action. We briefly outline practices and issues in the documentation of dance and the core problem that most contemporary choreography is not documented as a creative, developmental process. A survey of blogging then follows in Section 3. Next, in Section 4, we present our main theoretical frame centered on the work of Bakhtin. His core concepts of polyvocality, mediational tools and signs, and the chronotope are then applied to selections from *Docudancing* in Section 5. The chapter closes in Section 6 with a short discussion and some of the implications of using and studying blogs as ways of documenting creative processes in the arts. We conclude with a focus on the need to develop concepts for dynamic mediating artifacts and discourses in action.

INSIDE CHOREOGRAPHY VIA COMPOSITION

Utterance, Choreography, and Mediated Meaning Making

As a domain in the performing arts, choreography has been traditionally shaped and communicated through demonstration and rehearsal. Choreography may be seen as multimodal design for dance performance. Performatively—as a mode of expressive, creative discourse—a dance work is uttered via situated kinetics. The proxemic and proprioceptive unfolding of movement—from tightly marshalled moves of classical ballet to the freer forms of improvisation—is typically accompanied by multiple modes of staging, including light, image, and sound. A performance has the status of utterance. It exists through its embodiment in space and time, and thereafter the performance as text disappears (Phelan 1993). Dance is understandably often seen as product—a performance is the result of a creative design process, and it is performed before a live audience. Choreography also tends to be documented as a product on video, and this can be done through notation for movement. Performances are built across time and by groups of collaborators and participants. However, as performing arts have extended their relationships between body, stage, performers, staging, and audience participation (e.g., Thomas 2003; Thomas & Ahmed 2004), so, too, have processes and participation altered in choreography (Birringer 2005).

Blogs also may be seen as utterances, that is, as polyphonic discourse following Bakhtin. They are developed over time and across themes and topics. However, few are dedicated to the documentation of an emergent process that has a primary production goal. Here is Bakhtin's (1984) notion of the dialogical that interests us:

> Life by its very nature is dialogic. To live means to participate in dialogue: to ask questions, to heed, to respond, to agree, and so forth. In this dialogue a person participates wholly and throughout his whole life: with his eyes, lips, hands, soul, spirit, with his whole body and deeds. He invests his entire self in discourse, and this discourse enters into the dialogic fabric of human life, into the world symposium. (293)

The Weblog, or blog, is now a marked feature in the history of the World Wide Web, that übertext of the 'world symposium.' Blogs are used to cover a wide range of communicative purposes and modes of expression (Walker Rettberg 2008). They are constructed in a range of genres, and their context of use varies from sites of joint specialist research discussion and publication (Herring et al. 2004) and self mediation (Reed 2005). Educationally, in rhetoric and composition studies, blogs have been used to promote process-based writing, personal journals, and cross-curricular study, even at graduate level (Shultz et al. 2005). For Miller and Shepherd (2004: online), 'In a culture in which the real is both public and mediated, the blog makes "real" the reflexive effort to establish the self against the forces of fragmentation, through expression and connection, through disclosure.'

Docudancing is an investigation of how to compose a multiauthored, multimodal, creative ethnography through the exploratory use of digital technologies. It attempts to add to existing approaches to writing about dance and its design by paying particular attention to the multiple processes and participants involved in dance making. Further, blogging may be seen as an emerging mediated activity that has led to the growth of multigenre of Web media. Killoran (2005: 133) mentions that few studies examine diversity and 'diverse assemblages of discourses' in Web texts by way of analysis that is informed by Bakhtin's concept of dialogism between 'speakers' and 'respondents.'

Dialogism, however, tends to be cast in terms of spoken and written text and less the transposition of multimodal expression or processes of resemioticization (Iedema 2003). Apart from van Leeuwen's (1999) work linking speech, music, and sound, there is little mention of the kinetic, its shapes, and the performative in multimodal discourse. Thibault (2004) has addressed this in his work extending Lemke's (2000) social-ecological view of semiosis. Against this backdrop, the work of Susan Leigh Foster (1995: 9), concerned with 'history' in dance writing, resonates with our intentions to explore mediated activity as it emerges in the blog:

> How to transpose the moved in the direction of the written. Describing bodies' movements, the writing itself must move. It must put into play figures of speech and forms of phrase and sentence construction that evoke the texture and timing of bodies in motion. It must also become inhabited by all the different bodies that participate in the constructive process of determining historical bodily signification.

Blogging Choreographic Processes

Blog tools may be used to articulate a communicative purpose in which communication design supercedes functionalist approaches to interaction design. The *Docudancing* site has been built through collaborative use. It investigates ways in which the capacities of a blog may be used to convey a process of art making. For researchers and teachers of composition and rhetoric, for those in choreography and dance, as well as ethnography (Denzin 1997), *Docudancing* offers a sustained example of how process-related multimodal discourse about performing arts may be voiced and transversed. In discussing the multiple activities involved in choreographing, Blom and Chaplin (1982: 3) say that:

> You do not learn to choreograph by reading about it, hearing about it, or by watching major companies in concert. You learn by choreographing, by experimenting, by creating little bits and pieces and fragments of dances and dance phrases, by playing with the material of the craft over and over again until they become second nature. You learn by getting your ideas out and into movement, onto a body (yours or someone else's), giving your dance an independent existence. But where does one begin? and how?

Docudancing has been an experimental venture into blogging by doing. It is an instance of mediated social action (Scollon 1998). It introduces and draws together different elements and returns to many of them as the dance work takes shape. As its participants learn to get their ideas out and into the site, the blog begins to take form and develops a body and movement of its own.

Docudancing is an example of how a tool may be used in designing for multimodal composition. After Bakhtin (1986), *Docudancing* is a polyvocal text authored by a group of participants and through a variety of media types. There is space for individual reflections and postings authored via entries from the dancers, and by the production and research participants, in a variety of media. In this sense, drawing on activity theory, *Docudancing* is a mediating artifact. It functions as a site of composition where multiple media types are used to selectively portray a creative process by way of commercial blog software.

Choreography as 'Compositional Design'

As a process, choreography is commonly presented in the written biographical accounts of and by luminary figures in the field. These accounts are typically reflections on the development of works following their completion and often extensive performance. Photographs are an important part of these works, yet they freeze movement as image (Barthes 1981) and indicate the difficulty in representing and mediating a field of the performing arts in which movement and nonverbal communication are primary. Further, choreographic processes may be recorded via notational systems, drawings, and video. Most often these are not coordinated, presented, or distributed outside a choreographer's inner circle of collaborators and critics. Although notebooks may be a key part of the choreographer's creative processes, these are rarely revealed nor are public, written texts, generated during dance making, and connected to and reflecting on its processes of creative negotiation and formation. Yet making a dance work—an emergent act of composing—is an elaborate and multimodal process (see Figure 9.3). Choreographers, often dancers themselves, draw

Figure 9.3. Multiple activities in the rehearsal room.

and write (see e.g., Lee 2006); they dance and discuss their designs for movement with their dancers and with their peers. Seldom do we find accounts of the processes of dance making that may be seen as developmental, unfolding, and poised between the choreographer's vision and direction and the engagement of participants, moving and observing, writing and imaging their own perspectives as part of a shared object of construction. Analytical writing about dance is also not as prolific as written reflection and critique in other domains of performing arts. Martin (1995: 109) goes so far as to say that dance writing is underdeveloped and lacks a critically circulating discourse built on clear codes of interpretation and a secondary literature that has been shaped from dance and developed to account for nonverbal expression.

BLOGGING

Introduction

As text, blogs are mediated only online (Miller & Shepherd 2004). They are composed and communicated computationally as ergodic texts that require active and nontrivial engagement by readers (Aarseth 1997; Mortensen 2004a). At a technical level, the Weblog refers to the file logging of activity on the Web. This logging has been shortened in use to refer to publication of blogs on the Web via commercial software such as *MovableType* or *WordPress*. This software has been refined for ease of use, and it is this accessibility that has allowed millions of users to publish, distribute, and easily update their own perspectives and content on the Web (Blood 2002, 2004). In many respects, the blog has superceded the earlier publication of personal 'homepages' as sites for identity building and self-presentation.

Blog software typically includes a number of discursive features that have contributed to its popularity and coherence (Bonus et al. 2004). The 'new-to-top' structure of entries embedded in the software allows a mode of publishing the recent, current, and contentious in a diary-like form. This reverse chronology built into the software is one of the features that attracts bloggers (Nardi et al. 2004a: 43). Early writers on blogging (Mortensen & Walker 2002: 267) note that

> Blogs are chronologically ordered, rather than ordered according to the logic of an argument or the persuasive patterns of rhetoric. Entries bear a date, timestamp and permalink. Their order is determined by the time of thinking.

This refers to the notion of kairos—a 'time in between,' recognizing and acting at an opportune moment, not the sequential, marked time of chronos.

Blogs are already widely used in the teaching of composition and rhetoric as is evident in the *kairosnews* blog.[1] The blog is thus potentially a site for the articulation of multiple mediations and genres, yet these are constrained by the inherent qualities of the blog as application. According to Miller and Shepherd (2004: online), 'The cultural moment in which the blog appeared is a kairos that has shifted the boundary between the public and the private and the relationship between mediated and unmediated experience.'

Attributes, Motivations, and Discourse Moves

In conceptualizing blogs as multidimensional conversations, Krishnamurthy (2002) draws two classificatory attributes. These are focused on the space (personal vs. topical) and the organizational structure (individual vs. community). These attributes may be read across one another so that a diversity of purpose, motivations, and uses accrue when reading, using, and studying blogs. Blogs provide points of accumulative identity formation and expression online, and they allow astute bloggers to position their own utterances in relation to selected others (Nardi et al. 2004a). This may result in clusters of blogs (Kumar et al. 2004) that may be polyvocally linked and ventriloquize the related interests and discourses of other bloggers (Schiano et al. 2004).

Blogs are also often a hybrid of the personal and the public (Mortensen & Walker 2002; Mortensen 2004a). They exhibit mixed modes of expression within and across blog posts, categories, and other blogs. This finding suggests that they may be seen in terms of not only intertextuality but as what might be called *intergenre* composition. Aligned with news discourse, they may contain updates, features, and event-driven and opinion pieces (Krishnamurthy 2002; Schiano et al. 2004). Repeated entries serve to motivate readers and raise their expectations (Krishnamurthy 2002).

Although content matters immensely to bloggers, and formal features are what are shared, on the basis of their ethnomethodological approach, Miller and Shepherd (2004) are able to assert that bloggers highlight the importance of self-expression and community building (Blanchard 2004). The former functions to enact self-clarification and validation, perhaps adding to self-awareness and bolstering given values and beliefs, with the result that 'The blogger is her own audience, her own public, her own beneficiary.' In contrast, these researchers see blogs as realizing outward-reaching social action in which self-disclosure helps build connections and potential community.² In summary, the blog may be understood as 'a complex rhetorical hybrid.' Nardi et al. (2004b: 230) comment that blogs are '. . . a form of object-oriented communicative activity, enacting a wide range of social purposes.'

On Photo and Video Blogging

Developments in digital camera technologies and lower prices have resulted in a virtual explosion of digital imaging. Photoblogging has become an identified form of mediated blogging in itself. Services such such as *flickr* allow for annotation to photos and for their feed to blogs and across them. However, many photos appearing in blogs are not connected to longer term processes and their critical reflection. Cohen (2005) argues that the rise in digital image making has in many respects returned us to earlier theoretical discussions, such as realism. He see that

> As a result of this tendency to tether photography to questions of representation, the trajectory of photographic theory always arcs . . . from *the act* of taking the photograph to *the photograph* itself, straight from photography to photograph. (Cohen 2005: 884; italics original)

Taking a more ethnographic stance, Cohen presents a study of the practices of 30 photobloggers as a means to exemplify issues in the analysis of photographs and new media. For Cohen (2005: 886), 'text is to blogging as photographs are to photoblogging.' Miles (2005) reminds us that video blogging is not simply a matter of placing video in a blog tool.

Blogging and Research

Research-related blogging is now also an emerging domain of this polytextual online communication. Here the aggregative potential of linked online bloggers with known disciplinary domains, interdisciplinary settings, projects, and organizations adds blogging to academic networking already enhanced by lists and discussion groups. Writing has long been studied as a mode of arranging thought and argumentation through reflected action over time. Blogging also may provide space for reflected communication, but it is typically rapid and markedly deictic in its references to other online events, mediations, and conversations (de Moor & Efimova 2004). Researchers have used blogging to build their own mediated, reflective practice. The Norwegian researcher, educator, and blogger, Torill Mortensen, has named her blog *thinking with my fingers*. Writing for an audience can serve to structure thought and provide rehearsals and repositories for future use (Nardi et al. 2004a: 44-45).

Mortensen and Walker (2002) discuss the personal character of blogging as an online research tool. They reflect on the ways in which their own blogs have impacted on their research methods, thinking, and modes of writing. They note (Mortensen & Walker 2002: 252) that, although they find popular writings on blogs and a network of bloggers who feed one another's interests and knowledge, to date no research has been carried out on blogging. Their publication, therefore, offers a first: It points to their own experience as composers of blogs and as educators using blogs as part of their digitally mediated pedagogy. More important, as humanists, it is evidence of their hybrid writing. For Mortensen and Walker (2002: 261),

> Weblogs are written in order to share experiences rather than just display them.... Where academic writing is structured by the rules of the causal argument, a weblog is structured by time and impulses of the day, documenting rather than structuring the trail of thought.

For these researcher-bloggers, Web writing via blogs connects available information connotatively (Mortensen & Walker 2002).

Soon after Mortensen and Walker (2002: 250) each established their own blogs, these '. . . developed beyond being digital ethnographers' journals and into a hybrid between journal, academic publishing, storage place for links and site for academic discourse.'[3] Although blogger-researchers see blogging as a means of reaching beyond the formal discourses and arenas of the academy, they have pointed to the multigenre and multivoicedness of the professional and the personal in blogging. Their blogs became more than a means of multiple expression and linking; they became tools through which to reflect on and conduct research (Mortensen & Walker 2002; Kolb 1996). Yet few other scholars have noted that blogging may preempt more scholarly presentation of the innovative or insightful ideas that are the currency of academic success contained in formal publication (Mortensen & Walker 2002: 262-263).

Blogs and Process

In the writings of communicatively astute bloggers, entries anticipate that readers are following an unfolding process. Posts have an associative quality that promotes reading across individual entries and connects to other leading blogs. Yet entries often occur as the blogger finds the time, motivation, and need to publish them. Stylistically, they offer readers a domain in which fresh, noteworthy, and appointed views, information, and references may be consumed. Skilled bloggers create an appetite through their own posts, as each of these exists on its own or as a linked entry. Mortensen and Walker (2002: 266) claim that 'Weblogs are written continuously and published without being revised.' Tonally, they have a fresh, at times unfinished, spontaneous quality, but software allows revision. Mortensen (2004b) refers to the way in which a blog may be read as a dialogue in slow motion.

Blogs are also being used in experimental pedagogies. Krause (2004) reports that unclear instructions about students' participation, the number of expected posts, and processes of their discussion during a semester course can lead to disinterest and few entries being made over time. He sees blogs as not having the literal exchanges we see in e-mail or on lists. Developing a blog with a group of diverse participants, some of whom have choreography as their primary activity, can therefore also be rather risky. That dancers are often not encouraged to write about their dance making also adds to the potential for nonparticipation.

In *Docudancing*, we needed to find ways to include and motivate the dancers and other participants to engage in the overall project of making the performance work (shown in a visualization of the choreography in Figure 9.4) and finding different media to communicate their experiences and interests. The blog was, therefore, also a tool in the choreographic process: It was a site through which the dancers could view the processes of their own project work and many of the inner thoughts of the choreographer who had involved them closely in the design and development process. There appears to still be relatively little linking between blogging and ethnographic discourse production.

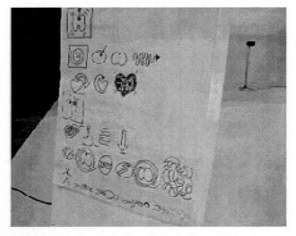

Figure 9.4. Photograph of schematic drawing of elements in the choreography always on the rehearsal room wall.

TRANSVERSING BOUNDARIES

On Mediated Action

In *Voices of the Mind*, Wertsch (1991) positions the work of Bakhtin and Vygotsky as central to developing a sociocultural approach to meaning making. In this approach, meaning making takes place through processes of negotiation and mediation. Analytically, we draw on the work of Bakhtin (1981, 1983) and his concepts of partiality or unfinishedness, addressivity, polyvocality, and chronotype. These concepts provide some means of getting at the processes and mediations of blogging as a socially mediated online activity (see e.g., Figure 9.5). Strong links between the

Figure 9.5. Entry by media researcher on polyvocal discourse.

social semiotic approaches to language and critical and mediated discourse studies and activity theory are not often made. We make a clear connection between situated and polyvocal articulations and their positions in the discursive contexts and traditions of dance writing and analysis. Attention to aspects of the discourse processes of blogging offers some material for further discussion of critical discourse analysis and online communicative processes as mediated action.

SOCIAL LANGUAGE AND SPEECH GENRES

Although there is a large body of work on Bakhtin and literary and genre studies, little work appears in applying the related approaches of activity theory to the activities and processes involved in artistic meaning making and less still to that of artists and researchers in the performing arts. To venture here is to broaden the attention that activity theory gives to language as the medium for meaning making into how 'languaging' via a medley of media may be understood in multiply made activities. Naturally, language does influence the histories and emerging practices of organizations and the socializations that influence articulations by individuals. Bakhtin named this 'social language,' referring to the fact that communication is always dialogic, shifting between parties to an event, or partners in what Wertsch calls 'communicative action.' However, these social languages are learned through exposure, participation, and use in context. Wertsch (1991) stresses the importance of appropriation of our social languages—that this is, in part, historical but also a process of acquisition and identity-building. In this process, we engage in layers of address and socially and culturally inherited ventriloquizing of communicative forms and formulations (Bakhtin 1984).

Where an individual speaker is always communicating in a web of discourse relations, Bakhtin also saw genre as critical to enabling and constituting such discourse. He used the term 'speech genres' to encompass the typical means and contexts of communicating on which we draw and without which we are not able to give shape to our utterances. These schematic aspects are, however, not necessarily visible to us in our uses of them. We need to pay attention to both the boundedness of genres and our expectations of them in contexts of use and dynamic enactment.

Bakhtin and Dialogicality

We refer closely to Bakhtin's concepts of polyvocality and chronotype. We see this move as enriching recent writings on multimodality that are grounded in social semiotic approaches to communication and its design, realization, and analysis (Kress & van Leeuwen 2001). Such approaches largely neglect intersections between rhetoric and interaction design, with blogs being a multigenre designed for active composition and online engagement. In his diverse writings, Bakhtin (1981, 1984, 1986) approaches language as the primary means of mediating social action. He argues that language needs to be viewed as a socially shaped engagement that is realized dialogically (Halasek 1999). In this realization, what is primary is the function of the utterance at the level of discourse as the motor for meaning making (and not so much lexicogrammar operating in the clause). 'Speech genres' was the term Bakhtin used to refer to this level of articulation.

Heteroglossia and Polyphony

This dialogical quality of communication is built pluralistically through multiple voices and perspectives. Bakhtin labeled this 'heteroglossia.' Multiple voices form a polyphonic text that necessarily inscribes preceding forms and functionalities. At the same time, communicative meanings are socially enacted through relations between the 'speaker' and the addressee. Although he viewed socially and historically tempered speech as polyphonic and emergent, living and vibrant in their responsivity, Bakhtin insisted that communicative events and their texturing always bear a surplus of meaning (see e.g., Figure 9.6).

The dialogical nature of such communication positions it as open to being specified and realigned in use through interaction and often without a specific predetermined structure. Our dialogizing as the active building of intersubjectivity involves us in the ongoing shaping of meaning beyond the inner speech of the individual and psychological models concerned with such representation. Our discourses remain unfinished works, in that they are in a process of being developed in time and space. Here, *différence* is important as a marker of the relationships that arise between utterances (e.g., Shields 1996). They are related to wider significations and intersections with other texts, patterns, and utterances in chains of ongoing addressivity. Further, when different voices speak, they invoke those of others, leading Bakhtin (1984) to call this ventriloquy.

Adding personal character is needed on the part of the speaker for this to change from being the recirculation of an inherited voice to that of his or her own. Here a move toward the expression and thus formation of identity shifts the speaker from a mode of mimicry to one of self-articulation and intentionality. Bakhtin also made extensive use of parody as a means of showing how different stances and reflexive overtones on positions and perspectives may be signaled and set against one another. Appropriation of speech conventions alone is inadequate; mastery of

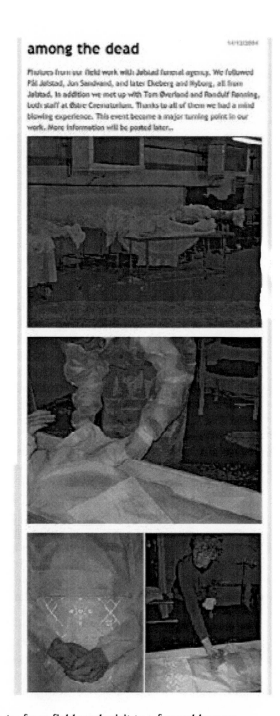

Figure 9.6. Images from field work visit to a funeral bureau.

272

them occurs through appointed, purposive ownership that is shaped through understanding the mutuality involved in making hybrid constructions and discourse.

Centifugal Forces

Language is more than a language: It is the medley of cultural and historical discourses, their layers, and the intertextualities that makes language a heterogeneous space of potential meaning making. The activity of language may be understood in terms of translinguistics. Here, Bakhtin (1981) made the key distinction between activities that authoritatively serve to fix or transform language, prefiguring much of the later work of critical linguistics and critical discourse analysis (see Chapter 2). Bakhtin saw forces that stablilize and maintain language roles and standards as centripetal.

Opposed to these are centrifugal forces that are associated with persuasion and transformation. They contribute to language as a multiply made resource for meaning making, in which emergence and change are partners. Text types, norms, and practices thus come into being through their enactment as socially produced discourse. Carrying with them their legacies, discourse is realized in and through social action. In studying emergent and centrifugal online discourses, we reach toward novel utterances possible through exchange and linked utterances that are built through the mixing and recombinations of elements that are at the same time known and evolving.

Chronotopic Discourse

Social language, as Bakhtin called it, also stretches across time and space. He used the term 'chronotope' to heuristically encapsulate these dimensions in 'Forms of time and of the chronotope in the novel: notes towards a historical poetics' (Bakhtin 1981). As a space-time figure (Allan, 1994), the chronotope is the place where narrative knots are tied and untied so that 'Time becomes, in effect, palpable and visible; the chronotype makes narrative events concrete, makes them take on flesh, causes blood to flow in their veins . . .' (Bakhtin 1981: 250).

In this giving of narrative life, the real and fictional or represented world is in mutual interaction, enriching one another. The real world continually feeds the constructed one that is the event narrated through the involvement and contributions of listeners and readers (Bakhtin 1981: 254). By extension, it is further constituted in other modes of discourse through more explicitly external production, as well as by speakers and writers. Bakhtin (1981: 254) continues to say that 'We might even speak of a special creative chronotope inside which this exchange between work and life occurs, and which constitutes the distinctive life of the work.' In such an elastic environment (see also Allen 1994), events and the words used to depict them take place in different times, have different duration, and occur in different spaces. They amount to a narrative, discursive, and communicative whole that Bakhtin sees as creating the fullness and indivisibility of the work.

Yet within the dialogical, their lies not just a distinction between story and discourse, or between plot and plotted, but the materialization of time in space—that is, between speakers and across utterances as discourse in the making. Here, discourse is embedded in action, and specific chronotopes may thus not be visible to participants in a discourse exchange or event. Further, as Scholz (1998: 161) argues, because a chronotope '. . . is a principle of sequentially and appositionally ordering of a manifold of events,' it needs to be seen as a principle for generating the plots of narratives. There are four levels: the concrete narrative text, its plot, the plot structure, and the related chronotype. In this way, Bakhtin diverts from Kant's abstract, given unitary time space and offers one in which manifold dimensions run across one another, historically, in their duration and in the immediacy of their enactment. Thus, as Scholz suggests, we are able to enter into the inside and the outside of the chronotope through attention to its multilinear temporality and thereby transverse time and space through their relations and intersections.

In a poststructuralist narrative and temporally acute landscape, we might also say that discourse as socially mediated action is in a state of perpetual becoming, in which pieces and parts intersect, recombine, and diverge in processes of understanding and interpretation. In this way, meaning making is shaped and emerges through the intersections of teller and tellings, reader-writers, and intertextual linkages (see e.g., Figure 9.7). This is especially so for Web text.

Hooman Shariffi at Mister India. Reflecting on my artistic exploration

a long evening with Hooman, discussing work, experiences and the politics of art (not so much art politics in general, but aims and direction in our work). He showed me the flyer of his new solo with the great title "we failed to hold this reality in mind", a quote from Virginia Woolf that he had found in Susan Sontags "Regarding the Pain of Others" (2003). A book that I have already got for my preparations working with Part 3. He reminded me of another voice in that respect: Hannah Arendt and her book "Judgement and Responsibility."

Figure 9.7. Entry on discussion with a fellow choreographer.

Bakhtin and Web text

Although Bakhtin's concepts were derived from and applied to the novel, they are well suited equally to digitally mediated domains. However, there appears to be relatively little use of his concepts in the study of more recent forms of Web text after that of earlier hypertext-imbued studies. Killoran (2005) refers to monologism and dialogism in the study of environmental discourse online, in which Web sites are rhetorically shaped to curtail or critique the nature of discursive debate about the environment, and forestry in particular. Through a dialogical analysis, Killoran shows how preferred governmental perspectives are mediated. Blogs may thus be seen as part of the emergent practice of civic discourse between publics and the state (Killoran 2003).

Wertsch (1991) discusses the centrality of meaning to a sociocultural approach to mediated action. Following Holquist, Wertsch suggests we extend the underlying Bakhtin question concerning addressivity 'Who is doing the talking'? to that of meaning-making processes by asking 'Who owns the meaning'? (see Pierroux, Chapter 13). Wertsch (1991: 86) says that, in Bakhtin's approach to meaning making 'It is by appropriating, or populating, social languages and speech genres that utterrances take on their meaning.' This appropriation takes places through the person as agent acting with the mediational means available to them. The unit of analysis that Wertsch (1991) hones in on is mediated action.

Meaning Making via Mediated Social Action

In the case of the blog as a site for social language, multiple voices may be included across time and the extent of the discourse embodied therein. Blog software provides an overall frame that needs to be given character in terms of genre. This demands choices and direction by the blogger. Different multimedia tools may be used to enable the 'talking,' that is, in terms of layout and styling via CSS, via photo software, video compression, and via written text. Who owns the meaning is ultimately a question of how polyphonic discourse is realized through utterances that are found in socioculturally situated contexts and modes of articulation.

As Wertsch (1991: 119) asserts, 'Only by being part of action do mediational means come into being and play their role. They have no magical power in and of themselves.' In the next section, we discuss how a particular authoring tool and a range of media types and software applications were used by a range of individuals taking part in a shared creative process of reflecting on dance making. As Wertsch (1991: 96) argues, we need to escape the notion of possession of mediational tools and offer '. . .

some sort of account of the organisation of mediational means. . . .' Here, we how and why different tools, modes, and media were taken up as part of our polyphonic online discourse processes.

ANALYZING DOCUDANCING

Orientation

We now look more closely at the dialogism of the blog through three main concepts 1) polyphony; 2) tools, signs, and mediation; and 3) chronotopic discourse. We offer a closer reading of the design, composition, and uses of the blog as process in which the overall ethos was one of a contextual, accumulative, participatory design.

Polyphony

The overall experimental, practice-based research and choreography project *Life & Death* has three parts. The first is strongly personal for Per Roar, taking the form of a danced solo memoria of a severely disabled friend, Martin Hoftun, who died in an aeroplane accident in Nepal. Documentary reaches into the performance space through video of movement within Oxford University, where they studied together, as well as of Martin's childhood self. The second work, discussed later, is more experiential and existential. It draws the dancers and audience into the projected movement of internal medical imaging technologies followed by procedures for cremation accompanied by the on-stage appearance of two funeral home professionals. The third work addresses communal, historical, and situated loss drawn from the war in the Balkans in the 1990s. This work, like the first one, included visits, rehearsals, and performances by the choreographer and dancers in context (see Figure 9.8).

At the widest level, the overall choreography project gives voice to these different perspectives around a common topos (Figure 9.9). The blog provides access to the three processes of design, development, and realization. The choreographer as writer is predominant in the blog; however, he often summarizes discussions and developments in gathering ideas, material, and processes involved in this. In addition, he provides overviews and insights into the events and collaboration on specific days when the process is particularly fruitful and challenging. He writes knowing that the dancers are his readers as well as contributors to the blog. Thus, the blog serves as a local externalization of a shared process so that the dancers who are busy on their actual dancing are also able to read and review their choreographer's reflections as the work progresses.

Visits to the funeral home, which included seeing their first dead bodies and learning about the processes of preparation for burial and cremation, were difficult for the dancers and the choreographer. They needed to observe the tone and sense of state, as well as think backward into the movement of life, of processes of gradual and rapid change, decay, and limitations on movement. The choreographer involved his dancers in understanding movement as also halted, interrupted, reduced, and graded across time and in time. The dancers would also be involved in conveying this to the audience through their own movements, showing changes in states from dying to deceased to disintegration. Each entry provides an angle on the process, and in the case of the visit to the funeral home, and later the Balkans, the dancers also blog on the same day, posting their own images, too. Photographs were important here, as is discussed later.

Figure 9.8. Blogging by bus, en route to rehearsal and review in Stockholm. Peder Horsen (left) and Terje Tjöme Mossige (right) with laptop and mobile phone.

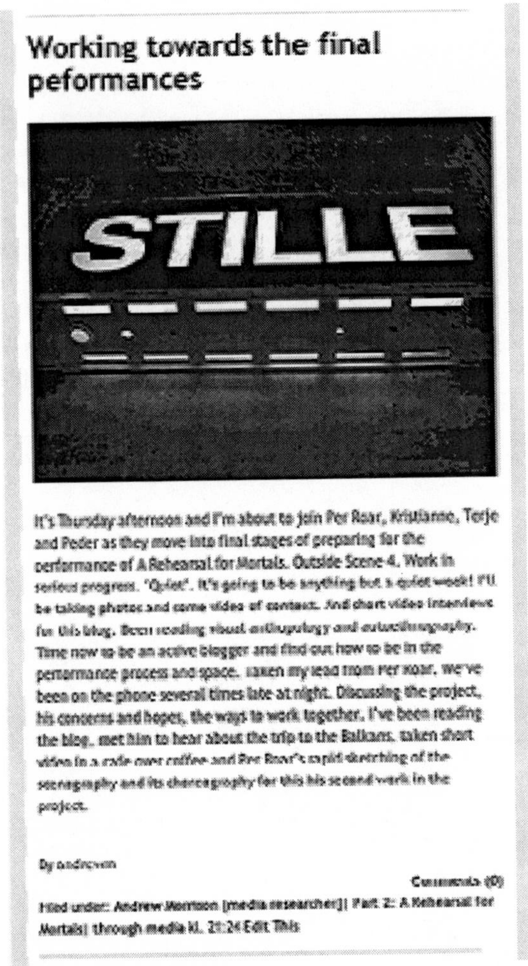

Working towards the final peformances

It's Thursday afternoon and I'm about to join Per Roar, Kristianne, Terje and Peder as they move into final stages of preparing for the performance of A Rehearsal for Mortals. Outside Scene 4. Work in serious progress. "Quiet". It's going to be anything but a quiet week! I'll be taking photos and some video of context. And short video interviews for this blog. Been reading visual anthropology and autoethnography. Time now to be an active blogger and find out how to be in the performance process and space. Taken my lead from Per Roar, we've been on the phone several times late at night. Discussing the project, his concerns and hopes, the ways to work together. I've been reading the blog, met him to hear about the trip to the Balkans, taken short video in a cafe over coffee and Per Roar's rapid sketching of the scenography and its choreography for this his second work in the project.

By andrcven

Commentals (0)

Filed under: Andrew Morrison (media researcher)| Part 2: A Rehearsal for Mortals| through media kl. 21:24 Edit This

Figure 9.9. Calm before the storm.

The original intention was that the dancers would also be active bloggers. In effect, their blogging was restricted by time—by their own creative processes that were being written in and through their bodies. In discussion, they often commented that they found the process of developing the choreography in which they had an active role to be intense. They needed to process much contextual material and develop aspects of it themselves, with the choreographer, and then together in rehearsal. Often they said they had little energy to blog after a long day of physical and creative work. However, they were usually motivated to discuss the process; Per Roar took the initiative to summarize their comments into the blog, ventriloquizing their views (Figure 9.10).

video editing yesterday's inspiration into tomorrow's moves

I am still looking at video shots of the dancers, apparently finishing my first rough drafts of the last 15 minutes by tomorrow morning. Then starts a week of work for the dancers to get that sketch into their bodies, before we can start to think about the stage presentation and to pull out the nuances in the material. One phase is nearly over for me, my eyes are sore and tired. Though it will still take some more hours before I am done.

By Per Roar

Comments (0)

Filed under: at work| Per Roar [choreographer]| Part 2: A Rehearsal for Mortals| through media id. 23:33

Figure 9.10. Relationships of live and stored performance.

Entries by the different participants in the project are also accessible via the blog menu; it is possible to see only the dancers' posts or those, for example, by the media researcher and his uses of photographs in the final rehearsal phase. Blog entries, as is usually the case, also point to external links, events, and views. However, *Docudancing* was largely a documentation and process site for the internal participants. At the time in early 2005, we found few other blog sites on dance that delved deeply inside the processes of choreography. We were fortunate to receive one such site via e-mail. Posts were also included from the blog site designer, a media researcher at the first full rehearsals of the work, and some of the audience members from the full performances.

No dancer or participant took over the main blogging role from the choreographer. He remained the primary blogger and presented his creative and reflective views on the process, often blogging at points of tension, need, and breakthrough. His posts record that close and detailed discussion has taken place offline, thereby voicing in digital from what has taken place verbally. These comments and discussion also took place during the dance sessions. The blog was also referred to in these discussions, providing a double loop between the already articulated and its critical review and connection (see e.g., Figure 9.9). For different participants and for the group, the blog functioned as a site for the processing of a process (Figure 9.11) and as a means of documenting this process in a more reflected, artistic, research voice. For Per Roar, this was particularly important in making a link between composing dance works involving documentary and documenting his creative process. As discussed later, video was also used in posts.

Figure 9.11. Kristianne Mo working with video of her own choreography-performance.

Tools, Signs, and Mediation

In an activity theory frame, blogging software operates as a tool, enabling online communication mediated through a variety of media types. These media types are employed to articulate the dance-making process and its related concepts, narratives, and content. These are each positioned in relation to four broad categories set up in the blog tool: 'at work,' 'through media,' 'in the world,' and 'as research.' The interface is not imported from a set of templates provided by a blog service. Specific styling is inscribed via the underlying CSS in the choices of fonts, color, layout, and weighting. Images and video are designed to appear within the main window of an entry.

Written entries vary considerably in length. This was a deliberate decision so as to motivate readers to look into the text, which was made of different layers and styles of writing. At times long texts are accompanied by images, but at times they are not (e.g., Figure 9.10). Equally, photographs and drawings are used alone, usually with a short contextual clarification, as well as with longer written pieces. Per Roar too uploaded entries on behalf of the dancers.

A digital video camera, still camera, and laptop were made available to the choreographer and dancers. All the participants also had mobile phones from which it was intended images and text would be uploaded. We discussed this as one means of entering short comments and insights, along with related images. Technically, this was harder for the dancers to use than anticipated, given their phone models and means of connection. The video camera was used to record sketching, early versions, and fuller rehearsal sequences. We anticipated that the laptop would be used to blog in the rehearsal room, perhaps between or at the close of sessions. In practice, this proved to be too diffuse an activity for the dancers and choreographer who needed to concentrate on their production of a dance work. Clearly, there were two different activity systems in play. Reflection and postings tended to follow long practice sessions and were often composed later at night. However, the camera and laptop came to be actively used in the rehearsal room. The camera was connected to a large monitor and used for quick replay and review. However, as the process of making the work was interrupted, in a sense, by the need to plan and prepare the third piece in the form of a visit to the Balkans, digitized video of the whole piece and individual elements and dancers' movements become crucial.

The dancers needed to refer back to this video as a point of prior achievement and reference. Here, the laptop became a tool not for blogging but for replaying video sequences in the desktop video software *iMovie*. In particular, one of the dancers, Kristianne Mo, made repeated and extensive use of the video sequences, often taking the laptop with her onto the stage and retracing aspects of her recent movement, splicing her actual just danced actions with those previously shaped (Figure 9.11). The material on the screen became a schema for reflecting on what she had immediately performed. What was interesting in this dancing with technology was that this dancer moved through her paces, as it were, turning and dipping, always with her eyes fixed on the screen, not unlike the ways dancers 'mark' their sequences rather than dance them out in full. That she did this without looking at the stage and that the others present did not interrupt her was also a specific feature of the way in which individual space for reflection, recall, and reshaping took form. Kristianne did not return to the original improvisational material developed at the start but to points in the compressed and resequenced material given by the choreographer. This took place alongside movements in which the choreographer joined the two other dancers to discuss an aspect of their dancing. Together, space and movement through it were multiply and simultaneously made. The edited video became a dancing artifact and an artifact that was danced. Photographs were included extensively in *Docudancing*, with permissions, from visits to the funeral home so as to also provide external participants with some sense of the context. In the blog, these also served to selectively situate the design and development process as documentary rather than to merely provide an extensive visual contextualization as has been criticized in some photoblogging (Cohen 2005).

In sessions on dance involving documentary media, photos also introduced strong images of stillness. Figure 9.12 is an assemblage of images from one of the visits to the funeral home. We see lives that have passed and are yet present, contained, yet poised in the back of a double-layer hearse. Absent are figures that are breathless and motionless, now lodged in the genre of the blog with its propensity toward active replacement, posts that are so often in motion, tumbling one after the other to the top of the screen.

Photos were often used to mark that the activity has been continuing. Sometimes these were used as placeholders for writing that was subsequently entered. Composite blocks of images were also included, varying the resolution and variety of visual postings. Large images were also often included so as to provide details and generate a blog that was visually varied and strong in character. In addition to photos of contexts such as the funeral home, we also included images from the performance space. The blog has images of the various participants at work: dancers, designers, choreographic expert. Images from the mixing desk are also included.

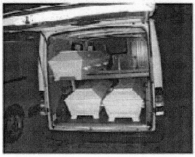

Figure 9.12. Transitional passages in *A Rehearsal for Mortals*.

Here (Figure 9.13), two images show long and near views. The first is of the number of screens and the large projection space at the back of the stage at first used for the projection of online Bingo. The performance begins with the audience filling in Bingo cards from a simulated live multi-venue Bingo game. Such games are directed by one caller and are displayed in multiple windows. The closeup is of the algorithmic arrangement of the digital video sequences and sound in *Max Studio Pro*. These trackings helped deliver images such as that shown in the entry 'Core images from performance.' The large landscape screen at the back of the stage was constructed to be raised and lowered, as well as to allow for images from two projectors.

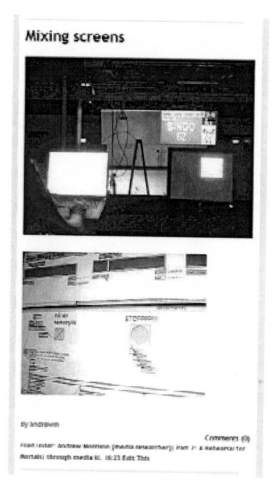

Figure 9.13. Views from the 'screening' room.

Chronotopic Discourse

Many blogs do not have a formal and explicitly long-term status. They are scripted by individual authors who have strong motivation and are keen to articulate their views, experience, and insights. Some blogs are dormant for long stretches, whereas others track a specific theme or interest and then move on to other ones. It takes effort to blog consistently and with quality. Multiply authored blogs such as some of those appearing in rhetoric and new media studies are the result of years of shared interest and at times copublication in other domains, such as Web projects and academic papers. Blogs such as these provide invaluable perspectives on contemporary issues and developments, as well as references to historical and related material. Project-based blogs, lodged between the academy and the art world, PhD-centered blogs, those by often younger untenured faculty, are bracketed by funding and participation connected to specific work, degrees, and courses. Through these blogs, rich resources and connections have been forged.

The *Docudancing* blog stretches over a 3-year period with three individual choreographic works. The blog shows that choreography is a multicursive activity. Earlier, we saw that a chart that visualized major components of the work was stuck onto the rehearsal wall. These components were developed as part of both a linear and nonsequential design process, as well as being potential elements in the combination of a coherent piece. This making and finding form occurred over time and was blogged as the work developed, turned back on itself, reappointed early movements, and began to take shape as a whole. The method of workshopping and building a dance work through collaboration is used in choreography, but this is what is often not documented as part of a creative, emergent artistic design process. Recombinations and refinements are thus mentioned and discussed in the blog. It provides traces of development over time.

During the developmental trajectory of the second dance work *A Rehearsal for Mortals*, it was necessary to begin the choreography of the third piece in the project, *An Unfinished Story*. Whereas *Rehearsals* involved the dancers and choreographer in visits to a funeral home, to meetings with experts on internal medicine, and to nights of rather unwilling competition in bingo halls, this next work included visits to the Former Republic of Yugoslavia (FYR), crossing war and peace lines, first to Sarajevo and then Belgrade. The first of these visits had a major impact on the dancers in particular. The choreographer had worked in the region prior to the breakup of Yugoslavia and the ensuing wars. In developing *Unfinished*, the dancers were drawn deeply into the context out of and about which the work communicates nonverbally. Having followed the lines of life and death inside and outside the body and with the living and the dead—from observing embalming and preparation for burial to seeing the mechanics of cremation—the dancers now encountered the complexities of collective and competing histories of war and survival.

Although two quite distinct artistic and choreographic activities were in progress, they had a clear influence on one another. The development of *Rehearsals* and the attention to the corporeal and the existential prepared the dancers for their entry into matters of how communities cope with loss as a shared, collective, and public process. *An Unfinished Story* is not designed as a dance drama but has been developed in conjunction with Bosnian and Serbian partners using nonverbal communication by sampling and incorporating traditional folk dance with contemporary dance vocabularies and movements. Here, the question, after Bakhtin, is one of who owns the answering. The dance work attempts to engage with painful and wrenching issues in recent European history and to take up the problems of public acknowledgment and private grief at a time when the Hague War Crimes Tribunal has been able to make limited progress.

The answering is a delicate move, offered through composition with local participants to audiences first in the FYR and only second in Oslo. In both of these dance works, however, the audience members are shown aspects of their own vitality and mortality, in works that are vicarious yet refer to loss, destruction, gradual decay, and sudden stoppage. In this sense, the blog entries are like a pulse that follows the dancer and choreographic progress into the performance space and then after its closure, its completion as timed utterance, back onto the screen as reflection and review.

In preparation for understanding this context of 'being' and movement, and some sense of the physicality and psychological trauma of the events, in July 2005, the choreographer and three dancers joined the 3-day march back to Srebrenica for the ceremony that marked the loss of thousands of Bosnian boys and men at the hands of Serb aggressors. The blog has entries on this visit and the dancers' views and feelings. Video in the blog also gives the dancers' own voicing about the importance of situated learning in *A Rehearsal for Mortals* and *An Unfinished Story*.

Although these two dance works crossed over and influenced one another, blending their outer narrative lines and inner processings, photographs became an important marker of the place and points at which the text could be read chronotopically. Reflections might refer to the events of one day or the wider sense of meeting a world recovering from but also concealing human tragedy and destruction.

CONCLUSION

Multifolded Mediation

In his reading of the dance piece *Panoramix* by La Ribot, André Lepecki (2006: 86) says it 'Acts in the present tense while pushing the past against the future of the memory.' Time, deixis, memory, movement. The same could be said about the nature of grief and the processes involved in the polyvocal and multimodal blogging of the ephemeral in *Docudancing*. Lepecki (2006: 86) continues:

> Here, the past emerges as contemporaneous to the present that has
> been and extends itself as matter-memory. And what is that being
> that constantly performs this weaving of contemporaneity into past-
> ness and back from the future if not the body–moving its presence
> not in a spatial grid, but in the multifolded dimensionality of its unsta-
> ble, slanted, oblique throwness into time?

In this chapter, we outlined how blogs may be realized as discourse in
action, by acts of not simply mediated action but *mediating* action. This is
both a matter of the ways in which mediating may be realized via media
and the processes of mediating action. The mediating artifact of the blog
offered an online means of composing and distributing a process of artistic development, broader than microlevel details of movements. We have
shown how photographs were used to mark various points in the process,
giving anchors for review and reflection, partnering the nonverbal movement of the dancers. Images and video were also accompanied by written
text varying in tone and text type. Material from the wider contexts on
which the works drew was included in posts that reached forward in
anticipation of the possible inclusion, albeit indirectly and indexically, in a
final live performance.

Together, through the structure of main categories, calendar, and thematic threadings across time, the blog may be said to be a site for multiple mediations as chrontotope. Mediated activity is narrated but in an
online domain in which movements occur from place to place, by category, from context of funeral bureau, medical imaging lab, laptop screenspace, video software, and the spatial and temporal arrangements of the
recontextualizations of these movements in a choreographic work. In
these transversals (Lemke 2005: 113-114), so too may *Docudancing* be
seen as a semiotic artifact that realizes differing but related timescales
(Lemke 2000). In this sense, it is also heterochronic.

Given this attention to tools and articulation, we may ask a key question: Did the blog make a change in the activity of the choreographic
process, and did it change practice? The blog did make a change in the
activity of the choreographic process. It provided the choreographer with
a 'stage' that called for a selection of entries. This stage challenged him
but also offered the choreographer a bird's eye perspective in the midst of
the heat of the work, by forcing him to situate and present the work
process as it unfolded. As the work with the blog developed, it became
clear that the entries were neither text nor images only, but rather the
composite of these two as well as in relation to earlier postings.

It became apparent rather immediately that the dancers used the blog
only when time was set aside during our rehearsal time because they were
involved with other engagements running parallel to the rehearsal period.
Inside the rehearsal itself, it was demanding for them to switch between

Departures

This is the final image we see as the audience after the dancers leave through this door in the foyer. The performances are now over. Sunday's being technically tighter. Per Roar's off to Belgrade on Saturday to plan the next work. No time to waste.

This image suggests a certain finality. The brushed concrete wall is immense, the doors firmly closed within them. Two panels, parallel. But there's also another sense. To the left the cloudy blue panel suggests a different space, one of light, of buoyancy and ultimately that of of progression. A space the audience shares. One that is constructed, has patterns and textures, where materiality is static and yet moves.

Figure 9.14. View after the performance.

intense states of physical exploration and to find adequate words for expressing these experiences. This process of working with the blog in the studio in the early period in Part 2 helped them to keep logbooks more diligently than they otherwise would have done. Although they maintained these logbooks throughout, they rarely transposed their comments over to the blog. The application of video for making short interviews as well as still images taken by the dancers later on in the process turned out to be more successful. However, this time it was the choreographer who was too busy to organize the editing of the material and upload to the blog. It became plain that to follow the process deeply, as an ethnographic account would have demanded, required an extra person who facilitated that process with uploading and formatting of images and video, but that would have been another project entirely.

For the dancers, the blog became a 'scroll' of the work, which impressed them as its depictions reminded them of the immensity of the activity and the intensity of exposures they had been processing. The blog made the work of making choreography visible and manifest as an object of itself in the world, and it contributed to their investment into the project. Through the blog as a mediating artefact, the project became visible as an endeavour larger than the dancers themselves and the choreographer's daily requests. It served to convey aspects of respect for delicate events and emotions, and it helped the dancers to be cautious or self-critical in their consideration of what to publish. Despite such a reserve and the boundaries on making entries, the blog enabled the dancers to think about articulation and situate themselves in a longer and complex process of becoming. For colleagues on site and for audiences online, closely following the project as it developed, the blog became a core of informed and critical mediation, which looked onward to the next public showing and opened out for view into its construction over time. By following the blog, these readers and commentators represented another kind of audience—they were not only looking for a spectacle to unfold but also were interested in how the process was manifested and could be related to its experimental staging.

Docudancing as 'Polyblogue'

In keeping with many of the writings cited earlier in the chapter, we see that blogs are indeed heterotopic spaces. Lambert (2005) argues that:

> Foucault's (1986) notion of heterotopic space (as sites of relationships that are always multiple) helps to account for some of the ways we inhabit so-called "real" space, network space, web space, and cyberspace at the same time. We crossover between physical/material spaces and conceptual spaces, with the ability to make multiple connections within each.

In its crossovers, *Docudancing* evinces many of the features of Bakhtin's dialogical, polyphonic, and chronotopic discourse. However, the blog is not merely the testimony, record, or musings of one individual but a shared space that is one part of a process of making three dance works over a period of 3 years. In this sense, *Docudancing* may be seen not merely as a Bakhtinian polylogue but a *polyblogue*, a mixture of speaking positions and their technologically mediated online articulations. 'Poly' refers to the diversity of authors, styles, and participants. 'Blog' refers to a potentially diverse genre of logged online communication characterized by it formal-informal and personal-public qualities. The tail end '-gue' refers to not just dialogue but both the polylogue and the blog as a site and an articulation of hybrid, multiple voices, and expressive forms.

The blog provides an experimental space for articulating a diversity of interlaced but also divergent ideas and perspectives. These are expressed in writing but also through other media. Here we may see this as choreographing a composition. When Peggy Phelan (1995) presented her influential 'Thirteen ways of looking at *choreographing* writing,' blogs did not exist—she might have included them as an addition. Beyond 'writing,' in *Docudancing*, a single photograph may be all there is in an entry, although usually some context is given. Yet this image functions differently for participants in the project, at once a reminder of an event, or a particular discussion, a place marker in a sequence, a still mirror for the moving self. As Brooke (2005) has observed, we meet

> . . . a relatively stable space for variation, a deictic system for writing, that only partly overlaps with the expectations typically found in the writing classroom. Blogs allow for a proliferation of discursive gestures, both centripetal and centrifugal, both inward and outward, but these various gestures aren't all equally valued in pedagogical contexts.

As an experiment in reflection on composition as composition, in *Docudancing*, multimodality found its own movement between the many demands of developing dance works collaboratively: participation was optional, production teams changed somewhat, and dancers were absorbed at times by other schedules and productions so that it was impossible to produce a tidy, seamless text. The rough edges and contours of anguish and relief as the works emerged are shown in the blog, so that the genres of diary, ethnographic reflection, and process reporting are copresent. In addition to mediating discourses of dance making in action in an online form, the blog also became a shared object for the discussion of creativity, art-based research, modes of writing about choreography, and research rhetoric online. In short, it was the chronotopic materialization of multicompositional process.

On Kairotopic and Kinetitopic Discourse

Docudancing offers a shared and emerging forum, both in time and in relation to dance discourse, for building a record of processes of making dance works and addressing their creative and collaborative genesis. It is partial, it addresses the ephemeral, and it is not a documentary or an ethnography composed by a lone writer from field notes, but a mode of noting in the field, as movement, reminding us of the insistent partnering of dynamic media and information systems in a digital age realized as mediated discourse in action.

In acknowledging and performing these articulations as dynamic and transformative compositions, we have taken up Bakhtin's concept of the chronotope. But for us there is now more. It is movement that also matters—as mediated scenography, in vlogging (video-based blogging), in our own paces, and in participation in mixed-reality environments. In digitally mediated compositions and multimodal discourse, we sense, experience, and analyze time space, that is, the chronotope. Yet increasingly we are caught up in mediating artifacts that are dynamic and demand us to shift, bounce, leap, and linger. This activity involves us in what we label the *kairotope:* being prepared for, recognizing, and acting at the opportune time. Rhetorically, this is now a matter for enactment in digitally mediated discourses. We also need to develop sharper means for analyzing the temporal and textual transversals in such movement space, that is, the *kinetitope*, or kinetic. At this point, these two concepts—*kairotope* and *kinetitope*—remain somewhat ephemeral, but blogging as mediated action has helped us to locate them, if only fleetingly.

NOTES

1. See http://kairosnews.org/node/3719?PHPSESSID = 3a1bdbe21ff59ada96ccd78 51491a511
2. See the Crooked Timber blog (http://www.crookedtimber.org/).
3. We acknowledge these Norwegian blogger researchers writing in English as influences on our research. Fagerjord: http://www.media.uio.no/personer/ andersf/blog/), Walker on hypernarrative (http://jilltxt.net/), and Mortensen (http://torillsin.blogspot.com/), especially on gaming.

REFERENCES

Aarseth, Espen. (1997). *Cybertext*. Baltimore: The Johns Hopkins University Press.
Allan, Stuart. (1994). '"When discourse is torn from reality": Bakhtin and the principle of chronotopicity.' *Time and Society*. Vol. 3, No. 2, 193-218.
Bakhtin, Mikhail. (1981). *The Dialogic Imagination: Four Essays by M.M Bakhtin*. Holquist, Michael. (Ed.). Emerson, Caryl & Holquist, Michael (Trans.). Austin: University of Texas Press Press.
Bakhtin, Mikhail. (1984). *Problems of Dostoevsky's Poetics*. Emerson, Caryl. (Ed. & Trans.). Minneapolis: University of Minnesota Press.

Bakhtin, Mikhail. (1986). *Speech Genres and Other Late Essays*. Emerson, Caryl, & Holquist, Michael. (Eds.). McGee, Vern. (trans.). Austin: University of Texas Press.

Barthes, Roland. (1981). *Camera Lucida: Reflections on Photography*. Howard, Richard. (Trans.). New York: Hill and Wang.

Birringer, Johannes. (2005). 'Dance and not dance.' *Performing Arts Journal*. No. 80, 10-27

Blanchard, Anita. (2004). 'Blogs as virtual communities: Identifying a sense of community in the Julie/Julia project.' In Gurak, Laura, Smiljana Antonijevic, Laurie Johnson, Clancy Ratliff, & Jessica Reyman. (Eds.). *Into the Blogosphere: Rhetoric, Community, and Culture of Weblogs*. Available at http://blog.lib.umn.edu/blogosphere/blogs_as_virtual.html

Blom, Lynne Anne, & Chaplin, L. Tarin. (1982). *The Intimate Act of Choreography*. Pittsburgh, PA: University of Pittsburgh Press.

Blood, Rebecca. (2002). 'Weblogs: A history and perspective.' In Rodzvilla, John. (Ed.). *We've Got Blog*. Cambridge, MA: Perseus Publishing. 7-16.

Blood, Rebecca. (2004, December). 'How blogging software reshaped the online community.' In *Special Issue: The Blogosphere. Communications of the ACM*. Vol. 47, No. 12, 53-55.

Bochner, Arthur, & Ellis, Carolyn. (Eds.). (2002). *Ethnographically Speaking: Autoethnography, Literature and Aesthetics*. Walnut Creek, CA: Alta Mira Press.

Bonus, Sabrina, Herring, Susan, Scheidt, Lois, & Wright, Elijah. (2004). 'Beyond The Unusual: Weblogs As Genre.' Panel presentation at Association of Internet Research. *AOIR 4.0. Broadening the Band*. Toronto. 16-19 October 2003. Available at http://www.ecommons.net/aoir/aoir2003/index.php?p=25

Brooke, Collin. (2005, Fall). 'Weblogs as deictic systems: Centripetal, centrifugal, and small-world blogging.' *Computers & Composition Online*. Available at http://www.bgsu.edu/cconline/brooke/brooke.htm

Cohen, Kris. (2005). 'What does the photoblog want'? *Media, Culture & Society*. Vol. 27, No. 6, 883-901.

de Moor, Aldo, & Efimova, Lilia. (2004). 'An argumentation analysis of weblog conversations.' In Proceedings of the *9th International Working Conference on the Language-Action Perspective on Communication Modeling*, New Brunswick, NJ. Available at http://www.scils.rutgers.edu/~aakhus/lap/Proceedings.htm

Denzin, Norman. (1997). *Interpretive Ethnography: Ethnographic Practices for the 21st Century*. Thousand Oaks, CA: Sage.

Engeström, Ritva. (1995). 'Voice as communicative action.' *Mind, Culture, and Activity*. Vol. 2, 192–215.

Engeström, Yrjö, & Miettinen, Reijo. (1999). 'Introduction.' In Engeström, Yrjö, Miettinen, Reijo, & Punamäki, Raija-Leena. (Eds.). *Perspectives on Activity Theory*. Cambridge: Cambridge University Press. 1-16.

Engeström, Yrjö, Virkkunen, Jaakko, Helle, Merje, Pihlaja, Juha, & Poikela, Ritva. (1996). 'The change laboratory as a tool for transforming work.' *Lifelong Learning in Europe*. Vol. 1, No. 2, 10-17.

Foster, Susan Leigh. (1995). 'Choreographing history.' In Foster, Susan Liegh. (Ed.). *Choreographing History*. Bloomington, IN: Indiana University Press.

Grimshaw, Anna, & Ravetz, Amanda. (2005). *Visualising Anthropology*. Bristol: Intellect Books.

Halasek, Kay. (Ed.). (1999). *A Pedagogy of Possibility: Bakhtinian Perspectives on Composition Studies.* Carbondale, IL: Southern Illinois University Press.

Heaton, Daniel. (2002). 'Creativity: Between Chaos and Order or My Life as a Messy Text-A Case Study and a Challenge.' *American Communication Journal.* Vol. 6, No. 1. Available at http://www.acjournal.org/holdings/vol6/iss1/special/heaton.htm

Herring, Susan, Scheidt, Lois, Bonus, Sabrina, & Wright, Elijah. (2004, January 5-8). 'Bridging the gap: A genre analysis of weblogs.' Proceedings of the *37th Annual Hawaii International Conference on System Sciences (HICSS'04).* Available at www.ics.uci.edu/~jpd/classes/ics234cw04/herring.pdf

Hine, Christine. (2000). *Virtual Ethnography.* London: Sage.

Iedema, Rick. (2003). 'Multimodality, resemioticisation: Extending the analysis of discourse as multi-semiotic practice.' *Visual Communication.* Vol. 2, No. 1, 29-57.

Jackson, Michael. (1998). *Minima Ethnographia: Intersubjectivity and the Anthropological Project.* Chicago: University of Chicago Press.

Killoran, John. (2003). 'Homepages, blogs, and the chronotopic dimensions of personal civic (dis-)engagement.' In Hauser, Gerard, & Grim, Amy. (Eds.). *Rhetorical Democracy: Discursive Practices of Civic Engagement.* Mahwah, NJ: Lawrence Erlbaum Associates. 213-220.

Killoran, John. (2005). 'ePluribus Unum? Dialogism and monologism in organizational web discourse.' *Journal of Technical Writing and Communication.* Vol. 35, No. 2. 129-153.

Kirklighter, Christina, Vincent, Cloe, & Moxley, Joseph. (1997). *Voices and Visions: Refiguring Ethnography in Composition.* Portsmouth, NH: Boynton Cook/Heinemann.

Kolb, David. (1996). 'Discourse across links.' In Ess, Charles. (Ed.). *Philosophical Perspectives on Computer-Mediated Communication.* Albany: State University of New York Press. 16-26.

Krause, Stephen. (2004). 'When blogging goes bad: A cautionary tale about blogs, emailing lists, discussion, and interaction.' *Kairos.* Vol. 9, No. 1. Available at http://english.ttu.edu/kairos/9.1/binder.html?praxis/krause/index.html

Kress, Gunther, & van Leeuwen, Theo. (2001). *Multimodal Discourse: The Modes and Media of Contemporary Communication.* London: Arnold.

Krishnamurthy, Sandeep. (2002, October 14-16). 'The multidimensionality of blog conversations: The virtual enactment of September 11.' *Internet Research 3.0.* Amsterdam, the Netherlands: Maastricht. Available at http://www.aoir.org/?q = node/350

Kumar, Ravi, Novak, Jasmine, Raghavan, Prabhakar & Tomkins, Andrew. (2004). 'Structure and evolution of blogspace.' *The Blogosphere. Communications of the ACM.* Vol. 47, No. 12. 35-39.

Lambert, Anthony. (2005, Winter). 'I connect therefore I am: Connectivity and networking in bodies, technologies, communities, and selves.' *Reconstruction: Studies in Contemporary Culture.* Vol. 5, No. 1. Available at http://reconstruction.eserver.org/051/lambert.shtml

Latour, Bruno. (1996). *Aramis or the Love of Technology.* Cambridge, MA: Harvard University Press.

Lee, Rosemary. (2006). *Passages*. An online choreographic notebook. Available at http://www.mdx.ac.uk/rescen/Rosemary_Lee/NOTEBOOKS/nbkThumb.html

Lemke, Jay. (2000). 'Across the Scales of Time: Artifacts, Activities, and Meanings in Ecosocial Systems.' *Mind, Culture, and Activity*. Vol. 7, No. 4, 273-290.

Lemke, Jay. (2001). 'Discursive Technologies and the Social Organization of Meaning.' *Folia Linguistica*. Vol. 35, Nos. 1&2, 79-96.

Lemke, Jay. (2005). 'Place, pace, and meaning: Multimedia chronotopes.' In Norris, Sigrid, & Jones, Rodney. (Eds.). *Discourse in Action: Introducing Mediated Discourse Analysis*. London: Routledge. 110-122.

Lepecki, André. (2006). *Exhausting Dance. Performance and the Politics of Movement*. New York: Routledge.

Martin, Randy. (1995). 'Agency and history: The demands of dance ethnography.' In Foster, Susan Liegh. (Ed.). *Choreographing History*. Bloomington: Indiana University Press. 104-115.

Miles, Adrian. (2005, May 19-22). 'Media rich versus rich media (or why video in a blog is not the same as a video blog).' *Blogtalk Downunder*. Sydney, Australia. Available at http://incsub.org/blogtalk/?page_id = 74

Miller, Carolyn, & Shepherd, Dawn. (2004). 'Blogging as social action: A genre analysis of the weblog.' In Gurak, Laura, Smiljana Antonijevic, Laurie Johnson, Clancy Ratliff, & Jessica Reyman. (Eds.). *Into the Blogosphere; Rhetoric, Community and Culture of Weblogs*. Available at http://blog.lib.umn.edu/blogosphere/blogging_as_social_action.html.

Mortensen, Torill. (2004a). 'Personal publication and public attention.' In Gurak, Laura, Smiljana Antonijevic, Laurie Johnson, Clancy Ratliff, & Jessica Reyman. (Eds.). *Into the Blogosphere: Rhetoric, Community, and Culture of weblogs*. Available at http://blog.lib.umn.edu/blogosphere/personal_publication.html

Mortensen, Torill. (2004b, July 5). 'Dialogue in slow motion: The pleasure of reading and writing across the web.' Keynote. *blogtalk 2.0*. Vienna.

Mortensen, Torill, & Walker, Jill. (2002). 'Blogging thoughts: Personal publication as an online research tool.' In Morrison, Andrew. (Ed.). *Researching ICTs in Context*. InterMedia/UniPub: Oslo. 249-279. Available at http://www.intermedia.uio.no/konferanser/skikt-02/docs/Researching_ICTs_in_context-Ch11-Mortensen-Walker.pdf

Nardi, Bonnie, Schiano, Diane, Gumbrecht, Michelle, & Swartz, Luke. (2004a, December). 'Why we blog.' *Communications of the American Association for Computing Machinery*. 41-46.

Nardi, Bonnie, Schiano, Diane, & Gumbrecht, Michelle. (2004b). 'Blogging as social activity, or, Would you let 900 million people read your diary'? *Proceedings Conference on Computer-Supported Cooperative Work*. New York: ACM Press. 222-228. Available at http://portal.acm.org/results.cfm?coll = Portal&dl = Portal&CFID = 64293533&CFTOKEN = 56681155

Norris, Sigrid, & Jones, Rodney. (Eds.). (2005). *Discourse in Action: Introducing Mediated Discourse Analysis*. London: Routledge.

Phelan, Peggy. (1993). *Unmarked: The Politics of Performance*. London: Routledge.

Phelan, Peggy. (1995). 'Thirteen ways of looking at *choreographing* writing.' In Foster, Susan Liegh. (Ed.). *Choreographing History*. Bloomington, IN: Indiana University Press. 200-210.

Reed, Adam. (2005, June). '"My blog is me": Texts and persons in UK online journal culture (and anthropology).' *Ethnos*. Vol. 70, No. 2, 220-242.

Richardson, Laurel. (1994). 'Writing: A method of inquiry.' In Denzin, N., & Lincoln, Y. (Eds.). *Handbook of Qualitative Research*. Sage: Thousand Oaks. 516-529.

Scholz, Bernhard. (1998). 'Bakhtin's concept of "chronotope": The Kantian connection.' In Shepherd, David. (Ed.). *The Contexts of Bakhtin: Philosophy, Authorship, Aesthetics*. Amsterdam: Harwood Academic. 141-172.

Schiano, Diane, Nardi, Bonnie, Gumbrecht, Michelle, & Swartz, Luke. (2004, April 24-29). 'Blogging by the rest of us.' *CHI 2004*. Vienna, Austria. 1143-1146.

Scollon, Ron. (1998). *Mediated Discourse as Social Interaction: A Study of News Discourse*. London: Longman.

Shields, Rob. (1996). 'Meeting or mis-meeting? The dialogical challenge to Verstehen.' *British Journal of Sociology*. Vol. 47, No. 2, 275-294.

Shultz Colby, Rebekah, Colby, Richard, Felix, Justin, Murphy, Robin, Thomas, Brennan, & Blair, Kristine. (2005, Fall). 'The role for blogs in graduate education: Remediating the rhetorical tradition?' *Computers & Composition Online*. Available at http://www.bgsu.edu/cconline/colbyetal/colbyetal.htm

Skjulstad, Synne, Morrison, Andrew, & Aaberge, Albertine. (2002). 'Researching performance, performing research: dance, multimedia and learning.' In Morrison, Andrew. (Ed.). *Researching ICTs in Context*. Oslo: InterMedia/ UniPub. 211-248. Available at http://www. intermedia.uio.no/konferanser/ skikt-02/skikt-research-conference. html

Taft-Kaufman, Jill. (2000, Fall). 'Critical claims, critical functions: Autoethnography and postscholarship.' *American Communication Journal*. Vol. 4, No. 1. Available at http://www.acjournal.org/holdings/ vol4/iss1 /special/taft.htm

Thibault, Paul. (2004). *Brain, Mind and the Signifying Body: An Ecosocial Semiotic Theory*. London: Continuum.

Thomas, Helen. (2003). *The Body, Dance and Cultural Theory*. Basingstoke: Palgrave Macmillan.

Thomas, Helen, & Ahmed, Jamilah. (Eds.). (2004). *Cultural Bodies: Ethnography and Theory*. Oxford: Blackwell.

Ulmer, Gregory. (1994). *Heuretics*. Baltimore: Johns Hopkins University Press.

van Leeuwen, Theo. (1999). *Speech, Music, Sound*. Basingstoke: Macmillan.

van Maanen, John. (1995). 'An end to innocence: The ethnography of ethnography.' In van Maanen, John. (Ed.). *Representation in Ethnography*. Thousand Oaks, CA: Sage. 1-35.

Walker Rettberg, Jill. (2008). *Blogging*. Cambridge: Polity.

Wertsch, James. (1991). *Voices of the Mind: Sociocultural Approach to Mediated Action*. Cambridge, MA: Harvard University Press.

10

DESIGN AS ALIGNMENT OF MODALITIES

Dagny Stuedahl

Ole Smørdal

THE DIGITAL MEDIATION OF CULTURAL HERITAGE

In this chapter, we ask how design of digital media can be supported by a conceptual framework focussing on meaning making within networks of practices, standards and agencies related to digital research mediation. We propose a framework that is derived from a design process related to the digital mediation of cultural heritage research. A combination of central theoretical concepts, such as alignment, configuration and negotiation, from Actor Network Theory (ANT), the understanding of tool and sign from Activity Theory and the notion of multimodality from media studies are proposed as a way of understanding the challenges and configurations needed to align networks of diverging practices, standards and agencies. This combination establishes a design framework that is based on an understanding of the meaning making with digital media as relative to the objects designed and the practices involved. Cultural heritage research is used as an example where digital mediation and its modalities are of fundamental importance for the building of new ways to mediate knowledge in future cultural heritage institutions.

Building on experiences from a collaboration between an ethnologist reconstructing excavated fragments from a Viking ship, and designers from cultural history and informatics, our claim is that digital research material can also be used for public mediation of research processes and that it can enable valuable insight into cultural heritage research for young audiences especially. With the help of digital media, digital documentation in archives and electronic publication systems, research and research mediation may be blended. Digital media can show diverging interpretations of a heritage object, as well as show how the research process is part of a larger scientific discussion on an institutional and academic level defining the context of the individual research. As a consequence, it is possible not only to divulge and display findings and results of research, but also the analytical and methodological work that lies behind them. Digital media make it possible to mediate the reflexive interpretations (Alvesson & Sköldberg 2000) that are involved in research, but also to mediate these in multiple narratives (Stuedahl 2007). In a sense then, we are able to move inside multimodal compositions in design research processes by using the notion of multimodality to develop a deeper understanding of media in a network-based understanding of mediation. This is to understand the relation between design and use of digital media.

Museums are currently being transformed from a concern with collections that has characterised much of their work with artifacts, repositories and exhibitions from the renaissance till today. The movement of modern museums called new museology (Vergo 1989) focuses on building new relations between museum institutions and the public, and has developed principles for radical public orientation and participation as well as ways of linking the past and present to the future (Hauenschild 1988; Duclos et al. 1986). In contrast, the traditional museum focused its work on documents and artifacts in relation to the imperatives of conservation and the notion of masterpiece (Hauenschild 1988), and mediated their collections through one official narrative legitimized by the institution. Convergence of new and old mediation challenges this focus (Stuedahl 2007) and suggest stronger attention to mediation processes in museum visits as well as in online communication with museum services.

The current transformation in museums can be related to new museology and other modern museum approaches that are related to the possibilities and challenges of mediation. This transformation can easily be tied to the processes of digitalization of cultural heritage (DigiCult 2006). Parallel to this, inside discussions on museum practice, multiple narratives and individual construction of meaning have become an overall issue for mediation in museums (Hooper-Greenhill 1992). This is relevant to the design of mediational means and narratives by which research is represented in museums. Digital media make it possible to open up and present research as a process of construction of meanings and interpretations. However, in many respects this poses considerable challenges to museum practice as well as research methods. These challenges need to be given attention in design and in the establishment of design frameworks.

Focus of chapter

In this chapter, we address these issues by reporting from a design-based research project that is centred on participation from a researcher, an ethnologist, working on a reconstruction of a Viking boat. The concepts alignment, negotiation and configuration from Actor Network Theory are used as design concepts for us as designers, one of us an information scientist and the other a cultural historian. The concepts are tools to be reflexive towards the multidisciplinary connections, and to be aware of the complexity of our goal of designing for linking research documentation with research mediation. This requires connecting research methods and institutional infrastructure for new sorts of empirical material to be added to museum collections. Here the concept of multimodality is used to realise the theoretical concepts related to mediation. The argument is that we need a deeper understanding of the variety of different mediational forms when we are designing for research documentation and research mediation. This is because mediation changes its character related to the goals of the activity. The project therefore spans the development of research methods and routines for storing empirical material, to designing solutions, as well as connections, across to discussions of categorisation, archiving and semantic levels of mediation.

On the design level the concepts alignment, negotiation and configuration complement the notion of multimodality derived from Kress and van Leeuwen (2001), in that they connect the issues of meaning making in media in use, to the process of analysis and reflexive understanding in the design work. This theoretical and conceptual approach to link the issues of use to issues of design is related to well known design discussions in information technology related fields like Participatory Design and Computer Supported Collaborative Work (CSCW).

In our joint inquiry, we have been developing principles of a system of annotation and archiving, making the content accessible in databases for narrative based mediation in museums and on the Internet. Our aim has been to devise a system that makes it possible to include multiple narratives derived from the same digital content in the databases.

Museums, Digitization, and Narrative

We argue that a multiple theoretical framework is important so as to integrate the diverging knowledge requirements in design of media that crosses disciplinary and institutional boundaries. In our case, the work of collecting, annotating, categorising, archiving the digital cultural heritage material and mediating research involves certain practices, agencies, routines as well as institutional conditions. To capture the issues of these aspects that are relevant for designing relations between categories, databases and narrative forms, what is needed is a theoretical framework for analysis that both allows for prescriptive answers and specific understanding of meaning making.

This chapter is structured as a dialogue between the empirical design case and a discussion of the theoretical framework, related to designing routines and infrastructure for the researcher, solutions to issues of standards for categorisation, and the type of digital empirical material, namely video recordings of processes. As a theoretical framework we introduce the actor network concepts that are relevant for the analysis of network of relations of which mediating processes are a part. Concepts such as negotiations and alignment between translations in networks, as well as modality of media are central for the design framework that we propose. This is because they make connections between issues of design and issues of use, which are hard to find in established design frameworks. The multimodality of the media is central in order to understand the design project from a user point of view. Multimodality will be used especially to discuss the concepts of mediation related to alignment and negotiation in Actor Network Theory.

ON DESIGN

Design Framework and Concepts

The design of Information and Communication Technologies (ICTs) that support the move towards a focus on narrative connections in museums requires new strategies (Dawson 2002). These strategies are required for the researchers, and their research methods, their relation to empirical material and techniques for analysing digital video recordings, photos and sound material they have collected in a qualitative research process.

By design approach we mean the theoretical and methodological framework we will use for planning and executing design of digital media that offers multimodal mediation of cultural historical knowledge. As Klaus Krippendorf (1995: 148) explains, design is deeply related to the meaning making level of artifacts:

> . . . no profession other than design is concerned with (the multiple) meanings of things, with how humans as knowledgeable agents interface with their material world, with how meaningfulness can be materially afforded.

The challenge is to find frameworks that offer concepts in support of the analytical work needed to capture the specifics of meaningful interactions as well as provide prescriptive solutions that can be implemented in the designed object of cultural heritage communication.

Digital media have had considerable influence on research methodology and research documentation (Svenningson et al 2003). The use of digital video cameras, digital audio players, and Internet-based communication arenas—such as wikis, blogs, and e-mail—represent valuable resources for the articulation of research processes and the sharing and discussions of empirical material (Johns et al.2004). The case described below illustrates how digital media represents infrastructures that connect individual practices with institutional policies and international infrastructures, and how concepts from actor-network theory and the concept of multimodality can build an analytical foundation for design work.

Designing for Mediation of Cultural Heritage Reconstruction Research

As a collaborative, multidisciplinary team of cultural historians, and information systems specialist, our design work concerns the mediation of a cultural historical reconstruction project of a Viking boat from one of the biggest excavations in Norway, the Gokstad excavation. The reconstruction, and the boatbuilding is carried out by an ethnologist and a small team of builders of traditional Norwegian wooden boats (Planke 2005). This is documented by digital video, audio and photo. The documentation represents the empirical material of our ethnologist. The ethnologist collaborated within our team to learn how to relate his recordings to modes of documenting and logging video as a research method. The categorisation and storage of the digital video material in database was also an issue in his participation in our design project.

ICT and digital media make it possible to document a research process in new ways. Hence, not only the research findings but also how the process of knowledge building can be mediated and articulated as part of the research findings. ICT and digital media also influence the methods used in the research process. One example of this is that the use of digital media, as for example digital video, changes methods in qualitative research. Traditional notions of emic and epic, meaning experiences of the world in contrast to analytical categories of the world, can become blurred when small, almost invisible digital cameras are positioned to document the same phenomena from different angles (Skaar 2005).

For the designers of such management of research material and mediation, it is important to understand how former reconstruction practices are bound to both conceptual and technical tools that play an important role for the ethnological analysis and understanding of the excavated objects and fragments. In the same way as digital media make it possible to sample and compare phenomena via comparative analyses, the old tools are still important for the ethnologist as well as the boatbuilder's understanding, because of their embeddedness in the ontological approach of the analyser. Old tools and old practices used for reconstructing the boat, are therefore important to understand thoroughly for design of new tools and practices for documentation and mediation as well.

One example of this need for integrating understanding of old tools and old practices is related to understanding the relation between the material of wood and the tools for handling the character of the material in the boat building tradition of the Viking times. To fully appreciate the requirements and limits of the oak wood, the researcher bases his reconstruction of the boat on a parallel reconstruction of the boat building skills, as well as understanding of sailing and rowing from the Viking times. The complexity of his interpretative process is one of the main challenges for the designers, both in the work to design solutions for documentation and categorisation, and in the work to mediate the process in an exhibition context.

The challenge of the design work is to build a solution that supports the ethnologist's analytical and interpretative work in the network between old fragments from the Gokstad excavation, the different theories of function of Viking boats, as well as discussions of the link between modern Norwegian wooden boats and the thousand year old Viking

Figure 10.1. The full-size reconstruction of the Gogstad boat (front); a paperboard model of the boat (back right).

boats. This design work is based on making digital solutions that connect the diverging activities of the ethnologist in this research network.

Concretely we have focused on designing systems of annotation, categorisation and archiving that make it easy for the researcher to analyse and carry out studies of metadata in museums within the digital material. The system should also make it feasible for the material to be accessible in public databases provided by the university collection of the Vikingship Museum and at the University of Oslo. For this we have negotiated with the standardized categorisation systems for metadata in museums, CIDOC CR. We have tried to identify connections between the system and the practices and needs of our researcher, and to find solutions that compromise between needs that do not converge.

The goal has been to make a system that allows for multiple narratives based on the same digital content in the databases. The principles we have developed to achieve this aim are related to making connections between annotation and archiving, and the search categories of the publicly accessible databases of the university. This is to provide the empirical material from the reconstruction process for the further development of narrative based mediation with personal media in museums as well as on the Internet. To be able to design these connections we have focused on the semantic level of categories and metadata, trying to align them with the categories of the researcher.

A number of research challenges related to design of digital media come to the fore in this process. What is required is a blending of modalities between the different forms of empirical material, such as sketches, photographs and recordings of hour long sessions in the workshop, as well as modalities related to empirical research procedures and categorization standards for storing the information in databases. The theoretical concepts and methodological frameworks that take up design as alignment of diverging modalities and translations, need to address design as network activities. Further, it is necessary to propose methods that support these.

MULTIMODALITY AND NETWORKS

Multimodality as an Addition to Signs and Tools

The concept multimodality provides aspects in social semiotic framework for studying the divergence between media and the meaning making processes related to them (Kress & Leeuwen 2001). For example, writing is stated as mode and the book as the medium that has shaped western imagination, forms of knowledge and practices of reading. In this perspective, meaning making is related both to discourse, design, production and distribution, and the choice of mode is of significant importance. Kress and Leeuwen (2001: 64) state that:

> . . . the design process in the multimodal world involves selection of discourses and selection of modes through which content-in-discourse will be realised. To use the mode of image to represent certain information means that the mode of writing is not used for that purpose. That will have an effect on the (elements of the) mode writing.

The multimodal theory of communication concentrates on the semiotic resources of communication, that is the modes and the media used, and the communicative practices, the discursive practices, production practices and interpretative practises in which these resources are used. This helps us understand how meaning making is related not only to language and conversation, but also to the modes and the materiality of media involved in communication. Design is understood here as a matter of choices in context, where choices are related to which mode is best for the content/meaning that is to be communicated (Kress 2004).

In stressing the role of material resources for meaning making, the concept of modality help highlight the physical character of meaning making (Kress & Leeuwen 2001: 28):

> A semiotics which is intended to be adequate to a description of the multimodal world will need to be conscious of forms of meaning-making which are founded as much on the physiology of humans as bodily beings, and on the meaning potentials of the materials drawn into culturally produced semiosis, as on humans as social actors. All aspects of materiality and all the modes deployed in a multimodal object/phenomenon/text contribute to meaning.

We argue that the mode of medium, according to Kress (2004), can be understood in terms of the sign characteristic of a mediating artifact. Meanwhile the tool aspect of the medium is weakly articulated in the theory of multimodality. In our case, where the medium is also used as tool for archiving and categorising, we need a notion of the multimodality of digital media that function as tool for the researcher.

The mediating artifact is a central concept in socio-cultural psychology introduced by Vygotsky in his activity oriented approach (Vygotsky 1978; Vygotsky 1986). Any artifact can be understood only within the context of human activity by identifying the ways people use the artifacts, the needs it serves and the history of its development (Kaptelinin 1996). Vygotsky distinguished between two interrelated types of instruments: signs and tools. According to Vygotsky (1978: 55) a sign ' . . . is a means of internal activity aimed at mastering oneself; the sign is internally oriented,' while the function of a tool ' . . . is to serve as the conductor of human influence on the object of activity; it is external oriented; it must lead to changes in objects.'

In our case, digital media can be regarded as tools, such as when the researcher uses it for annotating video, typing text, and drawing pictures. The signs have a different character and are means of thought, and of reflective and conscious actions. Digital media can be regarded as signs, for example when researchers use them for exchanging ideas, reminders of previous actions, a means for reflection, or using it for communication. The essence of signs is that they are basic instruments for intrapersonal processes that necessarily have a communicative form. However, it is important to remember that digital media can also be regarded as tools such as when new practices of categorising and archiving cultural heritage material are developed.

The selection of a mode for a tool in our case is concerned with the choice and interplay of devices, the graphical vs. textual representations, the selection of user interface metaphors (e.g., the degree of direct manipulation), the selection of infrastructure, the capability of mobile work, etc.

Actor-Network and Alignment

The perspective of understanding social processes as network activities has been introduced to analyse the complexity of knowledge production in science and society, especially to capture the role of the techno-social transformation processes. This is proposed as part of the social constructivist approach that takes departure in an understanding of technology and society as socially developed. The network perspective is relevant to design research to describe design as socially and technologically negotiated. The actor network (ANT) perspective (Latour 1999; Callon 1986; Law 2000) offers a framework that involves political, institutional and individual issues, which we in our case use to capture challenges of meaning making in design on the level of infrastructures, policies, of ideologies and of cultural aspects of the designed object.

ANT offers a framework for understanding the relation between the material-social on both macro level and micro level of knowledge negotiations (Law 1997). An important perspective of ANT compared to general network perspectives in sociology (Granovetter 1974) and theories of politics of knowledge production (Barnes 1974; Barnes 1977) is that ANT refuses to predetermine knowledge production belonging to either the material or the nonmaterial. Both humans and nonhumans are integrated in the understanding of knowledge production as well as in technical development.

In ANT this symmetry between humans and nonhumans, or between the social and the technical underlines the relation between the technical and human agency. It is because of this capability of transgressing well known dichotomies that the actor-network approach is used increasingly as an approach in studies of the relation between technology and society (Latour & Woolgar 1979; Callon 1986a; Callon 1986b; Akrich 1992; Latour 1999; Law 2000). Concepts such as actant, translation and alignment, mostly inspired by concepts from Greimasian structuralist semiotics, offer analytical tools for following technosocial relations as negotiations between human and nonhuman actors in network building processes.

Capabilities and potential are the main focus for ANT based analysis. Therefore the concentration on agencies instead of actors reminds us of Greimas' concept of actants, as the roles that makes the actors move in networks. The more correct concept would therefore be to speak about actants instead of actors, because it is the capabilities we are analysing. The actant can be individuals or collectives—humans or machines—but they are the driving force of the network building activities (Callon 1986; Latour 1991).

The actor-network approach provides a view for understanding ICTs as symmetrical to human actors in network building activities. This symmetry coincides with the symmetry between mode and medium in the multimodal framework for understanding meaning making with new media. The concept of modality supports a thorough concentration on the divergence of meaning making relative to the medium. A medium is understood as an actor in the alignment process.

Figure 10.2. The related web site comprised of text, images and video.

This semantic oriented approach offers us an important framework for understanding alignment processes between heterogeneous actors and their relations to media and other actors in the design of digital mediation. To an extent, it also allows us to understand how people and institutions collectively deal with heterogeneity related to the materiality of ICT-based meaning making. For this we propose the focus on negotiations given by the performative perspective of the actor-network approach (Callon 1986a; Callon 1986b; Latour 1987; Law & Singleton 2000). This approach conceptualises and studies alignments as a result of negotiation processes between actors with diverging understandings, goals and materiality.

The focus on modality draws attention to a weak point in the actor-network approach, where the role of mediation and meaning making is placed in the background of network building, and the agencies of the actors. In our design project we bring these questions to the front, as it seems that through digital mediation, modality makes a fundamental difference for meaning making related to digital cultural heritage.

The Researcher Mediating Multiple Narratives of His Reconstruction Work

It is by way of the researcher's struggle to archive his empirical digital material that we envisage that archives, collections and museums may be able to mediate several narratives and interpretations instead of being tied to one legitimated narrative. The design of the technical systems that support these kinds of multiple digital mediation, needs a deep understanding of how knowledge production and research are changed by the use of ICTs. However, at the same time the transformation of mediating practices need to be related to old frames.

The individual researcher faces major changes in his research, both on a methodological and on an epistemological level. First of all, during fieldwork, in this case in the workshop where the cardboard model of the Viking boat is reconstructed, he has to consider the angle and position of the video camera and the microphones, he has to plan discussion themes and be able to discuss these with his partner in front of the camera, so that the audio recordings give valuable documentation of the process. In the workshop where the Viking boat is built in full-scale, he has to consider the noise from the machines and tools, in relation to the types of the microphones. This gives an impression of the number of practical issues that have to be solved when video recording, categorising and analysing digital fieldwork material.

In addition to this, there is the amount of work related to the transcription and analysis of the video recordings. Because of the ease use of digital video recording equipment the hours of recordings easily increase in comparison with what was possible previously, when fieldwork activities was documented by notes and photographs. One example of the challenges of digital video recordings of fieldwork is related to finding sequences that are relevant for analysis. Still, the transformation of the mediation practices of the researcher also suggests potentials for the fieldwork and its analysis in that by the facility of digital video recording he can fully concentrate on his reconstruction process, well aware that he does not have to remember or note anything. His publication and mediation of his research may thus also be carried out more easily because he has complete documentation of the process.

The Design Network

We will now describe the network in which our researcher participates. We also describe how the object of research, that is the tools and the programme for his research, are parts of building the network of mediating cultural historical research. The agencies of the researcher need to be understood in relation to the network with which he has to negotiate during the activities with the fieldwork material and his analysis of the material. One of the agencies of the researcher is to mediate cultural historical research processes in a more reflexive way. He illustrates how reconstructions are based on interpretations, choices and priorities by managing the reconstruction in two versions as the boat gets its shape based on interpretations and choices, and he needs two versions of the boat to fully make any conclusions on his own interpretative work (Planke 2005). The agency of the ethnologist is to demonstrate how cultural historical reconstruction processes are placed in the knowledge context of present time, and how existing knowledge and political conditions influence reconstruction work.

On one hand this reflexive approach to cultural historical reconstruction represents a methodological shift in cultural historical research, while on the other hand it presents an entrance point for the use of digital media in mediating cultural historical research in new ways. The possibility of showing both the reconstructed boat and the video recordings of the process, when different parts of the boat were reconstructed give us valuable material for mediating the choices that had to be made during the reconstruction. This also provides us with important material for discussing alternative ways of reconstructing the boat. Digital media allow us, whether on a screen or a wall, to visualise the process of interpretation, experimentation and choices that were part of reconstructing the Viking boat, while the finished boat could be presented in the exhibition room. In this way, digital media make it possible for us to mediate the content by different media types in mixed media narratives in an exhibition or a museum.

The researcher, however, still needs to relate his mediation to the diverse institutional and professional levels in which his research is situated. First of all, there is the professional framework that the researcher is related to in his department that constitutes an important context for his approach on ethnological research related to reconstruction processes. His will to show reconstructions as interpretations, and his will to mediate the professional choices he has made during his research, are part of the reflexive turn he performs in relation to his institutional context.

Yet the researcher is also connected to the networks that will be presented later in this chapter. He refers to the CIDOC standard because he wants his research material to be part of the archival material of his university, and by that be accessible to other researchers and interested persons.

The theoretical framework is important as a means to integrate diverging knowledge involved in design. In our case the work of collecting, annotating, categorising, archiving and mediating digital cultural historical material involves certain knowledge, agencies, and routines as well as certain relations to the media and the mediation process. The design approach involves the theoretical and methodological framework that we use for planning the design project that leads to an awareness of the multimodal character of mediation processes related to cultural heritage research.

Configuration, Negotiation, and Alignment

Designing a process, a system and a practice of digital mediation of the reconstruction process consists of configuration and re-configuration of networks involving the researcher, the tools, the infrastructure, the institutions, and the research mediation tools and activities. Aligning all these heterogeneous actors poses a challenge for design and it presupposes an understanding of the positions and roles of the multiple parts. The concept of alignment from Actor Network Theory helps us focus on the adjustments that are needed by actors involved in the network related to the mediation of the Gokstad boat reconstruction.

One proposed approach related to design is to study the design process as a process of negotiation in networks (Newman 1998). The focus on the heterogeneous *translations* involved in design negotiations leads to problematising the involvement of diverging understandings in collaborative design processes. Translations can be the result of compromises and alignment between diverging agencies and actors. Translation can therefore also be understood as an 'agent' of network building activities, where the alliance around one relevant interpretation is a major part of the translation in the network. Translations are therefore also themselves results of negotiation process, where interpretations are examined, negotiated and adjusted. Above we have focussed especially on the concept of *alignment* between heterogeneous actors in design networks. Alignment processes are based on the translations that the involved actors are negotiating. Translations are products of compromises and mutual adjustment that is negotiated (Callon 1986; Latour 1987; Akrich 1992; Latour 1999). A concern with translation is that is focuses on the process of the mutual definition and inscription that make the alignment in the actor network. In a strongly aligned network, the translations are successful and relatively similar while in a weakly aligned network the translation does not fulfill these conditions.

In our view, then, to be a designer is to enter into networks of ongoing activities and negotiations. A designer should be able to identify and understand the networks of the user that require advanced analytical understanding. Entering a user's network implies connecting the user's networks with the networks of the designer. Design is therefore concerned with linking different networks of knowledge and practices. It is also a question of attaching different networks to each other in order for them to align so that the designed product will be built on the needs and requirements from participants in the design group. Describing these networks needs be carried out with help of the perspective of the practitioner.

Below, we describe the networks by following the activities of the reconstruction, and the digital media design and their relations with knowledge, infrastructure, standards, and practices. Negotiations are here not only understood from the perspective of one part of the negotiation, but takes the conditions under which different translations are aligned as departure point. In this way translations are understood by the way they point to transformations in the network building process. The changing positions of the actants in the network is another aspect of actor network perspective, which prevents a too fixed focus on one actant—and which strengthens the interpretation of actor networks as networks of relations (Law & Singleton 2000).

The understanding of networks as processes of knowledge negotiation between people, institutions and the material establishes the framework for an actor-network perspective on design (Stuedahl 2004). The perspective of network building is not based on a focus on the networks per se—but on what makes the actors capable of negotiating their own goals into other actors building activities (Latour 1999a; Latour 1999b).

This focus on capability and potential is relevant for design research and research-based design as it problematises the knowledge involved in design work. Design can be understood as inscribing the object, the medium or the material with competences, motives, and political prejudice. Akrich (1992: 208) notes that

Designers thus define actors with specific tastes, competences, motives, aspirations, political prejudices, and the rest, and they assume that morality, technology, science, and the economy will evolve in particulars ways. A large part of the work of innovators is that of inscribing 'this vision (or prediction about) the world in the technical content of the new object.

The goal for using an actor network perspective is a methodological one: the actor network approach does not offer a theory with a fixed set of concepts that reveals what is *actually going on* in practice. The point of an actor network approach is the opposite; it is to refuse to define in advance who the relevant actors are for understanding the building of the network (Gad & Jensen 2005). The purpose in using ANT for design processes is to avoid a pre-determined idea of actors. To follow this further, a pre-determined notion of actants is not compatible with the focus on alignment.

A design network can be built by heterogeneous actors who use their own configurations, with no incentive to be compatible with other actors involved. For example, this is so when modules and software are proposed from different actors that are not compatible and that still remain to be integrated into the network by the designer. In our interdisciplinary design team comprised of academics and practitioners, configurations were challenged by highly different goals and expectations related to the degree of compatibility of the digital fieldwork material between the university archive system and the mediation on web and mobile terminals. In reality, the required adjustments and alignments occurred on several levels, both technologically and practically. Technological development not related to the project helped clarify the goals from a technological level—while the expectations to the practical level of digital research methods was clarified and adjusted. The goals and the concepts that came out of the process were understandable for the team—and worked as boundary objects (Star & Griesemer 1989) for the further design work in the project. In design networks where negotiations have transformed the individual actors so that they align with the network, the alignment process may be seen to have adjusted knowledge and interpretations.

MULTIMODALITY, ACTORS, AND NETWORKS

Changes in Research Methods

On the level of design, the focus on modality draws attention to a weak point in the actor network approach. Analysing the modalities of the actants in the network, requires a shift of attention. It becomes clear that the role of mediation in ANT is placed in the background of a focus on the network building activities. The meaning making processes of the actants are implicit in the performative agencies of the actors. Meanwhile, building on experiences from our design project we propose to consider modality as prerequisite to performative actions. Modality gives important information to understand the alignment processes of cultural heritage research based on digital media, Also the concept of modality supports a thorough concentration on the divergence of meaning making relative to the medium. As the description from the case below will show, this is important to the analysis of the network building, as the medium is understood as an actor in the alignment process.

Digital Video as Research Tool

Digital media in the form of video and MP3 recordings are used in combination with the editing system AVID. Video and MP3 recordings are used to document the processes of building the cardboard model of the boat, as well as building the full-scale boat in wood. Several researchers have been using AVID for storing and categorising their digital empirical video recordings, using it for carrying out qualitative analysis and for presenting their research findings (Rasmussen 2005; Skaar 2005).

Using AVID for these analytical processes does indeed take some effort and time, as the system is not built for qualitative research, but for editing video recordings. This makes the system first of all time consuming to use: because annotating the different sequences of the empirical recordings is complicated and because the analytical annotation needs

Figure 10.3. Two video sequences, managed by the AVID video editing system, documenting the relationship between the excavated fragments and the construction of the paperboard model.

more text than annotating for editing purposes.

The Modality of Tools and Actors

The researcher's analysis of his empirical material in video, text and in sequences by annotation in the video editing tool AVID offers him ways to construct different interpretations related to the ways he conducted his data transcription and the ways he started his analytical process with the qualitative data. The modalities of AVID highlighted for him, first of all, physical constraints related to the management of the software, by being overly time consuming. Next, AVID posed increasing challenges to the work of annotating the video material. This was because the concepts that are used in the annotations needed to be consistent. The researcher decided to combine the different processes with the empirical material, and started annotation of the over 50 hours of videomaterial while he analysed them for the first time. Annotation of the video recordings happened too early in the research process as the researcher had not yet developed concepts and themes for the analysis of his research material. The modes of the well-defined and the not-yet-defined related to the use of AVID demonstrates the points where no alignments will be built in the network, as the researcher gave up on the annotation the vast material.

How does this framework help us understand the challenges for our design work? Finding that our design is concentrated on aligning networks that does not align well, the framework of modalities and medium helps us analyse why this may be so. The use of software tools as AVID, can be understood as media involved in the knowledge production that the researcher is part of when he performs his analysis of the digital video material. During the reconstruction an analytical understanding needs to be transformed into material artifacts (such as texts, diagrams, video recordings, annotations) and thereafter be translated into decisions in the reconstruction of the physical viking boat. In this process the media are regarded as tools for analysis and meaning making. The modes of the AVID tool do not support the meaning making process in the interpretative and reflective way that the researcher wants to achieve.

There are several reasons for this. First, the physical constraints with using AVID as a tool for transcribing video material are too great. Second, also splitting long video recordings in sequences, thematising them before an empirical understanding is fully developed is laborious. Third, the dilemma of having to work and rework empirical research material several times before the final thematising happens is well known but still a serious constraint. However, carrying this out digitally means that the categorising concepts develop during the research process and have to be altered as other material annotated with the same concept are annotated.

Building on the actor network understanding of a symmetry between human and non-human actors in transforming practice, AVID can be understood to be involved only relative to the mode of interpretation and meaning making it offers of the video recording concerned. AVID is a tool that offers a certain modality and, as described above, this modality does not meet with the modes of the researcher. AVID is therefore a weak actor in the network-building that does not align easily, and that does not translate well to the practice of the ethnologist. Important configuration work has to be done in the design to make this tool part of the network of tools and practices for digital research and mediation.

Modality of Standards

The empirical example we outline also demonstrates another set of conflicts of modality between the researcher and the standards of metadata provided by CIDOC CRM. The CIDOC CRM standard for metadata both systematises information and offers complex semiotic systems of categories and concepts to order digital information in museums and collections. To be able to store the empirical material from the reconstruction of the third Gokstad boat, it became important to use the standard of metadata required by the institution responsible for the research material, in this case the University of Oslo. The activity of systematising is not so directly bound to the technology as with the example of the editing software—but with the possibilities for ordering information in richer categories. It is therefore the categories rather than the technology that play an increasing role of transforming the CIDOC CRM standard into a mode and controlling how the researcher's meaning can be produced.

CIDOC as an Actant

The conceptual reference model called CIDOC CRM (The International Documentation Committee of the International Council of Museums), has been developed by ICOM (International Council of Museums) Data Model Working Group and elaborated to become an ISO standard (on CRM see http://cidoc.ics.forth.gr), The standard is based on object-oriented programming with a large group of categories describing the relation of the item, contextualising it both in its time, and in relation to other resources from the university databases. Examples of categories are; class, subclass, superclass, intention, extension, instance, property, sub property etc. These categories are defined as 'definitions and formal structure for describing implicit and explicit concepts and relationships in cultural heritage documentation' (Cofts, et al. 2005).

The very existence of the CIDOC CRM contributes in itself to the shaping of the activities, perspectives and concerns of researchers and designers in our case. The standards provide definitions of basic concepts used in cultural heritage documentation, with the highest level of abstraction defined by the five entities people, places, things, events, and concepts. The CRM is intended to promote a shared understanding by providing a common and extensible semantic framework that any cultural heritage information can be aligned with, such as metadata standards, formal data models etc. It is intended to be a common language for domain experts in museums, libraries and archives and well as for designers and implementers to inform information systems design and to serve as a guide for good practice of conceptual modeling, thus enable translation and negotiations between networks.

The CIDOC CRM emerged out of earlier approaches that only focussed on providing a general data model for museums. In 1996 the decision was made to engage in an object-oriented approach in order to benefit from its expressive power and extensibility for dealing with the necessary diversity and complexity of data structures in the domain, and after intense voluntary work over 10 years the CRM was submitted to ISO for standardization (International Standard ISO/DIS 21127). This means that the CIDOC bodies will make use of the services of ISO and negotiate with the respective ISO committees to ensure the widest possible agreement with the broader international community.

The categorization, storing, and archiving of the research documentation of the reconstruction process is influenced by the use of digital media. Digitisation projects on museums collections have shown that digital categorising systems offer the possibility of a broader presentation of the object both visually and in text. This generates challenges for the existing categorizing system used (Ore 2001).

For our ethnologist researcher, the object oriented character of CIDOC, as well as the event based focus of the semiotic framework does pose challenges when used as framework for archiving processes and trajectories recorded on video. Editing the video recordings of the reconstruction process demands a rather finished analysis of the material as well as of the reconstruction process. At the moment of annotating and storing the digital research material, the researcher is neither capable nor motivated to define his empirical material in categories provided by CIDOC.

The CIDOC standards for metadata annotation of digitalised empirical material in archives and stores are important for the design of specific routines and tools. But they are definitely made for archiving and storage as well as searching in vast digital cultural heritage material that is already analysed and categorised. This is a very different focus than to put cultural heritage research processes on show for the general public.

As demonstrated, the problems of diverging modalities is related to how well suited the defined entities of CIDOC are for documentation and structuring of information that is not yet analysed and categorised. The standard is an appropriate fit for structuring information that is established, but when entities and categories are not yet defined, the modality of the tool does not align well. The mode of the medium aligns poorly with the meaning making processes and negotiations of the researcher in the network of the reconstruction of the boat.

DESIGN AS ALIGNMENT OF MODALITIES

Design of Cultural Heritage Research Mediation

In this context of the documentation and archiving of the reconstruction of a Viking boat, we can say that the network between the researcher, AVID, CIDOC CRM standards and the databases of his university is not strong enough to lead to alignments since there are too many challenges and too many hindrances involved. The design of a system that translates annotations and metadata from one standard into another has to pay attention to the modes of the researcher's meaning making process.

Our interpretation of the networks and the actants that are involved in our case can be mapped schematically (see Figure 10.4). 'A' denotes the activity of reconstruction a viking boat, 'B' denotes the activity of the designers (aka the authors of this chapter). Strong relationships between actants are represented by short arcs, while weak relationships are depicted by longer ones. In the illustration below we define both the standard CIDOC, and the application AVID as actants in the network.

Using the perspective of actor-network as an analytical framework it is important to focus upon how the use of digital media changes the research methods, the agencies and the analytical work of the researcher. The understanding of existing practices, and how they are interwoven with standards and systems on an institutional level are important to designing. Yet, even more important for the design is to understand the role of modalities of the researcher in his knowledge building processes. To be able to align different actors in the network of mediating the reconstruction process, as normally is needed in design processes, our claim is that it is important to understand the modalities of the features involved in the network alignments.

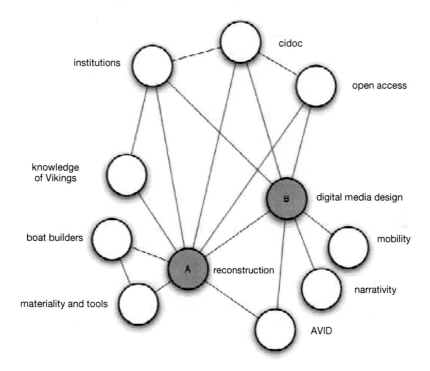

Figure 10.4. Design network of digital documentation and archiving of a reconstruction process.

Building Relations by Making Adjustments

We have illustrated the need for theoretical concepts and methodological approaches for design processes that can build relations between media, signs and tools. We have used alignment, negotiation, and translation from ANT in concert with the notion of multimodality to analyse how a particular standard and an application was introduced into a project, and how they were not successfully integrated in the networks.

Multimodality directs our attention toward the character of mediation and helps build understanding of the specifics of the medium involved, e.g., as tools and/or signs. The multimodal concept and its characteristics of the mediating and representational process offers a framework for understanding the relationship between the medium, mediation and the meaning making processes involved.

Regarding design as alignment of modalities allows us to be able to identify conflicts of modalities and meaning making related to modalities of media, signs, and tools. In this context, alignment puts weight on the meaning making processes in networks and conceptualises these as adjustments of the diverging meaning making.

Writing from a design project, we are in the initial phase of developing design concepts and approaches. We are not yet in a position to generalise our framework. For this we have to apply the design framework in diverging design projects. We argue however, that the design project that we selected is a rich and complex one, and that the concepts that we propose may translate also to other projects that are equally or less complex.

The project we have reported from is relevant, however, for both the discussion of the further development of ANT approach—that is towards using it as framework to understand complex processes—and for also understanding the reasons lying behind why some networks do not connect. Further, it is relevant for discussions of multimodal compositions, as alignment between actors and actants provides a good entrance point for understanding the techno-social issues of compositions and design.

ACKNOWLEDGMENTS

We would like to thank Dr. Terje Planke for his inspiring cooperation that made possible our design project, this research chapter and the contextual relevance of the work. We would also like to thank Even Westvang and Hans Magnus Nedreberg for their patient attention and practical contributions along the design process. Andrew Morrison has participated in our reflections from the very beginning of the chapter and has supported it with sharp comments and insightful discussions.

REFERENCES

Akrich, Madeleine. (1992). 'The de-scription of technical objects.' In Bijker, Wiebe & Law, John (Eds.). *Shaping Technology, Building Society: Studies in Sociotechnical Change*. Cambridge: The MIT Press. 205-224.

Alvesson, Mats & Sköldberg, Kai. (2000). *Reflexive Methodology. New Vistas for Qualitative Research*. London: Sage.

Barnes, Barry. (1974). *Scientific Knowledge and Sociological Theory*. London: Routledge and Kegan Paul.

Barnes, Barry. (1977). *Interests and the Growth of Knowledge*. London: Routledge.

Callon, Michel. (1986a). 'Some elements of a sociology of translation: domestication of the scallops and the fishermen of St. Brieuc Bay.' *Sociological Review.* Law, John (Ed.). London: Routledge and Kegan Paul. Monograph 32. 196-233.

Callon, Michel. (1986b). 'The sociology of an actor-network: the case of the electric vehicle.' In Callon, Michel, Law, John & Rip, Arie. (Eds.). *Mapping the Dynamics of Science and Technology: Sociology of Science in the Real World.* London: Macmillan. 19–34.

Croft, Brian, Doerr, Mike, Gill, Tony, Stead, Stephen & Stiff, Matthew. (2005). *Definition of the CIDOC Conceptual Reference Model.* Produced by the ICOM/CIDOC Documentation Standards Group, continued by the CIDOC CRM Special Interest Group.

Dawson, David. (2002). 'Inclusion and ICT: The challenge.' *Museum International.* Vol. 54, No. 3, 59-63.

DigiCULT. (2006). DigiCULT website. Available at http://cordis.europa. eu.int/ist/digicult/.

Duclos, Jean-Claude. (1986). MINOM Communiqué [MINOM Communique]. Grenoble.

Gad, Christopher & Bruun Jensen, Casper. (2005). *On the Consequences of Post-ANT.* Centre for STS Studies: Department of Information and Media Studies. University of Århus, Århus Denmark.

Granovetter, Mark. (1974). 'The strength of weak ties.' *American Journal of Sociology.* Vol. 78, No. 6, 1360-1380.

Hauenschild, Andrea. (1988). 'Claims and reality of New Museology; Case studies in Canada, United States and Mexico.' International Council of Museums (ICOM). Available at http://museumstudies.si.edu/claims2000.htm. (Accessed: June 11 2007).

Hooper-Greenhill, Eileen. (1992). *Museums and the Shaping of Knowledge.* London: Routledge.

Johns, Mark; Shing-Ling, Serina & Hall, Jon. (2004). *Online Social Research: Methods, Issues & Ethics.* Peter Lang: New York.

Kaptelinin, Viktor. (1996). 'Activity Theory: Implications for Human-Computer Interaction.' In Nardi, Bonnie. (Ed). *Context and Consciousness. Activity Theory and Human-Computer Interaction.* Cambridge: The MIT Press. 103-116.

Kress, Günther. (2004). 'Reading images; multimodality, representation and new media.' *Information Design Journal.* Vol. 12, No. 2, 110-119.

Kress, Gunther & van Leeuwen, Theo. (2001). *Multimodal Discourse. The Modes and Media of Contemporary Communication.* London: Arnold.

Krippendorf, Klaus. (1995).On the essential contexts of artifacts or on the proposition that "design is making sense (of things)." In Buchanan, Richard & Marolin, Victor. (Eds.). *The Idea of Design.* Cambridge: The MIT Press. 156-184.

Latour, Bruno. (1987). *Science in Action: How to Follow Scientists and Engineers through Society.* London: Open University Press.

Latour, Bruno. (1991). 'Technology is society made durable.' In Law, John. (Ed.). *A Sociology of Monster.* London: Routledge. 75-106.

Latour, Bruno. (1999a). 'On recalling ANT.' In Law, John and Hassard, John. (Eds.). *Actor Network Theory and After.* Oxford: Blackwell. 15-25.

Latour, Bruno (1999b). *Pandora's Hope. Essays on the Reality of Science Studies.* Cambridge: Harvard University Press.

Latour, Bruno & Woolgar, Steven. (1979). *Laboratory Life: The Social Construction of Scientific Facts.* Beverly Hills, CA: Sage.

Law, John. (1997). 'Topology and the naming of complexity.' Available at http://www.comp.lancs.ac.uk/sociology/stlaw3.html.

Law, John. (2000.) *'Networks, Relations, Cyborgs: On the Social Study of Technology.'* Available at http://www.comp.lanc.ac.uk/sociology/soc042jl.html.

Law, John & Singleton, Vickie. (2000). 'Performing technology's stories.' *Technology and Culture.* Vol. 41, No. 4, 765-775.

Newman, Susan. (1998). 'Here, there, and nowhere at all: distribution, negotiation, and virtuality in postmodern ethnography and engineering.' *Knowledge and Society.* Vol. 11, 235-67.

Ore, Christian-Emil. (2001). 'The Norwegian museum project. Access to and interconnection between various resources of cultural and natural history.' Available at www.muspro.uio.no/posterecdl.html.

Planke, Terje. (2005). 'Feltarbeid i fortiden' [Fieldwork in the past]. In Gustavsson, Anders. (Ed.). *Kulturvitenskap i felt. Metodiske og pedagogiske erfaringer [Cultural Science in the Field. Methodological and Pedagogical Experiences].* Høyskoleforlaget: Kristiansand. 203-217.

Rasmussen, Ingvill. (2005). *Project Work and ICT. A Study of Learning as Trajectories of Participation.* Unpublished PhD dissertation, InterMedia, University of Oslo, Oslo.

Skaar, Bjørn. (2005). *NettCase. Multimediale case i profesjonsutdanningen av lærere [The Multimedial Case in Professional Teacher Education].* Unpublished PhD thesis, InterMedia, University of Oslo, Oslo.

Star, Susan Leigh & Griesemer, Jeff. (1989). 'Institutional ecology, "translations" and boundary objects: amateurs and professionals in Berkeley's Museum of Vertebrate Zoology, 1907-39.' *Social Studies of Science.* Vol. 9, No. 3, 387-420.

Stuedahl, Dagny. (2004). *Negotiations and Persuasions. Multidisciplinary knowledge building in design of new ICT.* Unpublished PhD thesis, InterMedia, University of Oslo, Oslo.

Stuedahl, Dagny. (2007). Convergence, Museums and Cultural Heritage. In Storsul, Tanja & Stuedahl, Dagny. (Eds.). *Ambivalence towards Convergence.* Digitalization and Media Change. Gothenburg: Nordicom Press. 129-145.

Svenningsson, Malin, Lövheim, Mia & Bergquist, Magnus. (2003). *Att fånga nätet: kvalitativa metoder för internetforskning [Capturing the Net: qualitative methods for internet research].* Lund: Studentlitteratur.

Vergo, Peter. (1989). *The New Museology.* London: Reaktion Books.

Vygotsky, Lev. (1978). *Mind in Society. The Development of Higher Psychological Processes.* (Eds.). In Cole, Michael, John-Steiner, Vera, Scribner, Sylvia & Souberman, Ellen. Cambridge: Harvard University Press.

Vygotsky, Lev. (1986). *Thought and Language.* Cambridge: The MIT Press.

11

WHAT ARE THESE? DESIGNERS' WEB SITES AS COMMUNICATION DESIGN

Synne Skjulstad

EMERGING WEB MEDIATION

While trawling the Web, I come across a strange site that unfolds as I use it. The text moves. Unreadable, written words slide across the screen upside down. This is not a film, not an animation, nor is it an advert. It's not a standard net news site nor is it a typical web 'page.' A young man is pictured (Figure 11.1). Graphic blindfolds on, moving jerkily and abruptly in jump cuts. I click on every visible detail. He holds a glass of milk. He moves and shakes, not drinking much. I drag him across the screen. Screens within screens. Layers and navigational innovation. I notice that the site is part of an online portfolio. The designers' canny and artistic use of the medium entices me. This is a site that experiments compositionally. It's like others I've met. But I keep asking myself, 'What are these'?

In this chapter, I investigate the Web sites of two leading design companies, one in the United States called *Volumeone* and one in Norway named *Bleed*. These Web sites are instances of innovative digital compositions by designers who work at the experimental edge of dynamic and multimodal Web design. Highly crafted Web texts are the 'content' of these sites. The sites are examples of the changing character of Web design that blends media and transcends the standard formats of the 'Web page.' These are sites that are composed of diverse media and multiple mediations gathered in online portfolios. They are a means to exhibit

319

Figure 11.1. Consumed/perceived. Screengrab of experimental Web design in Volumeone.com.

work to clients. Accessible to other designers, they are openly available to general users, too.

My main argument is that such experimental texts are articulations of designers' own emerging and expressive professional work. This work needs to be seen in the wider context of the interplay of multimodal digital design that includes a variety of media types and their realizations via tools that allow for dynamic and nonsequential composition and mediation. The sites offer designers, customers, and other users some evidence of the potential intersections online of graphic design and information design. Yet often these fields are kept separate in the study of Web design. In analyzing the dynamic, textual environments of *Volumeone* and *Bleed*, I pursue a number of questions. What are these Web sites and how do they fit together and communicate? How might we approach them analytically as digitally designed and mediated texts? In what ways might we situate these texts as experimental and emergent forms of multimodal online communication?

The Importance of Communication Design

In answering these questions, I develop the notion of communication design as a macroconstruct that allows us to situate experimental, multimodal Web texts in their contexts of production and innovative mediational composition. A communication design perspective offers a related but alternative view to those of information and interaction design because it primarily focuses on communication as the outcome of design practice and textual mediation. A communication design-oriented analysis also may shed light on the multimodal, textual relations that generate communicative potential.

As instances of multimodal communication, these sites mix different modes, include a range of media, and draw these together as multimediational articulations. In contrast, views on Web sites have tended to be polarized: On one side are graphic design and visual elements, whereas on the other side are informational and structural concerns. From a media and communication design perspective, however, graphic and computational elements of a Web site may be considered equally important, intertwined, and inseparable. It is this integrated design that users meet and engage with in mediatized communication (Skjulstad & Morrison, 2005).

Both the selected sites present playful manifestations of the link between design practice and artful digital media underpinned by skillful information systems design. Although explicitly experimental, these sites are also instances of commercial Web design. They offer us examples of a merging of concepts commonly used in research discourse relating to the Web, such as form and function, window and mirror, and aesthetics and usability. I refer to these concepts, and I review them critically in framing my analysis. To analyze the expressive and emergent character of these sites, I have drawn up three related conceptual categories: *multimodal navigation, compositional density,* and *visual layering.* I apply these concepts to textual analysis of the two sites. I situate these three concepts in a communication design perspective that relates text to contexts and sees textual analysis of emerging textual forms as providing rich resources for understanding digital media in the making.

Outline of Chapter and Methods

My chapter has, as its point of departure, humanist traditions of text analysis applied to digital media (Bolter & Grusin, 1999; Liestøl, 1999; Fagerjord, 2003; Bolter, 2003a). In reaching toward an interdisciplinary communication design perspective, my analysis refers to research in design studies, media studies, and interaction design. Elements from these fields are combined in an interdisciplinary communication-oriented analytical approach related to social semiotics.

The two selected Web sites are drawn from hundreds of Web sites I have investigated since the late 1990s. This investigation has taken place alongside developments in the Web and with respect to the growing understanding of the Web as multiple media. Analytically, however, media studies research into Web media has often lagged behind 'designerly' and artistic innovation in Web design. My approach, therefore, has been developed through the interconnection of practice and theory and combinations of these (Bolter, 2003b). It is informed by my own Web use, my involvement in diverse and collaborative Web design development and its analysis (e.g., Skjulstad & Morrison, 2005), and by a collaborative study of related commercial Web media (Morrison & Skjulstad, 2007, Chapter 4). Selected screengrabs from the two Web sites form an important part of the chapter. I encourage readers to break the fold of these print pages and to access these sites and experience their dynamic properties for themselves.

The chapter is structured as follows: (a) Web sites as complex texts; (b) analytical concepts; (c) analysis, including design contexts, multimodal navigation, visual layering, and compositional density; (d) discussion; and (e) conclusion.

INTERDISCIPLINARITY AND WEB TEXTS

Media in Transition

Compositionally, digital media formats and new textual forms emerge as part of wider cultural changes that incorporate developments in communication technologies. However, new media forms are usually not entirely new. They emerge through social processes that are related to earlier mediational technologies and communicative practices (Bolter & Grusin, 1999; Thorburn, 2003; Gitelman, 2006), ones that are part of an ongoing process of change. Gitelman (2006: 5) views media as culturally and historically situated, reminding us that 'even the newest new media come from somewhere.' Similarly, Thorburn (2003: 21) observes that 'The new grows out of the old, repeats the old, embraces, reimagines and extends the old.'

Prior to the arrival of digital media, in the humanities, various media (e.g., the press, television) have been studied and critiqued, often with the aim of uncovering issues related to biased representations of power, class, race, and gender (see Bolter, 2003b). Media critique, together with creative practice, have contributed to the development and understanding of new media forms and genres. Several older media, such as television and film, have the common property that they unfold through time (Liestøl, 1999). Increasingly, this is also a feature of Web sites that have developed from early page-derived forms to more dynamic ones. Further, the boundaries among media, advertising, marketing, and art are often now blurred (Gibbons, 2005). In such a context, novel media expressions may challenge the analytical apparatus at hand for the close scrutiny of communication, especially when these entail multiple media in multiple relations. This is the case with Web sites in which multiple media are copresent and are in dynamic relations to one another.

Despite its spread and diversity, the Web is not widely studied as a medium that includes dynamic media expressions. Research on hypertext and hypermedia has been especially important in recognizing new multimediational practice in digital composition, as in the work of Landow (1997) and of Liestøl (1999) on hypermedia. On the Web, however, we may encounter texts akin to the one shown at the start of this chapter. Compositionally, such texts are realized through the mixing and combining of several modes, such as written text, images, animations, and music. They are instances of what is often referred to as multimodal discourse. However, contemporary multimodal discourse analysis rarely covers multilinear, digital mediation.

My approach is to view Web texts as examples of media in transition, in which dynamic multimediation occurs. I argue that closer attention is needed to the interdisciplinary linkages of form and function, of structure and expression, and of mode and medium. Together, these connections allow us to see the overall integrated communicational aspects of Web texts not only as media types or information structures but as designs for communication and articulations of communication design.

Promotional Design Discourses

Analysis of advertising forms part of the context for developing a communication design perspective on Web design. Advertising on the Web has often been perceived in terms of blinking banners, boxes with company logos, and annoying audiovisual noise. However, it increasingly takes on other forms (Morrison & Skjulstad, 2007, Chapter 4). Research on online advertising tends not to inquire into the textual levels of the mediationally marketed but rather focuses on audience behaviors, audience reception, and quantitative market-oriented analysis (Li et al., 1999; Chen & Rogers, 2006). Less apparent in the research on Web design and digital advertising, however, is attention to persuasive texts, where creativity and artistic skill is at the core of mediation online. Web designers need to mediate their own creative communicative talent and achievements so as to be present in the marketplace and to maintain and attract clients. Here, the genre of the Web portfolio is important (see below).

The Web sites I study are, however, rather different from traditional adverts that combine written text and images on a page, in a magazine, or on a poster (e.g., Kress & van Leeuwen, 1996). Within media studies, advertising has been discussed as social communication (Leiss et al., 1990) and as persuasive semiosis at the textual and ideological levels (e.g., Williamson, 1978/1994). As early as the 1970s, graphic design became important in giving companies a recognizable graphical profile (Hollis, 1997). Today, online advertising often fights for consumers' attention in the face of other user-driven interests and professional mediations. Recently, there has been a shift in advertising from informing the customer about the product, its price, and quality to attempting to persuade the consumer to purchase the product on the basis of its desirability or symbolic significance (Barnard, 1995: 33).

Advertising in the digital domain looks for ways to persuade us but also to engage us in contributing productively to the shared mediation of the marketed (Chapter 4). In recent years, focus has been placed on the phenomenon of branding (Moor, 2003; Arvidsson, 2005; Lash & Lury, 2007). With the advent of *YouTube* and other social networking applications and sites, attention is shifting to shared production of mediated advertising messages among corporations, advertising and Web bureaus and consumers. For Jansson (2002), this occurs to such a degree that he sees a merger of the research fields of media studies and consumption studies. Innovative Web sites are no longer only associated with net art or experimentation in Web design for its own sake. Dynamic and aesthetically designed Web interfaces have now become part of mainstream businesses on the Web. According to Engholm (2002), experimental avant-garde designer and 'branding sites' have many similarities in bringing an entire multimedia register into play. To date, few studies exist as to how this is articulated textually as communication design.

Through the genre of the Web portfolio, the item for sale in the two selected sites is predominantly the creative and experimental design solutions that the design companies may provide a potential client. Designers' online portfolios offer examples of Web expressions where multimodality is not only time-based and multilinear but where it is also situated in a media culture in which creativity and skills in visual design are integral to promotional strategies. Therefore, multimodal discourse needs to be attuned to the extra layers of media complexity in such Web sites, as well as the complexities of contemporary digital media culture.

Multimodal Digital Discourse: Modes and Media

A theory of multimodal discourse (Kress & van Leeuwen, 2001) has been developed to investigate the communicational strategies employed in various texts, contexts, and interactions. The theory has shifted from an initial focus on the 'language' of visual communication (see Kress & van Leeuwen, 1996) to communication involving multiple modes (Kress & van Leeuwen, 2001), such as video, text, graphics, and so on. These scholars have further reframed questions about what a mode is to ask how people use the variety of semiotic resources to communicate in concrete social contexts. In their framework, 'design' is defined as 'means of realising discourses in a communication situation, but designs also add something new: they realise the communication situation which changes socially constructed knowledge into social (inter)action' (Kress & van Leeuwen, 2001: 5).

This approach to design, however, is in need of some clarification if we are to relate it further to the Web. Kress and van Leeuwen regard design as separate from the material production of the semiotic product or the actual material articulation of the semiotic event (Kress & van Leeuwen, 2001: 6). For them design is about the provision of resources for meaning making by participants to a communicative event. Although this is, in itself, not an issue, these theorists see design as concerned with articulation and interpretation. In my view, this is logical, but it is also problematic. A multimodal discourse approach to communication emphasizes (a) semiotic resources for communication (the modes and the media), and (b) the communicative practices where these resources are used. To see multimodal discourse as the result of composition without examining the textual constructions as a part of such discourse weakens the understanding of what those resources for meaning making actually are. For van Leeuwen (2005), 'design' constitutes a communicative potential that is articulated through media texts, such as Web sites. How this potential is manifested in textual expression that is multimodally composed is therefore important.

Web Texts as Multimodal

The Web has come to a point where artistry and design are central to mediated communication (Hjort, 2001). In many sites, form and content are inseparable (Manovich, 2001; Bolter & Gromala, 2003). This is so in contemporary, artistic, or artful Web designs where embedded media files move and where a medley of media types are blended into a digital and dynamic montage (Skjulstad, 2007b). Many Web interfaces in this mould are graphically rich. A problem arises when the objects of study are Web sites rather than other media forms, such as a magazine. Web sites are not only multimodal, but also multilinear, and unfold through use over time. The combinations of semiotic resources in these texts may not present themselves in a given order but may be read and discoursed in a multiplicity of combinations over time.

Current approaches to social semiotics in a digital age, as advocated by Kress and van Leeuwen (2001), do not address what Liestøl (1999) refers to as discourse as discoursed. Multimodal online texts may be regarded as multimodal discourse as discoursed because of the proximity and relations of multiple modalities that are realized across links, windows, and sections of sites. They unfold through time and in use. At a macrolevel, multimodal Web site discourse needs to be understood as multilinear. At a more microlevel, the communicative discourse potential lies within the design for possible connections among parts of these dynamic compositions.

Web Sites as Multiple, Dynamic Compositions

Semiotic resources other than written text were integrated gradually into Web sites as the Web evolved multimodally. The Web is now a multi-medium. It borrows from older media conventions (Bolter & Grusin, 1999). However, the Web is not currently a set of refashioned and reme-diated old media expressions attuned to a new medium. In Web interface design, the potential for expression has been radically transformed since the inception of this communication medium. Early Web pages were remediations of written text on paper and eventually moved 'from page to screen' (Snyder, 1997). The range of Web site formats has increased since the early days of the medium; as a result, metaphors other than those derived from the book are now emerging.

Web interfaces, often composed through creative use of the applica-tion *Macromedia Flash*, may be described in terms of dynamic interfaces (Skjulstad, 2004). In dynamic interfaces, kinetic and time-based media types such as video and animation move. Dynamic interfaces also tend to have kinetic qualities dependent on or independent of users' actions. This movement is integrated into Web interfaces at a textual level, for exam-ple, through visualizations of transitions between sections of the site, by way of moving menus, and via internal navigation in single-screen inter-face environments (Skjulstad & Morrison, 2005). The kinetic qualities in dynamic interfaces, therefore, not only lie in the so-called content (see Liestøl, 2006) but also in the overall composition of a Web site. This 'con-tent' typically tends to be conceptualized as being placed in an informa-tion structure commonly referred to as the interface.

Interfaces are taken up in research on Human–Computer Interaction (HCI). However, research into Web design has often been polarized between approaches from HCI and those on graphic design. I address these briefly here because they impact on how Web sites are conceptual-ized and studied. Although both approaches have valid mutual critiques, elements of each are important in developing a fuller view of communica-tion design.

Visual Analysis and Web Sites

Because the main focus of research on Web site design has been strongly biased toward technical and functional issues, aesthetics and communica-tion have not been regarded as equally important (Thorlacius, 2004). Engholm and Salamon (2005), however, carried out a stylistic analysis of online banks in which a graphic design approach to interface design is evident. Such an analysis could have been conducted on adverts printed on paper. Its focus on the graphic omits attention to related structural analysis. However, Engholm and Salamon highlight how various Web sites communicate design norms and forms of social distinction and the role of graphics therein. Although it is now accepted that the difference in appearance and style are important for securing the attention of audiences (Crampton Smith & Tabor, 1995), the aspect of style, however, is also to be found, I claim, in more than the graphic design of a Web site.

In innovative Web design that stretches conventions, a site's functionality is often tightly integrated into its visual character. How the site looks and behaves is just as much a part of communication as are the texts and images that also constitute the site. Graphic design, then, becomes just as important as written text and is not reducible to what Garrett (2003) has labeled the 'presentational layer' in digital artifacts. To place the graphic design layer as the 'top' layer—the last and superficial part of a Web design project—makes perfect sense when describing how to develop Web sites from an information system developer's point of view. However, this truncates the textual aspects of compositions. Seeing graphic elements as merely 'skins' ignores what has already been designed, crafted, and published through the interrelationships among structure, modality and 'message.' A communication design view sees these elements as semiotically connected and not merely structurally layered.

The question 'What are these'? in the title to this chapter may be answered by conceptualizing Web sites such as *Bleed* or *Volumeone* as multimodal compositions. The communicational character and potential for user activity of these sites is more subtle than, for example, buying a book at amazon.com. Multimodally, the sites serve as examples of how Web design can be conceptualized and designed experimentally and as coherent texts for communication. Closer analysis is needed to further expand our notions of the Web as a medium in transition, where creativity, artistry, and skills help push the norms of generally 'accepted' Web design in a direction beyond existing normative and rule-based approaches.

Web Portfolios

Electronic portfolios are now important in professional contexts, including those of Web designers and design companies. The Web portfolio has evolved as a parallel genre to portfolio types already existing on paper (Linton, 2000). The portfolio is a promotional genre, related to advertising, and is now used to feature the creative work of Web designers. Web designers' portfolios provide rich examples of Web compositions designed to communicate multimodally. They achieve this goal expressively in an ensemble of graphics, media elements, interaction design, and site structure. An overarching portfolio-like structure is often used to show potential clients work that has been accomplished. It also demonstrates how the design companies choose to present and mediate themselves on the Web, not necessarily restricted by the demands of clients, thereby offering additional options, especially concerning Web interface design.

Form and Function Intertwined

The merging of professional roles, skills, and domains, described as a 'Bauhaus design in the service of information design' (Manovich, 2002: 1), are observable in the Web designers' sites selected here. Form and function are intertwined. The combination of skills and competence in interaction design, information architecture, graphic design, and commercial communication, combined with the ability to implement their ideas, make these designers' Web sites into instances of what Löwgren and Stolterman (2004) call 'dynamic gestalts.' The dynamic gestalt is viewed as an integration of various elements in interaction design, that is, .' . . the overall character of a digital artefact cannot be described by simply adding up a number of particular qualities. The artefact is more than the sum of its constituent parts–that is, it has holistic or emergent qualities' (Löwgren & Stolterman, 2004: 137). Dynamic gestalts are for interaction design what multimodal composition is for communication design.

In focusing on multimodal discourse and composition, interdisciplinary constructs are needed that assist us in examining textually the multiple relations within and across media, modes, and mediations. To connect the writings on multimodal discourse and interdisciplinary Web design to the types of texts that appear in Web designers' portfolios, I have devised three macroconcepts. These concepts combine aspects of related approaches presented earlier. The combinations are geared toward developing a more microlevel analysis in which combinatorial features are situated in relation to actual texts. This microanalysis and the macroterms both contribute to a wider view of communication design in which the intersections of the mediated, the graphic, information structures, and Web technologies all play a part.

ANALYTICAL CONCEPTS

Core Concepts for the Analysis

The three concepts I have developed are *multimodal navigation, visual layering,* and *compositional density.* Through these concepts, I show that we may move from a focus on modes in the study of multimodality to multiple media, multiple modes, and their articulations in dynamic, digital texts.

Multimodal Navigation

Navigation in Web sites refers to a user's movement through different parts and to the activity of a user engaging with a multilinear digital text, where the user has to follow links to access the various nodes. Navigation may be visualized in several ways other than the link convention of colored underlined words (Landow, 1997; Nielsen, 2000). In a more multimodal view of navigation, markers of points and spaces between links and destinations may be visualized by animated transitions or tunnels (Siegel, 1996), marking and integrating system and interface.

In experimental, emergent art sites on the Web, multimodal navigation is incorporated as part of their material articulation. *Jodi.org* is an important example. It offers an early example of how experimental navigation may be used as a strategy for estranging the user through making features in browsing Web sites into an arena for artistic practice. *Jodi.org* thus demonstrates that mediation takes place through the interconnections and interplay between the system and the surface of a Web site.

Jodi.org broke many conventions in Web navigation (Greene, 2004) by not providing users with any idea about what would happen when following a link, and by placing links randomly in several screens and using buttons, parodying mainstream computational styles, and visuals. Whereas Nielsen's (2000) usability norms are geared toward commercial communication and attuned to guiding users in their quest for information or purchases as effectively as possible, *Jodi.org* is designed as a metacomment to the entire Web medium. Navigating the site presents us with the unavoidable realization that artistic experimentation makes ironic existing hypertextual conventions of linking and navigation and our formalized expectations of them.

Such sites are examples of how experimental navigation with a strong focus in visual design adds a multimodal twist to conventions developed for verbal text markup that was then multimodally extended. Web design companies and their uses of portfolios often offer a medley of multimodal navigation as evidence of their professional Web design diversity. Multimodal navigation is also related to a second concept that concerns the layering of visual elements in a multimodal site. This further demonstrates that the textual articulation of interaction design for navigation may partly be merged with a site's 'content.'

Visual Layering

The metaphor of layering has been widely used in digital domains. The application *Hypercard*, according to Manovich (2002), was incremental in the conceptualizing of electronic texts as stackable 'electronic paper' based on the metaphor of playing cards. The application *Photoshop*, produced by Adobe, applies layers as a central metaphor. I apply layering to point to Web sites as multilinear and multimodal texts that allow for the creation of a 3D-like space, in which we see the stacking of thin and semi-transparent layers of different media compositions within a composition. Manovich (2001) points to a tendency within new media to move between textual coherence and assonance. He discusses this notion in terms of compositing versus montage. Although he regards montage as affording dissonances among the elements in a composition, compositing .' . . aims to blend them into a seamless whole' (Manovich, 2001: 144). Instead of only creating such seamless wholes in terms of temporal sequence, layering represents a strategy for extending such a seamless-ness in terms of screen space. A Web interface is essentially flat, and layering refers to strategies for extending the screen surface by placing elements on top of each other to increase the mediational space without disrupting the expressive composition. Layering also refers to ways that multimodality in Web composition is realized by placing various modes close to each other to achieve montage-like assemblies of different media expressions as part of a whole. This creates connections among separate entities in an interface so that together they are perceived as a whole, even if they are stored as separate files.

Layering is visible, for example, in the Web site by *Volumeone*. The site provides possibilities for a user to group separate mini-sites in relation to a background so that in sum they form a 'dynamic gestalt' (see Löwgren & Stolterman, 2004). In my view, seeing Web sites as dynamic gestalts does not reduce them to merely architecture, navigation, images, or links. It allows us to frame them holistically.

Compositional Density

Multimodal interfaces are characterized by a variety of media types and their intersections. They may be understood through what I term 'compositional density.' Bolter and Grusin (1999) use the term 'hypermediacy' to refer to a density in visual information in interfaces, often found in computer-mediated communication, as well as in older media forms such as television and even in pop art paintings. The layered and dense representation of and fascination for the medium, and indeed its materiality (as discussed by Bolter & Grusin, 1999), is further discussed by Bolter and Gromala (2003). They refer to the representational presence of computer-mediated interfaces in terms of mirrors. The window and the mirror are widely discussed and critiqued metaphors. The window represents the transparent flow of information, transmitted light, and the unmediated, whereas the mirror with its opaque and reflective surface denotes the opposite (Friedberg, 2006).

According to Bolter and Gromala, the metaphor of the mirror is helpful as a concept for approaching interfaces, which break illusions of transparency in mediated communication. They see the concept of the mirror as denoting interfaces that draw attention to the mediated and the medium, making our interactions with the medium into a mediational experience. The concept of the mirror, as a reflective surface, is proposed in opposition to the transparency of the window, where a direct access to 'content' or information is the main aim. The mirror as a mimetic metaphor may be slightly misleading in the context of electronic communication because what you ultimately see in a mirror is yourself. However, Bolter and Gromala see the design strategies of transparent windows and reflective mirrors as a continuum, where no interface can be fully reflective or wholly transparent. The strength of the two concepts lies in what they imply more than their practical application in actual textual analysis. Friedberg (2006: 15) argues that 'The metaphor of the mirror–producing substitutive, deceptive, illusory vision–and the metaphor of the window–producing direct, veridical, unmediated vision–imply very different epistemological consequences.'

Not having to meet demands of clients may provide designers and artists with artistic freedom to design beyond the conventions of more factual domains of online communication. Although the metaphor of the window represents domains of factual and conventional Web design, the mirror is applied as a metaphor for mediationally expressive texts. The concept of compositional density therefore lies closer to the concept of the mirror than the window. It refers to aesthetics and styles in interface design, as well as the complexity in all the connections among the various layers of copresent modes and media, which together saturate the site with multiple meanings. In the *Bleed* Web site, the entrance screen is composed through placing graphics and text on top of a photograph that covers the whole screen. Together, the combinations of these different modes underline the semantic meaning of the word 'bleed,' as I discuss later.

Compositional density is also a concept that distinguishes certain Web compositions from illustrated, written electronic texts. The written text in both the selected sites serves as a mode of communication and a semiotic resource; it does not hold a privileged position over that of images or graphics. Compositional density also refers to ways in which the transitions between sections of sites are visualized through animation. In dense, visual compositions, rich multimodal discourse is produced through combinations and juxtapositions of various modes in dynamic gestalts.

ANALYSIS

Design Contexts

Communicating Web Design as Commodity

The visual design companies, *Volumeone* and *Bleed*, promote themselves through alternative strategies in the form of innovative and comprehensive website design. Both *Volumeone* and *Bleed* are closely connected to a strand in advertising, where the product is not seen in isolation but is approached as a set of concepts or representations of certain styles or aesthetics connected to the product that is for sale. It is style, aesthetics, and skills in the case of *Volumeone* and *Bleed* that are the products for sale. The Web sites, therefore, need to make sure that this is communicated clearly and that visitors, consumers, and actual and potential clients all grasp this. They therefore do not sell commodities in a traditional, material sense but their communication expertise (Jansson, 2002; Lash & Lury, 2007).

The Interface Is the Message: Volumeone

Since 1997, *Volumeone* has produced media designs, as its Web site says, for a 'multi-disciplinary approach to the creations of visual solutions for print, motion, and digital media.' One of the main functions of the Web site is to mediate the company's design work and achievements. A section of the site is a portfolio that presents projects carried out for clients. Several functions are at play in the portfolio. First, the site operates as an overall design portfolio for the company. Second, sections of the site highlight work conducted for specific clients that may include more than one brief. This double function can be described as Linton (2000: 9) puts it: 'When I look at a design portfolio, I am interested in the content of course; but I am also interested in the design of the portfolio itself. Sometimes it tells me as much as the work it presents.'
Volumeone has a formal business-oriented section and an experimental section called 'seasons.' The 'seasons' section consists of small sites within the site, where each season (spring, summer, autumn, and winter) have a separate Web site. For each year, four seasons are added to the site. The main site contains 26 'seasons,' and each of these houses four different visual explorations, which are connected to a main site. They typically open up in one or two small pop-up windows. These pop-up windows are designed to be viewed together with the site that anchors the 'seasons' sites.
A third component to *Volumeone's* overall portfolio is also apparent in the subsections of the 'seasons.' This is the informal, experimental, and

emerging iterations of change over time, as the section titles suggest. This can be seen in one of the subsections (Figure 11.2), where a small visual experiment is shown as an overlay. Design elements from the seasons are used and redesigned in projects for clients. Their clients include brands such as MTV, Adidas, and DKNY, as well as less well-known ones.

In the site, *Volumeone* describes the designs in the 'seasons' section as 'conceptual narratives and personal visual works.' Through this selection of works, they present the range of the firm's design to potential customers. However, what is important is that this section also serves as a creative 'lab' for the development and experimentation outside of client-commissioned work. They use these as sources of inspiration and renewal (Grocott, 2003). Projects initiated by the designers' own interests may be productively channeled into projects paid for by clients. The 'seasons' sections exemplify a common design practice that extends beyond strict boundaries between autonomous artistic practice and commercial design projects. Projects initiated and funded by clients may provide designers with some means to follow their artistic interests that in turn may be developed further commercially.

The visual experiments shown in the 'seasons' section date from the late 1990s to the present. They contain several features of dynamic interfaces (Skjulstad, 2004; Skjulstad & Morrison, 2005). These features are, among others, dynamic transitions within the site, kinetic typography, experimental interaction design, extensive use of graphics, and an overall integration of 'form' and 'content' into an integrated unity, where the interface is the main feature. Together, we may see that these elements and their uses in particular designs are part of a wider communication design strategy adopted and enacted by this innovative company.

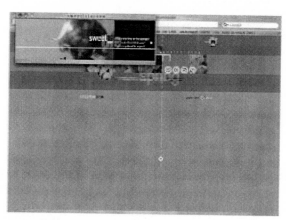

Figure 11.2. Screengrab from Volumeone.com 'seasons' section, 'spring fever' from 1999. The small window in the upper part of the screen shows one of the visual experiments.

The experiments in visual communication located in the 'seasons section' make little sense if seen from an informational task-oriented perspective, which values free and unhindered interaction with 'information' (e.g., Nielsen, 2000). It is therefore important to shift the set of premises on which this Web site is understood so as to account for other means of communication than a mere effective and information-centered notion of Web design. As a company that profiles innovation in Web design, *Volumeone* demonstrates that there are more ways of communicating than through a transparent interface filled with clear and uncluttered 'content.' A traditional distinction between content and form often found within Web-related discourse is not helpful in comprehending this site.

Selling Style: *Bleed*

Bleed was established in 2000 and covers various strands in the wider design field, such as design strategies, concept development, consultancy, project management, interaction design, graphic design, animation, and technical development. The main focus of the *Bleed* site is to showcase the group's design competence. This is carried out via the mediation of their overall Web site and through a separate portfolio section of work. The site demonstrates various visual techniques in online promotional design discourse that differ from those present in static and page-like Web sites. In short, this site is concerned with conveying multimodal design expertise (see Figure 11.3).

The *Bleed* site is structured around seven main categories (see Figure 11.3). It is composed in *Macromedia Flash*. This allows for dynamic transitions both within the site and among sections of the site. The overall organization and architecture of the site is at first glance quite conventional, but when taking a closer look, certain features stand out. Most of these are located in the portfolio section. In the following, I examine aspects of these features.

The portfolio sections of both *Bleed* and *Volumeone* show mediational strategies at work through more than what is commonly conceived of as 'content.' The concept of content in relation to Web design is not something one can pour into a container. For Liestøl (2006: 261), the '. . . term "content" is empty, or without content.' The content and the interface cannot be separated in a site that aims to experiment with and showcase Web design. As spaces where the designers for these companies can use their expertise as communicators, and extend the ways in which they can promote their work online, these Web sites also demonstrate that Web mediation may be regarded as taking place both through the surface, as well as through the structure of Web sites. I now apply the three concepts of experimental navigation, layering, and visual density to exemplify this idea.

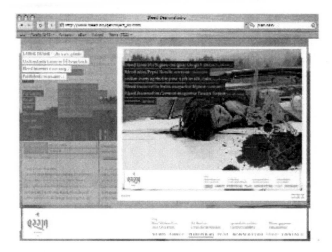

Figure 11.3. The Web site of the Norwegian company Bleed.no uses juxtapositions of different windows and visual layering as part of their self-presentation on the Web.

MULTIMODAL NAVIGATION

Finding and Changing Direction

One main feature, central in various research approaches related to the Web, is the notion of navigation. When the Web was launched, there was a need to ensure that users understood how to move within and among sites. The idea of easily understandable navigational systems was thus essential for the users' ability to access the Web. Earlier hypertext and hypermedia systems, especially the multimodalities of many CD-ROMs, were precursors to the vast number of sites and users that were ushered in by the specifically networked medium of the Web. Drag-and-drop navigation has been employed by Apple and many other producers of digital material but not primarily as a twist to conventional navigational strategies for Web sites. *Volumeone* experiments with such navigational strategies by way of tight integration of graphic design and site structure. Again, it is in the mediation that graphic design becomes intertwined with interaction design.

Volumeone: *Consume/Perceive*

The following images are from one of the online compositions in the 'seasons' section in *Volumeone*. This mini-site is named 'consumed/perceived.' It is made in *Flash*. It integrates still photo, animation, music, written, and moving text into one coherent composition. The written text serves more as a graphical decorative element than text for close reading. In the splash screen of this 'season,' an image of a plastic tray for making ice cubes is in the center (Figure 11.4). A small red circle is located above it. By clicking on this circle, the tray jumps up and down.

To the right of the ice cube tray are four small squares. To the left, there is one small square. By dragging one of the four squares into the square on the left and dropping it, the small subsite shown appears (Figure 11.5). This interface offers visual prompts to users. The composition is designed to only be completed through their active participation. The subsite is not apparent until this move within a dynamic interface is enacted, thus it enables discovery of several mediational layers.

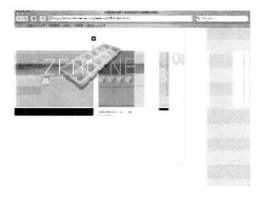

Figure 11.4. The splash screen of one of the 'seasons' called 'consumed/perceived.'

Figure 11.5. Screengrab from the subsite 'consumed/perceived' appears when dragging and dropping one of the squares shown in Figure 11.4.

Bleed: *Visualizing Navigation Through Layering*

The *Bleed* site also contains an interesting example of what I see as an experimental and unconventional navigation system. In Figure 11.6, the right area of the screen is covered by an image. A conventional navigational system would contain a 'close' button in the upper corner of this image. This convention is found in many operative systems and applications. In this site, however, to close the window, the user has to click on the background that surrounds the picture. This background is partly faded out by a grey, semitransparent layer. Although *Bleed* has incorporated unusual navigational features into its site, it is still not experimental to the degree that the novel navigation may be said to obscure access to the various parts of the site.

This example shows how novel solutions in Web navigation have begun to permeate commercial online discourse. This example from Scandinavia also shows the scope within which repertoires of online communication are being expanded outside the domain of art and are realized in creative approaches to commercial discourse online. Such layering aestheticizes navigation and brings surface and system design into one aesthetic mediation. Multimodal navigation thus becomes part of what is mediated in this site. Mediation transgresses functionality and design for user interaction but blends these into integrated parts of the communication design.

Figure 11.6. Screengrab from Bleeds' portfolio section. Here, images from a web development assignment Bleed has done for the Norwegian furniture design firm 'Norway says' is presented.

Aetheticization in Navigation: Movement

The Web is no longer a medium for static texts even if initially it may have been conceptualized as one. In the late 1990s, the Web designer and writer David Siegel (1996) provided examples of how a simple GIF animation could be integrated into a main Web site as part of its interface. He demonstrated that dynamic qualities to a Web interface could be realized without having to rely on high bandwidth.

In the *Bleed* site, motion is used, visualized, and aestheticized (see Welch, 1997) in the transitions from one section to another and as a means of signaling that specific categories in the menus are selected. The transition from one background image to another is made through a cutout figure. This shape resembles the Norwegian heraldic symbol of a lion. It is scaled until it completely covers the original image. These kinds of transitions are characteristic of sites crafted in the software *Flash*. Transitions are used in *Bleed* when a new page is loading; they provide continuous links among the different parts of the site (Skjulstad, 2004). These transitions correspond, in part, to what Siegel (1996) referred to as 'tunnels.' Then, *Flash* intros, providing dynamic entrances to Web sites, were widely used and eventually seen as annoying visual noise used to block direct entrance to a site's 'information' (Skjulstad, 2004). *Bleed* uses a new version of tunnels. It visualizes transitions between sections of the site with *Flash* animation. These animations do not run for long enough to be perceived as animations but operate as dynamic visual markers of a change of the users' location. Such connections work communicatively to visualize site structure. Via this visualization, *Bleed* integrates graphical and structural elements of the site into a compositional unity.

Motion is also used when signaling that a user has selected a link when mousing over a string of text in the left-hand submenu. In the menus, a moving blurring and greying out of the blackish background on which the text is written signals that these texts are links for potential selection. This is done through a vertical movement where these text fields are transformed from grey to white, aiding the navigation and recognition of links. By adding motion to this submenu, the user also gets feedback from the *Bleed* site and is likely to understand that the words are markers of links.

Navigation as Composition

Through making navigation part of the visual composition of a Web site, and by aestheticization of navigation, both *Volumeone* and *Bleed* demonstrate the interconnectedness of system and surface. The content and navigation as part of the sites' interfaces merge into single entities-they are equal partners in online compositions (Manovich, 2001). Navigation should be extended to account for more than a means of transport among various sections of a Web site and to being an integrated compositional feature in online multimodal and multilinear composition.

VISUAL LAYERING

Introduction

From hypertext research and theory, connections between nodes are usually represented as interlinked 'documents' (Landow, 1997). The links and relations among sections of a Web site are usually articulated as sequences in time. First, the user is placed in one screen, clicks on a link, and is transferred to another screen. A different way of expressing this relation among levels of information may be to borrow a term and a technique from the software Adobe *Photoshop*, namely 'layers.' In this instance, semitransparent screen designs are visually placed on top of each other, with the underlying one shining through. In this way, visual layering forms the basis of an online form of superimposition, instead of just multiple sequences (see Figure 11.7).

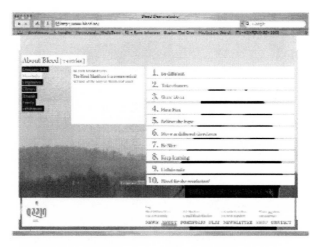

Figure 11.7. Submenu in Bleed. The white text boxes where the clickable menus are located are placed on top of the background photo, making it shine through the area for navigation.

Visual Layering in *Bleed*

The space in the middle of each screen in *Bleed* differs from many Web interfaces in that it is filled with photographs instead of being left empty for text and white space or filled with just a simple background colour. Another feature found in this Web site is transparency. My view of this concept differs from that given by Bolter and Gromala (2003). They regard transparency as an important aspect of electronically mediated interfaces as approached in terms of transparent windows through which it is possible to view information. The mediated surface is not given much attention as a mediational surface, with the result that the mediation more or less disappears. In contrast, in the case of *Bleed*, so as to use the screen space fully, the stacking and layering of information is made even more visible through making transparent layers of information placed one on top of another (Figure 11.8). As can be seen to the right, *Bleed* includes a site designed for the furniture designers *Norway Says*. This site within the site is displayed in windows that are gradually placed on top of the underlying background photography. On pushing a button that is provided, the presentation of the site is expanded for closer view.

In addition, when clicking, an interesting feature occurs: The main presentational window, a bigger version of the already visible window, is placed on top of all the other elements (see Figure 11.9). A new semi-transparent layer is overlayed on the previous screen. Here, the picture from the *Norway Says* site is enlarged, and a sub-submenu appears on top

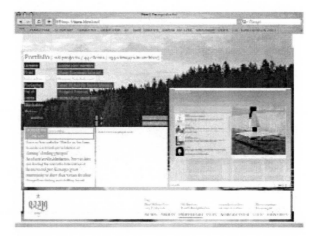

Figure 11.8. Example of layering in the Bleed portfolio. Here, the windows used to present a Web development project for the Norwegian furniture design firm, *Norway Says*, is overlaying the background photographs.

Figure 11.9. The window with the selected project in the portfolio is selected, and the background image is blurred out of focus by a transparent grey layer.

of the underlying menu. This is a semispatial way of simulating three-dimensionality in interface design, allowing the submenus to shine through from below. This technique makes visually dense interfaces manageable by partly concealing layers of information without removing them completely from sight, as is the case in an html 'jump' when a user moves from one html document to another (see Skjulstad, 2004; Skjulstad & Morrison, 2005).

In the *Bleed* site, layering is tightly interwoven with navigation. Layering becomes a navigational strategy through the stacking of elements on top of each other, instead of referring the user to another document via a link. Layering is designed to help the user stay in one place when searching for more information within a category. This is shown in the presentation of the Web design for *Norway Says* (see Figure 11.9). There is a pedagogical sense to this layering: It is designed to help the user not to lose sight of the part of the site from which she or he departs. The 'screen of departure' is visible beneath the semitransparent screen. Visual layering serves as both an expansion of screen space within a category and a means of going in more detail without leaving the context of departure. This is an example of how graphic design is also entangled with the structure and design for interaction. Graphic design cannot be regarded as mere decoration but rather as integral to the overall construction of the site

Visual Layering in *Volumeone*

Layering is also found in *Volumeone*. Here it is used differently than in *Bleed* and is a result of several windows in an audiovisual composition.

Many of the compositions found in the 'seasons' section are made up of combinations of several pop-up windows, and they are designed to relate to background screens. This layering is relational as the different windows are designed to be seen together and be moved around on the screen. The communicative resources applied in these online compositions are therefore arranged and composed so as to create several coherent combinations depending on the user's actions. Through this technique, *Volumeone* is designed to be discoursed in different ways.

Extending Space

Earlier I discussed instances of graphic design in Web sites that are tightly interwoven with the interaction design. Layering therefore works as a strategy for designing for user-friendly interaction within sites through placing several layers of information on top of each other to assist users in literally keeping sight of the point of departure when following a link. This is demonstrated in the portfolio section of *Bleed*. Layering also provides possibilities for extending the available screen space through stacking layers of information on top of each other instead of in temporal sequence. Layering therefore works as an alternative strategy to the more conventional screen organization and 'page' structure of traditional html-based Web sites.

Compositional Density

'Mirror Mirror'

What I term 'compositional density' occurs when a medley of modes and media co-occur in a Web interface in such a way that they do not stand out as separate elements but form rich and dense compositions. The various interfaces in the 'seasons' section in *Volumeone* may be seen in the light of the metaphor of the mirror described by Bolter and Gromala (2003). In their view of the interface, mirrors may be seen as reflective, and they draw attention to the interface. The mini-sites housed in the 'seasons' section draw attention to the visual design of the interface. Neither of them is designed as sites that contain only 'content.' The interfaces of these are the 'content.' These interfaces are designed so as to focus attention toward *Volumeone*'s abilities to design Web sites with kinetic and aesthetic qualities, visualization of experimental interaction design, and unconventional relations between users' actions and the dynamics in the sites. They function as prototypes, generators, and incubators of creative ideas that are embodied online and may be experienced by users and clients.

Typography

Font and typography are a major topic within graphic design. The role of typography is understated in academic discussions of Web design within Media and Communication Studies on the Web and 'new' media. van Leeuwen (2005) refers to typography as being transformed by new multi-modalities afforded by digital technology. He claims that a whole new way of writing has occurred in computer-mediated communication, where typography now is seen as multimodal and where image becomes more like writing and writing becomes more like image. However, if one looks back to medieval illuminated manuscripts, for example, the *Moralia in Job*, from Citeaux, France, from the early 12th century, one can see the letter 'R' represented through an illustration of a battle between George and the dragon (De la Croix et al., 1991). Here, illustration and type go together in a medieval multimodal composition, which forms the letter 'R.' Fonts and typography as a multimodal means of communication may not be attributed to the computer medium alone.

However, typography is an important feature of the *Bleed* site. The choices of and the blend of fonts are integral to this site. The *Bleed* logo is set in a gothic font. By contrasting this with white space, the lower area of the Web sites mixes a contemporary minimalist use of screen space with a traditional typeface, creating a strong stylistic contrast. In the main menu area, the font is static, and the area behind each written category name is a contrasting white or dark grey. The typography may at first appear to be moving, but the dynamic elements are really the back-grounds that move as the mouse is moved over them. The submenus in this site appear on the left-hand side. There, the blackish areas on which the different subcategories are written with grey-scale letters appear after the image has been loaded. The effect is that the menus look like they are stacked on top of the image.

In this mini-site, typography is not primarily used to provide meaning through words and sentences at the level of language. Typography is used as graphical elements that have the same function as the other semiotic modes in this composition. All the text is not even intended to be read because the text in the middle of the screen (as in Figure 11.10) is small. In the central left in this same image, the text is mirrored, as is the text underneath the central figure of the car and the woman. This text is as much a part of the visual design as it is part of the semantics of word-based graphology.

Figure 11.10. Screengrab from the 'breaking the rulez' mini-site in *Volumeone*'s Web site.

Multimodality at Work: Photo, Text, and Graphics

The opening screen of the *Bleed* site is a clear example of multimodality in a Web composition, where potential meanings are mediated through the interplay among the various modes. I go into detail concerning this interplay in the opening screen (see Figure 11.11). When looking closely at this opening, the use of various modes does not make sense if they are seen separately. The potential meanings of this composition lie in the connections and interplay among the various semiotic resources involved.

Figure 11.11. Opening screen of Bleed.

When the various modes are seen in relation to one another, a specific meaning may be read from them. The meaning of the name *Bleed* supports this reading across modes, graphic and photographic. A lion with a sword (shown in a line drawing) is about to swing it toward the woman's neck shown resting on a cabriolet in a realist photographic style that fills most of the screen. Superimposed graphical blotches represent the splash of blood from this action. This pictorial narrative employs a compositional element referred to as a vector, a graphical device for indicating which element is acted on in a narrative image (Kress & van Leeuwen, 1996). Anna Munster (2006) draws parallels between digital media and baroque. By extending this analogy toward this specific screen design, there is a parallel in motif, as the typical baroque motives are caught in a split second before action is about to take place. That is what is going on in this composition.

Other images that are used as background in *Bleed* depict the same young woman. For example, the image in the 'play' menu is a cropped portrait of the woman (Figure 11.12). We see that her hair covers most of her face. This generates the same ambiguity as the photography discussed earlier when seen together with the words 'play' and 'bleed.' This suggests that this play is not totally without risk. The snapshot aesthetic in this image is at the same time an example of the 'wannabe' coincidental, unarranged, and unprofessional snapshot, and simultaneously it looks like fashion photography through the precision of its planned cropping and the model's pose.

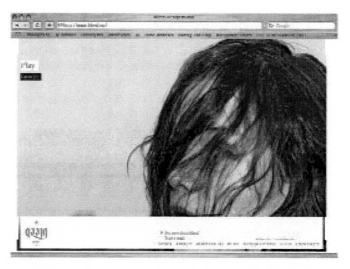

Figure 11.12. Portrait of woman in the Bleed site, serving as background for the category 'play.'

Volumeone: *Grasping Screen Space-Photography and Graphics*

Graphic design creates meaning by presenting and visualizing structures of information that are important to an audience. The most prominent visual elements in many dynamic interfaces are photographs and graphics. Web sites are often elaborate pieces of graphic design. Graphic design aspects might be integrated into the interface, logics, and architecture of Web sites. In *Bleed,* the images are large and cover expansive stretches of the screens throughout the site. Information related to each main category is placed on top of the images, sometimes almost covering them completely. The photographic style employed here is closely connected to the photography found in fashion and lifestyle magazines. Fashion photography typically plays on ambivalence and mystique, along with the bizarre and sometimes even repulsive, in contrast to other renderings of 'beauty' (Andersen, 2006).

The compositional density of both *Bleed* and *Volumeone* is made possible through the layering and stacking of windows. These are examples of multimodal and multilinear compositions. The now widely considered troubling concept of interactivity (e.g., Jensen, 1998) complicates a conception of online multimodal composition. This is because there are many variations on how the different elements of the composition are placed together. In the 'breaking the rulez' mini-site from *Volumeone* discussed earlier, one of the main elements is the person with sunglasses who may be moved across the screen. The small video window besides this person may also be moved around while it plays. Each of the four compositions in this season has a sound track with rock music. On following a link, a new soundtrack plays. While jumping back and forth between the different parts of this mini-Web site within this 'season,' a sonic montage of four different musical tracks is generated. Such montages are examples of multilinear multimodal discourse as discoursed in use, over time. This is because meaning is created through a user's own movement across the possible routes of the multilinear composition.

The style of the images in *Bleed* differs from those in online news sites. They may be seen as remediations (Bolter & Grusin, 1999) of fashion photography. They may also be understood through what Kress and van Leeuwen (2001: 10) refer to as the principle of provenance, where meaning is imported from one area into another. The photographic style borrowed from fashion magazines also emphasizes the importance of the ability of visuals to project a certain look or style online. This use of fashion photographs as wallpapers in this site may be seen as a strategy for indirectly drawing in an element of fashion into *Bleed's* self-presentation.

The style and aesthetics of the use of image in this site are also closely linked to strands of art photography that generally has a tense relationship with commercial and fashion photography. Constructing a relationship between art and fashion photography, to a certain extent, may be used to legitimize politically incorrect imagery. Issues of race, sex, violence, gender, abuse, and so on are explicitly explored in some strands of art photography. By stylistically linking the fashion photography to the art photography, these issues are easier to import into a more commercially oriented design setting, such as a promotional Web site. Compositional density may therefore also refer to a meta-level in these texts. The rich intertextual referencing among various domains such as graphic design, art, and advertising add another level of indirect density.

Graphic Design With Systems Design

Together, the concepts of multimodal navigation, visual layering, and compositional density make visible various connections between what is often presented as a separation between the top layer of a Web site and its underlying system. These connections are typically not discussed in much depth because Web sites tend to be understood in terms of either site usability and/or graphic design (see also Munster, 2003; Skjulstad, 2007a). Whereas a medley of modes and media are in intricate dialogue with each other, sites tend to be visually dense. Through this density, they draw attention to themselves as mediated communication (see Bolter & Grusin, 1999; Bolter & Gromala, 2003). Compositional density not only occurs as a superficial graphical layer on top of the sites' overall design but is interconnected with the sites' inner workings on the system level as well. By making the navigational system in a site part of the visual compositions, both *Volumeone* and *Bleed* demonstrate that Web design cannot be understood only in terms of graphic design or as systems' design.

In the sites discussed earlier, compositional density draws attention to the companies' mastery of designing both system and surface as integrated elements in online composition. Both *Bleed* and *Volumeone* demonstrate that potential for meaning making is not only located at specific places within each mode, but that it lies in the connections and dialogues among the various elements at work in them. Kress and van Leeuwen's theory of multimodal discourse does not fully take such considerations of multimodal, but also multilinear, online compositions into account. The communicational connections among the various modes become problematic. It is this issue that I now discuss further in a wider discussion of multimodal composition.

DISCUSSION AND CONCLUSION

System and Surface Entangled

The sites discussed earlier are instances of Web design that depart from the underlying metaphor of electronic paper central to earlier approaches and practices. They demonstrate intersections among interaction design, graphic design, and underlying system design. These closely interwoven complex compositions are difficult to discuss distinct from their various contributing designs. Experimental yet successful Web design companies such as *Volumeone* and *Bleed* mediate such design complexity. These Web sites work to provide innovative, publicly accessible multimodal Web sites that have been designed to be discoursed in multiple ways. They ask that we, too, as users and consumers are open to such innovation that plays with our expectations and with Web conventions. The sites remain goal-oriented yet are tailored for commercial communication by being different from the Web newspaper or personal homepage. These sites show how communicative resources are drawn together in an interplay of components. In this interplay, multimodal and multilevel compositions are constituted.

To some extent, the modes and media as communicative resources discussed earlier correspond to what Kress and van Leeuwen (2001) refer to as communication modes and resources. In Web design, modes exceed those found on a page in a magazine or a poster ad. The resources at play may include ways of visualizing the functionality and structure of a site and how this is reflected in the interface. The mediating and communicating elements in a site move between the underlying system and the 'presentational layer.'

Kress and van Leeuwen (2001) refer to a move from monomodality to multimodality in communicative practice. They see a shift to selective use of various modes for optimal meaning making in a communication situation. Critically, '. . . meaning is made not only with a multiplicity of semiotic resources, in a multiplicity of modes and media, but also at different "places" within each of these' (Kress & van Leeuwen, 2001: 111). On the Web, these resources may co-occur in an integrated multimodal text and not simply as a fragmented collection of various modes of expression. The question is not which modes are at play, and how they communicate in isolation, but how they are interrelated communicatively.

Multimodal Meaning Through Co-Occurrence

My aim has been to investigate how modes and media interact in online compositions, instead of applying a detailed 'grammar' of any of the modes in use. I argue that the relational quality found in the co-occurrence of various communicative resources in interfaces, such as those discussed here, mediate a complex interplay that is realized by, and in use, over time. As textual coherence, this aligns with the concept of dynamic gestalts mentioned earlier.

Kress and van Leeuwen (2001: 2) partly miss the point when they state that new, digital technologies stimulate the question 'Shall I express this visually or verbally'? In multimodal, Web-based discourse, multiple articulations are often made through the use of multiple modes in one text. These articulations, therefore, cannot be seen as diffuse multiples when it comes to communication. Their communicative intent-always open to interpretation-is not geared toward making several mode-specific meanings but rather providing resources that afford certain meanings through their co-occurrence. It is fruitful not to only see the elements that make up a Web site as a medley of different modes and media. It is rather fruitful to investigate how these elements constitute multimodal compositions through their interplay.

Relational Multimodality

To focus on experimental navigation, visual layering and compositional density in Web sites is to draw attention to a multimodal complexity that involves visualizations and aestheticizations that include the underlying systems in Web compositions. Through breaking conventions of navigation, as well as aestheticizing navigation, both *Volumeone* and *Bleed* make visible important connections between interface and system. These sites use experimental navigational techniques as an artistic strategy for commercial and effective communication, and through this they partly bridge the gap between artistry and commerce, interface and system.

Moreover, the sites demonstrate that the visual design of a Web site is not only located in the graphic design at a superficial level. Integrating navigation into both the aesthetics and style of a Web site makes navigation more than a procedural operation. It becomes part of the overall communicative composition. When modes, such as image and animation, as in the case of *Bleed*, are employed as communicative resources for visualizing a user's possible transition from one section of the site to another, this is an important part of the potential for communication mediated by the site.

By subtle application of layers of communicative resources within *Volumeone* and *Bleed*, screen spaces are used dynamically and may not be regarded as interlinked stacks of electronically mediated paper. The metaphor of layering shows how multimodality in online compositions occurs relationally. Different spaces are still part of the same composition because they lie on top of each other and can be moved around. Layering also refers to the possibilities of expanding screen space by letting the informational level below a certain position in a site shine through, as in *Bleed*. This demonstrates a linkage between graphic design and the technical and organizational composition.

Through the design of visually dense screen spaces made up of different modes that move and may be moved by users, rich examples of multimodal discourse may direct users' attention to the designers' and companies' design skills. These skills are manifested textually in what is referred to as 'content.' In a communication design-oriented view, the overall Web site and its mediational character constitutes this content. Both *Volumeone* and *Bleed* show that the potential for multimodal communication lies in the complex of relations among these. I term this a *relational multimodality*. This is what is being enacted textually and is in need of further analysis. The application of the three concepts developed may be extended to include various types of montage (Skjulstad, 2007b). A better grasp is possible of how designers' Web portfolios are multilinear and multimodal, yet coherent, communicative texts. The concepts of visual layering and compositional density, combined with notions of multimodal and multilinear montage, may contribute to a more comprehensive textual analysis of designers' Web portfolios and their Web sites.

Toward Communication Design

The chapter has aimed at showing how one might take up the challenge of regarding visually rich and experimentally marked Web sites in terms of multimodal mediation for communication. A communication design perspective opens up for discussions of Web design outside of theoretical frameworks made for either developing or evaluating Web sites. A communication perspective on Web sites allows sites that exist outside the borders of established design conventions to be discussed as both commercially oriented, creative, and artistic communication, as well as multimodal composition. Such a perspective allows designers and analysts to incorporate important knowledge from adjacent and relevant fields, such as interaction design, HCI, graphic design, and social semiotics, as well as from media practice.

The textual analyses of designers' portfolios given earlier demonstrate that there is a need for further inquiry into textual analysis of expressions mediated online. Textual analysis within the humanities needs to take on board challenges posed by contemporary digital media practice where multimodality in digital texts reaches beyond what is typically recognized as media. A communication design perspective can help us meet some of the challenges that dynamic interfaces pose to our understanding of text norms, genre crossing, and innovation in digital media.

Kress and van Leeuwen (2001) claim that the age of monomodality is defunct. Once separated, design and production practices may be connected through digital technology. How multiple modes intersect in digital, multilayered, and nonsequential multimodal texts is not fully taken up or applied to the workings and articulations of Web texts. In multimodal online texts, the user's encounter with the text is often both time-based and multilinear. The user's Web discourse is thus made possible through her movement through a dynamic text (Skjulstad & Morrison, 2005). This movement may take place in both a dynamically composed interface and the dynamic modes such as animation, which are integrated into an interface as part of this kinetic communication. In such an environment, different modes may not necessarily be regarded as separate entities or modes by a user. This suggests that such dynamic sites and users' actions in constituting them may be enriched through being seen in the wider complex offered in a communication design-oriented perspective.

When I first encountered the Web sites profiled previously, I asked myself, 'What are these'? In these pages, I have replied that they are multimodal and multilinear online compositions. I argued that these compositions might spur us into expanding prevailing conceptual approaches to the analysis of Web sites. These sites may be understood as media texts in a communication design frame. As the Web continues to emerge in and from use, we are likely to meet further compositions 'on the move,' part known, part freshly designed, and realized in use. In the evolving relations between text and context in Web design, we are also likely to continue to ask 'What are these'? and to continue to refer to close textual analysis of emerging articulations and situated uses.

ACKNOWLEDGMENTS

At the University of Oslo, my thanks to: Andrew Morrison, the MULTIMO project and InterMedia, Gunnar Liestøl, Even Westvang, Ragnhild Tronstad, the PhD group at Department of Media and Communication, project members from *Aesthetics at Work* (the Norwegian Research Council), and related doctoral research funding from that project.

REFERENCES

Andersen, Charlotte. (2006). *Modefotografi: En Genres Anatomi (Fashion Photography: Anatomy of a Genre)*. Copenhagen: Museum Tusculanums Forlag.

Arvidsson, Adam. (2005). 'Brands: A critical perspective.' *Journal of Consumer Culture*. Vol 5, No. 2, 235-258.

Barnard, Malcolm. (1995). 'Advertising: The rhetorical imperative.' In Jenks, Chris. (Ed.). *Visual Culture*. New York: Routledge. 26-41.

Bolter, Jay. (2003a). 'Critical theory and the challenge of new media.' In Hocks, Mary, & Kendrick, Michelle. (Eds.). *Eloquent Images*. Cambridge, MA: The MIT Press. 19-36.

Bolter, Jay. (2003b). 'Theory and practice in new media studies.' In Liestøl, Gunnar, Morrison, Andrew, & Rasmussen, Terje (Eds.). *Digital Media Revisited*. Cambridge, MA: The MIT Press. 19-36.

Bolter, Jay, & Gromala, Diane. (2003). *Windows and Mirrors*. Cambridge, MA: The MIT Press.

Bolter, Jay, & Grusin, Richard. (1999). *Remediation*. Cambridge, MA: The MIT Press.

Chen, Quimei, & Rogers, Shelly. (2006). 'Development of an instrument to develop website personality.' *Journal of Interactive Advertising*. Vol. 7, No. 1. Available at http://www.jiad.org/article86

Crampton Smith, Gillian, & Tabor, Philip. (1995). *The Role of the Artist-Designer*. In Winograd, Terry. (Ed.). *Bringing Design to Software*. New York: ACM Press. 37-57.

De la Croix, Horst, Tansey, Richard, & Kirkpatrick, Diane. (Eds.). (1991). *Gardener's Art Through the Ages*. 9th ed. New York: Harcourt Brace Jovanovich.

Engholm, Ida. (2002). 'Digital style history: The development of graphic design on the Internet.' *Digital Creativity*. Vol. 13, No 4, 193-211.

Engholm, Ida, & Salamon, Karen Lisa. (2005, May 29-31). 'Web genres and styles as socio-cultural indicators: An experimental, interdisciplinary dialogue.' *In the Making. First Nordic Design Research Conference*. Copenhagen. Available at http://www. tii.se/reform/inthemaking/files/p119.pdf

Fagerjord, Anders. (2003). '*Rhetorical convergence: Studying web media*.' In Liestøl, Gunnar, Morrison, Andrew, & Rasmussen, Terje (Eds.). *Digital Media Revisited*. Cambridge, MA: The MIT Press. 225-293.

Friedberg, Anne. (2006). *The Virtual Window*. Cambridge, MA: The MIT Press.

Garrett, Jesse. (2003). *The Elements of User Experience*. New York: New Riders.

Gibbons, Joan. (2005). *Art and Advertising*. London: I.B. Tauris.

Gitelman, Lisa. (2006). *Always Already New*. Cambridge, MA: The MIT Press.

Greene, Rachel. (2004). *Internet Art*. London: Thames and Hudson Ltd.

Grocott, Lisa. (2003). 'Speculation, serendipity and studio anybody.' In Laurel, Brenda. (Ed.). *Design Research*. Cambridge, MA: The MIT Press. 83-93.

Hjort, Mette. (2001). 'Aesthetic approaches to the Internet and new media.' In Nissenbaum, Helen, & Price, Monroe. (Eds.). *Academy & the Internet*. New York: Peter Lang Publishing. 196-224.

Hollis, Richard. (1997). *Graphic Design*. London: Thames and Hudson Ltd.

Jansson, Andre. (2002). 'The mediatization of consumption: Towards an analytical framework of image culture.' *Journal of Consumer Culture*. Vol. 2, No. 1, 5-31.

Jensen, Jens. (1998). *Multimedier, Hypermedier, Interaktive Medier* (Multimedia, Hypermedia, Interactive Media). Aalborg: Aalborg Universitetsforlag.

Kress, Gunther, & van Leeuwen, Theo. (1996). *Reading Images*. London: Routledge.

Kress, Gunther, & van Leeuwen, Theo. (2001). *Multimodal Discourse*. London: Arnold.

Landow, George. (1997). *Hypertext 2.0*. Baltimore, MD: Johns Hopkins University Press.

Lash, Scott, & Lury, Celia. (2007). *Global Culture Industry*. Cambridge, MA: Polity Press.

Leiss, William, Kline, Stephen, & Jhally, Sut. (1990). *Social Communication in Advertising*. London: Routledge.

Li, Hairong, Kuo, Cheng, & Russell, Martha. (1999). 'The impact of perceived channel utilities, shopping orientations, and demographics on the consumer's online buying behavior.' *Journal of Computer-Mediated Communication*. Vol. 5, No. 2. Available at http://jcmc.indiana.edu/vol5/issue2/hairong.html

Liestøl, Gunnar. (1999). *Essays in Rhetorics of Hypermedia Design*. Unpublished doctoral dissertation, Department of Media and Communication, University of Oslo, Norway.

Liestøl, Gunnar. (2006). 'Conducting genre convergence for learning.' *International Journal of Continuing Engineering Education & Lifelong Learning*. Vol. 16, Nos. 3-4, 255-270.

Linton, Harold. (2000). *Portfolio Design*. 2nd ed. New York: W.W. Norton.

Löwgren, Jonas, & Stolterman, Erik. (2004). *Thoughtful Interaction Design*. Cambridge, MA: The MIT Press.

Manovich, Lev. (2001). *The Language of New Media*. Cambridge, MA: The MIT Press.

Manovich. Lev. (2002). 'Generation Flash.' Available at www.manovich.net. 1-18.

Moor, Elisabeth. (2003). 'Branded spaces: The scope of "new marketing".' *Journal of Consumer Culture*. Vol. 3, No. 1, 39-60.

Morrison, Andrew, & Skjulstad, Synne. (2007). 'Talking cleanly about convergence.' In Storsul, Tanja, & Stuedahl, Dagny. (Eds.). *The Ambivalence of Convergence*. Göteborg: NORDICOM. 217-335.

Munster, Anna. (2003, May 19-24). 'Compression and the intensification of visual information in Flash aesthetics.' In Proceedings of DAC 2003 conference, Melbourne. Available at http://www.msstate.edu/Fineart_Online/Backissues/Vol_17/faf_v17_n08/reviews/munster.html.

Munster, Anna. (2006). *Materializing New Media*. Hanover: Dartmouth College Press.

Nielsen, Jakob. (2000). *Designing Web Usability*. Indianapolis: New Riders.

Siegel, David. (1996). *Creating Killer Websites*. Indianapolis: Prentice-Hall.

Skjulstad, Synne. (2004, November 17-21). 'Flashback: Tracing developments from electronic paper to dynamic digital environments in the software Macromedia Flash.' In Proceedings of the Future Ground Conference,

Melbourne. Vol. 2. Design Research Society/Faculty of Art and Design Monash University, Melbourne, Australia.

Skjulstad, Synne. (2007a). 'Clashing constructs in Web design.' In Melberg, Arne (Ed.). *Aesthetics at Work*. Oslo: UniPub. 81-103.

Skjulstad, Synne. (2007b). 'Communication design and motion graphics on the Web.' *Journal of Media Practice*. Vol. 8, No. 3, 359-378.

Skjulstad, Synne, & Morrison, Andrew. (2005). 'Movement in the interface.' *Computers and Composition*. Vol. 22, No. 4, 413-433.

Snyder, Ilana. (1997). *Page to Screen*. New York: Routledge.

Thorburn, David. (2003). 'Web of Paradox.' In Thorburn, David, & Jenkins, Henry. (Eds.). *Rethinking Media Change*. Cambridge, MA: The MIT Press. 19-22.

Thorlacius, Lisbeth. (2004). 'Visuel kommunikation på WWW' ('Visual communication on the WWW'). In Engholm, Ida, & Klastrup, Lisbeth. (Eds.). *Digitale Verdener (Digital Worlds)*. Copenhagen: Gyldendal. 79-100.

van Leeuwen, Theo. (2005). *Introducing Social Semiotics*. London: Routledge.

Welch, Wolfgang. (1997). *Undoing Aesthetics*. London: Sage.

Williamson, Judith. (1978/1994). *Decoding Advertisements*. London: Marion Boyars.

PART V

REFLECTING

PREFACE

FOLLOWING A PLENARY ADDRESS

Sinfree Makoni

MULTIMODAL, NEGOTIATED MEANING MAKING

I read the chapters in the book that Andrew Morrison has competently put together as I prepared for a plenary session on September 29, 2006, in South Africa, which I titled 'Reflections on the Social Sciences and Applied Humanities in the Human Sciences Research Council (HSRC) in South Africa.' I am going to explore how reading the chapters in the book influenced the arguments that I subsequently made in the plenary.

The HSRC is a state-governing body created in 1968 and mandated to carry out social science and humanities research within South Africa. I delivered a paper on Alternative ways of conceptualizing language in multilingual contexts, so I also try to draw parallels between the book and the discussions currently taking place as Applied Linguists explores possibilities of reimagining ways of thinking about the nature of language and language learning, particularly in non-Western multilingual contexts.

As I read the chapters in this part (and several others in the book), a number of issues quickly dawned on me. Principally, these were that there are no firm boundaries between the humanities and social sciences, and that technology, as Morrison and his colleagues aptly remind us, has not only had an impact on society, at times adversely, but it has radically altered the ways in which we conceptualize our role in society and ourselves as well. It is a combination of changes in history with developments in ways of thinking that Morrison and his coauthors forcefully highlight.

EVOLVING EXPERTISE

In my plenary generously drawing on this book, I argued that one of the challenges which social scientists in Africa are confronted with is how to address the various ways in which learning and communication takes place when one is learning to be a social scientist or, indeed, a scholar. I found the overall argument that communication is multimodal and does not reside in language alone compelling. The multimodal and negotiated nature of meaning was extremely powerful to an audience inclined to regard communication as a one-way flow and meaning as prefigured and preassembled rather than emergent and flexible. The idea of meaning as negotiated and learning as collaborative struck a right chord with me because I was addressing an audience to which I felt I was an outsider.

The sociocultural perspectives that are the overriding principles on which the book is based enable us to account for the nature of learning and how expertise evolves across time and even at the same time in different contexts. Morrison and his colleagues—in a manner that is reminiscent and reinforces some current versions of Dynamic Systems (De Bot & Makoni, 2005) approach to language—argue quite effectively that expertise is always emerging, it never has a finite or an end state, it is always fluid, and it is always open ended.

The idea of a continuously evolving expertise has clear political consequences because it forcefully suggests that we need to keep continuously updating our expertise because we can never reach an end goal. From that perspective, the authors argue quite effectively that expertise is always provisional; it is something that may constitute a challenge to orthodox thinking about the nature of expertise. It is because expertise is always provisional and subject to contestation that it creates opportunities for change.

As I read the chapters in this part, I was also struck by the similarities with the arguments that are being made in alternative ways of reimagining the nature of language learning in multilingual contexts (Makoni & Pennycook, 2006). In both traditions, the emphasis has shifted from conceptualizing learning as being carried out by a lonely individual to an emphasis on the collaborative nature of learning. Both traditions, although drawing inspiration from different sources, stress the role and significance that interaction plays in learning. However, interaction in Vygotskian thinking can also take place even within the same individual: private speech. In other words, we do not necessarily need other people to interact.

DISCOURSE ANALYSIS
AND OLDER MEDIA

Wenche Vagle (Chapter 15) adopts a diachronic analysis of radio texts by introducing an important discourse analysis slant to a book exploring the role and centrality of technology. In an informative chapter, Vagle outlines some of the changes that have taken place in the way radio was conceptualized going back to some of the early writings in the early 20th century. We have all gotten used to the radio so that at times we need to be reminded about the impact radio had on the various ways in which individuals conceptualized language and the human possibilities it engendered. An analysis of the historical aspects of the development of our thinking of radio is also illuminating because it enables us to capture some of the changes in conceptualizations that have taken place about radio and technology over the last century.

Philosophically, the analysis is also valuable because it is by subjecting the past to a critique that we are best able to gain a firmer understanding about the nature of the present and the possibilities that the future creates. Furthermore, we are always preoccupied by the past because we are always re-creating it for our contemporary purposes so the past is a never-ending story. Vagle's chapter is also intriguing because it combines an analysis of historical documents with a combination of anthropological analysis and systemic theory, drawing on the work by Goffman (1959) and Halliday (1978) to provide a more rigorous understanding of the nature of radio, which is referred to as 'the blind medium.' By combining Goffman (1959) and Halliday (1978) in the analysis, Vagle demonstrates convincingly the importance of theorizing our experiences in multiple ways.

SHAPING AND BEING SHAPED
BY CULTURAL PRACTICES

The book is worthwhile reading even for those who work in the so-called 'developing countries' because it theoretically stresses the importance of grounded analysis, which goes beyond political rhetoric. The book is also able to foreground notions of how scholarship in itself is a type of cultural practice that is in turn influenced by and influences how we appropriate technology for our cognitive and social purposes.

REFERENCES

De Bot, Kees, & Makoni, Sinfree. (2005). *Language and Aging in Multilingual Contexts*. Clevedon: Multilingual Matters.

Goffman, E (1959) *The presentation of self in everyday life*. Ann Arbor, MI: University of Michigan Press.

Halliday, M. (1978). *Language as Social Semiotic: The Social Interpretation of Language and Meaning*. London: Edward Arnold.

Makoni, Sinfree, & Pennycook, Alastair. (2006). *Disinventing and Reconstituting Language*. Clevedon: Multilingual Matters.

12

MULTIPLE ACTIVITY–
MULTIPLE MEDIATION

CONCEPTUALIZING AND FURTHERING
THE USE OF WIKIS

Andrew Morrison, Ole Smørdal

Andreas Lund, Anne Moen

THE CHALLENGES
OF MULTIPLE ACTIVITIES

Rapid and innovative changes in digital technologies and related communication practices may challenge the theoretical and analytical frameworks we employ to account for them. This is currently the case with several types of networked communication in the domains of online work and learning. Generally, networked communication in these domains is characterized by being emergent, flexible, and reconfigurable. However, it is specifically the collaborative character of meaning making in networked communication that increasingly places demands on educational designers, teachers, and researchers.

Recent developments in social software and tools for Web-based collaboration have been taken up in user-driven purposes and contexts of need, exchange, and reconfiguration. We argue that the wikis is one particularly interesting example. Briefly, this can be attributed to its collectively oriented nature; its open, networked, and nonhierarchical structure; and its potential for epistemological reorientation, especially involving a shift from individual to collective cognition. These qualities are further pursued in the course of the chapter with reference to three projects.

CHARACTERIZING WIKIS

Although there seems to be no precise definition of a wiki, Désilet, Paquet, and Vinson (2005: 3) find that there is general consensus about characterizing a wiki as 'a collective website where a large number of participants are allowed to modify any page or create a new page using their Web browser.' Typically, a wiki will afford a series of meta-features, such as the history of a page (including comparison of versions and rollback to earlier versions), notification of revisions, and discussion spaces assigned to particular pages.

Although this involves technical innovation, the focus in the present chapter is on the ways that wikis mediate meaning making through collective epistemic agency (Scardamalia & Bereiter, 2006). Although artifacts come with certain affordances and potential, these materialize only through socially object-oriented enactment (e.g., Lund, 2008). In the projects referred to (see Section 4), this involves a radical shift in epistemology and communicative practices. Wikis accentuate this shift but are just one instance of a plethora of technologies that transform our approach to knowledge advancement, meaning making, and the way we organize such efforts.

Blogs, wikis, and social networking environments such as *MySpace* are now apparent across different domains of interest, in informal and formal educational settings, and, to a large extent, in popular culture. Large multiparty research projects funded by the European Union include wikis as part of their platforms for collaborative knowledge building so that varieties and diversity of competence and interest may be purposively converged across distance and time.

New modes of working and learning are developing that are multimediational and are often built from the intersections of theory and practice. They involve multiple actors (humans and machines) in varied settings, across and within time frames, and in relation to shifting competences in contexts of collaboration. Coordinating this multimediational activity and the resulting modifications in practice requires new forms of working together, especially when this cooperation is only possible by way of collaborative processes that cannot be completely prefigured. New work practices may be conceptualized in terms of multimediational networked activity.

At the widest level, these developments and the demands they make may be understood from a knowledge-building perspective (e.g., Scardamelia & Bereiter, 1999, 2006; Hakkarainen et al., 2004). Knowledge building refers to the changing nature of collaborative meaning making in organizations and groups involving relationships between the uptake of new tools for shared activity and the transformations of existing practices. Multimediational activity is at the heart of changes in practice. In this chapter, we focus on multimediational activity in relation to wikis and the affordances they offer for collaborative meaning making.

MODELS, REPRESENTATIONS, AND COLLABORATIVE KNOWLEDGE BUILDING

Much of the linguistic and semiotically inflected approaches to multimodal discourse and its application to learning and multimediational literacy (e.g., Kress, 2003; Jewitt & Kress, 2003; Jewitt, 2006) do not refer in any detail to the now immense literature on information and communication technologies (ICTs) in informatics or net-based learning (e.g., Wasson et al., 2003). We argue for and demonstrate the significance of informatics in net-based institutional discourses and distributed learning as central to enlivening multimodal discourse that extends beyond the composition of Web pages in html or advances in computer-based writing as composition.

At a meta-level, for us this is a clear indication that design matters. It matters in that the designing for collaborative knowledge-building activities is now possible with vastly improved and openly available software tools. These tools and their use in constructing communicative artifacts are also the 'matter' of design. As Löwgren and Stolterman (2004) argue, what is needed is an overall conceptualization of the design of information as a gestalt. Taking this into the analysis of dynamic Web sites, Skjulstad (Chapter 11, this volume) argues that we need to extend this to an understanding of a communication design. This is not an idealistic, modernist holism but rather an overall perspective of how multiple elements, media, and modes converge and are designed to enable effective and elegant multiple combinations and configurations. Our interest as educational researchers is also on how the practices of learning and communicating via wikis may function as a heuristic for investigating collaborative knowledge building in which networks of relations are central.

RESEARCH QUESTIONS AND OUTLINE OF CHAPTER

The previous outline provides some context for situating the main research questions we address in this chapter. These are:

- How can we conceptualize digitally mediated meaning making in networked knowledge-building activities?
- How can we inform design and configuration of digital environments for such activities?
- How can we inform further development of wikis?

In the following section, we include a short literature survey with relevance for our approach. In Section 3, we examine approaches to multiplicity. In Section 4, we refer to three main domains that refer to projects on wikis: (a) semantic wikis mediating learning and research rhetoric, (b) networked wikis mediating and translating institutional and personal voices, and (c) meta-level features for teachers in wikis. In applying our framework in these domains, we refer to empirical material from three projects. The first investigates archaeology and learning. The second takes up the uses of wikis in supporting and enabling 'living well' in contexts of chronic illness. The third refers to a longitudinal intervention study at a Norwegian upper secondary School. In Section 5, we propose that the concept of the artifact be expanded to include two additional concepts that help us understand the complexity of the relations between 'multiple activity and multiple mediation.' Finally, in Section 6, we close with a short discussion of technology-enhanced literacies. We now move to Section 2 and a more detailed presentation of wikis.

ON WIKIS

What Are Wikis?

The history of wikis is a short one. The first wiki (from Hawai'ian 'wiki-wiki,' meaning quick, fast) was created in 1995 by Howard Cunningham as a novel way to develop private and public-knowledge bases (Leuf & Cunningham, 2001). The most famous offspring is the online encyclopaedia Wikipedia < www.wikipedia.org >, which, in January 2010, with its 91,000 active contributors and 15,000,000 articles in 270 languages, embodies the idea of a potentially collective, democratic, open, and dynamic design.

However, wiki applications may not only accommodate encyclopedic approaches. Other types of wiki applications can be used for collective content management, as well as personal knowledge management, community building and support for project groups, agile software development, and semantic webs (Schaffert et al., 2005; Lund & Smørdal, 2006). Also typical is the use of a wiki as a staff Web site that is continually evolving as a result of staff input. Such a wiki can be placed up front (as in the case of the University of Minnesota Libraries Staff < http://wiki.lib. umn.edu/ >) or integrated with Web page and blog (as in the case of the authors' working environment at InterMedia, University of Oslo < http://www.intermedia.uio.no >). Thus, we see an increasing growth in public use, as well as in fields of research and development. The reason may be found in the wiki's deceptively simple interface but radical episte-mological implications. Some of the implications are briefly discussed later. However, first we need to relate such a discussion to already exist-ing studies of wikis.

Research on Wikis

Judging by the existing and rapidly increasing scholarly literature on wikis, we argue that studies addressing technical features, programming, and software design dominate. However, there is an increasing number of studies that addresses wikis in education and in particular collective knowledge creation.

For instance, Scaletta (2006) demonstrates how wikis can be used as collaborative writing spaces in higher education. Such spaces are used for teaching consensus building, as well as identifying and organizing differ-ent facts and opinions.

Lund and Smørdal (2006) report on a longitudinal intervention study in which learners in a Norwegian upper secondary school used the MediaWiki application (identical to the one used by Wikipedia) throughout two projects in English as a Foreign Language (EFL). Findings showed that learners produce a lot of material, but that budding and seeding dominat-ed over linking and revision. They conclude that what is needed is a focus on collective task construction, teacher role in a wiki, and the importance of the epistemological shift from individual to collective composition.

Grant (2006) addresses wikis as knowledge-building networks and finds that they serve as environments for knowledge advancements, as well as the reified artifact of communal practices. However, she also points to the fact that students did not automatically adopt shared prac-tices but stuck to individually oriented writing typical of institutionalized educational practices. We find this tension to be emblematic when intro-ducing a collectively oriented cultural tool in a historically solitary prac-tice, such as writing and composition (for similar findings and a more detailed overview of literature, see e.g., Lund & Smørdal, 2006; Carr et al., 2007).

A regularly updated (although somewhat incomplete) overview of research on wikis can be found in the Wiki Research Bibliography (part of the WikiMedia wiki) at < http://meta.wikimedia.org/wiki/Wiki_Research_

Bibliography > . It, too, reflects a growing interest in communication change, transformed literacies, knowledge community building, and collaborative authoring.

Still, the mediational aspects of wikis seem to be somewhat underresearched and (hence) undertheorized. How wikis afford collaborative, multimodal composition requires a focus on shared spaces for meaning making and how symbol processing and appropriation of the cultural tool together add up to wiki practices. Garza and Hern (2005) analyze writing practices in wikis and how wikis emerge as cultural tools, as well as contexts for composition (i.e., a space for a particular cultural practice). In the following, this space is elaborated with a view to the complex mediation involved.

Wiki Characteristics

What separates the wiki concept from other online, distributed environments, such as Learning Management Systems (LMS) and groupware applications, is their open architecture. The networked structure is not imposed or predetermined but emerges as a result of use and participation. Thus, the functionality of a wiki is highly situated and, unlike a word processor, does not come with a spread of built-in features. The networked structure is built from within by means of a simplified hypertext markup language; it is the collective activities around the wiki syntax that give rise to content formation and revision, structure, and (indefinite) growth.

The central principle is that of collective ownership—that anyone can create, edit, and delete material. It is, however, important to stress that this is not a technology-driven truism but a complex process of semiosis, mediation, and use of artifacts that involves a repositioning of the *composer*. Although most wikis are text oriented, we choose to expand the notion of writer to that of composer in light of the network construction that is just as important as the added text. Also, several wikis hold graphics and mixed-media affordances, meaning that the semiotic budget exceeds that of traditional writing environments.

Although there would hardly be any disagreement over regarding writing as a particular type of social practice, the cultural tools involved may not always have received sufficient attention. Moving from the feather to the ball point pen, from the typewriter to the word processor, and from paper to digital space involves not just increased efficiency but a cultural change. The process of communication changes—what it involves in terms of aesthetics, construction of meaning, and audience orientation.

What we currently witness is that every day professional modes of communication are changing with an increased use and variety of digital media. Technologies and their many cultures of use constitute a mutual relationship where communicative activity articulates as well as transforms the larger culture. How we think is deeply intertwined with the technologies we use (for extensive studies, see Ong, 1982/1988; Heim, 1987).

In the case of wikis, they not only afford collective production, networked structures, and shared spaces but they require them (Garza & Hern, 2005). Consequently, wikis lend themselves to the Bakhtinian notions of dialogicality, polyvocality, and heteroglossia—that we come to knowledge through adding ours to the many and different voices that envelop us. Moreover, the wiki not only documents the product of these processes but also documents the process, even over long time scales, due to the history feature of each page in the rhizome. Wikis change the way knowledge is produced but also the way they are disseminated and circulated. The implication is that the writer(s) are immediately deeply involved in developing structure as well as content instead of putting words into a confined space, either by adding, revising, or opening new pages on the fly by adding simple code to a word or term that will open a new opportunity for content formation. In summary, in wikis, we see a systemic environment for collective meaning making and one that makes visible the processes entailed.

What this amounts to is a shift in epistemological position for those involved in wiki practices as compared with much of the other writing/composing assisted by technologies. Working with wikis involves going from individually acquired to collectively generated knowledge. The first mode is historically and institutionally linked to schooling (individual grades, exams), where individual reproduction and problem solving have dominated. The second mode points toward what educational researchers (e.g., Engeström 1987; Bereiter, 2002; Hakkarainen et al., 2004) identify as the major challenge for knowledge advancement: how to make epistemic artifacts conducive to knowledge creation. The wiki may emerge as a shared object that mediates collectively oriented activities conducive to such knowledge creation.

In conclusion and in a larger perspective, it would seem that the concept of wikis dovetails with the emergence of an increasingly more networked society and its resulting need for networked and multimodal literacies. The concept of a network can be imbued with a sociological perspective as one type of social organization (Castells, 1996), or it can be regarded as a philosophical notion of system of connected nodes that is always in flux, a rhizome (Deleuze & Guattari, 1988). These two perspectives span the artifact as well as the semiotic aspects of multimodal and networked literacies and, in turn, the cultural tool as well as the social system of signs that materialize in a wiki and wiki practices. The cultural tool mediates the object-oriented activity and the semiotic mediates social interaction (Vygotsky, 1978).

EXAMINING APPROACHES TO MULTIPLICITY

Artifacts: Tools and Signs

Mediation through artifacts (sometimes referred to as cultural tools) is one of the key concepts in sociocultural theory (e.g., Vygotsky, 1978; Wertsch, 1991, 1998), cultural psychology (e.g., Cole, 1996) and activity theory (e.g., Engeström, 1987). The basic assumption is that we do not act directly on the world but through mental, symbolic, and material auxiliaries. The relation between artifact and mediated action is important in Vygotsky's activity-oriented approach (Fjuk & Smørdal, 2001). It is the context of human activity that allows us to understand artifacts. The history, use, and needs of an artifact are central to understanding mediated meaning making (Kaptelinin, 1996). Tools function to conduct our influence on the object of an activity, and they are external and need to lead us to changes in those objects (Vygotsky, 1978). Signs are internal; they are centered on thought and its manifestation and representations in texts, such as a wiki. Social dialogues become internalized in each of us, as well as within our mediated representations. In the case of the wiki, a typical sign is the use of square brackets to represent invitations to knowledge advancement by adding and revising information. What is in play is the interrelatedness of the communicative aspect of mediated action at the level of the sign and the operational aspect of the action as tool. Cole (1996: 117) defines an 'artifact' as 'an aspect of the material world that has been modified over the history of its incorporation into goal-directed human action.' Artifacts come with a dual nature, in that they are simultaneously ideal (or conceptual, shaped by language and interaction) and material.

Let us briefly look at a few typical examples: the ploughshare, the watch, the alphabet, and the computer. What they have in common are historically accumulated insights into particular domains of knowledge and human activity (agriculture, organization, communication, and multi-literacy). As such, they will at one time in history function as passage points for enculturation, as well as 'glue' for members of that culture. Imagine a typical Western culture without the sense of time manifested by the watch.

However, artifacts also hold the potential to change cultures. The alphabet is indefinitely powerful in creating new insights (scientific articles), artistic experiences (poetry, novels), and regulating mechanisms (laws, procedures). Such artifacts transform the conditions under which we live, work, and learn, but they also have the potential to change the way we think. They add up to 'the cultural mediation of thought' (Cole, 1996: 119). Thus, artifacts are not 'things' in an ontological sense but intimately interwoven into activities and practices. In a meaning-making perspective, we need to have the activity between production and consumption in the foreground but also consider collective aspects. The duality of artifact mediation in all these relationships constitutes our understanding of complex mediation. In Actor Network Theory (ANT), such relations are seen as mediating the networks that constitute social worlds.

Epistemic Object and Artifact

The qualities listed previously are present in the wiki. It represents an aspect of collective activity but one that is clearly modified from earlier conceptions, such as Leont'ev's famous depiction of the hunt as a multifarious collective endeavour. We have discussed (see Section 2) the wiki's potential for epistemological change. When we relate this potential to the notion of artifacts, we also see how a wiki with its networked nature holds the potential to change the way we think. Wikis (the ideal as well as the material aspects) can be said to act as a cultural gatekeeper as well as cultural 'glue' in a society that is increasingly networked (Castells, 1996).

The potential of artifacts to mediate cultural change is an especially interesting notion when we consider knowledge advancement and innovation. According to Scardamalia and Bereiter (2006: 97), 'Ours is a knowledge-creating civilization.' These authors find that some artifacts are distinctively epistemic (i.e., 'tools that serve in the further advancement of knowledge'; (Scardamalia & Bereiter, 2006 :99). Hakkarainen (2006: 17) approaches the epistemic *object* of activity in similar terms with its 'focus on issues that are currently beyond the agents' knowledge and understanding and at the edge of the epistemic horizon.'

Thus, the notion of an epistemic object dovetails with the epistemic artefact, as well as the knowledge creation metaphor referred to previously. The epistemic artifact mediates the activities oriented toward the epistemic object. From the potential we have outlined in wikis, we argue that they qualify as such epistemic artifacts. They provide a response to what we increasingly see as a quest for knowledge-advancing practices—practices that are beyond the individual and require collective and distributed approaches (for essential studies, see Hutchins; 1995; Valsiner & van der Veer, 2000; Hakkarainen et al., 2004). Of course, the epistemic agency involved would not be a cause-effect relationship between a particular technology and the results it may produce but rather a carefully developed social practice in which activity structures, multiliteracy, and artifacts are mutually constitutive of knowledge advancement. Hence, the introductory emphasis is on the social enactment of technological affordances.

Wiki and Wartofsky

Also, and as a consequence of the prior argument, a wiki would seem to emerge as a manifestation of Wartofsky's (1979) three levels of artifacts. On one level, the wiki appears as a primary artifact in the sense that it is directly used in production—in this case, composition of collectively generated rhizomatic texts. On another level, the wiki architecture, including meta-features, represents the mode of action that produces such texts. It makes visible and accessible the norms and conventions that go into such a venture. In the case of the wiki, these would typically entail dialogue that weaves resources into the spiraling, 'feedforward' process so crucial to knowledge advancement (Scardamalia & Bereiter, 2006).

Along with the epistemological implications discussed earlier, the wiki also influences the way we come to see the world and transforms the practices that constitute this world. As such, the wiki, a tertiary artifact, has an impact on our perception; it mediates our epistemological transition from the individual consumer *or* producer of linear text to the collective consumer *and* producer of multilayered and multimodal meaning making that is so typical of a networked and knowledge-creating society. If anything, the immense popularity and growth of Wikipedia testifies to such a potential.

Networks of Activities Mediated by Interrelated Tools and Signs

Following developments in generations of Cultural Historical Activity Theory (CHAT; see e.g., Chapter 2), Engeström (1996) has developed a model whose objective is to consider the socially based nature of human activity by including rules of communication and division of labor. However, in this approach, there is a problem related to the notion of artifact mediation, that is, to the duality between sign and tool.

Drawing on their own contextualized inquiry into changing work practices involving technologies in mediation, Bødker and Bøgh Andersen (2005) see mediation as being complex. They view this complexity as being heterogeneous, dynamic, and comprised of webs of mediators that may be used simultaneously, linked in chains, or organized in levels related to automation or intention of the activity. In seeking to account for this complexity, they juxtapose perspectives on mediation drawn from activity theory (AT), accentuating its dialectical materialist origins, and from semiotics with a focus on processes of individual meaning making, or semiosis, derived from the semiotics of Peirce rather than the structuralist approach of Saussure. Bødker and Bøgh Andersen (2005) point out that we need to distinguish between the notions of mediation used in AT and semiotics: '. . . tools mediate between subjects and material objects, signs mediate between subjects. . . .'

In viewing mediation as meaning making, communication may be more indirect than instrumental. In a dialogical framework (e.g., Wells, 2002; see also Morrison & Thorsnes, Chapter 9; Pierroux, Chapter 14) its realization and success depends on the activity involved in a negotiative encounter. As Bødker and Bøgh Andersen argue, the object of the 'conversational' encounter is its topic or theme, not the participant. Although this is wholly logical, how this topic or theme comes to shape the negotiation is a matter of alignment and a rather different notion of how negotiation unfurls. This we see as linked to core concepts in ANT (see Stuedahl & Smørdal, Chapter 10; Morrison, Chapter 2). This is important, as Bødker and Bøgh Andersen (2005) argue, because mediators are not single and do not refer to one activity at one level. As a consequence, we need to design for multimediation that acknowledges chains and practices of co-occurring meaning making. It is to this that we now turn in the form of three projects.

FURTHERING THE USE OF WIKIS

Orientation

Taking the conceptual outline into consideration, we may start to investigate how these concepts may influence further development of wikis, in terms of both their use and infrastructure. We are involved in a number of research projects that explore wikis in new domains. We outline three of these projects and suggest how the concepts may explain and suggest further design of wikis. The domains are:

- Semantic wikis mediating learning and research rhetoric
- Networked wikis and institutional ownership, and
- Meta-level features for teachers in wikis.

Semantic Wikis Mediating Learning and Research Rhetoric: Project 1 – *Open Archaeology*

Open Archaeology is a Web-based learning resource targeting both the national curricula in Norway on cultural heritage and the needs of the general public. The goal of the project is to let pupils use a wiki to formulate hypotheses based on field studies and on the resources provided in the core Web site. The wiki pages, through semantic information provided, may link to databases with cultural historical content, such as pictures, diagrams, texts, objects, and GIS information (e.g., layered maps).

The wiki facilitates several narratives about the same phenomenon. In this way, it allows for the expression of alternatives and doubts about objects and imagined events related to, for example, an excavation. In *Open Archaeology*, the wiki pages may refer to items in cultural historical databases. This is facilitated by including a cultural historical ontology (the CIDOC CRM) as part of the shaping of that database and by providing technology that support semantic Webs.

There is a growing interest in the combination of semantic technology for the Web and wikis. Semantic wikis are suggested as a combination of wiki and semantic Web technologies (Tolksdorf & Simperl, 2006). It has been suggested that Wikipedia be enhanced with typed links between pages (Haller et al., 2006). The type can indicate the nature or quality of the relationship between those pages, be used to enhance the navigation elements, and give the user more understanding of the information design. SweetWiki is an approach using typed links and semantic embedded meta-data in the Web pages (RDFa: using RDF to annotate a Web page with meta-data) (Buffa & Gandon, 2006).

In developing *Open Archaeology*, several relationships have needed to be balanced at the level of design. One of these relates to the parameters of CIDOC as an ontology that is maintained by an international body of researchers and practitioners. Then, there are the curricula needs, the custodian of which is the Ministry of Education. Given this content domain, there are also the archaeologists and their need for digital tools and infrastructure in research. In addition, we meet the needs of museums in renewing the genres of research rhetoric, in contrast to maintaining a pure focus on recording and documenting their collections.

Taken together, these intersecting interests may be seen as an instance of what Scollon (1998) calls a meeting or nexus of discourse. However, as argued elsewhere with respect to ANT (see Stuedahl & Smørdal, Chapter 10), what is involved is more than a meeting of diverse elements and interests but the discourses in action, that is, in their alignments, their processes of negotiation, and the manner in which they tackle their different traditions and indeed preconceived expectations when these come into direct contact with those of others (e.g., Law & Singleton, 2003). Employing wikis in such meaning making across, between, and within intersecting domains, each with their own valences and interests, allows for the design of communication that is coconfigured collaboratively.

Here semantic Webs are both embedded in document specification in informatics, as well as composed rhetorically through the collaborative articulations in wiki spaces. Concerning the mediation of research as rhetoric—between the researcher's specialization and the versioning for different audiences and layers of participation—wikis offer access to processes of shared meaning making, as well as pathways to situating products of mediation and their location in different combinations in specific 'views.' Thus, it is possible to conceive of the blend of the process and the product, where both are locatable, diachronically shaped, and contemporaneously accessible via shared meaning-making activities. The potential gains and tensions in representing and mediating the views of multiple participants is now taken up in relation to our second project.

Networked Wikis Mediating and Translating Institutional and Personal Voices: Project 2 – *ChronICT*

ChronICT (ICT-based information and communication resources for patients, their families, and health care providers dealing with chronic disease) is a research project focusing on persons with a health problem and their families handling, coping, and living well given a congenital condition. The clinical case for ChronICT is 'anorectal anomalies.' The malformation is treated surgically but still leading to many, also unknown, problems in the course of daily living. In the case of ChronICT, when the condition is permanent but is a hidden handicap, learning and mastery in ongoing self-care and symptom management are required. Therefore, what are needed are opportunities for knowledge building and communication among and between peers, but also providers representing different constituencies. In support of this, infrastructures that allow simple and timely access to and contribution of relevant resources would be necessary.

ChronICT as an information and communication resource will be developed in a participatory process with several iterative development cycles. People with the condition, family members, health care providers, and the design and research team members are involved in the processes. Focus is on experiences and strategies to live well with anorectal anomalies as a chronic/permanent condition and hidden handicap. What solutions to these various needs might be found through the multiple mediations possible through wikis?

Our solution to providing connections among various resources and perspectives/voices is based on two interlinked wikis. One would provide health care providers' contribution with their insight and cumulative experiences, such as description of diagnoses, treatments, suggested self-care, procedures, and so on. The other wiki provides a channel for the experiences of the persons with the condition and facilitates peer communication. The coping and learning about everyday experiences to 'live well' would be mediated by through the collective production of knowledge by the persons with the condition and their families. On the technical side, a parallel to the blogs trackback facility will be developed for these wikis to exchange information on related content in the connected wikis. The trackback will be based on both explicitly given semantic information and reasoning about semantic information. Being able to discern different 'views' is not only important in settings such as this health-related one but also in other educational settings.

The idea is to let the wikis cross-reference each other based on semantic information. The contributed information in the connected and lined wikis inform, enhance, and nuance each other. This provides a means for recontextualization of information in both wiki spaces. Polyvocality (Bakhtin, 1981, 1986) is afforded by breaking down a traditional model force through the dual ownerships of the wikis (on polyvocality, see also Morrison & Thorsnes, Chapter 9). Multiple speaking positions may criss-cross one another in loose couplings and through the building and support of different perspectives.

What is interesting here is also how to design for these perspectives and their potential relations without overdetermining specific roles and rights. A parallel to Wikipedia is the idea of the neutral point of view (NPOV). The NPOV is a policy that is applied to each article in this gigantic site so as to include all relevant positions on a given case. In ChronICT, personal points of view given your role as person with the condition, family members, as well as providers or even teachers are encouraged. In addition, there is also a focus on the interdependence of their information and the meaning-making process. How the involved collectives of persons with the condition, their family members, and health providers will take this up is still to be evaluated.

Meta-Level Features for Teachers in Wikis: Project 3 – *Plicte* (Productive Learning in ICT-Rich Environments)

The first project shows the aggregated and transformed representation of archaeology as a semantic Web, and the second project shows the multi-voiced participation of actors in a domain traditionally reserved for experts (medicine). This third project addresses the field of secondary education but embodies both approaches reported on in the previous projects; there is knowledge construction beyond the contribution of a number of individuals, as well as overlapping and contesting voices.

The setting is an upper secondary school (foundation course, age 17) in Norway, and the subject is English as a Foreign Language (EFL). The school has a history of collaborative approaches to learning (learners work in groups of four to five on projects spanning several disciplines). Hence, the introduction of a wiki can be seen as an intervention to observe, articulate, and support collective practices that address often complex learning objects that may escape the capacity of even resourceful individuals.

Two intervention studies (Lund & Smørdal, 2006; Lund, 2008) document the activities that develop when a digital technology with collective affordances is integrated in the historically and institutionally anchored practice of individual writing. In the first study, the learners were asked to give their collective perception of the United States; in the second study (and as an effort to make the task even more collective), learners were asked to construct a textual (and partly graphical) typically British town with its history, population, businesses, public sectors, tourist attractions, and so on.

Our findings point to three vital areas for research, design, and support of knowledge-creating practices. The empirical support for these claims is gleaned from video- and audiotaped lessons, the wiki log files, and a response sheet filled in by the learners who used the wiki. Observation notes and ongoing informal talks between researcher and teacher add to the multilevel methodology approach to the phenomenon examined.

Perhaps the most dramatic outcome from these studies is a strong indication of an epistemological shift. Writing is historically and culturally a solitary experience with (as a result) a sense of private ownership to the product (the school essay, diary, letter). However, practices and responses from participants point to a different notion of 'authorship.' Videotaped material shows how learners gradually move from local (dyadic, small-group) production to a networked (whole-class), nonfinite state of production as growth, budding, and branching instead of production as a means to a finished product to be handed in for assessment. The response forms, adding a 'lived' experience to these observations, testify to this interpretation. Of the 31 learners, only 1 found the experience to be without relevance, whereas typical of the majority are responses such as:

- I like this because we so easily can compare and share information on what we know and what we do not know about the American way of living.
- I like this because it is a win/win situation. To help others and get help back is nice. Cooperating is important in our daily lives and our future jobs!
- It doesn't matter if it is yours or others. This way it is possible for people to argue and discuss.
- The subject will be shown from many persons' view and not from one singular person [...]. I feel like part of a team.

These responses indicate an important shift in perspective—reciprocity, trust, altruism, and collectivity. However, some voices articulate that this shift does not come without a price:

- Someone can change what you have written even when you know that what you have written is correct.
- My texts got deleted.

The implication for practice is that collective approaches to wikis are definitely afforded by the technological design but that these are not enough to overcome the tensions when moving from one cultural-historical practice and toward one that is epistemologically radically different. This is an undertheorized issue (at least in education, but see Valsiner & van der Veer, 2000) and, hence, needs to be pursued.

Following this, we ask whether wikis can be developed to offer design features that support collective knowledge construction. The typical educational fallacy of so-called LMS is that they seemingly offer collaborative spaces but are designed with folders and feedback mechanisms that embody individual learning. Thus, a crucial question for future wiki design is how to maintain the balance between its open architecture and reciprocal vision with a more object-oriented and, at the same time, multivoiced approach. Structure *and* anarchy may seem like an oxymoronic pair but can be said to guide wiki designs.

The question of balancing structure and creativity is perhaps the most challenging issue in modern education (Sawyer, 2004). Although numerous technologies have been introduced with a rhetoric of innovative and knowledge-construction features, practices have been shown that practices show that change and development are incremental and carry substantial impact only over longitudinal time scales (Ludvigsen, 2005). Consequently, the role of the teacher emerges as particularly significant. Along with the design features referred to earlier, we see a definite need to afford teacher spaces in a wiki so as to initiate, support, and sustain practices of collective knowledge advancement. The 'wiki-in-the-wild' projects at the secondary school from which we report reveal that, although learners appropriate collectively oriented practices, there is a greater potential to be harvested, and there are some tensions that need to be managed constructively.

In summary, the projects referred to here indicate that wikis change representations of knowledge as well as our approach to knowledge. Wikis can be said to embody epistemological shift as well as semiotic expansion. With the intense research and development currently going on with semantic Webs and multimodal representation, we expect these issues to increase in significance in the near future.

STRETCHING THE CONCEPT OF ARTIFACT

The Value of Theoretical Artifacts

We have already argued that wikis challenge our notions of network communication and meaning making in a wider literacy and knowledge-building perspective. Our experience in using, designing, and studying wikis, some of it in process, has convinced us that we need some concepts for the design and study of multiple mediation in wiki environments and potentially others similarly complex ones.

Wartofsky (1979) was concerned with how we can extend our perception and conceptualization of meaning imaginatively and the ways in which artifacts may be a part of reaching for a new understanding of representation and reflection. He reminds us that 'We become theoretical in knowing ourselves to be theoretical; and we know ourselves to be theoretical in the very act of creating theoretical artifacts' (Wartofsky, 1979: xxv-xxvi). It is possible, then, to see the wiki as a theoretical artifact, too. To take such a view is perhaps also coherent with the collective approach to taking on complex problems that typify the 'knowledge society.'

Two Proposed Concepts

We see a further need to design for complex mediation and meaning making in networked communication. This implies that we need concepts to address and structure problems of mediation and concepts that contribute to the design or redesign of these environments.

The conceptual approach is based on a combination of basic concepts from AT and core concepts from ANT. There has been discussion on the ontological problems on this combination (cf. Miettinen, 1999). However, we will combine these approaches on a conceptual level, leaving the theory building and integration for future investigation. We therefore offer what Engeström (1996) has labeled 'intermediate concepts.' The two concepts we propose are *translating artifact* and *prosuming artifact*.

The concept of the *translating artifact* refers to the conjunction of the notion of translation from ANT and that of the interrelationship between tool and sign from AT. Further, this entails the coupling of the notion of the boundary object much referred to in Science and Technology Studies (STS; Starr, 1987) and that of the sign originating in social semiotics (see also Morrison, Chapter 2, this volume). Taken together with the notion of complex mediation, from Bødker and Bøgh Andersen (2005) as outlined earlier, we may conceptualize the process of activity as a site and an instance of negotiation and thus redesign. This concept may be partnered with that of the mediating artifact proposed by Wartofsky, where attention is less on the transferral of meaning between the elements listed earlier and more on imaginative modes of perception and their embodiment (see also Morrison, Chapter 13).

We have found it difficult to find an apt term in English to coalesce the emerging relations between production and consumption that is possible in environments such as wikis and their attendant mediated meaning making. We have coined the term 'prosuming artifact' to encompass the breakdown of the earlier distinctions of production and consumption. In wikis, what occurs is that participants constitute the discourses themselves but that they do this in concert with one another. Their emerging textualizations serve as further moves for additions and distinctions to which they may read, hear, or watch, as 'consumers' but located within discourse chains that are built through mediated action online. Where production is connected to tools and consumption is connected to signs and cultural expressions, production of signs also occurs as does the uptake and uses of tools. Tool-sign relation is thus recast 'prosumptively.' Again, we see the concept as a partner to that of the mediating artifact but a partner that now allows us to hopefully further conceptualize the processes and dynamics of collaborative meaning making. For us, this is a meaning making that is challenging our notions of mediated literacy and especially our formulations of written discourse and its patternings.

CONCLUSION

Extending Notions of Literacy

There has been so much written about shifts in our notions of literacy in the past 20 years or so that it is possible to see the affordance and constraints offered by wikis as being just another small step in a larger progression of technology-enhanced learning. In many senses, this is of course the case, yet we hope to have shown that, wikis and multimodality, taken together, do indeed challenge us to rethink notions of authorship, collaborative meaning making, and the role of the teacher. The qualities of the dialogical discourse that emerges between participants and also across their proximal interests and articulations demands that we also extend our earlier notions of polyvocality to the study of texts that are the outcome of shared meaning making (Roth, 2001).

In wikis, we need to understand the multiple contexts and contributions that are part of the making and use of complex multimodal discourse. This is a discourse that transverses earlier important characterizations and discussions of links and locations of them in and across documents. Wikis ask that we attend to processes of meaning making in which copresence, delay, and anticipation are also features of the composition of networked communication. We have referred to this both empirically and theoretically. From our experience so far, and that made visible by our students and partners, our understanding of wikis is unfolding. This occurs through the collaborative character of production-based research projects that involve multiple actors in complex, multimodal mediations.

We see that it is also important to conceptualize these as they are realized in networks of meaning making. Further development and application of the concept of the translating artifact we propose may help us to move closer into the situated and empirical study of wikis. Our concept of the prosuming artifact also allows further scrutiny of the intricacies involved in the complex relations between production and consumption that wikis, and indeed other domains of 'social software,' make possible.

On Dialogue

Katherine Hayles' (2005) recent book is called *My Mother Was a Computer*. Referring to the manual work of data entry that was typically carried out by women in the United States in the 1940s and 1950s, she reassesses her earlier writings on being posthuman in a digital age. Our chapter is about a rapidly emerging digital artifact, the wiki, that is beginning to be used in schools and higher education in learning activities that are group based and involve a fair degree of process for all genders (and interests in meaning making). Closer study of the dialogical character of meaning making in wikis is needed by delving deeper into the actual discourse of participants in their negotiations in its shared shaping, as Arnseth and Ludvigsen (2006) argue. Perhaps in time we might not only say, 'My mother was a computer . . .' but perhaps also that 'Our Dialogue was a Wiki.'

ACKNOWLEDGMENTS

This chapter refers to work on three projects at InterMedia: (a) *Open Archaeology* involves the codevelopment of learning resources on Archaeology with InterMediaLab funded by the Flexible Learning Program at the University of Oslo. (b) The clinical case for ChronICT concerns living with a rare physical, congenital malformation. The project aims to explore and assist in the challenges and support of 'living well,' with attention to self-care and symptom management activities. The project is funded by Knowledge Practices Lab (EU), InterMedia, and the Centre of Rare Diagnosis, Rikshospitalet, Oslo. (c) The PLICTe project (Productive Learning in ICT-rich Environments) investigates interactions among technology, school subject matter, and collective learning and is part of the EU-Kaleidoscope program and the CMC program at University of Oslo.

REFERENCES

Arnseth, Hans Christian, & Ludvigsen, Sten. (2006). Approaching institutional contexts: Systemic versus dialogical research in CSCL. *ijcscl*. 1(2). Available at http://www.ijcscl.org/?go = contents&volume = 1 &issue = 2

Bakhtin, Mikhail. (1981). *The Dialogic Imagination: Four Essays by M.M Bakhtin.* Holquist, Michael (Ed.). Emerson, Caryl & Holquist, Michael (Trans.). Austin: University of Texas Press.

Bakhtin, Mikhail. (1986). *Speech Genres and Other Late Essays.* Emerson, Caryl, & Holquist, Michael (Eds.). McGee, Vern (Trans.). Austin: University of Texas Press.

Bereiter, Carl. (2002). *Education and Mind in the Knowledge Age.* Mahwah, NJ: Lawrence Erlbaum Associates.

Bødker, Susannne, & Bøgh Andersen, Peter. (2005). 'Complex mediation.' *Human-Computer Interaction.* Vol. 20, 353-402.

Buffa, Michel, & Gandon, Fabien. (2006, August 21-23). 'SweetWiki: Semantic Web enabled technologies in Wiki.' *2006 International Symposium on Wikis.* Odense, Denmark.

Carr, Tony, Morrison, Andrew, Cox, Glenda, & Deacon, Andrew. (2007). 'Weathering wikis: Net based learning meets Political Science in a South African university.' *Computers and Composition.* Vol. 24, No. 3, 266-284.

Castells, Manuel. (1996). *The Rise of the Network Society.* Cambridge, MA: Blackwell Publishers.

Cole, Michael. (1996). *Cultural Psychology. A Once and Future Discipline.* Cambridge, MA: Belknap Press.

Deleuze, Gilles, & Guattari, Felix. (1988). *A Thousand Plateaus. Capitalism and Schizophrenia.* (Brian Massumi, Trans.). London: Athlone.

Désilet, Alain, Paquet, Sébastien, & Vinson, Norman. (2005, October 16-18). 'Are Wikis Usable?' Paper presented at the WikiSym'05, San Diego, CA.

Engeström, Yjrö. (1987). *Learning by Expanding: An Activity-Theoretical Approach to Developmental Research.* Helsinki: Orienta-konsultit.

Engeström, Yrjö. (1996). 'Development as breaking away and opening up: A challenge to Vygotsky and Piaget.' *Swiss Journal of Psychology.* Vol. 55, 126-132.

Fjuk, Annita, & Smørdal, Ole. (2001, March 22-24) 'Networked computers' incorporated role in collaborative learning.' Presented at *Euro CSCL,* Maastricht McLuhan Institute, Maastricht, The Netherlands. 245-252.

Grant, Lyndsay. (2006). 'Using Wikis in schools: A case study.' Retrieved June 5, 2006, from http://www.futurelab.org.uk/research/discuss/05discuss01.htm

Hakkarainen, Kai. (2006). *Scientific Challenges of Knowledge-Practices Laboratory (KP-Lab)* (Working paper). Helsinki: University of Helsinki Press.

Hakkarainen, Kai, Palonen, Tuire, Paavola, Sami, & Letninen, Erno. (2004). *Communities of Networked Expertise: Professional and Educational Perspectives.* Amsterdam: Elsevier.

Haller, Heiko, Krötzsch, Markus, Völkel, Max, & Vrandecic, Denny. (2006, August 21-23). 'Semantic Wikipedia.' Paper presented at the 2006 International Symposium on Wikis, Odense, Denmark.

Hayles, N. Katherine. (2005). *My Mother Was a Computer.* Chicago: University of Chicago Press.

Heim, Michael. (1987). *Electric Language. A Philosophical Study of Word Processing.* Foreword by David Gelernter (2nd ed.). New Haven & London: Yale University Press.

Hutchins, Edwin. (Ed.). (1995). *Cognition in the Wild.* Cambridge, MA: The MIT Press.

Kaptelinin, Viktor. (1996). 'Activity theory: Implications for Human-Computer Interaction.' In Nardi, Bonnie. (Ed.). *Context and Consciousness. Activity Theory and Human-Computer Interaction.* Cambridge, MA: The MIT Press. 103-116.

Kress, Gunther. (2003). *Literacy in the New Media Age.* London: Routledge.

Law, John, & Singleton, Vicky. (2003). 'Object lessons.' Lancaster, UK: Centre for Science Studies, Lancaster University. Available at http://www.comp.lancs.ac.uk/sociology/papers/Law-Singleton-Object-Lessons.pdf

Leuf, Bo, & Cunningham, Ward. (2001). *The Wiki Way: Quick Collaboration on the Web.* Boston: Addison Wesley.

Ludvigsen, Sten. (2005). 'Læring og IKT-Et perspektiv og en oversikt' (Learning and ICT-a perspective and an overview). In Brøyn, Tore, & Schultz, Jon Håkon. (Eds.). *IKT og tilpasset opplæring (ICT and adapted learning).* Oslo: Universitetsforlaget. 158-183.

Lund, Andreas. (2008.). 'Wikis: A collective approach to language production.' *ReCALL.* Vol. 20, No. 1.

Lund, Andreas, & Smordal, Ole. (2006, August 21-23). 'Is there a space for the teacher in a Wiki'? Paper presented at the 2006 International Symposium on Wikis, Odense, Denmark.

Miettinen, Reijo. (1999). 'The riddle of things: Activity theory and actor-network theory as approaches to studying innovations.' *Mind, Culture, and Activity.* Vol. 6, No. 3, 170-195.

Ong, Walter. (1982/1988). *Orality and Literacy. The Technologizing of the Word.* New York: Methuen.

Roth, Wolff-Michael. (2001). 'Situating Cognition.' *The Journal of the Leaning Sciences.* Vol. 10, Nos. 1&2, 27-61.

Sawyer, Keith. (2004). 'Creative teaching: Collaborative discussion as disciplined improvisation.' *Educational Researcher.* Vol. 33, No. 2, 12-20.

Scaletta, Kurtis. (2006 July 28). 'Teaching with Wikis.' Retrieved August 9, 2006, from https://wiki.umn.edu/twiki/bin/view/TeachingWithWikis/WebHome

Scardamalia, Marlene, & Bereiter, Carl. (1999). 'Schools as knowledge building organisations.' In Keating, Daniel, & Hertzman, Clyde. (Eds.). *Today's Children, Tomorrow's Society: The Development of Health and Wealth of Nations.* New York: Guilford. 274-289.

Scardamalia, Marlene, & Bereiter, Carl. (2006). 'Knowledge building: Theory, pedagogy, and technology.' In Sawyer, Keith. (Ed.). *The Cambridge Handbook of the Learning Sciences.* Cambridge: Cambridge University Press. 97-115.

Schaffert, Sebastian, Gruber, Andreas, & Westenthaler, Rupert. (2005, November 23-25). 'A semantic wiki for collaborative knowledge formation.' Paper presented at *Semantics 2005*, Vienna, Austria.

Tolksdorf, Robert, & Simperl, Elena. (2006, August 21-23). 'Towards Wikis as Semantic Hypermedia.' Paper presented at the *2006 International Symposium on Wikis*, Odense, Denmark.

Valsiner, Jaan, & van der Veer, Rene. (2000). *The Social Mind. Construction of the Idea.* Cambridge: Cambridge University Press.

Vygotsky, Lev. (1978). *Mind in Society: The Development of Higher Psychological Processes.* Cambridge, MA: Harvard University Press.

Wartofsky, Marx. (1979). *Models: Representation in Scientific Understanding.* Dordrecht: D. Reidel Publishing Co.

Wertsch, James. (1991). *Voices of the Mind: A Sociocultural Approach to Mediated Action.* Cambridge, MA: Harvard University Press.

13

BORDER CROSSINGS & MULTIMODAL COMPOSITION IN THE ARTS

Andrew Morrison

TWO SENSES OF DEVELOPMENT

This chapter is about three cases of student composition using a variety of media types and discourse modes. The cases relate to projects involving Zimbabwean students, both in Harare, Zimbabwe, and Oslo, Norway. In these cases, development is seen to have two senses: (a) developmental processes in student learning, and (b) student learning in development-oriented contexts, that is, in 'developing' countries. This chapter draws these two senses together and shows that they may enrich one another, theoretically and practically, by accessing two core concepts: border crossing and multimodal composition.[1]

With regard to developmental processes in student learning, I refer to border crossing in terms of students' engagement in experimental processes—by shaping digitally mediated art and performance works as mediating artifacts, and by communicating about those works academically. I use the term 'multimodal composition' to encompass students' creative and critical constructions in fine and performing arts as part of their own emerging electronic multiliteracies. In the second sense of development, the chapter refers to how inquiry into the implementation of information and communication technologies (ICTs) in learning involving Zimbabwean students has moved between two geographically remote countries, Zimbabwe in the 'south' and Norway in the 'north.' The material presented shows that perspectives, pedagogies, and innovation may also move from their local genesis in a resource-strapped African higher educational and development setting to experimental works relating to Zimbabwe at a major university in one of the world's most technologically endowed countries.

Three Cases Relating to Zimbabwe

The three cases that are presented,[2] may be seen as instances of how students' uses of ICTs may generate new knowledge for both themselves and for the research projects connected to them. The cases offer empirical evidence on ways in which experimental multimodal discourses may be built through student collaboration, via access to different media and modes of communicating, and in interdisciplinary partnerships. At a time of considerable political turmoil surrounding access to land in Zimbabwe, these student projects offer creative, constructive, and culturally articulated contrasts to the self-destructive political policies about land redistribution there. These student works show what it was possible to develop locally via a large project *HyperLand,* from which the first case on fine art is drawn. *HyperLand* had the overall goal of motivating and supporting students' critical investigations of representations and mediations of 'land' as part of their production-based learning about content, culture, and ICTs. This approach was extended to the interplay of digital scenography in collaborative processes of choreographing and performing dance works. In all of these cases, students managed to locate and negotiate important cultural inheritances and traditions and to include them as meaningful resources in their own digitally mediated learning.

A Sociocultural Approach to Learning

The three cases were each framed in a sociocultural approach to learning (Vygotsky 1962, 1978; Wertsch 1991, 1995) related to cultural historical activity theory (CHAT), in which students' agency and creative voices are important. In each case, students developed digitally mediated artifacts through collaboration, via the uptake of new tools, as inscriptions of earlier practices and in the form of new expressions.

The chapter argues that earlier notions and practices of composition—from academic communication and rhetoric—may be recast in an expanded learning frame (Engeström 1987, 2001). Here, student 'composition' may be seen to be moving from writing into experimental and emergent multimodal discourses. This may extend students' academic literacies (Johns 1998) to include a range of digital media types and discourse modes, that is, as electronic multiliteracies. Learning through multimedia production (e.g., Buckingham et al. 1995) is in a sense learning to 'write the technology' (e.g., Haas & Neuwirth 1994) and thereby also a means of investigate changing meaning making in expository and expressive discourses (Diaz-Kommonen 2002, 2003). In the context of the arts, it is about building links between the material and the virtual (e.g., Brown 2006).

Outline of the Chapter

Research questions related to the cases are covered in the following sections on each case. The main research issue has been how to understand and analyze the intersections and differentiations of multiple participant roles and the various ICTs involved in collaborative, experimental student productions.[3] The next section refers to interdisciplinary inquiry by use of the concept 'border crossing.' This is followed by a section on multimodal composition. Cultural historical activity theory is then covered. The three cases follow. A final concluding section discusses directions for multimediational and polyvocal composition.

BORDER CROSSINGS

Making Multimodal Discourse

The metaphor 'border crossing' is now used by several disciplines in the human sciences as part of conceptualizing subject-specific concerns over how knowledge is made and communicated (e.g., Cohen 1999 on anthropology). It also appears as part of the repertoire of reflexive methods in poststructuralist inquiry (e.g., Chambers & Curti 1996 on cultural studies; Atkinson & Breitz 1999 on contemporary art in southern Africa). Earlier disciplinary distinctions and subsequent notions of multidisciplinarity have been rephrased through the intersections of parts of disciplines, resulting in transdisciplinarity. Transdisciplinarity has come to be framed in, through, and as negotiations and translations. Here, 'border crossings' refers not only to the inclusion or importation of concepts from a related or distant field but to the ways in which knowledge may be formed through the linkages, convergence, and recombinations of elements from and across different domains (e.g., Seaman 2002 on visual poetics). Knowledge making is now acknowledged to be a process and not only directed toward the shaping of an end product. In this view, it is seen to be epistemically in a state of flux; creation and contestation, contradictions and shared resolutions are thus central to the making and analysis of multimodal composition.

Border crossing is included here as part of a conceptual apparatus for investigating how multimodal digital compositions might be understood as multiply scored, arranged, and performed—and by students. I refer to the empirical shaping of multimodal discourse in learning in fine and performing arts. This discourse is characterized by students' collaborative involvement in making multimediated texts of their own, that is, both expository and expressive discourse. The student works are instances of voicing degrees of fluency with new tools; they are also instances of finding ways of applying digital tools to educational tasks and wider forms of enculturated expression in digital domains.

This said, however, the chapter presents crossings that are not often mentioned in the numerous studies on ICTs and learning. This refers to both teachers and students moving between and across two geographically remote countries with varying cultural, technical, and educational contexts. Border crossing is used to point to ways in which student learning may be realized through local, culturally situated articulation, in which students' own compositions are paramount and where local is not seen to be culturally isomorphic with geographical place. The three cases refer to connections between Zimbabwe and Norway; both Harare (fine art with hypermedia) and Oslo (mediated scenography with choreography), however, may be seen as local contexts for collaborative, multimodal composition.

MULTIMODAL 'COMPOSITION'

Multimodal Discourse

'Multimodal discourse' has become a vogue term in the past few years, often informed by the work of Kress and van Leeuwen (2001). Their approach has been applied largely to school-based and informal learning. Relatively little use has been made of their core concepts in the form of student authoring or composition with ICTs in higher education.

The 'digital discourse' to which this chapter refers is that generated through student 'composition.' Academic writing may be supplemented in learning through and by communicating in a variety of modes (e.g., drawing, video, dance, and animation; Bolter 1998). Attention to such modes in shaping multiliteracies (Kress 2003) takes place through collaboration involving working with the known and the familiar but also the uncharted and risky. Here, multimodal composition refers to learning to make multimodal discourse, in which there is a convergence of tools, content, and culture (e.g., Myers et al. 1998; Wysocki 2004).

Electracies

To draw together these lines of argument, I refer to the notion of multiple electronic literacies or, as I have termed them, 'electracies' (Morrison 2001, 2003a, 2003b). I have adopted the term 'electracy' from Ulmer (1997, 1998), influenced by his book, *Teletheory*, from 1989, in which he discusses the changing nature of electronic communication, especially video. Drawing on Derrida, Ulmer enacts grammatology to address the histories and theories of writing and more recently electronically mediated communication (Ulmer 1994a, 1994b, 2002). He applies the term 'electracy' to signify a paradigm shift from literacy to electronic literacy:

> A new name such as electracy helps to distinguish this epochal possibility that what is at stake is not only different equipment but also different institutional practices and different subject formations from those we now inhabit. This much the theory shows us, even if theory is not 'cause,' not determinism, but a guide for action. Poststructuralist theory of grammatology shows us the scale and scope of our problematic. It is not a matter of taste: whether one does or does not honour and love the achievements of literature, the greatness of our nation, the rights of individuals. It is not a matter of whether these qualities are in flux, but to what degree we have any influence in shaping the outcome. (Ulmer, 1998, p. xii; italics original)

I developed the term 'electracies' to refer to a compendium of literacies in higher education and the mediation of research that reach beyond written communication, which may be combined to generate new forms and practices (Johnson-Eilola 1997; New London Group 2000). Buckingham and Sefton-Green (1997) point to the need to look at expanded notions of media literacy in media studies. Wysocki and Johnson-Eilola (1999) remind us, however, that we should be wary of using literacy as a metaphor to account for all that takes place in learning with new technologies. These literacies are multimodal: They demand our ongoing work and competence with a range of software and systems, and they may include still and moving images, illustrations, and texts written for screen spaces, to mention a few.

Extending Communicative Repertoires

Traditional pedagogy in higher education does not typically encourage process-based experimentation with new genres, forms, and expressions through and as multimediated communication. Each of the projects presented next took a specific experimental stance, yet was contextualized within an explicitly situated approach to learning (Lave & Wenger 1991). This method was to adopt a motivatedly investigative, experimental approach to learning with technologies that encourage and encompass curiosity on the part of humanities students (e.g., Green 1995). In terms of collaboration, however, art, design, and performance studies offer a medley of modes of communicating that may be usefully added to and combined in our changing, yet often written, electronic discourses. In short, this is to look into ways of building an expanded communicative repertoire.

CULTURAL HISTORICAL ACTIVITY THEORY

A Theory of Change

CHAT is adopted as an overarching conceptual framework (Engeström 1999a; Engeström & Miettinen 1999) for the analysis of these three cases. It offers some means of critically mapping and understanding how the changing terrain of expository and expressive literacies may be inscribed as part of pedagogies in higher education. However, this approach as applied here is also threaded through the unfolding practices and knowledge formations in and through electracies. Although participation is central to such an approach, activity theory provides a powerful multilevel conceptual apparatus for getting at the role of technology as a mediating tool that helps facilitate expansive cycles of learning. Expansive learning is one approach within CHAT that pays attention to the dynamics of cycles of transformation (Engeström 1999b). It is presented and then applied to the three cases. In the knowledge creation framework of CHAT, collaboration is that '. . . process mediated by shared objectives on which the participants are working' (Lipponen et al. 2004: 41). For these researchers, what defines creative collaboration is its focus on '. . . certain shared objects, knowledge-laden or conceptual artifacts and the agents' relationships to them' (Lipponen et al. 2004: 41). CHAT sees the activities of learning as occurring in a context and a community. In this context, the subjects' actions are influenced by rules and roles. Through intersecting with dynamic relationships with divisions of labor and the functioning of mediating artifacts and tools, additional activities or artifacts may result, that is, as outcomes (Engeström et al. 1998).

A wide sociocultural approach to learning focuses attention on what participants actually do within a communicative process and the ways in which their compositions or mediating artifacts may be understood contextually. In a sociocultural view, the 'meaning potential' of language and social semiotic approaches to communication, learning, and composition (e.g., Halliday 1996; Halliday & Hasan 1985; Kress 1998, 2003) may be seen as more than the collaborative construction of an activity. As the following cases illustrate, this is also about how such compositions, and indeed their experimental character, may be viewed in terms of their cultural significance, that is, interpersonally and institutionally. This is to accentuate that learning to compose is a situated, shared activity that also needs to be contextualized and yet remain tentative and open to change as part of ongoing learning with and through ICTs.

Third-Generation CHAT

In the formulation of what is called a third generation of CHAT, a number of key features have now been identified: cultural diversity, multivoicedness, dialogue, macrolevel networks, networks of activity, and boundary crossing.[4] Boundary zones refer to what lies and is constructed among different, intersecting systems of activity. Such 'crossings' may be understood in terms of 'motives.' Interest is also in collective artifacts, that is, in their shared making and interchange. Artifacts are seen as multiple and multiply mediated. How such shared and situated knowledge comes to be achieved may be studied less by seeing developmental change on a vertical axis and more in terms of its horizontal character and constitution. The features–cultural diversity, multivoicedness, dialogue, macrolevel networks, networks of activity, and boundary crossing–help us to analyze how different activity systems intersect and what 'travels' or may be exchanged between them (Gregory 2000).

Part of adopting such an approach is also to see CHAT as referring not only to a historically and contextually framed inquiry but one within which cross-cultural communication is important (e.g., Cole 1988). Here what is needed is the integration of activity systems and elements of them in which language and expression, modes and discourse processes, and the articulations of situated experience are central 'resources' in cross-cultural communication.

Expansive Learning

Engeström (1987, 2001) has conceptualized this third, synthetic phase of CHAT in an expansive theory of learning. He argues that we can identify five main principles: 1) The activity system as the unit of analysis, 2) multivoicedness, 3) historicity, 4) contradictions, and 5) expansive transformations.

In his model, Engeström outlines the following stages in cycles of transformation: (a) questioning existing practices; (b) analyzing existing practices; (c) collaboratively building new models, concepts, and artifacts for new practices; (d) examining and debating the created models, concepts, and material and immaterial artifacts; (e) implementing these; (f) reflecting on and evaluating the process; and (g) consolidating the new practices (Engeström 2001; Lipponen et al. 2004).

For Engeström, learning is a state of becoming—that is, for persons and institutions; it is unstable, ill defined, and often not yet understood. There is a transformative component to this theory, in that we need to learn new forms of activity that are not yet crystallized but are in the process of emergence. For Engeström (2001: 139), 'Expansive learning activity produces culturally new patterns of activity.' These patterns need to be seen against the summative dimensions of the entire system, just as learning needs to take place in interconnected, dynamic activity systems (see also Wells 1999).

It is also important to study the background and context of these intersecting activity systems. Historicity is one of the main characteristics that Engeström argues we need to include in a thorough model. In a southern African educational setting, this is part of the daily enactment of understanding inherited structures and constraints as well as developing alternatives to evade, erase, and replace them. Engeström also argues that we should add to this approach acknowledgment and analysis of contradictions, which arise in overlapping relations and outcomes. Here, disturbances, conflicts, and challenges posed by intersecting systems need not be seen as negative; they are part of the processes of negotiation and transformation. This he takes up in the final component of expansive transformations. When cycles of change are lengthy, individuals may begin to deviate from conventions and their individual secure practices and concepts. For Engeström (2001: 37), 'An expansive transformation is accomplished when the object and motive of the activity are reconceptualised to embrace a radically wider horizon of possibilities than the previous mode of activity.'

Engeström (2001) positions his five principles of activity systems (unit of analysis, multivoicedness, historicity, contradictions, and cycles of expansion) against four questions in the shape of a matrix. The questions focus on the learners. The questions are: Who is learning? Why are they learning? What are they learning? How are they learning? I now apply this framework to the three experimental, innovative projects in which Zimbabwean students were primary collaborative actors.

CASE ONE: *HYPERPOTTERY*

This first case and unit of analysis centered on an existing ceramics course and learning about traditional pottery involving student collaborative and multivoiced production of a hypermedia Web with support from peer tutors. The case was developed in Zimbabwe. The software *Storyspace* was used as the main authoring tool. The resulting Web was a hybrid of media types and discourse modes: print text, photographs, and video; face-to-face and electronic interviews; on-screen categorizations; a short narrative with drawings; and hyperlinking. The students developed work in the form of a hypermediated portfolio, to which they each contributed and commented on shared inputs and one another's work (Morrison 1997). The overall research question behind this was: How might fine art higher education students in an African setting collaboratively compose content-rich, hypermediated learning resources where few formal documents and limited research are publicly available?

On the *why of learning*, as one part of the overall *HyperLand* project, a Web was developed to support learning about visual arts in Zimbabwe at the Department of Graphics and Fine Art at the Harare Polytechnic. Called *HyperVision*, this Web contained a variety of art resources (writings, still images, video annotations of exhibitions) that were compiled with input from artists, critics, and students. The contents of the *HyperVision* Web are shown in Figure 13.1. Given that, since Independence in 1980, much art interpretative discourse has been written by white English-speaking Zimbabweans and European scholars (albeit sensitive to local context), the project also aimed to encourage students to see art criticism and visual literacy in cross-cultural perspectives (e.g., Phillipson 1995; Messaris 1997).[5] Local texts, images, gallery visits, and video material were hyperlinked to produce a novel structure and a resource for expansive learning. The students' own expansive learning would contribute to this discourse, content-wise and rhetorically.

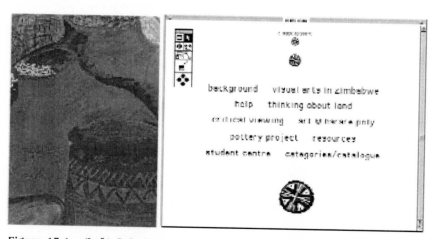

Figure 13.1. (Left) Painting developed by ceramics students for Zimbabwe International Book Fair 1996; (Right) Start screen of *HyperVision* Web.

Final-year ceramics students were asked to develop a hyperweb of their own to investigate the cultural context, design, uses, and production processes of traditional pottery (Morrison 1997). They were asked to use a diversity of modes and media in shaping such a Web as part of learning how to articulate their own learning multimediationally. This is indicated in the painting to the left in Figure 13.1, which was created by the students and used in the opening screen on the final version of the pottery project rather than a photograph of a pot. This shows that multivoicedness may be seen not only as a written or spoken polyvocality but also as a mix of media types and modes of artistic expression. The motive of this Web was also to build contextual resources around a specific domain of material culture and as material for a hypermediated interpretation.

In terms of historicity, the pottery project aimed to develop situated, local knowledge resources alongside the students' own practice in pot making and related interpretation. The Web was intended to be a record of students' creation of a multimodal artifact rich in content, modes of communication, and media types. Yet it was also designed to provide them with experience in learning processes through cycles of transformation, questioning their own practice in relation to existing ones, and reflecting on their own art making and analysis and the contradictions and new horizons arising from these.

In terms of the 'who of learning,' the group consisted of six students, five women and one man. They were all taking a course in ceramics and made use of the *HyperVision* Web (used more generally in other classes),

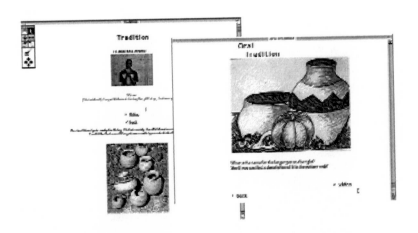

Figure 13.2. *HyperPottery.* (Top Left) Video on value of tradition; (Below Left) Photograph of pots having been fired in the earth; (Right) Student drawing for section with their writing on Oral Traditions in conveying knowledge.

with guidance from specially trained peer tutors from the *HyperLand* project. Support importantly came from the head of the department, Jane Shepherd, and her staff. At a macrolevel network, the ceramics lecturer, Alison Brayshaw, saw a possible connection of the *HyperVision* Web to her course in ceramics. Of British origin, she admitted she had little knowledge of the forms and functions of traditional Zimbabwean pottery. We discussed how a student-based hypermedia production might involve ceramics students in moulding more than just clay but in building an experimental web of material and reflection on traditional pottery. This would involve them in networks of activity with their aunts, grandmothers, a gallery director, an art lecturer, another ceramic lecturer, and the four peer tutors involved in the *HyperLand* project. The fact that pot making along traditional lines is a female-gendered activity also meant that gender was an ever-present element. The one male student in the group found he was not only working with five motivated female colleagues but that he had restricted access to the gendered transmission of knowledge on pot making. He discussed this in a video file, in which he mentioned his own understanding of the contradiction of being asked to learn about embellishment and diverse styles and uses of pots while not having an inherited role from which to access such historical knowledge.

On the 'what of learning,' the students developed a novel and information-rich Web, in which they demonstrated their own work processes and results. Their Web included written texts, summarized from the few print publications they were able to locate in libraries and the National Archives, but also written by them. There were tables categorizing, naming, and describing a range of pots and their functions. A hypermedia story was developed with illustrations by the students so as to show contexts of cultural use of pots. Special attention was given to the role of women in making pots and in their handing down of knowledge to novices. The project was patterned around the categories of Background, Usage, Process, and Intepretation. The group learned that knowledge about traditional pots lay not only in books and their classroom. They visited their families in rural parts of the country and through interviews learned about the value of oral culture as a repository of knowledge. This was echoed in their own spoken contributions to the Web. The project clearly introduced a range of voices and perspectives, and the possible contradiction between oral culture and technodeterminism of a hypermedia system was avoided through the production of a synthetic text: The students all commented that the possibility of continually changing their inputs and links in the hypertext system meant that they were able to work through cycles of reflection and improvement of their contributions.

The group also learned to work together collaboratively in contributing material to the dynamic structure the members presented as work in progress and that was redesigned with help from the lecturer and the researcher-educational designer. In terms of hypermedia, the students developed a multimodal text of their own, drawn to different modes of presentation and cross-linking by virtue of the material they gathered. However, they were also able to use the functions in *Storyspace* and quickly alter how content was linked. They clearly demonstrated skill in how to think and link across factual content, narrative, photographic, and hand-drawn representations.

Concerning the 'how of learning' and historicity, these students were actively involved in meeting and translating their own cultural heritage and representing it as a digital, cultural one in a form of collage-like writing and imaging (Landow 1998). They were involved in conducting primary research, the documentation of field interviews, and the generation of new textual representations. They did this with support from their lecturer with her background in education, as well as from the researcher-designer and the three peer tutors in the *HyperLand* project. The students also consulted other lecturers in the department and, most challengingly, in terms of Engeström's conflictual questioning and 'multi-voicedness' and 'dialogue,' gave a diskette with interview questions to one lecturer who had designed a series of postage stamps on Zimbabwean pottery. The students asked her to give an account of her own knowledge on Zimbabwean pottery. The lecturer's replies were included in the Web. The students also included the earlier photographic documentation by one of their lecturers of traditional methods and contexts of production (from shaping to firing). The students made their own voices heard through short videos. They used these to annotate their contributions to the Web and also to reflect on them. For example, the male student reflected on how he had learned more about the value of women as bearers of cultural and artistic knowledge through researching gender in pot making; this video could be seen alongside those by the women students. As part of composing their Web, the students had several sessions in the networked computer lab at the University of Zimbabwe. Here they were able to work collaboratively in structuring, linking, and annotating their material. In terms of multiple activity systems, this student project was also incorporated in the many sessions on the broader *HyperLand* project for students in the humanities department at the university.

This student work was an example of 'rearticulating hypertext writing' (Johnson-Eilola 1997) that would break out of known modes of formal project presentation in the art institution as well as by extending notions of hypertext writing to multimodal 'composition.' Further, as a 'translation,' this student project took a multimedia tool and used it to articulate new views on gaps in the small body of print sources. It augmented these through short accounts of field visits, via individual entries, through the narrative piece linked to a formal typology of pottery artifacts, and in video meta-reflections on the process included as guides to other users. Gender perspectives on the gendered activity of pot making were also linked in the model of expansive learning to another Web developed by law students on women's rights to land, inheritance questions, and connections to a women and law research project. This also reached into a different activity system, in which women law students were codesigners of a learning task for their large class of peers on learning how to generate a genre of written legal discourse.

In reading the pottery project in terms of meta-media literacy (Lemke, 1998), the students all commented favorably that the experience had given them insight into their own cultural heritage, into how to use digital media as a research and recording tool for reflection, into new ways of understanding visual arts as multiply constructed discourses, and especially into the role of women as bearers of traditional culture. This was clearly to move beyond the hype over hypertext (Snyder, 1998). As an educator and researcher interested in the transformative aspects of an activity theoretical approach to sociocultural learning, the project most clearly was a case, in Engeström's words, of developing 'a wider horizon of possibilities.' One of the students, Victor Mavidzenge, expressed this as follows:

> I don't think I'd be seeing as far as I do now. It was really inspira-
> tional. It's hard to express how much it did for me because you know
> words are very limiting, but the innermost feelings are what counts as
> I see it. So it was more like a new door opening to me you know, so I
> don't think I'd be thinking like I do now (laughs).

In terms of 'boundary crossing,' the pottery Web included a variety of successful use of modes and media (video, drawing, and interviews). These were positioned in an integrated articulation of making and interpretation that broke out of the predominantly art-making pedagogical frame for the institution. Students' own prototypical and hypermediated discourse illustrated how collaborative, peer-based authorship might be achieved through creative processes and in building content along with situated interpretation.

As expansive learning, the pottery project may be seen as an instance of the collaborative design of a new activity. The case offers empirical evidence of how the conceptual frames of CHAT may be anchored in actual production and reflection on learning. Students' own experimental production generated a newly textured body of work. The means and content of this work were embodied in a new mediating artifact.

CASE TWO: *BALLECTRO*

The second case involved six choreography students in the collaborative design of a dance work with digital media scenography produced by three media researcher-designers in Oslo, Norway. Here there was a blend of face-to-face communication, live workshopping, and improvisation with video feedback, choreography, and performance involving live and stored digital media. This mixed-reality approach took the media off the desktop computer screens and into a shared collaborative devising and development space, with the overall goal of live performance. The project is conveyed in the form of a multimodal Web site, the *BallectroWeb* (see Figure 13.3).[6]

The main research question was: In what ways might the inclusion of digital technologies impact on the compositional processes and outcomes of collaboratively developed choreography for dance performance? The changing horizon of possibilities in the model of expansive learning was enacted through collaboration on dance making, in which digital media was to be a partner. In expressive digital arts and culture, in which performance and performativity are being reconstituted (e.g., Birringer 1998; Schieffelin 1998), new modes of public expression and screen-based mediations are beginning to be documented (e.g., deLahunta 2002).

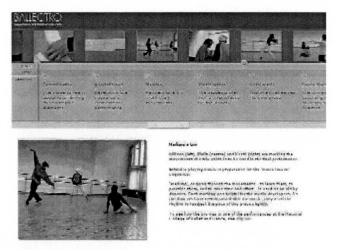

Figure 13.3. The integrated interface in *BallectroWeb*. (Top) An item on rehearsing a trio is selected from one of 80 videos in a horizontal scrollable video menu. The video plays in the large window (bottom left). One of three tracks (dance, media, learning) has been selected from the bar below the video menu; a corresponding text appears to the right. The large video window has controls built in (pause, frame-by-frame moves, etc.).

This project involved participants in collaborative design processes based on methods from the performing arts but also from experimental digital media production (e.g., Halskov Madsen 2003) and iterative design. The merger of real-time and recorded mediations of both dance and digital media may result in a different hybrid digital poetics (Qvortrup 2003). As Seaman (2002) argues, it is the potential and practice of the recombination of elements in such a poetics that challenges us to see per-fomativity differently. This is a performativity in which the relationships between human performer and media as actor alter earlier notions and expectations of stage and staging (Sparacino et al. 2000). These are envi-ronments that are labeled mixed or augmented reality and extended to media as responsive participants through sensors and location-aware technologies (e.g., Sha & Kuzmanovic 2000). In our setting, and given that this was our first foray into such a project, we would concentrate on com-puter-based and live projection and multiple screens as the main means of creating an extended stage and staging.

Concerning the 'why of learning,' we wanted to involve choreography students in critical, recombinatorial practices in dance design, in which mediated scenography would be a part of their designing along with attention to other para-performative aspects, such as lighting and music. For the choreography teacher, the project was a means of providing a col-laborative, experimental space for dance making, in which students could develop their own contributions in a horizontal and sideways move, rather than the characteristic vertical one of expert-to-novice learning processes (Engeström 2002). This was to see how to relate their own solo and duet components to those of other participants and to produce an integrated, varied whole. As educators, therefore, we were concerned to introduce choreography students to digital media in dance as an asset and as a complement to their own competences and dancers and as learner choreographers. For the Zimbabwean students in particular, this was an introduction to digital media in performance as well as to a shared, itera-tive design process in dance making. It also involved them in direct col-laboration with designer-researchers who were learning about digital media as dynamic scenography in live dance performance.

On the 'who of learning,' the *Ballectro* project was a collaboration between six final-year choreography students at the National College of Dance in Oslo and InterMedia. Two of these students were financed on a collaborative study program between Norway and Zimbabwe. There were three male dancer-choreographers in this group, two of whom were from Harare. The group was taught by a freelance choreographer and dancer, as well as by three media researcher-designers from InterMedia at the University of Oslo. The aim of this partnering with the college was origi-nally to provide some video-based documentation of dance performance.

However, in practice, this collaboration was quickly extended to a shared process of designing, learning, and performing a dance work over one semester.

On the 'what of learning,' the student and development group learned about the complex and recursive possibilities in developing a dance performance work in which digital media elements could be included and at different levels of centrality in a final performance. They saw how improvisation with video feedback could generate ideas for designing movement. Such aspects were included in the final performances. Further examples of the 'what of learning' as process and as product can be seen in the project Web site. The students learned about the cycles of transformation in the varied intersections among digital music, animations in the software Flash, and their dancing with live projected images of themselves (e.g., see Figure 13.4). The videos in the Web site show, for example, links between rehearsals and final performance material by Koshiwayi Sabuneti from Zimbabwe.

About the 'how of learning,' the project explicitly faced a number of potential contradictions on learning and performance design as process. These centered on the negotiation of real-time, recorded dance and media and their intersections as mixed or augmented reality performance. Here students were working with new modes of interconnecting composition. We used workshopping sessions with improvisation of both dance and media. One of the contradictions we quickly encountered was that dance students were able to turn on their heels and rework movements, whereas it took more than a few hours to change some of the digital media elements. Initially, the dance students were impatient; however, they came

Figure 13.4. *Ballectro*. Live video projection of Willson Phiri from an ensemble with two dancers.

to understand that, other than the immediate and playful character of video feedback, digital scenography takes time to generate and redesign.

The 'composition' went through many cycles and reordering of elements. At first, some of the students commented that this was confusing; toward the end of the experience, Willson Phiri from Zimbabwe commented that this was a completely different way of learning to dance and to choreograph: Improvisation and expressivity were not necessarily centered around a musical score, as has been the approach in most of the choreographers' education. The Web site demonstrates the variety and cycles of process-driven creativity. In addition, and especially for the Zimbabwean students, the choreography teacher was open to exploring alternative solutions and framings of parts of the dance piece. They were able to see a choreographer at work with experimental media and see how a recombinatorial design process could bear fruit. Further, these students could extend their experience from that of their traditional classes at their own dance school to include collaborating with researcher-designers at an educational research and experimental media lab. This was similar to Engeström's concept of change laboratory. The multilevel composition *Ballectro* functioned as a mirroring device for the participants: Whereas different elements were known to different participants, it was the combination of these and the interplay among them that resulted in a new activity or unseen horizon of possible expression. Through this activity, it was also possible to refract the main concepts back to the whole group, not always in a strict activity theory vocabulary, but through discussions on problems and potential of mediated dance and its shared design or composition. In terms of border crossing and multimodal composition, the integrated performance work included 'traditional' Zimbabwean dance blended with 'contemporary' Western dance movement, accompanied by animations in *Flash*. Traditional Zimbabwean mbira music was played live but also remixed electronically in collaboration with material by a young Norwegian electronic musician. In summary, these multimodal compositional elements were also combined, with the overall result that the students developed a new, integrated activity in and through which their own blends of knowledge and cultural expression were realized.

CASE THREE: EXTENDED

In the third case, *Extended*, the interplay between media and dance shifted to one between choreography and media students in Oslo (see Figure 13.5). In this partnering, four works were developed, each an experiment in collaborative learning and hybrid performativity. Media and dancers

Figure 13.5. Startscreen of student initiated and designed website developed in Flash for *Extended*, with term papers containing video of projects and of *Ngirozi*.

were active contributors to an overall creative co-construction. One work, *Ngirozi*, by the Zimbabwean participant, Jimu Makurumbandi, is presented in detail (Figure 13.6). This was a narrative piece with a mix of southern African dance styles (Morrison 2003b). The overall research question was: What issues of cross-cultural communication emerge in the development of digital scenography for narrative-led dance performance work?

Concerning the 'who of learning,' this was a second choreography project between the National College of Dance and InterMedia. This time, however, the four dance students involved were choreographers, and they did not necessarily need to dance their works. In contrast with the *Ballectro* project, the media elements of these works were designed, developed, and performed by two master's students in Media and Communication at the University of Oslo. In the case of *Ngirozi*, the choreographer, Jimu Makurumbandi, also chose to dance his work. This involved the participants in unique relationships not present elsewhere in the project.

On the 'why of learning,' the concept 'extended' was introduced to challenge both choreography and media students to rethink their notions of performativity and to find ways of reaching beyond their given experience and competencies by way of collaboration. For the choreography students, this was to think creatively about how the body and movement might be extended performatively. For the media students, who were taking a course in new media production and critique, the aim was to investigate how digital media as scenography could be integrated as part of the overall composition. In the student-developed Web site shown in Figure

Figure 13.6. Stills from *Ngirozi*. On the left, digital scenography fills the right hand side of the image; to the right, the dancer in full motion is pictured in a still from a digital camera.

13.5, the students listed the following questions as part of their process of defining their joint creative experimentation: What is integration? Where does the physical room end? Can it be extended into a virtual one? Is there an overlap between the rooms? If so, what happens to the dancer? Is the extended body within reach? What is digital scenography? How can we use it? The students were explicitly asked to face one of the main contradictions experienced in the *Ballectro* project—namely, that the choreographers' design took primacy over the media. In this new project, the aim was to find out how movement, space, body, and media could complement and play off one another.

This was to give the students a difficult challenge in developing their own blended and collaborative learning experience; it also asked that they achieve this artistically and for live performance.[7] Here, with little work published on digital scenography (e.g., Morrison et al. 2004), the students needed to draw on their own ingenuity in devising, workshopping, and reformulating dance and digital media as composition and simulation (see e.g., Penny 2004). As researchers, we have attempted to analyze their works and to develop further the concept of performativity.

On the 'what of learning,' Jimu Makurumbandi chose to design and dance his work as a solo (see Figure 13.6). He was the only student who was not Norwegian and also a male choreographer. He wanted to develop a work that would be an invocation of ancestral spirits in the setting of a cave. This led to discussion about how to create a cave-like scenography in which animated figures would dance on the rockface as a backdrop as the dancer moved through the space and into such projections. This raised many questions about the ethics and aesthetics of such mediations. The Norwegian media students were requested not to produce hackneyed images of San rock paintings, which would be at odds with the views and cultural understanding of their codeveloper. However, the students were asked to not merely reproduce images from key print texts on San rock painting in the region. In time, they developed a short dance work together, in which a small screen was placed at the front of the stage to demarcate two different narrative zones in the choreographed movement. Pixellated animations were projected of shadowy figures moving on the rock face. The choreographer reflected positively on his own learning through such coordinated activity in designing and in performing. In particular, as the dancer in the piece, he also felt connected to the animated figures dancing on his body (Morrison 2003b).

On the 'how of learning,' in addition to the same modes of improvisation, sketching, and workshopping collaboratively, the media students also came with preprepared scenography for discussion and adaption. There were compromises on the depiction of the cave and the character of the animated figures. Despite the openness to experiment on the part of this Zimbabwean choreographer, who had not worked with digital project and blended movement with digital scenography, we encountered a substantial contradiction in terms of activity theory. In CHAT, analyzing contradictions is important so as to identify changes that might be needed and the processes involved in effecting them. The contradiction was that, despite being visible on the computer screen, the main animated figures were not easy for audiences to see when the stage was lit and when the projection was a major source of light. Although the dancer commented that he saw new relations and dimensions to his performance because he almost felt the figures dancing on his skin, audiences did not have this experience in the way this was intended. In developing this scenography, the media students had had to pay attention to four dance works in all; perhaps they had also been too careful about avoiding the clichéd literalism of uses of San rock paintings in advertising. As a consequence, the figures that were developed were not distinct enough, nor was there adequate contrast in their projection onto the dancer. This led us all to reconsider the entire scenography as a tension, in Engeström's terms, in need of resolution.

The *Extended* project produced four new digitally mediated dance works. For undergraduate choreography students, it provided an opportunity to work with fellow media studies master's-level students and learn about ways of seeing performance as more than driven by dancers. In this new activity, the media students also came to see how to design moving media as part of dynamic performance. For the Zimbabwean student, this was his first engagement with digital scenography as part of artistic and cultural expression. However, because this scenography was at times difficult to see, we discussed ways to adapt it in a new cycle. This was taken up in a project on multimodal discourse and augmented space. We called this redesign of the digital scenography and the performance work *Extended +*. As can be seen in Figure 13.7, the earlier sepia and ochre tones have been replaced by figures much more visible and all the more so on the dancer's moving body (Morrison et al., 2004).[8] For us, this reworking was a clear example of an expansive learning style and a shift from a student to a professional production, one in which similar collaborative workshopping methods were used. Makurumbandi has also been able to include this work in his emerging portfolio and as part of his experimental repertoire in new choreographies with Zimbabwean dancers.

Ultimately, the projects into extended dance and mediated performance showed that, in terms of intersecting activity systems, choreographic and scenographic design cannot be effectively developed as separate entities. They need to be understood as embedded in a complex of negotiations between the kinetics of dance design and the dynamics of shaping digital scenography.

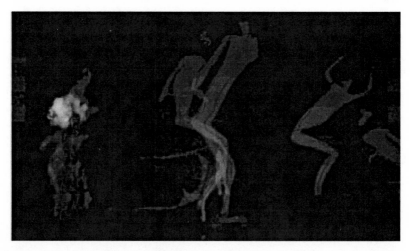

Figure 13.7. Reworked scenography for *Ngirozi* with altered colour palette and increased scale of animated figures as presented in the project *Extended +*.

CONCLUSION

Border Crossings and Multimodal Composition

ICTs are now apparent at different levels of complexity and use in many higher education institutions. In the arts, working out ways in which they can be applied to articulate educational needs and give shape to cultural expression is as much a part of finding apposite means of articulation as it is learning how to compose through multiple media types, software applications, and underlying information systems. Each of the three cases presented earlier indicates how ICTs have been taken up in the processes of meaning in the making. It is this making that transverses the cases.

Through exploratory and student-generated production, new knowledge, fresh mediating artifacts, and intersecting activity systems were generated. As shown, this is a question of relating content and materials to context (Coniglio 2006). This generative aspect of learning through production included important open-ended tasks where student collaboration was built as and through 'dialogue' with existing knowledge and via the emergence and related synthesis of new knowledge for the participants. This transformation was facilitated through processes of improvising, devising, and trialing the intersections of artistic expressions, digital technologies, and multiple participants.

The initial open-ended nature of these activities placed high demands on students' engagement with negotiating digital technologies in shaping their creative expression. The resulting works indicate the importance of interdisciplinary collaboration in shared creative processes, where technologies have a role as compositional and performative 'actors,' as is argued by actor network theory. However, in these three cases relating to Zimbabwe, the participants working with new software and media types (hypertext and video) and in cross-border collaboration (between media studies and choreography) generated new cultural resources, knowledge through use, and art and performance works. In terms of border crossings and multimodal composition, these matter at the level of cultural significance, that is, as cultural articulations digitally composed and mediated.

Reconsidering Expansive Learning

Through a sociocultural approach to learning, it is possible to situate students' experimental engagements with digital media and information systems, such as these, in terms of expansive learning. In the cycles that characterize this approach, an activity system is transformed and, along with it, new motives and objects are generated (Lipponen et al. 2004). In this change process, actors in the activity system reflect on their own reconceptualizations of the system. They assess shared objects and relations. The actors '. . . negotiate a shared understanding of the new activities and artifacts, and in this process something new is created and emerges.'

These three projects demonstrate that the theory and model of expansive learning provide a useful frame for understanding the emergence of digitally mediated communication in higher education relating to the southern African region. Students' roles in acquiring individual literacy knowledge and practices may be seen in their productions and reflections on them in a CD-ROM Web, in a project-based Web site, via a student Web site, and through live performance with mediated scenography. Art and choreography students' participation in co-constructing new knowledge about content and fine arts and modes of performing is crucial in the building of a fuller understanding about multimodal composition.

Inquiry into understanding and analyzing the multiple constructions of hybrid, mediating artifacts and embodied interaction may benefit from closer study of creative and expressive processes and modes of performativity in fine and performing arts. In further investigating creativity, expressivity, and performativity, an integrated approach to communication design is needed. Projections are light sources; dynamic media need to be rehearsed with dance moves; choreographers and media designers need time to familiarize each other with their practices and adaptative workarounds; media leaves computer desktops and needs to be integrated with electronic mixing desks in real-time performance. Designing digital media as part of choreography demands rethinking interaction design, scenography, and dance. Together these design elements may be recast as the choreography of dynamic, emergent, and expressive multimodal discourse.

Taken together, these components and intersecting activity systems may be seen in terms of co-configuration (Engeström 2004). Whereas earlier research has focused on work environments, such as medicine, this chapter points to the applicability of CHAT and expansive learning in the expressive and performing arts. CHAT provides a robust theoretical frame for analyzing the complex, intersecting processes and systems involved in learning about multimodal authorship in ceramics and digital dance. In this sense, the chapter aimed to draw together a developmental learning and design process and resulting mediated artifacts as change experiments with a situated and artful integration of multimodal composition relating to cultural and historical contexts. This was to venture into what was not known or co-configured as building a radical localism (Engeström 2004). Macrolevel analysis of the type presented here might in time also be supported by microlevel interaction analysis. To adopt this delicate approach is to move closer to participant discourses in and as multimodal composition processes and as part of our understandings of them as situated multimodal interactions (see Pierroux Chapter 14).

On Reciprocity

The three projects relating to Zimbabwe presented here may each be seen as part of learning how to negotiate the interplay of digital tools and the articulation of culturally situated artifacts within a wider postcolonial frame.[9] The cases show how collaborative engagements with ICTs and with one another are part of developmentally and ecologically emergent experiences in knowledge making. These experiences are situated culturally and historically yet are also translocal (place, discipline, skill, and person), as has been discussed in several domains within postcolonial studies. Hall (1996: 255), sees 'the status of the 'post-colonial' as an espisteme-in-formation.' It is possible then to view a multimodal multiliteracy not only as the production of a product, a policy, or a result, but also as a process in which learning may be conceptualized as potentially ongoing transformation. In such a process, student compositions may be seen as mediating artifacts that allow us to see the 'translation' of local knowledge domains into newly shaped digital environments and modes of articulation.[10]

Hall (1996) also argues that we need to engage in a reading of a double inscription of difference. He foresees that the value of postcolonial studies 'lies precisely in its refusal of this "here" and "there," "then" and "now," "home" and "abroad" perspective' (Hall 1996: 247). For Hall, the global should be seen as neither universal nor nation/society-specific. What is important is how 'the global/local reciprocally re-organise and re-shape one another.' This may be connected to the concerns of third-generation CHAT and the approach of expansive learning. Key concepts of cultural diversity, multivoicedness, dialogue, macrolevel networks, networks of activity, and boundary crossing have been shown to be present in intersecting activity systems concerning a dynamics of learning how to apply ICTs in fine and performing arts.

ACKNOWLEDGMENTS

The *Hyperland* project was supported by the Linguistics Department and the Media Programme at the University of Zimbabwe, and by the Department of Media and Communication at the University of Oslo and NUFU. The *Ballectro* and *Extended* projects were made possible through grants from the Faculty of Education at the University of Oslo. *Extended +*

was part of the MULTIMO project (Researching Multimodal Discourses) financed by the KIM programme at the Research Council of Norway. Thanks to Sten Ludvigsen, Sinfree Makoni, Even Westvang, and Synne Skjulstad for their comments; my thanks also to the many participants in these projects. An earlier version of this chapter appeared in the online journal *IJEDICT*.

NOTES

1. An earlier version of this chapter, in html and PDF formats, can be seen at http://ijedict.dec.uwi.edu/viewissue.php?id = 4#Refereed_Articles
2. The first case is from 1996, the second from 2001, and the third from 2004.
3. The chapter does not present a detailed interaction analysis of processes of negotation and breakdown.
4. Engeström (2001) has described activity theory as passing through three phases, culminating in multiple activity systems. In the first phase, centered on Vygotsky, relationships were posed around subject-object-mediation relations. In the second phase, influenced by Leont'ev, differentiation between individual and collective action was made. The third phase now ushers in concern with multiple, interrelated activity systems. In this third phase, Engeström (2001) suggests we need to develop concepts and tools to account for dialogue, multiple perspectives, and networks of these intersecting systems. Boundary crossings occur when the outcomes of these systems overlap. For Engeström (2001: 139) the learning challenge therefore 'is to acquire new ways of working collaboratively.'
5. Later in the decade, in the region there appeared vibrant, challenging publications on interpretation, visual arts, and identity (e.g., Deepwell 1997; Enwezor 1997).
6. As media and education researchers involved in this codesign, we have published several print pieces on this project (e.g., Skjulstad et al. 2002). We have also attempted to communicate the project online in the form of a seminar presentation (Morrison et al. 2004) linked with an actual performance and a Web site, the *BallectroWeb*. This Web site is a resource for contextualizing the project especially via video (see Figure 13.5). It links research publications to contexts of production and performance-based learning. I encourage readers to refer to the site themselves. Its interface allows users to trace comments on the videos from three perspectives while scrolling across the menu of videos. This Web site has been invaluable in explaining such inquiry as exhibition, performance, and creative co-construction. This has referred to not only dance design and performance but as the role of dynamic software and media in generating movement in the interface (Skjulstad & Morrison 2005).
7. In doing this, we were also concerned as researchers to see how production-based learning and collaborating in a production and a performance could raise new issues and perspectives for critical theory and new media (MacIntyre 2003).

8. This scenography was developed by one of the original media researchers in the *Ballectro* and *Extended* projects, Synne Skjulstad, and one of the media students from *Extended*, Idunn Sem. Jimu Makurumbandi was again central to this process, and in his own words, this was part of a reshaping of possibilities and expression, or in expansive learning frame, a clear cycle of expansion that came about through designing via interative changes and in performance. The resulting redesigned scenography was performed three times in a choreography festival in Spain.
9. See Sylvester (1999) for a discussion of linkages between development studies and postcolonial studies, with reference to Zimbabwe.
10. If we take the second sense of development to refer to ICTs in development-oriented institutions and societies, we find that development discourses are framed by terms such as the 'digital divide,' 'technology transfer,' and the transformative power of ICTs to overcome fundamental and embedded development needs. In such settings, ICTs have often been directed toward the material sciences. In such targeted investment, technologies have been perceived drivers of wider economic change. In contrast, one seldom comes across research papers about creating, teaching, or researching electronic arts relating to African contexts and cultures. Even less often do these perspectives on electronic arts travel 'north' and have a presence there in negotiations of learning with and through digital tools and modes of composition and reflection.

REFERENCES

Atkinson, Brenda, & Breitz, Candice. (Eds.). (1999). *Grey Areas: Representation, Identity and Politics in Contemporary South African Art*. Johannesburg: Chalkham Hill Press.

Birringer, Johannes. (1998). *Media & Performance*. Baltimore, MD: Johns Hopkins University Press.

Brown, Carol. (2006). 'Learning to dance with Angelfish: Choreographic encounters between virtuality and reality.' In Broadhurst, Susan, & Machon, Josephine. (Eds.). *Performance and Technology: Practices of Verbal Embodiment and Interactivity*. Basingstoke, UK: Palgrave Macmillan. 85-99.

Buckingham, David, Grahame, Jenny, & Sefton-Green, Julian. (1995), *Making Media: Practical Production in Media Education*. London: The English and Media Centre.

Buckingham, David, & Sefton-Green, Julian. (1997). 'Multimedia Education: Media Literacy in the Age of Digital Culture.' In Kubey, Robert. (Ed.). *Media Literacy in the Information Age*. New Brunswick, NJ: Transaction Publishers. 285–305.

Chambers, Iain, & Curti, Lydia. (Eds.). (1996). *Common Skies, Divided Horizons*. London: Routledge.

Cohen, Anthony. (Ed.). (1999). *Signifying Identities*. London: Routledge.

Cole, Michael. (1988). 'Cross-cultural research in the sociohistorical tradition.' *Human Development*. Vol. 31. No. 3, 137–151.

Coniglio, Mark. (2006). 'Materials vs content in digitally mediated performance.' In Broadhurst, Susan, & Machon, Josephine. (Eds.). *Performance and Technology: Practices of Verbal Embodiment and Interactivity.* Basingstoke, UK: Palgrave Macmillan. 78-84.

deLahunta, Scott. (2002). 'Virtual reality and performance.' *Performing Arts Journal.* Vol. 24, No. 1, 105-114.

Deepwell, Kay. (1997). 'Introduction.' In Deepwell, Kay. (Ed.). *Art Criticism and Africa.* London: Saffron Books. 9-13.

Diaz-Kommonen, Lily. (2002). *Art, Fact and Artifact Production.* Helsinki, Finland: University of Art and Design.

Diaz-Kommonen, Lily. (2003). 'Expressive artifacts and artifacts of expression.' *Working Papers in Art and Design.* Vol. 3. Available at http://www.herts.ac.uk/artdes1/research/papers/wpades/vol3/ldkfull.html

Engeström, Yrjö. (1999a). 'Activity theory and individual and social transformation.' In Engeström, Yrjö, Miettinen, Reijo, & Punamaki, Raija-Leena. (Eds.). *Perspectives on Activity Theory.* Cambridge, UK: Cambridge University Press. 19-38.

Engeström, Yrjö. (1999b). 'Innovative learning in work teams: Analysing cycles of knowledge creation and practice.' In Engeström, Yrjö, Miettinen, Reijo, & Punamaki, Raija-Leena. (Eds.). *Perspectives on Activity Theory.* Cambridge, UK: Cambridge University Press. 377-404.

Engeström, Yrjö. (2001). 'Expansive Learning at Work: Toward an activity theoretical reconceptualization.' *Journal of Education and Work.* Vol. 14, No. 1, 133-156.

Engeström, Yrjö. (2004). 'New forms of learning in co-configuration work.' *Journal of Workplace Learning.* Vol. 16, Nos. 1/2, 11-21.

Engeström, Yrjö, & Miettinen, Reijo. (1999). 'Introduction.' In Engeström, Yrjö, Miettinen, Reijo, & Punamaki, Raija-Leena. (Eds.). *Perspectives on Activity Theory.* Cambridge, UK: Cambridge University Press. 1-16.

Enwezor, Okwui. (1997). 'Reframing the black subject: Ideology and fantasy in contemporary South African art.' In Hope, Marianne. (Ed.). *Contemporary Art from South Africa.* Exhibition catalogue. Oslo, Norway: Riksutstillinger. 20-36.

Gregory, Judith. (2000, July 9-12). 'Activity theory in a "trading zone" for design research and practice.' In Durling, David, & Friedman, Ken. (Eds.). *Proceedings of Doctoral Education in Design: Foundations for the Future.* International conference, La Clusaz, France. Staffordshire, UK: Staffordshire University Press. Available at http://heim.ifi.uio.no/~judithg/.

Haas, Christina, & Neuwirth, Christine. (1994). 'Writing the technology that writes us: Research on literacy and the shape of technology.' In Hilligoss, Susan, & Selfe, Cynthia. (Eds.). *Literacy and Computers: The Complications of Teaching and Learning With Technology.* New York: MLA Press. 319-335.

Hall, Stuart. (1996). 'When was the "post-colonial"? Thinking at the limit.' In Chambers, Iain, & Curti, Lydia. (Eds.). *Common Skies, Divided Horizons.* London: Routledge. 242-260.

Halliday, Michael. (1996). 'Literacy and linguistics: A functional perspective.' In Hasan, Ruqaiya, & Williams, Graham. (Eds.). *Literacy in Society.* Harlow: Addison Wesley Longman. 339-376.

Halliday, Michael, & Hasan, Ruqaiya. (1985). *Language, Context and Text: Aspects of Language in a Social-Semiotic Perspective.* Geelong: Deakin University Press.

Halskov Madsen, Kim. (Ed.). (2003). *Production Methods: Behind the Scenes of Virtual Inhabited 3D Worlds.* London: Springer.

Johns, Anne. (1997). *Text, Role, and Context: Developing Academic Literacies.* Cambridge, UK: Cambridge University Press.

Johnson-Eilola, Johndan. (1997). *Nostalgic Angels: Rearticulating Hypertext Writing.* Norwood, NJ: Ablex Publishing.

Johnson-Eilola, Johndan. (1998). 'Negative space: From production to connection in composition.' In Taylor, Todd, & Ward, Irene. (Eds.). *Literacy Theory in the Age of the Internet.* New York: Columbia University Press. 17-33.

Kress, Gunther. (1998). 'Visual and verbal modes of representation in electronically mediated communication: The potentials of new forms of text.' In Snyder, Ilana. (Ed.). *Page to Screen.* New York, NY: Routledge. 53–79.

Kress, Gunther, & van Leeuwen, Theo. (2001). *Multimodal Discourse.* London: Arnold.

Kress, Gunther. (2003). *Literacy in the New Media Age.* London: Routledge.

Landow, George. (1998). 'Hypertext as collage-like writing.' In Lunenfeld, Peter. (Ed.). *The Digital Dialectic: New Essays on New Media.* Cambridge, MA: MIT Press. 150–170.

Lave, Jean, & Wenger, Etienne. (1991). *Situated Learning: Legitimate Peripheral Participation.* Cambridge, UK: Cambridge University Press.

Lemke, Jay. (1998). 'Metamedia literacy: Transforming meanings and media.' In Reinking, David, McKenna, Michael, Labbo, Linda, & Kieffer, Ronald. (Eds.). *Handbook of Literacy and Technology: Transformations in a Post-Typographic World.* Mahwah, NJ: Lawrence Erlbaum Associates. 283-301.

Lipponen, Lasse, Hakkarainen, Kai, & Paavola, Sami. (2004). 'Practices and orientations of CSCL.' In Strijbos, Jan Willem, Kirschner, Paul, & Martens, Rob. (Eds.). *What We Know About CSCL and Implementing it in Higher Education.* Dordrecht: Kluwer. 31–50.

MacIntyre, Blair, Bolter, Jay, Moreno, Emmanuel, & Hannigan, Brendan. (2001, October 29-30). 'Augmented reality as a new media experience.' In *ISAR 2001.* New York, NY. Available at http://www.cc.gatech.edu/projects/ael/papers/newmedia.html

Messaris, Paul. (1997). 'Visual "literacy" in cross-cultural perspective.' In Kubey, Robert. (Ed.). *Media Literacy in the Information Age.* New Brunswick, NJ: Transaction Publishers. 135–162.

Morrison, Andrew. (1997). 'What happens when you let go?.' *KTK seminar manuscript series on Communication, Technology & Culture.* University of Oslo, No. 6. 1-14. Available at http://www.ktk.uio.no/notater/notat6.html

Morrison, Andrew. (2001). *Electracies: Investigating Transitions in Digital Discourses and Multimedia Pedagogies in Higher Education. Case Studies in Academic Communication From Zimbabwe.* Unpublished doctoral dissertation, Department of Media & Communication, University of Oslo.

Morrison, Andrew. (2003b). 'Dancing with postcolonial theory: Digital scenography and the performance of local culture.' *Norsk medietidsskrift* (Norwegian media Journal). Vol. 10, No. 2, 28–56. Available at http://www.medieforskerlaget.no/nmt_arkiv/2003-02/index.htm.

Morrison, Andrew, Skjulstad, Synne, & Smørdal, Ole. (2004, November 17-21). 'Choreographing augmented space.' Paper presented at *FutureGround* Conference, Melbourne. CD-ROM Proceedings.

Myers, Jamie, Hammett, Roberta, & McKillop, Ann Margaret. (1998). 'Opportunities for critical literacy and pedagogy in student-authored hypermedia.' In Reinking, David, McKenna, Michael, Labbo, Linda, & Kieffer, Ronald. (Eds.). *Handbook of Literacy and Technology: Transformations in a Post-Typographic World.* Mahwah, NJ: Lawrence Erlbaum Associates. 63-78.

New London Group. (2000). 'A pedagogy of multiliteracies: Designing social futures.' In Cope, Bill, & Kalantzis, Mary. (Eds.). *Multiliteracies: Literacy Learning and the Design of Social Futures.* London: Routledge. 9-37.

Phillipson, Michael. (1995). 'Managing "tradition": The plight of aesthetic practices and their analysis in a technoscientific culture.' In Jenks, Chris. (Ed.). *Visual Culture.* London: Routledge. 202-217.

Schieffelin, Edward. (1998). 'Problematising performance.' In Hughes-Freeland, Felicia. (Ed.). *Ritual, Performance, Media.* London: Routledge. 184-207.

Seaman, Bill. (2002). Recombinant poetics: Emergent explorations of digital divide in virtual space.' In Resier, Martin, & Zapp, Andrea. (Eds.). *New Screen Media.* London: BFI. 237-255.

Sha, Xin Wei, & Kuzmanovic, Maja. (2000). 'From representation to performance: Responsive public space.' *DIAC 2000.* Available at http://www.f0.am/publications/2000_diac/index.html

Skjulstad, Synne, & Morrison, Andrew. (2005). 'Movement in the interface.' *Computers and Composition.* Vol. 22, No. 4, 413-433.

Skjulstad Synne, Morrison, Andrew, & Aaberge, Alberine. (2002). 'Researching performance, performing research: Dance, multimedia and learning.' In Morrison, A. (Ed.). *Researching ICTs in Context.* Oslo: InterMedia/UniPub. 211-248. Available at http://www.intermedia.uio.no/konferanser/skikt-02/skikt-research-conferance.html.

Snyder, Ilana. (1998). 'Beyond the hype: Reassessing hypertext.' In Snyder, Ilana. (Ed.). *Page to Screen: Taking Literacy Into the Electronic Era.* London: Routledge. 125-143.

Sparacino, Flavia, Davenport, Glorianna & Pentland, Alex. (2000). 'Media in performance: Interactive spaces for dance, theater, circus, and museum exhibits.' *Systems Journal.* Vol. 39, Nos. 3&4. Available at http://www.research.ibm.com/journal/sj/393/part1/sparacino.html

Sylvester, Christine. (1999). 'Development studies and postcolonial studies: Disparate tales of the "Third World."' *Third World Quarterly.* Vol. 20, No. 4, 703-721.

Ulmer, Gregory. (1989). *Teletheory: Grammatology in the Age of Video.* Baltimore, MD: Johns Hopkins University Press.

Ulmer, Gregory. (1994a). *Heuretics.* Baltimore: Johns Hopkins University Press.

Ulmer, Gregory. (1994b). 'The Miranda warnings: An experiment in hyper-rhetoric.' In Landow, George. (Ed.). *Hyper/Text/Theory.* Baltimore, MD: Johns Hopkins University Press. 344-375.

Ulmer, Gregory. (1997). 'The grammatology of distance learning.' *TEXT Technology.* Vol. 7, No. 3, 5-20.

Ulmer, Gregory. (1998). 'Foreword/forward (into electracy).' In Taylor, Todd, & Ward, Irene. (Eds.). *Literacy Theory in the Age of the Internet*. New York: Columbia University Press. ix–xiii.

Ulmer, Gregory. (2002). *Internet Invention. From Literacy to Electracy*. New York: Longman.

Wells, Gordon. (1999). *Dialogic inquiry: Toward a Sociocultural Practice and Theory of Education*. Cambridge, MA: Cambridge University Press.

Wertsch, James. (1991). *Voices of the Mind. A Sociocultural Approach to Mediated Action*. Cambridge, MA: Harvard University Press.

Wertsch, James. (1998). *Mind as Action*. Oxford, UK: Oxford University Press.

Wysocki, Anne. (2004). 'Opening new media to writing: Openings and justification.' In Wysocki, Anne, Johnson-Eilola, Johndan, Self, Cynthia, & Sirc, Geoffrey. *Writing New Media*. Logan, UT: Utah State University Press. 1-41.

Wysocki, Anne, & Johnson-Eilola, Johndan. (1999). 'Blinded by the letter: Why are we using literacy as a metaphor for everything else?' In Hawisher, Gail, & Selfe, Cynthia. (Eds.). *Passions, Pedagogies and 21st Century Technologies*. Logan: Utah State UniversityPress. 349-368.

14

GUIDING MEANING ON GUIDED TOURS

NARRATIVES OF ART AND LEARNING
IN MUSEUMS

Palmyre Pierroux

BRIDGING THE GAP BETWEEN DISCOURSES
OF ART AND LEARNING

Contemporary art theory operates with the tenet that artworks are open to multiple interpretations and that different strategies may be employed to draw out and reflect on a work's meaning. At the same time, interpretations produced by scholars, curators, critics, and artists are deeply rooted in perspectives on how people experience and learn about art, what Kress and Leeuwen (2001) call 'rhetoric/epistemological frames.' Professional art discourse, implicitly if not explicitly, draws on these frames when interpreting a work's meaning, historical styles and influences, and artists' intentions and productions.

In art museums, professional interpretations become embedded in a strata of potentially meaningful semiotic resources, which include the museum architecture, labels, exhibition displays, catalogues, guided tours, selection of museum objects, and the objects themselves (O'Toole, 1994; Kress & Leeuwen, 2001; Ravelli, 2003). A common approach to the design of semiotic resources entails the use of narrative, a primary mode of communication that provides meaning and engages visitors in museums. In this chapter, I explore the guided tour as a semiotic resource, the narratives that characterize this communication mode, and how narratives are used to mediate meaning-making activity.

In guided tour practice, it is possible to distinguish two familiar narratives on how meaning in art is learned and experienced. On the one hand, although not mutually exclusive, there is a perspective that meaning in art is produced in individual perception and experience through exposure to art. This view is common in art history, aesthetics, visual culture studies, and social semiotic approaches, whereby learning becomes associated with vague notions of neural patterns, perception, and affective response. On the other hand, there is a perspective that meaning in art is produced by art history and its discourses. This view is associated with contextual approaches in art history and assessment concerns in formal education.

In this chapter, I investigate the rhetoric/epistemological frames in art and learning discourses, theoretically, and the practice of these discourses in museums, empirically. This innovation on traditional analytical approaches makes it possible to address the 'gap' between contemporary art discourses, on the one hand, and learning concepts that inform art museum education practice, on the other hand. I bring to this study of museum practice my background as an art historian and a sociocultural perspective on learning. The latter entails an understanding of learning as emerging through social interaction, mediated by cultural tools and artifacts.

FOCUS OF THE CHAPTER

The focus of this study is the meaning-making activity of high school students on guided tours in modern art museums. I present empirical material gathered from observations of guided tours, which are analyzed as communicative events mediated by signs and tools, including the work of art, but also speech, gestures, and text, in the broadest sense. I explore narratives about art and learning that are embedded in concrete discourse in art museums, and I investigate the role of art history in meaning-making activity on guided tours.

The chapter is organized in the following manner. I first present the theoretical significance of a situated, mediated understanding of human activity for studies of meaning making. I then present case studies of guided tours with museum educators who consciously use contrasting narratives to frame their discursive activity. I conclude by discussing the contributions of this study to museum research and the implications of the findings for bridging the gap between art and learning discourses.

THEORETICAL PERSPECTIVES

Mediated Activity

Sociocultural perspectives build on the Russian cultural-historical school of thought from the 1920s and 1930s. However, since the translation and publication of key works by psychologists Vygotsky (1978, 1986), Leontev (1978, 1981), and Luria (1976, 1982), a broad range of sociocultural research traditions and interests has developed in the human sciences. It is nonetheless possible to say, in general, that sociocultural approaches aim 'to explicate the relationships between human action, on the one hand, and the cultural, institutional, and historical situations in which this action occurs, on the other' (Wertsch et al., 1995: 11). The key to explaining these relationships is the concept of *mediation action*.

The principle of mediated action is that the mind develops through social interaction and that historical-cultural 'tools and signs'—physical orientations, semiotic resources, language, and particularly speech—powerfully influence this development (Wertsch, 1985, 1998). Moreover, just as semiotic resources mediate human development on the individual level, so too are 'cultural tools' in constant transition across different temporal and spatial scales through use. From a sociocultural perspective, cultural tools are taken as 'acquired knowledge that is objectified into a collective memory' (Engeström et al., 1984).

In this sense, cultural tools may be understood as integrated in all aspects of bodily and mental interaction with the world. To understand meaning making in encounters with art, then, analysis must take into account the interactions of actors as they are mediated by specific cultural, historical, and institutional settings. Meaning-making processes are seen as grounded in the material body of the actor(s) but also in collective, cultural activity, through discourse and interaction (Roth & Pozzer-Ardenghi, 2005). Therefore, meaning is not understood in an isolated, abstract, or disinterested sense but as a multimodal composition that is 'generated by a particular semiotic activity and a particular social language' (Wertsch, 1991: 85). At the same time, as an inherently social process, there is an *expressive and relational* aspect to meaning making, as dialogical event. This is the influence of Bakhtin (1986) on sociocultural perspectives on discourse, which stress the inherently dialogical character of meaning as emerging in the relationship between utterance and speech genre. In this study, meaning making on guided school tours in art museums is explored as such a dialogical event.

Narratives as Mediational Means

The most important tool in museums for mediating meaning is narrative. It is, as Roberts (1997) puts it, the 'heart and soul' of what museums do. Although I do not focus on narrative theory as such, narratives are conceptualized and explored in this chapter on several levels. First, narratives in art museums are taken as value-laden discourses that have developed over time into institutionalized ways of thinking, collecting, and explaining art. In this sense, narrative is produced by and reproduces cultural-historical practices evolving on quite long time scales and may be analyzed as such (Lemke, 2000). Embedded in cultural and social practices in museums, narratives are *mediational means* and may be studied as 'part of the "cultural tool kit" that characterizes a sociocultural setting' (Wertsch, 2002: 57).

Which narratives shape practices in modern and contemporary art museums? As mentioned earlier, the answer to this depends on whether one is investigating the *production* of narratives about art in curatorial practice or examining narratives as *mediational means* in educational practice. Although curators engage with political, feminist, and sociological discourses to interpret contemporary artistic practices, there appears to be what Ricoeur (1981) calls a 'temporal lag' between curatorial narratives and those that museum educators draw on in their discursive practices. In my study of art museum education theory and practice, I have chosen to explore two familiar narratives as they are used in guided tour activity. The one narrative posits the significance of art history as central to art's meaning. The other narrative about art's meaning stresses the direct relationship between artwork and the observer as subject. I refer to these familiar, contrasting narratives as contextualism and formalism, respectively. On guided tours, contextualist and formalist narratives are resources on which educators draw in their discursive practices, consciously or unconsciously, intentionally or not.

However, these narratives have not only developed from contrasting views on the nature of art, but they also represent different notions about what counts as knowledge. Although debate about whether 'information' compromises aesthetic encounters is familiar to museum curators and educators, the underlying epistemologies of these respective views are rarely explored. Therefore, the first question posed in this chapter is: What are the learning perspectives underlying formalist and contextualist narratives in art museum education?

It is in regard to learning, or what I will call meaning-making processes, that a second understanding of narrative is useful. Describing the tensions that arise *between narratives* in processes of collective remembering, Wertsch (2002) puts forward an understanding of the 'dialogical function' of narrative. Wertsch argues that, although specific narratives are embedded in concrete discursive practices, they are also open to contestation, negotiation, mastery, and appropriation. It is this dialogical activity of mastery and appropriation, as I have argued elsewhere (Pierroux, 2005), that *becomes* learning in museums. My second research question thus explores the dialogical function of contextualist and formalist narratives in museum education practice. How do these narratives enter into meaning making processes on guided tours in art museums?

Guided Tours: A Communicative Genre

My decision to use data from guided tours is based on the assumption that narratives will be more apparent in this institutionalized discursive setting between educator and high school students than in settings where casual museum visitors 'pick up' narratives in their talk from museum texts or other mediating resources. Is it possible to reconcile an emergent, dialogical concept of meaning-making with the guided tour, an event that is organized, structured, and purposive? In the museum research literature, the guided tour, as an activity that is constrained both verbally and physically, is frequently contrasted with 'free choice' learning, with visitors moving about freely. Guided tours may be considered a communicative genre, which in Linell's (1998: 239) terms is 'originally interactionally developed, then historically sedimented, often institutionally congealed, and finally interactionally reconstructed in situ.'

Yet it is this *in situ* aspect of guided tours, as a face-to-face, discursive activity with speech the essential tool, that allows them to be conceived dialogically. The role of speech is crucial to sociocultural understandings of mediation, as Wertsch et al. (1995: 12; italics original) explain: 'For [Vygotsky], speech is a *process, if not a form of action*, that uses language as a *means*.' Speech is not only a mediating tool, but is, in itself, an active reconstruction process, a 'dynamic merging' of word and thought in socially situated communication and discourse. Therefore, although guided tours give the impression of being monological rather than dialogical, as a communicative genre, they also may be 'more or less open' depending on unfolding activity in different situated social encounters (Linell, 1998). Accordingly, guided tours are considered in this study as multimodal experiences and discursive sites in which participants' utterances come into play and exchange, with each other but also as responses to narratives specific to this institutional practice. It is thus through studying discourse and interaction at Bakhtin's 'utterance level,' as Billig (2001) points out, that both emergent and ideological meaning may be identified, that is, *inside* multimodal compositions.

Formalist and Contextualist Narratives

The two contrasting narratives that I call 'formalism' and 'contextualism' are systems of beliefs that are rooted in antiquity and run as an undercurrent in literary discourse through aesthetics, art history, visual studies, and art education. That these narratives are relevant today became apparent during my study of how modern and contemporary art is taught in museums, specifically during my observations of guided tour discourse with middle- and high school-level students and through my interviews with museum educators.

Although contextualist and formalist positions overlap and merge, the practical problem that stems from these narratives is familiar to museum educators: how to balance an object-based focus on the artwork with information from the disciplinary domain of art history? In the instance of guided tours for school groups, for example, art history is information that teachers often expect from museum educators. Yet museums frequently posit the primacy of the art object over correct meanings, contending that language—particularly complex theories—hinders (aesthetic) art encounters and undermines observers' opportunities to make their own meaning. In the following, I briefly sketch the histories of these narratives.

Formalism in Art Museum Education

A formalist perspective considers form inseparable from content because it is grounded in the social and cultural conditions of a specific time by means of the creative act. This makes it possible to analyze or decode the meaning of an art by relating grammar, composition, style, and palette to the historical and cultural conditions of its making. Recent studies within linguistics and semiology that adopt such formalist strategies include systemic functional linguistics (SFL) analyses of visual and 'displayed' art (O'Toole, 1994; Kress & van Leeuwen, 1996) and, more recently, multi-modal analyses of visual images, museum architecture, and art exhibitions (Fei, 2004; Hofinger & Ventola, 2004). In terms of reception, the art object is seen as a system of (more or less arbitrary) signs, a composition, to which the observer relates intuitively and directly, that is, through cognition and senses.

Learning theories grounded in formalist approaches in art museum education thus stress unmediated, visceral response as the most genuine. They may also take the pragmatic view that most observers do not have disciplinary knowledge to bring to bear on their experiences of artworks, and that in contemporary art every meaning is valid (Yenawine, 1991). The observer constructs meaning ever more deeply through increased 'exposure' and perception is central. Such exposure theories are based on the premise that cognition is not passive, but that

> we learn constantly through experience and exposure (. . . .) As is common elsewhere, the appreciation of art is likely to be partial at first, but it can be developed subsequently by a kind of bootstrapping, without resort to the formal study of theory or history. (Davies, 2006: 75)

Philip Yenawine, former Director of Education at the Museum of Modern Art (MoMA), New York, has developed a particular approach that I situate among formalist educational practices. Yenawine works with developmental psychologist Abigail Housen and promotes an educational method in art museums called the *Visual Thinking Strategy* (VTS). This inquiry-based strategy supports young (elementary school) or inexperienced observers as they construct meaning by cultivating rather than 'moving beyond' intuitive responses. Based on Housen's research on aesthetic understanding, VTS recognizes that concepts in art history and aesthetics, particularly in modern and contemporary art, are typically beyond the young or inexperienced observer's understanding (Housen, 1999).

Housen and Yenawine propose that observers instead be taught how to develop their perceptual and reasoning skills over time, empowering them to develop aesthetic understanding based on close looking and a guided inquiry-based strategy. VTS is a quite specific but also open-ended approach to meaning-making that has been likened to the creative act of the artist. Yenawine explains in a demonstration video (Yenawine & Rice, 1999) titled *Contrasting Practices III*:

> It begins with asking people to look in silence at the work, and I follow a period of examination with questions. What's going on here? What do you see that makes you say that, and (. . .) what more can you find? I paraphrase what people say. And I link answers that relate one way or another. I also point to what people mention as they talk.

Contextualism in Art Museum Education

Response to VTS has been quite positive among museum educators. However, such object-based, 'formalist' approaches are contested in museums' work with schools, which prioritize assessment and disciplinary content, that is, art history. Kemal and Gaskell (1993: 1) provide a useful general definition of art history as 'seeking to define the circumstances in which the art object was initially produced and perceived, and to follow its reception through time.'

Protests against a formalist approach generally follow the argument voiced by Associate Director of Education Danielle Rice at the Philadelphia Museum of Art. Rice is concerned that viewers may walk away with misunderstandings and 'wrong answers' without contextual information. She maintains that specialized disciplinary knowledge is expertise that viewers seek from contemporary art museums, and educators are obliged to share contextual information in a manner that enriches encounters with art. Rice also participates in the demonstration video *Contrasting Practices III* (Yenawine & Rice, 1999), and she argues:

> I think listening is really important...but I do also believe that it's very important to get them inspired and motivated to want to go out to learn more and . . . to figure out how to interpret objects by bringing their own responses to bear and the responses of historians, artists, critics, etc.

Summing up

To go over the main points thus far, I propose that formalism and contextualism represent specific narratives (Wertsch, 2002) within aesthetics and art history concerned with the ontology of art: questions of what constitutes a work of art. In the formalist perspective, the art object is constituted through subjective perception of its formal characteristics. In the contextualist position, perspectives in art history about the significance of object, artist, and its making are essential to understanding an object as art. Moreover, in the context of an educational setting, I propose that formalist and contextualist narratives bring central epistemological problems to the forefront: questions of what constitutes knowledge about a work of art. In my view, formalist understandings are at the core of the VTS, which situates meaning in individual cognitive and sensory processes, while contextualist strategies in museum education prioritize art history and thus bring social and cultural resources into encounters with works. As mentioned, these are complex philosophical positions necessarily reduced for analytical purposes.

METHODOLOGICAL PREMISES

Interaction Analysis

The methods used in this study are grounded in Interaction Analysis (IA) (Jordan & Henderson, 1995), an interdisciplinary approach to studying human interaction. IA has roots in ethnomethodology, ethnography, and conversation analysis, among other disciplines, and has the larger goal of identifying how actors organize and use social and material resources in activity. An important premise for conducting research in IA is that theories of knowledge and action must be grounded in empirical evidence, that is, in verifiable observations of moment-to-moment verbal and nonverbal activity in social settings. This means that, to the largest extent possible, analysis is free from predetermined categories about mental faculties and human behaviors (Jordan & Henderson, 1995).

In sociocultural studies, detailed attention to social interaction is important to understanding the relevance of language, semiotic resources, the physical setting, and participants' physical orientations and gestures for meaning making. Video recordings are made to capture this level of detail and to make interactions accessible for multiple replayings and collaborative interpretations with other researchers. In this study, the argument of 'contrasting practices' put forth in the demonstration video became a theme for analyzing the interactions and discourse of the participants. This video was then analyzed in relation to video and audio data that I had collected in Norwegian and North American art museum guided tours from 2002 to 2004. Video analysis sessions were conducted with InterMedia researchers to look at the raw video data and discuss its character and possible means of selection. These sessions informed the approaches I have used to study contrasting narrative practices and how they organize and structure guided tour discourse and meaning-making processes.

In the following section, I present the data and the methods used to code and analyze discursive moves. I discuss this first analysis and then move on to a sequence analysis of selected discourse segments. I conclude with a discussion of these two methodological approaches in terms of their relevance for my research questions.

Discourse Analysis Methods

It is important to acknowledge that classroom and museum discourse studies build on broad and established traditions in conversation, interaction, and discourse analysis. I draw on familiar tools from these traditions, among them, the analytical concepts *moves* and *functions*. In this study, moves are 'utterances,' the basic discourse unit determined by the change of speaker. In analyzing the moves in the data, I observed characteristics of an Initiation-Response-Feedback (IRF) pattern (Sinclair & Coulthard, 1975; Mehan, 1979; Mercer, 1995), which involves three moves: the educator's initiation, the student's response, and the educator's follow-up. However, it should be noted that moves in the turn-taking pattern are conceptualized as relational entities. In this sense, 'a move's "own" content is always understood in relation to its local (and other) contexts' (Linell, 1998: 175). A dialogical perspective such as the one I adopt thus entails a more open understanding of discourse than the IRF model may suggest (Wells, 1999; Rasmussen, 2005).

I also noted that each move generally contains more than one function. Function is an analytic category based on the concept that language may be used in a regulatory manner and that different communicative functions may be identified in individual parts of the move (Halliday, 1978; Wells, 1999). The purpose of using a coding scheme in this bottom-up approach, which is based on replayings of video recordings and analysis of the unfolding interaction of participants, is to identify similarities in the organization and structure of talk in the different guided tours—the kinds and instances of communicative functions the educators used in their discursive strategies and the responses these elicited (Wodak, 2001).

Following analysis of the coded discourse, and to explore more deeply the relations between the structure and organization of discourse, social interactions, and meaning-making processes, I select segments of talk in the data and analyze the sequential development of meaning *as it unfolds*. This method of sequential analysis corresponds with the fundamental dialogical perspective that utterances should not be analyzed in isolation from their relational positions (Linell, 1998). I conclude with a discussion of what kinds of information, practices, and understandings are made apparent by using these different methodologies: coding and sequence analysis.

DATA

The *Contrasting Practices* (CP) Video Data

As mentioned earlier, museum educators Yenawine and Rice demonstrated and documented their respective approaches to gallery teaching in a video titled *Contrasting Practices III*. In this video (CP), taped at the Philadelphia Museum of Art in 1999, two different classes from the same middle school were invited to discuss the work titled *Tori*, which was made by by artist Eva Hesse in 1969 (Figure 14.1): one class with Yenawine and one with Rice. In the introduction of the tape, these two educators explain that the video has been produced with the express aim of demonstrating two contrasting teaching methodologies.

Figure 14.1. *Tori* (Hesse, 1969).

This video serves as the foundation for my empirical analysis. Furthermore, the video invites comparison with my own observations and analysis of guided tours with school groups, and it frames my main research questions: How are formalist and contextualist narratives embedded in art education discourse? What is the role of art history as mediational means guided tour discourse?

The primary data in this study are these two different 'gallery talks' with middle-school students in the CP video. These different groups of students were similarly seated on chairs in front of Hesse's sculpture, which was placed on a raised platform. The educators stood in front of their respective classes and moved about during the talk, pointing and calling on the students as they raised their hands. However, because the CP video had been edited, and to give a richer description of the school field trip experience, I include in my analysis recorded observations of two additional tours with high school students at the Philadelphia Museum of Art (PMA) and the Museum of Modern Art (MoMA), New York, respectively. The data set thus comprises four gallery talks: two 10-minute talks in the CP video and two 1-hour tours that I observed and recorded in 2004.

The latter were selected from a larger corpus based on their suitability as comparative data; these two tours had approximately the same number of students (12–15), the same age (15–17 years), and were from the same kind of schools (public) as the students in the CP video. All of the museums included in this study are located in the same part of the United States (northeast), and all of the educators are familiar with the VTS. In addition, similar types of art works (modern, contemporary, and abstract) were discussed on all of the tours and are part of the permanent collections at each museum.

The MoMA data

In contrast to the discussion of one work each in the CP video, the MoMA data includes discussions of three different works on the tour, and each discussion has been analyzed separately. It is a thematic tour ('landscapes and cityscapes'), and the educator had visited the students at school the previous week to introduce the theme, presenting and discussing slides. The classroom teacher was present on the tour and engaged in 'whole-class' conversation at one point during the tour.

The MoMA tour data is audio recordings, supplemented with field notes to record physical activity. Although video data are considered ideal for interaction analysis, the lack of visual data is not considered a disadvantage here because participants' orientations and the physical exhibition space are managed quite similarly in all of the data. The students' movements are confined in the sense that they are closely seated on folding chairs while educators stand and move about. Similar, too, is the use of hand-raising and pointing as the main gestural means, not unlike whole-classroom discourse settings.

The PMA Data

The PMA data also include discussions of three works on the tour, with each discussion analyzed separately. Like the MoMA data, it is a thematic tour ('modern and contemporary art'). The classroom teacher was present here as well, occasionally reminding the students that they had seen or discussed a reproduction of a particular work of art in class. In all, there were three such instances of teacher comments during the 60-minute tour.

The data from the PMA tour are video recordings. A single handheld video camera was used, making it possible for me to capture participants' talk and orientation to each other, to artworks, and to other artifacts at a detailed level. The museum educator used a remote microphone, allowing two sound feeds and the possibility of isolating each track in playback. Because the students were stationary and seated in a large group in front of artworks when the educator was talking, it was a relatively simple setup and thus possible to capture most of the interactions and discourse. I had met and recorded the students the previous week in their classroom and they seemed comfortable with the camera.

Finally, regarding the data, it is important to point out that neither the MoMA nor the PMA museum educator I observed had formally been trained in VTS. However, the MoMA guide reported that this specific questioning strategy is taught during their training, although the use of theme-related and contextual information to supplement this approach is also encouraged.

In this sense, there is a similarity between the specific questioning methods used on the MoMA tour and Philip Yenawine's method on the CP video. Likewise, the educator I observed on the PMA tour aimed to convey art historical information, not unlike the method endorsed and demonstrated on the CP video by Danielle Rice. In contrast to MoMA training, however, no explicit methods are taught as part of the training at PMA, and educators employ a broad range of approaches that have been developed on both an individual and collaborative basis. These similarities, between the MoMA tour and the formalist approach in the CP video, on the one hand (no or little information), and the PMA tour and the contextualist approach in the CP video, on the other hand (emphasis on art historical information), were considerations that entered into the data-selection process.

CODING ANALYSIS

Functions

As mentioned, classroom discourse structures have been identified as features embedded in gallery tour activity (Xanthoudaki, 1998; Pierroux, 2005), with museum educators guiding discussion using a triadic dialogic structure (IRF) that is common to whole-classroom interaction. Because the students were on school field trips in museums, a coding scheme was developed to be sensitive to both types of institutional talk, drawing on conventions from classroom (Cazden, 1988; Wells, 1999) and museum discourse analysis (Leinhardt et al., 2002).

Moves/Functions

The talk from each of the four tours (CP formalist, CP contextualist, MoMA, PMA) was first transcribed in its entirety from video and audio data in keeping with interaction analysis conventions (Jordan & Henderson, 1995). Each tour transcript was analyzed using a 'bottom-up' approach. In the initial phase of analysis, talk functions were quite broadly defined. During analysis of participants' orientations to previous and subsequent utterances in context, multiple functions *in each move* were identified and defined in the transcripts using *HyperResearch* as a tool. The video recordings and field notes were occasionally consulted during this process to support inferences about participants' interactions and talk functions. Similarities between functions were identified and organized into categories.

The categories of these 'communicative functions' were developed based on Wells' (1999) research because of parallels (such as the IRF pattern) between educator-led discussions in classroom settings and museum educator-led discussions on guided tours. Wells' methodology is rooted in a sociocultural view on language, which he combines with Halliday's (1978) concepts of genre and register, extending them to encompass social action beyond linguistic behavior. The researcher tool *Hyper Research* was used to organize, compare, and eventually label the functions in each move directly from the transcripts. The categories in Figure 14.2 describe the functions in the educators' moves.

Reformulating & summarizing.

Rephrasing a student response as a question to be confirmed, making previous utterances a possible focus for the next utterance, labeling utterances as arguments; repeating utterance. Used in conjunction with physical pointing, connecting, and extending.

Connecting.

References to either ideas in previous utterances (possibly from discussions of other works in the same tour) or themes.

Requesting explanation & requesting further explanation.

Keep talk afloat in the form of open questions prefaced with 'what, where, and what more.'

Requesting opinion and information.

Questions that require yes or no answers or request specific information.

Extending.

In a reformulating move, information or observations are added to the previous utterance.

Providing information.

Educator contributes art historical information, observations, or personal interpretations.

Figure 14.2. Functions in educator talk.

To label the functions in student moves, I use perspectives from classroom and museum discourse analysis. However, the function categories were also developed to be sensitive to the interpretive nature of the students' activity, drawing on interpretation perspectives in art history

(Baxandall, 1985). The function categories for student talk shown in Figure 14.3 thus reflect characteristics of interpretative processes, such as making associations and inferential explanations. Specific analytic attention was paid to semiotic resources used in art museums: object-related talk and gestures, disciplinary terms, concepts, and rhetorical and narrative elements, museum labels, and texts.

Analyzing.

Talk that is often phrased as questions, involves reflection on how objects were made (cause and effect), intentions, materials, and processes.

Describing.

Indexical, object-related observations that compare and note resemblances to other things in the world.

Interpreting.

Proposes a mood, intent, theme, idea, narrative, and includes personal associations such as 'it reminds me of' and 'it seems like.' Often includes aspects of analysing and describing.

Giving opinions.

Brief answers containing information, yes or no responses.

Clarifying and extending.

Responses to educator's request to build on or relate to previous utterances, either their own or others.' Clarifying is often object-related and involves pointing and describing ('up in the middle there'). Extending is a continuation of a previous utterance to further develop an idea.

Arguing.

Expresses disagreement with a previous utterance.

Figure 14.3. Functions in student talk.

In addition to categorizing the functions of talk in each move, I have noted the frequency of directly object-related talk among both students and educators. By this I mean that the object is pointed at, either physically or through reference. The following table presents all of the talk from the two sessions on the *CP* video coded according to the communicative functions in educator and student moves.

Contrasting Practices Video

Teacher moves	Formalist	Contextualist	Student moves	Formalist	Contextualist
Reformulating & summarizing	62%	26%	Analyzing	14%	0
Connecting	27%	15%	Interpreting	22%	27%
Req. explanation, further explanation	44%	20%	Describing	25%	0
Req. opinion & information	0	26%	Clarifying & extending	38%	14%
Extending	19%	13%	Using art concepts & terms	4	5
Providing information	0	11%	Giving opinions	0	20%
Using art concepts, terms, theme	8	5	Arguing	4	4
Directly object related	55 (48%)	10 (11%)			

Coding Results

I first discuss the communicative functions in educator and student talk on the two tours in the CP video. In keeping with the analytical distinction made earlier, the 'visual thinking' questioning strategy of Philip Yenawine (PY) is presented as formalist, whereas the gallery talk with Danielle Rice (DR) represents a contextualist approach. The frequency of each function in relation to the total moves is represented in percentile. The percentages for each tour add up to more than 100% because there was more than one communicative function identified in many of the moves. It was not possible to compare total moves in the different tours since the CP tape had been edited. However, the IRF pattern was consistent across the data, with teacher and student moves equally divided.

I then consider data from the formalist tour in the CP video in relation to the MoMA tour and discuss similarities between them. Next, I present codes from the contextualist data in the CP video alongside the PMA tour and consider similarities between the two contextualist approaches. I conclude my coding analysis by considering similarities and differences between the discursive functions of formalist and contextualist approaches.

Formalist Tour-CP Video Data

Most striking in the CP formalist educator moves is the high frequency of *reformulating and summarizing* (62%), *requesting explanation* (44%), and *connecting* (27%) activity. Also salient is the total lack of *providing information* (0%) and the use of a large amount of *object-related* talk (48%). Student moves mainly involve *clarifying and extending* (38%) and *describing* (25%) activity. Students are not engaged in *giving opinions* (0%) but spend a good deal of time *interpreting* (22%) and *analyzing* (14%). In general, the coding suggests that all educator initiate and follow-up moves support the building of student responses based on object-based descriptions. Accordingly, student interpretations are closely linked with *describing* activity, both their own and that of other students. This further suggests that interpretations are based on a joint, collaborative process in which descriptions and ideas of fellow students are picked up, elaborated on, and argued against. The talk is mainly *object-related*.

Contextualist Tour-CP Video Data

In the CP contextualist approach, the educator almost equally divides her time among *reformulating and summarizing* (26%), *requesting opinion* (26%), and *requesting explanation* (20%). By the educator move *requesting opinion*, I mean instances in which the educator first makes statements and provides information to which the students are expected to directly respond (giving opinions in the form of agreement, disagreement, or brief answers). In addition, the educator *provides information* (11%), *makes connections* (15%), and *extends* (13%) student responses. The educator uses less talk (11%) that is directly *object-related*. Student moves mostly involve *interpreting* (27%), *giving opinions* (20%), and *clarifying and extending* (14%). In general, the coding suggests that students give opinions and make interpretations based on information provided by the educator. The educator initiate and follow-up moves elicit opinions and information-based interpretations rather than support student responses based on *describing* or *analyzing*. The talk is mainly information-related.

However, it is important to note that the CP tape was edited for demonstration purposes, which may explain why it was not possible to identify any *describing* or *analyzing* activity in the student moves here. It is apparent that the educator encouraged some describing activity in the first few minutes of the talk that was edited, although neither the students nor the educator took up or referred to these descriptions again in the talk that is presented on the video.

To sum up the analysis of the CP video thus far, in the formalist data, students appear to make interpretations based on the object-related descriptions and analyses of fellow students because these are clarified and extended through the specifically structured communicative genre that characterizes the VTS. In the contextualist data, students make interpretations and give opinions based on information supplied by the educator rather than on their own object-related descriptions and analyses.

Comparing Formalist Tours-CP Video and MoMA Data

I next consider how the formalist tour in the CP video data compares with my own observations of a MoMA gallery tour, in which a similar questioning strategy was employed. As explained earlier, the session on the CP video consisted of one discussion of one artwork with duration of approximately 12 minutes. The MoMA tour had duration of approximately 45 minutes, with three 12- to 15-minute talks about three different works. Therefore, in coding talk from the MoMA data, instances of each function were first totaled for all three discussions and then averaged for a representative mean.

The most important difference to be mentioned is that, because the MoMA tour was thematic, information was introduced during the tour (5%). This difference is perhaps reflected in the lesser amount of time that students spend *describing* (8%) than on the CP video (25%). However, the data also suggest several important similarities between these two formalist strategies. Significantly, talk on both tours is largely *object-related* (48% and 45%). Furthermore, both educators stress *requesting explanation* (what, where, and what more questions), *reformulating* (rephrasing student responses), and *connecting* (referring to previous utterances) as their main discursive strategies. This similarity suggests that the most important activities for educators working with a formalist approach are to support an ongoing dialogue among the students. Similarities between student responses in the two groups are apparent as well because both spend the most time *clarifying and extending* (building on or relating to previous utterances), *interpreting* (proposing a mood, intent, theme, idea, and narrative), and *analyzing* (reflection on how objects were made, intentions, materials, and processes). This suggests that students are mainly encouraged to jointly construct meaning through works of art when VTS questions are the mediating tool: what's going on here, what do you see that makes you say that, and what more can you find?

Comparing Contextualist Tours-CP
Video and PMA Data

Like the MoMA tour, instances of function types for all three discussions on the PMA tour were first totaled and then averaged for a representative mean. Also similar is the thematic framing of the PMA tour. However, in contrast to formalist approaches that downplay the use of information in principle, both contextualist educators consider art historical information an essential part of a guided tour. This is reflected in the data in the frequency of *providing information* in both contextualist tours.

The PMA tour has a slightly higher frequency of *providing information* (15%) than the CP contextualist tour (11%). At the same time, student *interpreting* is much less (11%) in the PMA tour than in the CP contextualist tour (27%). This may perhaps be explained by the more frequent use of art concepts and terms in the PMA tour, which was thematic. A greater emphasis on art terms and concepts may also figure into the high percentage (59%) of *analyzing* talk, which in any case is a strong contrast to the apparent absence of analyzing talk among students on the CP video contextualist tour. In other words, the PMA educator supports talk that analyzes works of art (reflection on how objects were made, intentions, materials, and processes) rather than interpreting them (proposing a mood, intent, theme, idea, and narrative). How is this done?

The answer seems to lie in that the PMA educator frequently *requested explanation* (53%) in conjunction with *providing information* and *using art terms* in comparison with the CP video contextualist data (20%). There was also more directly *object-related* talk (34%) in the former than in the latter (11%). This suggests that information was provided in a manner that kept talk afloat by means of open questions, linked to the artwork, and prefaced with 'what, where, and what more.' That talk is 'kept afloat' more in the PMA contextualist data is seen in an overall higher frequency of student responses and student *analyzing* (59%) and *clarifying and extending* (31%) responses.

This is an important contrast between two contextualist approaches. The students spend most time of all tours *interpreting* (27%) in the CP video when the contextualist educator *provides information* (11%). When the PMA educator provides (even more) information but also combines this with moves that keep talk afloat, the students spend less time *interpreting* (11%) but are more active, use more art terms, extend and clarify their responses, and make object-related analyses. In other words, comparing the two contextualist approaches, the PMA tour has more dialogic characteristics.

Discussion of Coding Analysis

What kinds of conclusions may be drawn from this analysis of the communicative functions in educator and student talk? First, we see that it is possible to identify characteristics of guided tours as a communicative genre in that similar moves and functions are identified in all of the data; educator initiate and follow-up moves include *reformulating, requesting opinion and explanation, connecting,* and *extending* activities, and student response moves include *interpreting, analyzing,* and *describing.*

Second, there are similarities in the kinds and instances of talk in the respective *Contrasting Practices* tours and the two museums that adopt (more or less) these two practices. This suggests that there are functions and patterns in discourse that are characteristic for the contrasting practices of formalism and contextualism. In other words, there are connections between specific narratives in art and learning theory, formalism and contextualism, and their manifestation in concrete discourse as compositions. In the formalist approaches, interpretations of art are based primarily on student descriptions and analyses, whereas in contextualist approaches, students make interpretations and analyses based on information from the educator. A similarity between theory and practice is apparent in both the formalist and contextualist data.

To summarize, in this analysis, museum educators consciously or unconsciously use types of utterances oriented toward the production of the specific narratives I have identified as formalist and contextualist. Embedded in what the educators call 'contrasting practices' are ontological and epistemological positions in art and learning theory, fundamental views on what counts as art, and what counts as knowledge about art. Analyzing aspects of discourse in terms of functions in utterances and the frequency with which they occur provides information about 'modes of instruction,' narratives, the patterns of participation that are produced, and the types of knowledge and activities that are favored and embedded in these contrasting narratives (Rasmussen et al., 2003).

SEQUENCE ANALYSIS METHOD

Unpacking Categories

Yet insight into the kind of discursive work that is being done still leaves me with questions about *meaning-making* as a dialogical process and an intersubjective, situated activity. As a method, coding enforces an analysis of discourse that is deliberately and conventionally abstracted from dialogue and the multimodal experience. In this sense, the coding scheme represents what Bakhtin (1986: 75) calls 'potential meaning,' making generalizations that overlook the dialogic overtones of 'real-life dialogue.'

A dialogic approach allows me to unpack the categories that I have developed and examine the emergent nature of talk and interaction, in sequence and inside the guided tour as a 'multimodal composition.' Meaning is analysed as co-constructed sequence by sequence, even when one participant has unequal topic control, as in the guided tour setting (Wells, 1999). In particular, I am interested in exploring the category *interpretation* as it emerges in sequential talk. *Interpreting* has been identified in the data analysis as a function that proposes a mood, intent, theme, idea, and narrative and includes personal associations such as 'it reminds me to' and 'it seems like.' As a category, however, *interpreting* gives little information about the content of meanings that are produced in the chain of communication. This raises the question of what similarities and differences there might be in the interpretations?

In the following, I first present segments of talk, in sequence, which I have selected from the formalist tour in the CP video. All segments were selected according to their relevance as data for analyzing *interpreting* activity. I analyze these data and continue by presenting and analyzing segments of talk from the CP contextualist tour. I conclude the sequence analysis by reflecting on similarities and differences in interpreting and meaning-making on the respective formalist and contextualist tours.

Sequence Analysis: Formalist Data

The questioning strategy recommended in the VTS entails asking three questions: 'What is going on here?,' 'What do you see that makes you say that?,' and 'What more can you find'? The formalist CP video session thus begins with the educator (E) asking the question what is going on here'? In the ensuing discussion, students analyze processes of making (molded, paper-mâché, sloppily made); physical characteristics of the objects are described (different heights and sizes, glassy appearance, randomly placed, dull in color, transparent), as are resemblances (raviolis, unironed clothing, cocoon, beehive, pea pod, and overstuffed pillows, hot dog roll, swaddling). Educator moves are concentrated on *reformulating, requesting further explanation*, and *connecting*. Well into the discussion, building on descriptions and referencing previous comments, an *interpretation* of a more somber nature is put forward:

Sequence 1

  1. P: It looks like it's the aftermath of the birth of something and they all, everything came out and left the shells there, sort of in a big pile. (*interpretation*)

  2. E: OK, so this is like the shell after—

  3. P: Just, like the pods or the cocoon—

  4. E: Yes, so that idea of either pods, or cocoons, or something else and these are, these are left over after the event, a kind of birth event has occurred. Good, what more can you find?

  5. H: A hotdog roll, put the hot dog inside. ((laughter))

  6. E: OK, good, so maybe it's waiting for the hotdog. Yep?

  7. J: Kind of like after war or crime, like, the body bags, cause there are these bags and they kind of have a slit, like, where you keep the person, especially the one, the very back one, looks like you could put a human, or a dead animal or something, and zipper it up. (*interpretation*)

  8. E: Right, this is interesting, because we have had ideas about birth, or things coming out of it like a chrysalis, but this is the opposite end of the life, thing, where maybe these are body bags, but the bodies have been removed. Yes?

At this point, students begin to argue with emerging interpretations and position themselves in relation to what in a sense become reified meanings.

Sequence 2

((tape edit))

  9. E: Oh, yeah, not pigs in a blanket, but babies in a blanket. ((laughter)) So maybe like, they call them a sort of a blanket that you swaddle a child in when they are little? Yes, swaddling clothes, OK, great. Yes? You. ((points to a student))

 10. P: I think that the general theme is aftermath, whether it's about a football game, a crime scene, war, death, whatever it is. It has definitely happened after something (interpretation)

 11. E: OK, so sort of thinking about a lot of these different ideas that have been brought up, so you're thinking that the aftermath, whether, whatever it was, battle, football game.

 12. P: [...] whatever it was, it was the aftermath of something. (*interpretation*)

 13. E: This is after something has happened and some kind of ending, yeah?

((tape edit))

14. P: Well, we are definitely drawn to some sort of action [...] whether it was before, during or after, but it is such a still piece, so its really so weird that we draw action from something so still. (*interpretation*)

15. E: OK, good, it's kind of ironic that something that seems so still is, has all of these ideas important about some kind of action.

((fade out))

Analysis of Formalist Sequences

In the previous sequences, interpretations are based on what the students see, that is, art's formal characteristics. Significantly, no contextual or disciplinary information is provided. Following a relatively long period of describing, several students begin to argue for a definitive interpretation of Hesse's sculpture that is somber rather than trivial in nature. The museum educator remains impartial, indicating no preference for one interpretation or another, as students begin to associate the work not only with war, abandonment, and chaos, but hot dog rolls and swaddling blankets as well.

Implicit resistance to interpretations that are not 'serious' enough becomes apparent, however, when P breaks (2: 10) with the more tentative character of the talk and makes the exploratory hypothesis that the 'general theme is aftermath.' In tracing the development of this interpretation, we see that P is actually extending a previous utterance (1:1: 'It looks like it's the aftermath of the birth of something . . .'). This utterance is then picked up several turns later by J (1: 7), who connects the work to 'war, crime, and body bags' while ignoring a third student's more playful 'hot dog' comment (1: 5). The boldness of P's interpretation (2: 10: 'It has definitely happened after something') suggests a personal responsibility for her thinking, an appropriation of a meaning that nonetheless developed over several turns through peer comments about pea pods, cocoons, birth, and death. It is in this sense that Bakhtin's (1986) notion of addressivity, or the speaker's response orientation, is useful in understanding meaning making as a process.

Sequence Analysis: Contextualist Data

The next CP session begins with the educator (E) announcing that she is going to try something; she is going to provide the students with three different kinds of information, and she is going to ask their opinion about whether it makes a difference in how they see the piece. However, instead of providing information, she first asks the students what kinds of materials are typically used to make sculpture. The students respond with materials such as clay, wood, and metal. She then points out that this particular sculpture is made of fiberglass and that, according to the students' answers, it is 'an unusual material for a sculpture.' The educator then requests explanation (3: 1) about what makes a good work of art.

Sequence 3

1.   E: And, when you think of what makes a good work of art, what are some of the criteria that you use? What makes a good work art? What's important? Yeah?

2.   J: Well, like, it should catch the person's eye, like, it needs to be interesting.

3.   E: It should be interesting. ((points to a student))

4.   L: It needs to be, like, different from others.

5.   E: It needs to be original, it needs to be new, different, right? OK, what else? What else is important in a work of art? (5.0)

6.   E: It needs to say something, communicate something. It needs what? ((bends towards a student in the front row))

7.   P: It needs to catch your eye.

8.   E: It has to mean something. ((points to a student))

9.   J: It needs to have a lot of different meanings.

10.   E: Yeah, it could have a lot of different meanings, in fact, the best works of art have a lot of meanings, you all saw different things in this piece. ((reference to describing activity edited from tape)) Well, the reason I ask you that is because the first piece of information that I'm going to give you is about the artist's importance. Obviously if a work of art is in this museum, the artist was important. Her name was Eva Hesse, and she was important because she was one of the first artists to make art out of new materials like fiberglass, artists before that only used wood and metal and clay ((pointing to different students as she mentions the materials)) and all those things you said, and the other reason she was important is because she was one of the very first artists to make sculpture out of lots of different similar pieces ((gestures indicating many several pieces placed together)). If you think of a sculpture, right, ((moving her hands up and down)) it's usually a thing, and she made sculptures with all these

different pieces. So, this was one of her contributions to, uh, contemporary art and many other artists thought wow, this is really interesting, and this is really important, and she became very important. Now, does that piece of information make anybody feel differently or see something different in the piece? (3.0) Yes? No? (Several students shake their heads no, but no one answers.) Not very much.

As the students respond (3: 2–9), the educator *reformulates* their responses using art terminology. We see this in (3: 4–5) when the student's use of the word 'different' is reformulated with the more correct art term 'original' and again (3: 7–8) when the student says 'it needs to catch your eye,' which the educator reformulates as, 'it needs to mean something.' Examining the follow-up move of reformulating *in sequence* makes apparent how the educator both extends or translates students' everyday knowledge using vocabulary from the disciplinary domain of art history and enculturates the students in the production of certain narratives or ways of talking about art. The educator signals the next student response (3: 9) 'it needs to have a lot of different meanings' as a good place to present the first piece of information.

First, however, the authority of the art museum, and hence the significance of the information she is about to provide, is asserted in the next sentence when the educator emphasizes the artist's importance by pointing out that the work would not be in the museum otherwise. She then confirms that the use of fiberglass, as a new and unusual material, is one reason that the artist is important, and she *connects* this to an earlier discussion ('artists before that only used wood and metal and clay and all those things you said'). The other reason that the artist is important, she explains, is because Hesse was the first artist to make a sculpture consisting of many similar pieces. The first piece of information, then, is that the artist is important because, in art history, she was one of the first to work with fiberglass and the first to make a sculpture consisting of many similar pieces. In other words, specific narratives in art history about the 'new' and the 'genius artist' explain the artist's importance. The educator then (3: 10) asked the students to *give an opinion* about whether the contextual information made them *feel* differently about the piece, and the students respond (by not responding or shaking their heads) that this piece of information did not make them feel differently.

In the next sequence, the educator provides biographical information about the artist Eva Hesse and tells the students about Hesse being born Jewish in Germany during World War II, escaping to Amsterdam when she was a child, and losing many family members in the Holocaust. The following sequence begins with the educator then *requesting explanation*.

Sequence 4

11.	E:	OK, now take a look at the piece. So, now we have a piece of information about the Holocaust and her early history of it. What are you thinking?
12.	A:	Well, it looks like dead bodies. (*interpretation*)
13.	E:	You're thinking what?
14.	A:	Like it's dead bodies.
15.	E:	Dead bodies.
16.	A:	Like, it's a little more depressing. (*interpretation*)
17.	E:	You're seeing it slightly more depressing. Does anybody else feel like that? Yeah, what were you going to say?

[…]

18.	E:	Speak up just so I can hear you and the camera can pick you up.
19.	K:	[…] like it's not happy colors. (*interpretation*)
20.	E:	Not happy colors. Yeah. ((leans towards the student))
21.	J:	It looks like sort of like an opening wound. (*interpretation*)
22.	E:	An opening wound, there's something about that slit. Well, he was already saying paper-cut, but maybe it's the seriousness of the wound that is now changing it a bit.
23.	V:	Somebody put something inside that, you know, like…why is everybody, it's, it could be…
24.	E:	Uh-huh?
25.	V:	shells or…I don't know, it could be anything. (*interpretation*)
26.	E:	Ahh.
27.	V:	It doesn't have to be dead bodies, or dead people's fingers, or—
28.	E:	Oh, OK, so you're moving in a more positive direction, are you?
29.	V:	Yeah.
30.	E:	Ah-huh, interesting. Yes?
31.	A:	Well I definitely don't think it is positive, I don't feel like they are like pasta or like they are fingernails anymore. I think it's, like, depressing.
32.	E:	OK, my telling you that piece of information about the Holocaust kind of made the other stuff about pasta and fingernails seem a little trivial? ((A nods))

33.   A: Yes.

34.   E: And the piece seems more serious to you now? ((A nods))
            Uh-huh, interesting.

Analysis of Contextualist Sequences

After hearing about the Holocaust and tragic details of the artist's life, the students immediately respond with a myriad of appropriately gloomy associations ('dead bodies,' 'bones,' 'wounds,' and 'depressing'). As discussed, this is a specific narrative in art theory that links an artist's biographical details to the meaning of a work of art. However, a student (4: 23) contests the grim nature of these interpretations in the utterance 'why is everybody, it's, it could be (. . .) anything.' I propose that this break in a pattern of consensus may be understood as resistance to the educator's somewhat leading use of narrative as 'mediational means.' At the same time, the dialogic function of narrative is also apparent in its contestation by the student. In other words, this might be an authoritative narrative that is understood and 'mastered' as a piece of information—but it is not appropriated, or made the student's 'own.'

The educator reformulates this utterance by attaching a value to the student's position and then requesting confirmation (4: 28: 'So you're moving in a more positive direction, are you'?). This follow-up move reifies interpretations of the work as 'serious' or 'not serious' and creates a polarizing effect, as another student argues against a meaning of the work as not serious (4: 31) with the following quick and bold response: 'Well I definitely don't think it is positive. . . . I think it's, like, depressing.' In the utterances that follow (4: 33–34), the student confirms her opinion that the information makes the work seem more serious.

DISCUSSION OF SEQUENTIAL ANALYSIS

Talk as a Tool

In the formalist data, different interpretations emerge through a specific dialogical structure (IRF), and new meanings are constructed through the 'interanimation of voices' (Bakhtin, 1986). Narratives, in the sense of cohesive but seemingly inexhaustible explanations, develop in joint collaborative activity through associations, descriptions, analyses, and the process of clarifying and extending previous utterances. In this sense, the excerpts support Leinhardt and Knutson's (2004: 159) studies of museum conversations in which 'talking is a tool for socially constructed thought, not just evidence of it.' This corresponds with the aims of VTS, in which the development of critical thinking skills is valued more highly than art historical information in student encounters with art. As an art museum education theory, this means that there is no correct meaning, and the interpretation of Hesse's work is thus owned as much by the students as it is by art history.

However, just as the educator does not provide students with art history information neither is there any mention of art historical knowledge by the students. In the quite controlled discursive structure that is VTS, the educator poses the question 'What do you see'? and not 'What do you know'? This sets the frame of the discourse as a multimodal composition. Without discursive space to take up the disciplinary domain of art history, students draw on everyday concepts and knowledge to construct meaningful narratives. In other words, although meanings emerge from students' responses rather than from information provided by the educator, there is nonetheless a narrative that is guiding meaning in the VTS approach—namely, a learning narrative that emphasizes critical thinking skills over disciplinary knowledge. In the same way, then, that narratives in art theory may discursively narrow the field of interpretive possibilities, so too may perspectives on unguided learning direct and frame interpretations through specific discursive structures.

In contrast to the formalist emphasis on supporting the students' own interpretations, guiding meaning is an explicit aim in the contextualist narrative, and Rice maintains that meaning should be directed based on 'interesting and worthwhile' information (Yeanwine & Rice, 1999). This presupposes a normative distinction between good associations, that is, meaning constructed through contextual information, and those made based on students' previous knowledge and what they see. Although the latter may be valued for contributing to 'a sense of confidence in their abilities to look carefully at an object,' the former are valued more highly for 'also engaging in the external discourse of art history scholarship,' as Rice explains in the CP video (Yenawine & Rice, 1999).

What does art history scholarship consider important about Eva Hesse and, in particular, her artwork *Tori* (1969)? Several books have been written about Hesse (Lippard, 1992; Sussman, 2002), in which we can read an art historical analysis of the artist and her work, Hesse's reception at the time in relation to her more 'successful' male artist colleagues, her contribution to the new trend of 'anti-form,' and her overall production. In addition to her groundbreaking work with the fiberglass, Hesse's artistic interests are described as

> repetition, forms in isolation, similar forms repeated, fixed and
> unfixed, hard and soft, her variations on formal themes, her desire to

make sculptural elements absurd in themselves and in their multiplicity. . . . (Lippard, 1992: 132)

In the contextualist data, then, arguably the most worthwhile art historical
information that the educator provides concerns Hesse's use of fiberglass-
a new and 'undignified' material for sculpture and her use of multiples or
serial forms (3: 10). In terms of Hesse's significance within art history, it
is this contrast between explorations of geometrical order and forms
using new and seemingly dissolving, 'anti-form' materials that has earned
her a prominent place in minimalist art. Yet this piece of valuable disciplinary information, key to mastering the art historical narrative about
Hesse's contribution to modern art's development, was not appropriated
as particularly interesting or meaningful in the students' opinion.
Moreover, it did not make them feel differently, another narrative in aesthetics to which the educator (intentionally or not) refers when linking
affective response to meaning making.

The disturbing narrative about the artist's personal history that the educator chooses to tell the students as the next piece of information is funda-
mentally different in character. As mentioned, a significant part of any
explanation by art historians will tend to focus on the artist as maker
(Mansfield, 2002), and the biographical model that links artist to the structural and formal characteristics of a work is quite prevalent. In Lippard's
(1992: 156) interpretation of *Tori*, for example, the artist's early and tragic
death by brain cancer is featured: 'It is impossible not to read into these
broken and barren forms-like seed-pods past their prime-the downward
plunge of Hesse's life at this time.' In this sense, the use of biographical
information in the data demonstrates not only the dialogic use of art history
as a narrative but also the rhetorical character of art history as a discipline.

Finally, I note that students make striking similar *interpretations* in
the two groups despite being 'guided' by contrasting practices.
Specifically, several students in both groups associate the artwork with
death (1:7 'body bags' and 3: 13: 'dead bodies'). Descriptions based on
the work (the shapes resemble body bags) elicit interpretations akin to
those based on contextual information (the artist escaped the
Holocaust), and on the whole, rather gloomy interpretations prevail. Yet
analysis of meaning as it unfolds reveals that, in the formalist sequence,
a student argues for a serious interpretation of the artwork (aftermath)
in dialogue with other student responses. In the contextualist data, a student argues against a serious meaning (dead bodies, depressing) in
response to the educator's initiative. In this sense, it is possible to say
that meaning as it unfolds in dialogue is quite different in the respective
settings, although the content of the interpretations appears similar. By
analyzing discourse in sequence, we see that the similarity lies not in
interpretations of the work as serious but in the wish to be taken seri-

ously as meaning makers. In analyzing meaning making as an unfolding process in discourse and social interaction, it is possible to discern 'Who owns the meaning'? In contemporary art theory, there is perhaps no more fundamental question.

CONCLUSION

On the Two Methods

As described in the introduction, a basic tenet in contemporary and modern art museums is that works are open to multiple interpretations. In this chapter, I have used two approaches to demonstrate how such interpretive processes are enacted, as compositions. In the coding analysis, *interpreting activity* was identified empirically in both the formalist and contextualist tours. In the second approach, *interpretation* was explored in terms of meaning making, as a process unfolding inside the multimodal composition of the guided tour.

The first method of coding and analyzing guided tour compositions provided me with information about 'who is doing the cognitive work,' 'which activities are favored as meaning making,' and 'how these activities are supported' in each of the tours. In addition to allowing comparisons across data sets, coding discourse structure called attention to certain phenomena, or *potential meaning*, for closer analysis. That the 'formalist' educator provides no disciplinary information, for example, suggests that students focus mainly on keeping the dialogic process going, relying on perceptions of the art object and everyday concepts to make meaning. Similarly, that the 'contextualist' educator does provide information suggests that student interpretations are rooted in art history. This is one way that coding discursive structure makes it possible to identify how philosophies of art enter into and become perpetuated in museum discourses and educational practices, as compositions.

In the sequential analysis, moving inside the compositions, I found that *multiple interpretations* of the artwork's meaning were indeed made by students in both formalist and contextualist tours, and that some of these interpretations were in fact quite similar in content. Yet the sequential analysis also revealed an important aspect of the interpretation process that is not apparent in the coding analysis: the meaning making that happens in the negotiations, agreements, and disagreements inside interpreting activity. In the formalist tour, for example, students demonstrate a sense of ownership, or appropriation, toward interpretations that developed over many moves in a joint, collaborative process that links identity and knowledge construction.

Such exchanges were not as apparent in the contextualist tour data, where educators guided more forcefully the content of the interpretations. In fact, a student protests against the interpretations that emerge precisely because of a lack of ownership. Yet I would argue that such 'disappropriation' may *also* be understood as museum learning, as the student critically argues the conditions for her disagreement. In contemporary art, an important part of engaging critically with works is calling into question the conditions under which they may be considered 'art.' In this sense, these two approaches demonstrate a need to articulate, differentiate, and broaden the conditions under which meaning making in museums may be understood as learning.

Guiding and Making Meaning in Museums

In this study, I aimed to identify the characteristics of what I have termed 'formalist' and 'contextualist' narratives in art museum guided tours and to explore how these enter into meaning making processes. In the two 'formalist' guided tours, I found that the educators are mainly engaged in discourse that supports ongoing dialogue among the students about the artworks before them. Requesting explanation—*and requesting further explanation*—while continuously summarizing and reformulating student responses mediate this process. This approach means that students concentrate on clarifying and extending their own responses and that analyzing and describing artworks based on these responses is the foundation for the meaning-making process.

In the two 'contextualist' guided tours, there are similarities but also some important differences. The strategy of providing information clearly supports *interpreting* activity on the part of the students, by which I mean that students propose meanings that are guided by the educator. Accordingly, meaning making here is an interpretive process grounded in art historical information. The other contextualist educator also provides information, including many art terms, but uses more object-related talk, frequently requests students to explain, and reformulates and summarizes their responses. As in the formalist data, these moves engage students in more kinds of discursive activities.

Providing information while requesting that students explain and clarify their responses creates some striking contrasts. The finding is that formalist and contextualist education ideologies may actually be working at cross-purposes. First, in contrast to the aims of formalist approaches that emphasize object-related talk and perception, it appears that critical thinking skills may be better supported when disciplinary knowledge is introduced. In the formalist approach, the educator consciously uses a specific discourse structure for the purpose of mediating students' critical thinking and supporting students' interpretations based directly on *object-related experience*. However, in examining the meaning-making process as it unfolds in sequence, I conclude that, although the students have a sense of owning the everyday or spontaneous (Vygotsky, 1986) meanings that emerge, these are in fact strictly guided by the discourse structure that effectively inhibits potential utterances containing disciplinary knowledge. Furthermore, the introduction of disciplinary 'scientific' concepts through instruction is, in a Vygotskian perspective, considered essential to the development of meta-cognition, a characteristic of critical thinking. An alternative view on the significance of a formalist approach, then, is that this guided discourse supports the appropriation of the meaning as it is dialogically produced by the students and empowers them to form identities as meaning makers in museum institutions.

In the sequential analysis of contextualist discourse, I show that, although students make interpretations based on art historical information, the meanings that emerge are not necessarily considered their own. Although students may master norms of what counts as knowledge in art museums, meanings may be countered—or disappropriated—because of this lack of ownership. In this sense, although aiming to support the mastery of art historical narratives, contextualist approaches may work at cross-purposes when the student is not participating as a meaning maker. According to their respective normative educational aims, then, there is a sense in which each approach fails. At the same time, by moving inside compositions of guided tour discourse from a sociocultural perspective, we see how narratives of art and learning guide meaning in certain directions and also allow for and support other forms of knowing.

ACKNOWLEDGMENTS

I would like to thank InterMedia, University of Oslo for supporting this research. I am grateful to Andrew Morrison and Sten Ludvigsen for their participation in the video analysis sessions and for their constructive comments on numerous drafts of this chapter. Dagny Stuedahl and Ingvill Rasmussen also provided useful comments in their review of an earlier draft. Particular thanks are extended to the museum guides, teachers, and students who participated in this study, and to Victoria Lichtendorf, Curator, and Deborah Schwartz, Deputy Director of Education at Museum of Modern Art, New York.

REFERENCES

Bakhtin, Mikhail. (1986). *Speech Genres and Other Late Essays*. Austin: University of Texas Press.

Baxandall, Michael. (1985). *Patterns of Intention*. New Haven, CT: Yale University Press.

Billig, Michael. (2001). 'Discursive, rhetorical and ideological messages.' In Wetherell, Margaret. (Ed.). *Discourse Theory and Practice*. London: Sage. 210-221.

Cazden, Courtney. (1988). *Classroom Discourse. The Language of Teaching and Learning*. Portsmouth: Heinemann Educational Books.

Davies, Stephen. (2006). *The Philosophy of Art*. Malden, MA: Blackwell.

Engeström, Yrjö, Hakkarainen, Pentti, & Hedegaard, Mariane. (1984). 'On the methodological basis of research in teaching and learning.' In Hedegaard, Mariane, Hakkarainen, Pentti, & Engeström, Yrjö. (Eds.). *Learning and Teaching on a Scientific Basis: Methodological and Epistemological Aspects of The Activity Theory of Learning and Teaching*. Aarhus: Aarhus University, Institute of Psychology. 119-189.

Fei, Victor. (2004). 'Problematising "semiotic resource"' In Ventola, Eija. (Ed.). *Perspectives on Multimodality*. Amsterdam: John Benjamins. 51-62.

Halliday, Michael. (1978). *Language as Social Semiotic*. London: Arnold.

Hofinger, Andrea, & Ventola, Eija. (2004). 'Multimodality in operation. Language and picture in a museum.' In Ventola, Eija. (Ed.). *Perspectives on Multimodality*. Amsterdam: John Benjamins. 193-209.

Housen, Abigail. (1999, September 27-29). 'Eye of the beholder: Research, theory and practice.' Paper presented at the conference *Aesthetic and Art Education: A Transdisciplinary Approach*, Lisbon, Portugal.

Jordan, Brigitte, & Henderson, Austin. (1995). 'Interaction analysis: Foundations and practice.' *The Journal of the Learning Sciences*. Vol. 4, No. 1, 39-103.

Kemal, Salim, & Gaskell, Ivan. (Eds.). (1993). *The Language of Art History*. Cambridge, UK: Cambridge University Press.

Kress, Gunther, & van Leeuwen, Theo. (1996). *Reading Images: The Grammar of Visual Design*. London: Routledge.

Kress, Gunther, & van Leeuwen, Theo. (2001). *Multimodal Discourse. The Modes and Media of Contemporary Communication*. London: Arnold.

Leinhardt, Gaea, Crowley, Kevin, & Knutson, Karen. (Eds.). (2002). *Learning Conversations in Museums*. Mahwah, NJ: Lawrence Erlbaum Associates.

Leinhardt, Gaea, & Knutson, Karen. (2004). *Listening in on Museum Conversations*. Walnut Creek, CA: Altamira Press.

Lemke, Jay L. (2000). 'Across the scales of time: Artifacts, activities, and meanings in ecosocial systems.' *Mind, Culture, and Activity*. Vol. 7, No. 4, 273-290.

Leontev, Alexei N. (1978). *Activity: Consciousness and Personality*. Englewood Cliffs, NJ: Prentice-Hall.

Leontev, Alexei N. (1981). *Problems of the Development of the Mind*. Moscow: Progress.

Linell, Per. (1998). *Approaching Dialogue. Talk, Interaction and Contexts in Dialogical Perspectives*. Amsterdam: John Benjamins Publishing.

Lippard, Lucy. (1992). *Eva Hesse*. New York: Da Capo Press.

Luria, Alexander R. (1976). *Cognitive Development: Its Cultural and Social Foundations*. Cambridge, MA: Harvard University Press.

Luria, Alexander R. (1982). *Language and Cognition*. New York: Wiley.

Mansfield, Elisabeth. (Ed.). (2002). *Art History and Its Institutions*. London: Routledge.

Mehan, Hugh. (1979). *Learning Lessons: Social Organization in the Classroom*. Cambridge, MA: Harvard University Press.

Mercer, Neil. (1995). *The Guided Construction of Knowledge*. Clevedon: Multilingual Matters.

O'Toole, Michael. (1994). *The Language of Displayed Art*. London: Leicester University Press.

Pierroux, Palmyre. (2005). 'Dispensing with formalities in art education research.' *Nordisk Museologi*. Vol. 2, No. 2, 76-88.

Rasmussen, Ingvill. (2005). *Project Work and ICT: Studying Learning as Participation Trajectories*. Oslo: Unipub.

Rasmussen, Ingvill, Krange, Ingeborg, & Ludvigsen, Sten. (2003). 'The process of understanding the task: How is agency distributed between students, teachers, and representations in technology-rich learning environments'? *International Journal of Educational Research*. Vol. 39, No. 8, 839-849.

Ravelli, Louise. (2003). 'Renewal of connection: Integrating theory and practice in an understanding of grammatical metaphor.' In Simon-Vandenbergen, Anne-Marie, Taverniers, Miriam, & Ravelli, Louise. (Eds.). *Grammatical Metaphor. Views From Systemic Functional Linguistics*, Vol. 236. Amsterdam: John Benjamins Publishing. 37-64.

Ricoeur, Paul. (1981). *Hermeneutics and the Human Sciences*. Cambridge, UK: Cambridge University Press.

Roberts, Lisa C. (1997). *From Knowledge to Narrative. Educators and the Changing Museum*. Washington, DC: Smithsonian Institution Press.

Roth, Wolff-Michael, & Pozzer-Ardenghi, Lillian. (2005). 'Tracking situated, distributed, and embodied communication in real time.' In Vanshevsky, Michael A. (Ed.). *Focus on Cognitive Psychology Research*. Hauppauge: Nova Science. 237-262.

Sinclair, John, & Coulthard, Malcolm. (1975). *Towards an Analysis of Discourse: The English used by Teachers and Pupils*. Oxford, UK: Oxford University Press.

Vygotsky, Lev. (1978). *Mind in Society*. Cambridge, MA: Harvard University Press.

Vygotsky, Lev. (1986). *Thought and Language*. Cambridge, MA: The MIT Press.

Wells, Gordon. (1999). *Dialogic Inquiry. Toward a Sociocultural Practice and Theory of Education*. Cambridge, UK: Cambridge University Press.

Wertsch, James. (1985). *Vygotsky and the Social Formation of Mind*. Cambridge, MA: Harvard University Press.

Wertsch, James. (1991). *Voices of the Mind. A Sociocultural Approach to Mediated Action*. Cambridge, MA: Harvard University Press.

Wertsch, James. (1998). *Mind as Action*. New York: Oxford University Press.

Wertsch, James. (2002). *Voices of Collective Remembering*. Cambridge, UK: Cambridge University Press.

Wertsch, James, Del Rio, Pablo, & Alvarez, Amelia. (1995). *Sociocultural Studies of Mind.* Cambridge, MA: Cambridge University Press.

Wodak, Ruth. (2001). 'The discourse-historical approach.' In Wodak, Ruth, & Meyer, Michael. (Eds.). *Methods of Critical Discourse Analysis.* London: Sage. 63-95.

Xanthoudaki, Maria. (1998). 'Is it always worth the trip? The contribution of museum and gallery programmes to classroom art education.' *Cambridge Journal of Education.* Vol. 28, No. 2, 181-195.

Yenawine, Philip. (1991). *How to Look at Modern Art.* New York: Abrams.

Yenawine, Philip, & Rice, Danielle. (1999). *Video: Contrasting Practices III.* Produced by Visual Understanding in Education. Available at http://www.vue.org/.

15

IN THE BEGINNING THERE WAS ONLY ELECTRICITY– TOGETHER WITH WORDS, MUSIC AND SOUNDS

FRAGMENTS OF THE SEMIOTIC HISTORY OF NORWEGIAN BROADCAST RADIO

Wenche Vagle

What strikes everyone, broadcasters and listeners alike, as significant about radio is that it is a blind medium. We cannot see its messages, they consist only of noise and silence, and it is from the sole fact of its blindness that all radio's other distinctive qualities—the nature of its language, its jokes, the way in which its audience use it—ultimately derive. (Crisell, 1986: 3)

* * *

The first microphone reportage was successful. The event was praised both in newspapers as in a number of letters. It is something new and inconceivably fantastic that people in 'Bardu [name of a place in Northern Norway] are able to ascertain with grievance that Ole Hegge fell in his first jump,' that they are able to hear the ovation of the audience when the King, the Queen and Prince Eugen arrive at the ski jump, that they can hear the clearance signal for each jumper and hear their skis when they touch the ground *before* the audience down by the tarn have perceived the same noise with the use of their personal—and in relation to the radio receivers almost slow-functioning—hearing device. (statement by Programme Secretary Thorstein Diesen; cited in Hougen, 1932b: 81)[1]

ALL CATS ARE GREY IN THE DARK

Why are we crazy about dinosaurs? They were huge, and their disappearance from earth remains to be fully explained, that is so. But the main reason is, I think, that they may inform us not only about the past but also about the present and the future. When examining today's array of digital media and multimodal resources, many observations come easily. Yet, 'all cats are grey in the dark,' as the saying goes in Norwegian. What is needed to make their colors stand out is light and comparison, whether implicit or explicit, whether cross-cultural or cross-temporal. The observation that humankind tends to see the 'otherness' of others but be blind to the specificity of their own culture is the gist of prominent humanistic traditions of the 20th century, such as critical hermeneutics and the sociology-of-knowledge school (Berger & Luckmann, 1966).

Although there is no escape from the frame of mind construed by socialization and naturalization, there *are* ways of enhancing cultural reflexivity. To view things in a historical perspective brings awareness to the fact that the studied phenomena are not what they are by nature but rather by culture. As everything else, semiotic resources are continually in the process of being created. To track their formation and evolution may help us to understand what they are. For these reasons, historical reflection—to look backward and situate the multimodalities of today with respect to the ecologies and evolutionary processes of former times—should be part of our resources for understanding multimodality.

Multimodality is not new, nor does it have to be visual. The theme of the present chapter is the semiotic resources of broadcast radio. At the heart of the discussion is a diachronic analysis of the semiotic and generic conventions that were developed on Norwegian broadcast radio during its first 15 years of operation from 1925 to 1940.[2] Because the production technologies and facilities of a medium are fundamental to the materiality and textuality of its texts, the chapter also addresses the capabilities and limitations of the radio's production and distribution technologies at the time.

Radio Research Revisited

By now, media discourse has become an established research field. As is well known, it is part of a larger field of inquiry known since the mid-1980s as discourse studies. Most of the research dealing with media discourse has *contemporary* texts and genres as its empirical object—that is, from the time of the study. Regarding broadcasting research, the label is nearly coextensive with television research in the Nordic countries, as in most parts of the world. The contemporary focus is dominant also within the relatively restricted bulk of broadcasting research devoted to the radio's programming (Åberg et al., 1999; Vagle, under review). Yet for some reason or other, quite a few of the studies that actually deal with the radio and its sounds incorporate a historical component at the fore of their argumentation (see e.g., Nørgaard et al., 1975–1978; Cardiff, 1980; Jonsson, 1982, 1991; Nordberg, 1991, 1998, 2003; Bruck, 1993; Scannell, 1996; Åberg, 1999a; Dahlén, 1999a, 1999b; Hartenstein, 2001; Nyre, 2003; Poulsen, 2006; Vagle, under review).[3]

Without means of expression, nothing can be expressed. That is the reason why the radio's semiotic resources and conventions have been essential to my research into the early text history of Norwegian radio (Vagle, under review). More specifically, the work to be presented here was originally carried out as part of a study that aimed at reconstructing the changing contextual frames within which the discursive practices of Norwegian radio were embedded in the 1920s and 1930s. The focal point of this context reconstruction was the formation and first development of the radio's genre system in the interwar years, which the study attempted to describe and explain. To make the context clearer, the motivation for this undertaking was the observation that historical texts represent a special hermeneutical problem for present-day readers/listeners/viewers. When we interpret texts, we rely not only on 'what is in the text' but also on contextual resources. To arrive at historically acceptable interpretations and explanations of texts from former times, we therefore need to gain some kind of access to the far-gone contexts that once engendered them (Rüppel, 2002; Vagle, 2006).

METHODOLOGY

Perspectives

Methodologically, my research on the history of text and contexts on Norwegian radio has been based partly on three different text-context perspectives, partly on a temporal or processual model of explanation. The main function of the text-context perspectives was to guide the exploration of the historical data so as to identify the relevant situational features and explicate the various relations holding between them (causal, consequential, circumstantial, semiotic, etc.). The perspectives were: Halliday's (1990 [1978]) structural correlation model, the multistratal realisation model developed within social semiotics (Barthes, 1969; Eco, 1979; Ventola, 1987; Martin, 1992; Matthiessen, 1993), and Goffman's (1986 [1974]) laminated frame model.[4]

The Multistratal Realization Model

Whereas Goffman's analytical scheme is to approach a discursive event 'from the outside in,' the sociosemiotic strategy is to move 'from the bottom up' (i.e., to start the analytical process of 'opening' the text at the level of the text's selected lexicogrammatical expressions and end up by interpreting their ideological implications at the macrostrata of culture and society). The ultimate objective of social semiotics is to explain how the social system is expressed through linguistic structures in texts. To reach this end, the theory operates with a multileveled norm concept. This theoretical construction schematically displays the organization of articulation in advanced semiotic systems such as language. This basically Hjelmslevian model can be represented diagrammatically (see Figure 15.1). The notation is inspired by Hjelmslev (1943), Barthes (1969 [1967]), and Martin (1992).

The bottom part of the figure represents language 'proper' as a tristratal system consisting of phonology, lexicogrammar, and semantics. Language is a denotative semiotic system because it has its own means of organizing expression—phonology (recodable in the form of orthography) and lexicogrammar (words, grammatical constructions, and prosodic features).

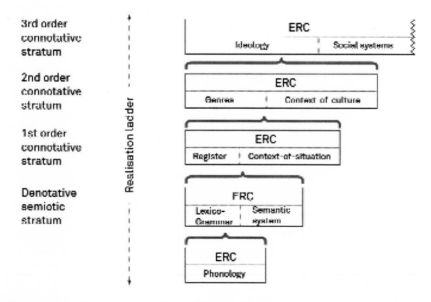

Figure 15.1. The realisation ladder between ideology, genre, register and language.

According to the sociosemiotic theory of language, the individual sign functions of language fall into three classes or meta-functions: the ideational, the interpersonal, and the textual. Language users employ ideational functions for presenting 'states of affairs'—experiences with the 'inner' and 'outer' world, as well as experiences that have already been formulated in signs. In alluding to the binary 'form/content' partitioning of the message that prevails in mass communication research, one could say that it is this meta-function that infuses texts with 'content.'

Interpersonal functions enable actors to partake in social relationships and to mark them on the dimensions of social hierarchy and solidarity. A separate subgroup of interpersonal functions, sometimes referred to as expressive functions, holds means for expressing subjectivity and social identity. Textual functions are used for combining the different meanings of a message into a composite text and for anchoring the text to its context.

The other strata in the model do not have their own articulations. Rather, they use the stratum 'beneath,' which is a semiotics in its own right, for their expression. This is why they are called connotative systems. Registers are varieties of language that correspond to or encode varieties of situations. Registers are realized through language, as already indicated—yet not directly, but rather by way of systematic variation within the linguistic system. (The term 'register' is more or less synonymous with style in the sense known from rhetorics and stylistics.) Genres are schemata of language-based activity types, which specify: (a) the components of the genre, (b) the components' canonical order, and (c) the goal of the genre. The level of ideology is realized through genre—yet not directly but rather through variation in the ranges of genres accessible to different groups in society. Thus, ideology is a system of coding orientations that positions speakers/hearers in such a way that options in genre, register, and language are made selectively available.

Goffman's Frame Model

Goffman's frame model indicated early answers to the empirical questions about what 'materials' radio contexts are made of and what kind of relationship exists among the various contextual factors. According to this model, radio contexts can be said to consist of six layers, or factors, of contextual 'material' (see Figure 15.2). A relation of determination is thought to be holding among the layers so that each layer delimits the possibilities on the layer above it.

Halliday's structural correlation model provided support in answering the question about the connection between the configuration of radio contexts and the medium's discursive practices. The model suggested

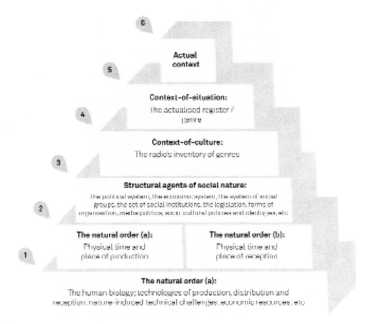

Figure 15.2. The multiple layers of radio context.

that the properties of radio contexts having a conditioning effect on the medium's discursive practices belong to the situational component of mode (means of communication in a wide sense) and tenor (social identities and role relationships). The present chapter presents my findings on one of the mode structures—the one that I have called 'basic semiotic resources.' As already indicated, it extends to one of the structures situated on Level 1, the one that I have called 'production technologies and facilities.'

Questions for Discussion

Since the recent expansion of visual culture, broadcast radio has become known as a 'blind' medium (see the prior citation from a well-known textbook on radio semiotics by Andrew Crisell). This characterization refers to the fact that it is an auditory medium founded on technologically reproduced sounds, sound waves, and the sense of hearing. However, at the time when the medium was young and the surrounding media culture was dominantly chirographic, it was not so much the absence of images and other visual codes that made a difference in people's experience. What was remarkable was the presence of sounds, the temporal immediacy, and the transgression of spatial distances (compare the contemporary statement by Programme Secretary Torstein Diesen in the second citation). In 1925, the development of sound media was in its early stages. Edison's phonograph had been invented only a few decades ago, the gramophone was still an acoustic medium, and the film remained without voice until well into the 1930s.

The physical-perceptual base of the radio medium has consequences for the kind of semiotic mediation that it is capable of supporting. Herein lies the topic of the present analysis, which seeks answers to the following questions:

> Given the nature of the medium itself, what are the *elemental semiotic resources* by which it is possible to create meaning on the radio?
>
> If compared to meanings coded with the use of semiotic systems using light-waves as their carrier, is it significant that the radio's meanings are carried by sound-waves?
>
> Does it affect the signification taking place on the radio that it is a 'live' medium uniting the communicating parties in the same 'now'?
>
> Founded on the 'raw material' of sound, music, language and silence, which semiotic conventions have evolved on the radio? *How* and *when* were they originally taken into use?
>
> When did the radio become a truly multimodal medium?
>
> Under which natural and technological restrictions did the radio's semiotic conventions evolve?

Method and Data

The method that I have used for reconstructing the contextual frames of early broadcasting can be characterized as a reconstructing empirical-explicative method. It critically involved two kinds of data and methodical procedures: (a) systematic reading of historical sources (primary and secondary) dealing with Norwegian broadcasting, and (b) listening to historical recordings.

Methods for examining the sources were fetched from documentary and discourse analyses. Primary and secondary sources were exploited in an integrated fashion. The most extensively used sources were: (a) previous research, (b) the official and near-contemporary history about the first private broadcasting company in Oslo (Hougen, 1932a, 1932b), (c) NRK's Annual Reports and official presentation (Klæbo, 1954 [1953]), and (d) NRK's radio program archive.

There is not much research literature on the radio's semiotic conventions (see Vagle, under review). As for the history of those conventions (especially those involving music and sounds), it remains to be written. In the case of Norwegian broadcasting, observations on this part of the medium's text history are few and far between in the literature.[5] What I have chosen to do in this chapter is to take Andrew Crisell's theory from the mid-1980s about the signs, codes, and conventions by which the radio codes its messages (Crisell, 1986) as a point of departure and confront it with the conjectures that I have been able to make on the basis of relevant pieces of information in my historical sources.

RADIO AS REPRODUCED SOUND

The Radio's Fundamental Channel Characteristics and Production Regime

Broadcast radio is a one-way auditory channel. Materially, its messages consist of sounds. What is special to the sounds of radio is that they are not natural, but electronic reproductions of natural sounds. Therefore, their presence, immediacy, and physical radiation into a locality can be controlled in ways that depend on the technical features of the equipment, as well as on the producers' and listeners' competence in using that equipment (Nyre, 2003). In the early decades of the 20th century, radio transmission constituted a new possibility to control sounds, and this possibility founded the miracle of the wireless in the 1920s: the totally new configurations of time and space where the communicating parties could be spatially separated while temporally united. The rudimentary sound preservation media that were taken into use in the 1930s represented further possibilities for controlling the radio's sounds.

Until the coming of magnetic tape recorders in the 1950s, the production of radio programs was subject to the premises of the continuity realism regime, to use Lars Nyre's (2003) descriptive label. Compared with the established written media, this regime involved three striking constraints, of which the first two apply to the radio medium generally and the last one distinguishes continuity realism from later production regimes in broadcast media. The first constraint is that verbal material must be articulated through human voices in acoustic habitats. The second is that the produced text, as experienced from the perspective of the receiver, continuously keeps disappearing because sounds exist as a succession of events in time. The third constraint, which is specific to the continuity realism regime, is that production and reception processes have to take place at the same time because radio transmissions were almost always live. Before the introduction of the first sound preservation media in the mid-1930s, transmissions were by necessity live. Also in the latter half of the 1930s, the larger majority of programs were live productions. The few programs that were produced with the help of the early recording equipment bore the marks of the continuity realism paradigm all the same. In combination, the two last-mentioned constraints had the effect of producing programs with high *event fidelity*. In other words, the programs tended to reproduce the temporal succession of events in a straightforward, linear fashion (Nyre, 2003).

The Radio's Elemental Semiotic Resources

It is time to start answering the questions that were posed earlier. The first question—What are the elemental semiotic resources by which it is possible to create meaning on the radio?—is fairly easy to answer. The radio's elemental semiotic resources are speech, music, sounds, and silence. The next question—Is it significant that the radio's meanings are carried by sound waves?—takes a few more words to address. What is particularly noteworthy about meanings carried by sounds is that they have a special authority or 'naturalness' that stem from the materiality of the sign carriers. The special 'realism effect' of sounds is produced by two qualities that set them apart from most visual carriers of meaning. The first distinguishing feature is that sounds exist as incessantly changing events in time. Whereas the normal case for meanings expressed through visual codes is to have a prolonged life in space, which enables them to be reused,[6] sound-carried meanings disappear immediately on production, leaving no physical trace (Nyre, 2003). The other distinguishing feature is that sound-carried meanings have a more direct connection to the material world than what is usually the case with light-carried meanings. As Crisell (1986: 47) has pointed out, sound is 'a form of signification which exists "out there" in the real world.' Although meanings to be taken in by the eye are normally coded with the use of symbolic or iconic signs, sound-carried meanings are mostly based on indexical signs (i.e., signs that are directly linked to their referents, often in a causal or sequential way). This account of the expressiveness of sounds draws on the semiotic theory of Charles Sanders Peirce—more precisely, on his categorization of signs into icons, indices, and symbols. The basic criterion by which this categorization is made is the relationship between sign and referent. To quote from Fiske (1985 [1982]: 50):

> In an icon the sign resembles its object in some way, it looks or sounds like it. In an index there is a direct link between a sign and its

> object, the two are actually connected. In a symbol there is no connection or resemblance between sign and object: a symbol communicates only because people agree that it shall stand for what it does. A photograph is an icon, smoke is an index of fire, and a word is a symbol.

As the previous citation by program secretary Thorstein Diesen bears witness to, the medium's capability of rendering authentic sound documentation from reported events was highly appreciated by program makers and radio listeners alike in the early days. Let us look at the four elemental resources in turn.

Sounds

Of course, it is an oversimplification to say that sounds are indexical signs. They may also be simulations or 'images' of naturally occurring sounds, in which case they can best be described as iconic indices. If the reportage is the genre that makes the greatest use of naturally occurring sounds, then the radio drama is the genre where sounds, like everything else, are make-believe. As an example of the simulation involved in the radio drama's use of sounds, one can mention the clapping together of coconut shells faking the hooves of a galloping horse, which has become a cliché. The degree of artificiality in the radio drama's production of sounds is no longer a secret. In the early years of the medium, however, producers were often secretive about their use of artificial sound effects because they worried about spoiling the illusion. In time, it has been realized that sounds, even when simulated, retain their communicative force—feeding, as it were, on the realism effect characteristic of naturally produced sounds (Crisell, 1986).

As anyone familiar with radio broadcasting will know, the presence of sound combined with the lack of visual input gives rise to semiotic possibilities that are special to the medium. Most famous is the appeal to the imagination. By inviting the receiver to fill in the rest, sounds can be used to establish settings and create stories with a minimum of effort. Fantastical or impossible scenes represent no hindrance (see Crisell, 1986).

Music

From a semiotic point of view, music represents a riddle. The question is whether music can be said to signify—let alone to 'refer to' or 'represent' anything in the conventional sense. This is not the time and place for a full discussion of that question. Suffice it to say that it is generally acknowledged that music is capable of coding textual and interpersonal meanings,[7] as well as imprecise connotative meanings of various kinds. Based *either* on private experiences *or* on more or less conventionally established relations, music can evoke associations to all sorts of things. Furthermore, music—like sounds generally—has an indexical aspect. It can be heard as an index of the instruments or musicians that are playing (Kjerschow, 1978; Crisell, 1986; van Leeuwen, 1999; Larsen, 2005).

Writing from the perspective of the mid-1980s, Crisell (1986: 51) points out that music seems to perform two main functions on the radio. In its first and basic function, music is 'an object of aesthetic pleasure in its own right, in record shows, concerts, recitals, and so on.' In its other, and ancillary, functions, music is put to use for signifying something outside itself—either by itself or in combination with words and/or sounds. With implicit reference to British and North American radio in the 1980s, Crisell identifies five such ancillary functions that music has on the medium. First of all, music can function as a framing mechanism, which identifies or 'frames' a particular radio station or radio program—infusing it with an overall style that will be familiar to its audience. The text elements performing the framing function are known as station jingles, program signatures, or—because they function to identify stations or programs—simply as IDs. Incidentally, such elements can also be verbal, or they can be made from a combination of music, words, and sounds.

The second ancillary function that Crisell identifies for music on the radio is that of being put to use as a cohesive device. Music can be employed either to set segments of a program apart or to provide a bridge between them. In its third ancillary function, music is used as a background element to create a certain mood or comment on what is being told or shown within in the ongoing narration or drama. The fourth ancillary function, according to Crisell's list, is the job that music can do as a stylized replacement for naturalistic sound effects in radio drama. Fifth and last on to this list, music—like any other naturally or culturally produced sound that is part of the ordinary sounds of the world—can appear within actuality programs and other factual genres, in which case the music is interpretable as an indexical sign (Crisell, 1986).

On most radio channels, music holds—and has always held—a dominating position in terms of its share of the channel's total hours of broadcast. It is nonetheless language in the form of speech that is the primary means of meaning making on the radio. Compared with sounds and music (and many other nonverbal systems of signification), language has the functional advantage of enabling the coding of precise meanings and thereby of making references clear and specific. In radio contexts, as in many other multimodal contexts, linguistically coded meanings are required to contextualize meanings coded with the use of other types of signs (Crisell, 1986).

Language

What is special to language in the form of speech as compared with language in written form is that it is 'a binary code in which the words themselves are symbols of what they represent, while the voice in which they are heard is an index of the person or "character" who is speaking' (Crisell, 1986: 46). Let us take a closer look at the two parts of this code in turn, starting with the indexical one, so as to link up with what was said earlier on sounds as signs.

It is the normal situation that linguistic utterances—when realized through the human voice—are intrinsically indexical of the person who is talking. Whether intended or not, spoken utterances convey paralinguistic connotations about the speaker's age, gender, social class, geographical origin, discursive role, emotional state, and so on. On broadcast radio, voice-carried indexical meanings are often highly complex because of the complicated settings actualized on the medium. To quote again from Crisell (1986: 47):

> A voice may be interpreted merely as the index of a human presence; or on another level as the index of a personality (a country bumpkin, seductive French woman, and so on); or on yet a third level as the index of a programme, broadcasting institution or entire nation.

In its capacity as a symbolic sign system, language is a multileveled articulation system consisting not only of a denotative stratum but also of several *connotative* strata (i.e., register, genre, and ideology). Although the denotative stratum of language came forward as a basic constraint on content with radio broadcasting, the connotative strata also proved to be of uttermost importance because they encode sets of values and identities related to specific countries/societies (Nyre, 2003). We return to these aspects of language later when dealing with the historical dimension of the radio's four elemental semiotic resources. Let us first look at the fourth, and last, of the radio's basic semiotic resources, silence.

Silence

Writing from the perspective of the mid-1980s, Crisell (1986) identifies three functions of silence on broadcast radio and comments on their place within the aesthetics of British radio at that time. To take the most obvious function first, a silence that persists for more than a few seconds on the radio can mean that nothing is happening on the medium for the moment. Because 'dead air' is a fatal sin on modern radio, the normal interpretation by modern standards would nonetheless be that there is a dysfunction or nonfunctioning somewhere in the technical channel. Either the transmitter or the receiver has broken down or been switched off.

If the silence appears on a station with a traditional 'sound' and is not overly long, it can be acting in the second function identified by Crisell— as a framing mechanism that makes a space around a program or program item. If the silence forms an integral part of a text sequence, it can be acting in its third, and fully semantically loaded, function. Depending on the context, silences may encode meanings that the speaker for some reason or other has chosen not to express with sound-carried signs. In audiovisual media, semantic silences are visually filled. On the radio, however, they are left totally open for the listener to fill with meaning using inferences and her own imagination. This type of silence is a powerful sign because it can be used to create many kinds of effects (Crisell, 1986).

A PERIODIZATION OF NORWEGIAN RADIO HISTORY

Periods

Before diving into the empirical matter of this chapter concerning early Norwegian radio, it can be helpful to have an idea of the overall history of the medium. Space prevents me from giving more than a nut-shell version, which I do in the form of the periodization to which my research has given rise. This periodization corresponds fairly well with a widely accepted periodization of Norwegian 20th-century history (see Figure 15.3).

Part of the basis for my periodization of Norwegian radio history is the development of the radio's production equipment, which falls into three phases. The era of Very Old Radio (1925-1933) saw beginning progress in the radio's primordial production facilities and apparatuses— production rooms, microphones, amplifiers, batteries, cables, telephone lines, and tools for combining sounds from different sources. The courses of improvement that were established in the 1920s have continued ever since—in step with expanding budgets and inventions in electronics. What was qualitatively new in the period of Old Radio (1933-1981) was the advent of sound-preservation media, editing techniques, and mobile production units. During the periods called Transition (1981-1993) and New Radio (1993 onward), digital equipment gradually replaced the original analogue appliances. But so far, DAT recorders, compact discs, and computerized editing benches can hardly be said to have revolutionized the production practices that had already taken shape under the influence of the properties of the analogue tools.

The history of Norwegian radio broadcasting	The general history of Norway in the 20th century		
	'The new working day' & world war I (1900–1920)		
VERY OLD RADIO (1925-1933)	The interwar period I: Social crisis and splitting forces (1920–1935)		
OLD RADIO	PHASE 1 (1933-1940)	The interwar period II: Towards a new social order — the dawn of the welfare society (1935–1940)	The Social-Democratic Order (1933–1973)
	WAR PARENTHESIS	The German occupation (1940–1945)	
	PHASE 2 (1945-1950)	The restoration (1945–1952)	
	PHASE 3 (1950-1960)	The social-democratic order I: Growth & hope (1952–1961)	
	PHASE 4 (1960-1968)	The social-democratic order II: Growth & protest (1961–1973)	
NEO-OLD RADIO (1968-1982)	The oil age and the crisis years (1973–1981)		
TRANSITION (1982-1993)	Back to the market (1982–1993)		
NEW RADIO (1993 onward)	Postindustrial society (1993 onward)		

Figure 15.3. The history of Norwegian radio broadcasting correlated with the country's general history.

SEMIOTIC RESOURCES ON NORWEGIAN RADIO IN A HISTORICAL PERSPECTIVE

The First Development of Semiotic Conventions

It may be that the functions of silence, when viewed in isolation, were more or less the same in the early days of the medium, but their role and distribution within the overall aesthetics of the medium were certainly different—a point to which we now turn. Of course, Crisell's identification of the semiotic functions performed by the four elemental semiotic resources on British radio in the mid-1980s cannot be generalized across time and culture. The empirical reality of Norwegian radio in the 1920s and 1930s was certainly different. As a matter of fact, what can probably be discerned in the early days of the medium is the first emergence and beginning development of the conventions that Crisell was able to identify as fully grown forms 50 to 60 years later.

As already mentioned, the history of sounds and music on Norwegian radio has not been properly researched. Based on scattered observations in the research literature, I have nevertheless attempted to offer a historical overview of the radio's semiotic conventions and practices, which may be used as a point of departure for future research into the history of semiotic resources on Norwegian radio.[8] The list focuses mainly on the interwar years but also includes a few observations on the postwar decades. Naturally, the list contains early semiotic functions that had become extinct at the time when Crisell compiled his inventory. Under the restrictions set by the available sources, I have identified the semiotic functions and practices listed in Figure 15.4.

To get an overall impression of what the radio sounded like in the 1920s and 1930s, one would need to know how much of each ingredient on the list that the listeners used to be served—spread over the 24 hours that make up a day. In the early period, the listeners had large amounts of silence in the function 'no transmission.' On average, they had 20 hours and 40 minutes of 'nothing' in 1925, sinking to 14 hours and 24 minutes in 1938-1939. Owing to various technical shortcomings that prevailed for decades, the listeners would also have pauses of various length among the individual programs—and often also within the frames of one and the same programme (Dahl & Bastiansen, 1999). In addition, they had irregular amounts of silence due to dysfunctions somewhere in the technical channel, especially in the 1920s.

When there was something on the air to listen to, it would primarily be one of two ingredients: music in its normal aesthetic function or scripted language read aloud. Of the total number of broadcast hours, 58% would be music in 1925, sinking to 42.1% in 1931, only to rise again to 48% in 1938-1939. As Crisell notes, music is and has always been a mainstay of radio's output. According to Crisell's (1986) analysis, the reason is that it is highly suited to the medium—so suited that it does not need any 'adaptation' to be reproduced on it. In the VOR era, music was considered to have the advantage of being better suited for the reception through headphones than the human voices (Dahl, 1999 [1975]: 78f). The rest of the program was dominated by speech delivered from manuscript.

When it comes to sounds, the most characteristic one to be heard on early radio was the time signal, which was broadcast twice a day (from Nauen at 12:55 p.m. and from Oslo at 20:00 p.m.) (Hougen, 1932b: 79). Otherwise, there were only three genres in the VOR era that accommodated semiotic sounds: church services, reportages and drama productions (including the drama productions broadcast within the frames of the Children's Hour). This is to say that the exploitation of sounds was closely

Time of introfuction [9]	Elemental semiotic resource	Semiotic functions and practices	Tradition of the convention / practice
Day 1	Silence	No transmission	New
Day 1	Silence	Dysfunction somewhere in the technical channel	New
Day 1	Silence	Production - technically induced pauses in the transmission	New
Day 1	Language	Scripted speech based on the written standard Riksmål	Taken from situations of public oratory
Day 1	Music	Object of aesthetic pleasure in its own right	Old art form
Day 1	Sound	Natural, indexical sounds in actuality programs	New
Day 1	Sound	Time signals	New (?)
Day 1 (app.)	Music	Gramophone music used as pause fill	New (?)
Day 1 (app.)	Sounds	Artificially producved sound effects in drama productions	Taken from traditional art forms
Day 1 (app.)	Music	Music used as a cohesive device in drama productions	Taken from traditional art forms
1920 (?)	Music	Music used as a background element to create a certain mood (in drama productions)	Taken from traditional art forms
1933	Language	Scripted speech based on both written standards of Norwegian	Taken from situation of public oratory

1933	Language	Unscripted, but planned, speech based on dialects	Taken from situations of formal speech in private settings
Mid-1930s (?)	Music/sound	Station jingle	New
Mid-1930s (?)	Music/sound	Pause signal	New
1946 onward	Music/sound	Program jingles	New
?[10]	Music	Music used as a stylised replacement of naturalistic sounds	Taken from traditional art forms
1980s	Music	Music used for profiling a radio station to the tastes of specific listener groups	New

Figure 15.4. The use of language, music, sound, and silence on Norwegian radio—a historical overview.

465

linked to the development of these genres. There was little drama on the programme (around 1 or 1.5% of the total number of broadcast hours), and not much reportage either in the very first years (0.3% in 1925). However, the amount of actuality material quickly started to rise so as to reach 7.1% in 1931. Regarding church services, they figured heavily on the programme all through the 1920s and 1930s with percentages between 6 and 9. Of course, the actual use of sounds cannot be read out of these statistical figures alone. What one also needs to know in order to get an impression of their role within the radio's output is that all these genres remained dominated by the scripted word throughout the interwar period—with a possible exception for drama productions, where changes set in with the turn to studio productions after a few years. As for the development of radio drama on Norwegian ground (or air!), it lagged behind the flourishing growth that the genre experienced in other North-European countries (Dahl, 1999 [1975]: 270). To begin with, radio-distributed drama existed in two forms: (1) live transmission of performances staged by theatres in Oslo, and (2) studio recitations of dramatic literature. It was immediately realised, however, that transmissions of ordinary theatre performances were not satisfactory for ear reception and that special adaptation for the radio medium was required. Studio productions therefore came to be favoured. Two different lines of development start at that point: (1) the staging of plays originally written for the theatre, and (2) the staging of dramatic pieces created specifically for the radio (known as *Hörspiel* in German or *hørespill* in Norwegian) (op cit: 89ff). To return to the few sounds that occurred within reportages and church services in the 1920s and 1930s, they were salient, but represented little more than small dashes of seasoning.

THE RADIO BECOMES MULTIMODAL

From Musical Station Jingles Onward

In step with improvements in the radio's production technology, the medium slowly started to grow more truly multimodal in the early 1930s. Spurred by the coming of mobile production units and new production technologies in the mid-1930s, the breakthrough of that process came in the latter part of that decade. Perhaps the introduction of musical station jingles[11] and pause signals can be said to mark the stage in the developmental process when the new medium acquired a semiotic-material quality of its own deserving the name 'radiophonic.' In that case, the 10 years spanning the mid-1930s to the mid-1940s seems to be the correct dating in a Norwegian context. That period was also the time when the new, and truly multimodal, genre with the name (Norwegian) '*hørebilde*'[12] was formed and had its first growth. It was also the time when the School Broadcasting Department started to illustrate its talks, dialogues, and sound pictures with sound samples fetched from the newly established archive of recorded sounds. Furthermore, it was the time when the Radio Theatre Department, which had just acquired a park of professional sound machines, started to overdo the use of sound effects so as to cross the border to parody according to critical voices in the press (Hartenstein, 2001). Another aspect of the new multimodality was that the radio from now on created its own semiotic conventions to a greater extent than before. As commented on in Figure 15.4, many of the first semiotic conventions to be established on the medium had been fetched from existing contexts of public speech and from traditional art forms.

Developments on the Levels of Genre and Register

Having commented on developments in the use of silence, music, and sounds, I go on to say something about the use of language—the radio's primary bearer of semantic meaning. The normal situation for language is to be in a constant state of change, which also applies to the language heard on Norwegian radio. Throughout history, both the denotative stratum and the connotative strata have gone through a series of changes. Periods of relative stability have shifted with 'moments' of more vehement restructurations.

As for the processes of change affecting the connotative strata, I only give a glimpse of them in this chapter. Figure 15.5, which is organized according to a simplified 'before-now' distinction that is widespread in Nordic broadcasting studies, may serve as a first overview.

On the level of genre, the programs of the 1920s were mostly imperfect reproductions of existent cultural forms. Yet a beginning modernization of the genre repertoire took place in the 1930s. Whereas the rudimentary genre repertoire of the 1920s was built up by way of plain copying from other domains in society, the latter half of the 1930s saw the introduction of a more advanced genre-generating process, whereby new genres were formed through the mixing of two or more existing norms.

A number of developmental trends, which have marked the evolution of the radio's registers and genres ever since, appeared already in the 1920s. The patterns of change go in the direction of greater diversity and variation in forms and contents, enhanced continuity, shorter texts, serialization, fixed scheduling, multivoice formats, greater mixing of elements within programs, and growing accent on the communicative goals of information/actuality and entertainment. After the nationalization in 1933, a couple of new developmental patterns emerged: (a) a shift from a nar-

	'Before'	'Now'
Ideology third-order connotative stratum	Enlightenment Universalism Pluralism within a framework of cultural unionism Nationalism Traditionalism Bureaucratism Authoritarianism Paternalism <u>1950s, 1960s,and 1970s:</u> Decentralization/regionalism Political enlightenment Critical journalism	Consumerism Marketization Commercialism Commodification Populism Individualism Diversification Americanisation Internationalization Localism
Genre second-order connotative stratum	Homogenous genres Traditional art forms & traditional models of public speech: Content?	Hybrid/newly synthesized genres Genres resembling those of private face-to-face interaction: Tension between information and entertainment, Tension between public and private domains
Register first-order connotative stratum	Written forms of language: Content?	Spoken forms of language: Conversationalization (informality, intimacy, [pseudo] spontaneity, immediacy, naturalness, authenticity, spokenness,quasi- symmetric authority relations ...)

Figure 15.5. Connoted signification in Norwegian radio—'Now' versus 'Before.'

row focus on culturally highbrow bourgeois topics toward a broader and more popular selection of topics, and (b) a change in linguistic norm from the exclusive use of the traditional Dano-Norwegian standard (*Riksmål*) toward a more inclusive language policy allowing different varieties of the two written standards of Norwegian, as well as dialects and sociolects.

Around 1930, the inventory of the radio's genre system consisted of:

> *Traditional genres from the public sphere* (concerts and other kinds of musical performances, dramatic pieces, cabarets, sketches, operas, talks, causeries, academic lectures, church services, formal speeches, programme announcements, gymnastics instruction, dialogues),

Genres from modern media (other than the radio)(commercials, news telegrams, weather reports/forecasts, various other kinds of announcements, reportages, 'kronikk-s,' linguaphone-like language teaching), and,

Genres from the intimate sphere (children's hours, prayers, songs, recitation of prose and poetry, soirees).

The first years under the NRK saw the introduction of a handful of new genres, which fall into two groups. The first group consisted of multiparty formats (the classroom lesson, the conversation [an enlightenment genre], the discussion, the debate); the second of the radio's first truly radiophonic genres (the composite program, the 'microphone rolling' format, the sound picture). From a present-day perspective, the composite program is of special interest because it inaugurated the shift from genre to format as the basic principle of the radio's aesthetics.

The Use of Language in the Early Period

Regarding the denotative stratum—the coding relations holding between semantic meanings, on the one hand, and words and grammatical structures, on the other hand—nothing has as yet been said. As a matter of fact, there is not so much to say. During the decade and a half that we are focusing on in the present context, a certain number of new words did of course come about, and a few old ones went out of use or had their meanings slightly shifted, but the time span is too short for noteworthy changes to have occurred on this plane. Nonetheless, changes of consequence on the denotative stratum did actually take place—not within a specific linguistic code but in the selection of linguistic codes in use on the radio.

Ever since the late 19th century, Norway has enjoyed the luxury of having two written standards of Norwegian, plus a host of dialects that are widely used in formal as well as in informal contexts. In the VOR era, however, the range of linguistic varieties that could be heard on the air was practically restricted to one single variety. The language of the private broadcaster in Oslo was 'Riksmål,' the traditional Dano-Norwegian standard. Dialects and *Landsmål* (the standard that had been created in the 1850s on the basis of rural dialects from the western part of the country) were practically not heard on the air. With the nationalization in 1933, the expansion to new groups of listeners, and the coming of the ideology of nationalism, a broadened language policy was taken on by the NRK. From now on, the other official standard, *Nynorsk*[13] (formerly *Landsmål*), also started to be allotted substantial shares of broadcast hours. Even dialects were occasionally heard in reportages from the districts. The share of New Norwegian grew within the announcement service, within newscasts (where it had been nil), within programs generally, as well as within NRK's external communication with the authorities and the Norwegian society. In 1933, only about 3 or 4 percent of the verbal output had been in New Norwegian. By 1936, the percentage had risen to 9, and it continued to grow after the war (Dahl, 1999 [1975]). In this connection, it could be mentioned that NRK's first Chief-of-Programming, Olav Midttun, was a prominent advocate of New Norwegian and remained in the mentioned chair for almost 30 years. The language issue (in Norwegian: målstriden), which later became a lasting controversy in Norwegian broadcasting, was not an issue of debate as long as 'Riksmål' ruled supreme. It was when 'Nynorsk' began to be used on the air that the struggle started. The expansion of New Norwegian in broadcasting stirred strong reactions in the Norwegian society. Ever since, the language question has continued to run as a leit-motif in the public discussion about the NRK (see Dahl & Bastiansen, 1999).

The restructuration of the Norwegian broadcasting system in 1933 also gave rise to other changes in the selection of linguistic codes. During the VOR era, the programming of the private Oslo company, which was aimed at an urban bourgeoisie audience, contained quite a few talks and recitations in foreign languages—in Danish and Swedish, as well as in German, French, and English (Hougen, 1932b; Dahl, 1999 [1975]). When new social groups became radio listeners and the principle of 'Norwegianness' was implemented in NRK's programming, the international orientation dwindled so as to become next to extinct. (Of course, foreign languages remained an important element in educational broadcasts). The other Nordic languages could still be heard, but not often. The statistics of the budgetary year of 1938-1939 can illustrate the situation with respect to both the *Bokmål/Nynorsk* ratio and the low share of foreign languages. Figure 15.6 provides the relevant statistics.

	Recitations	Talks (incl. causeries, discussions, debates)
Bokmål	163	418
Nynorsk	61	79
Swedish and Danish	4	7
Esperanto		3
German		1
Foreign literature (translated to Norwegian)	9	
Total	224	508

Figure 15.6. **Use of languages and written standards of Norwegian in recitations and talks (1938-1939).**

MATERIALITY, TEXTUALITY, AND PRODUCTION TECHNOLOGIES

Sounds Sources and Their Flexible Mixings

The production technologies and facilities of a medium are fundamental to the materiality and textuality of its texts. In the case of a sound medium, the capabilities and limitations of its production technologies play a decisive role in the sound reproduction. As for the textuality of auditory texts, it hinges on two factors: (a) the supply of sound sources, and (b) the available techniques and apparatuses for switching between the sound sources, mixing them, and sampling within the stretches of sound. Variation in time and place of production is an issue with the supply of sound sources (studios vs. outdoor locations; live vs. prerecorded inputs). Variation in content and coding resources is another. Is the content coded with the use of language, music, or other kinds of sounds—or by way of a combination of these elemental semiotic resources? The answer to this question largely depends on the available techniques and technologies for producing, transferring, and preserving sound. In these processes, technical installations and appliances such as networks, microphones, gramophones, recorders, sound machines, and sound archives are instrumental. Given the limitations of the human body, the size, weight, and practicability of the appliances are important aspects of their functionality.

The Radio's Original Production Technologies in Relation to Its Programming

> Broadcasting technology comprises one acoustic component related to the studio and the place of reception, one electric component consisting of the microphone, the loudspeaker or the telephone, amplifiers and the wire to the transmitter, and yet another electric component comprising the transmitter itself, the mediation through the ether and the reception by way of the receiver apparatus. (Hougen, 1932b: 88)

This definition of broadcasting technology was formulated around 1930 by Kringkastingselskapet's chief engineer Fritz Gythfeldt. He describes broadcasting technology as an integrated (re)production and distribution technology. Most of the mentioned elements belong to the distribution and reception parts of the technical channel: the wire from the microphone to the amplifier, the amplifier, the wire connecting the amplifier to the transmitter, the transmitter, the electromagnetic waves, and, finally, the receivers with telephones or load speakers. The production technology was simple, comprising only two elements: the microphone (in singular form) and its acoustic surroundings (i.e., the studio), which together form the first link of the technical chain connecting radio performers to their audiences. As compared with the production technology of later times, there are two conspicuous gaps in the short list of elements: the lack of recording machines and devices for mixing and switching between sounds from different sources.

The production technologies of the new medium developed in a dialectic relationship to its programming. In the beginning, the medium used technologies that had been worked out for ordinary telephony. But after a few years, it started to develop its own apparatuses. Production facilities, as well as routines and competence, were built up more or less from scratch. During the first years of operation, technical problems seem to have been the rule rather than the exception, but fairly quickly solutions to many of the production-technical problems were reached through experimentation. Two different concerns, which were sometimes at odds with each other, guided the development—then, as they still do: (a) the ambition of the technical personnel to heighten the quality of the sound reproduction, and (b) the program makers' need for practical and workable tools to be used under demanding circumstances (Ormestad, 1975, 1993; Andersen & Bernstein, 1999).

To begin with, the medium's technical resources only allowed it to function as a simple reproduction and distribution technique. This was particularly evident with outdoor broadcasts. In the 1920s, these were merely direct sound representations of happenings taking place in society—caught by the microphone and transmitted through the ether without any kind of journalistic processing or medium-minded shaping and adjustment (Åberg, 1999a).

Many of the characteristics of early studio broadcasts derived from the constraints imposed by the production facilities of the time (Åberg, 1999b). Using only one studio fitted with a single immovable microphone, one could hardly produce anything but homogenous programs. Lectures, recitations, and musical performances were by necessity packaged within the frames of separate programs. Regarding verbal formats, the single microphone arrangement strongly favored monologue formats. Because it takes time to move people in and out of a studio (especially if a whole orchestra is to take position), pauses between programs were inevitable. Performances by sizable ensembles such as the philharmonic orchestra could only be scheduled at the end of the day's program (Hougen, 1932b; Dahl 1999 [1975]).

From Day 1, the five following production-technical areas called for attention: (a) the microphones with their impracticable weight, poor

sound rendition, and lack of direction sensitivity; (b) the supply and organization of production rooms; (c) the acoustic properties of the studio(s);
(d) the connections to outdoor locations from which transmissions were
to be arranged; and (e) techniques and tools for switching between and
mixing sounds from different sources (be they studios, telephone connections, or wired locations such as churches and theatres).

Technological Developments and the Fostering of a New Radiophonic Textuality

Measured against the production-technological revolutions that were to
come in the second half of the 20th century, the first improvements in the
radio's production technologies were moderate. They nevertheless enabled
the initiation of the developmental trends going in the directions of greater
diversity and variation in form and content, enhanced continuity, shorter
texts, greater mixing of elements within programs, and more use of multivoice formats. The production technologies of the 1930s also played a role
in the formation of truly radiophonic genres, such as the sound picture, the
composite program, and the 'microphone rolling' format.

On a basic level, the 1920s and 1930s notably saw the following
improvements: an increasing number of production rooms, a more ample
supply of long-distance telephone lines and other technologies for fetch-
ing programming from outside the station, the coming of tools for switching between different sound sources in the early 1930s and of recording
technologies and mobile production units in the mid-1930s, and, finally,
the construction of the so-called 'high-frequency channel' in the latter half
of the 1930s.

With these developments, the radio's supply of sound sources kept
increasing—with part of the growth laying the ground for the new senses
of time and space to be fostered in the latter half of the 19th century and
the other part furthering the growing multimodality of the medium. To be
specific, what we are talking about is the increase in the number of microphones, studios, and connections to outdoor locations and other stations,
as well as the coming of sound-generating machines and appliances, such
as the gramophone, the sound machines, the pause and time signal generators, the recording machines, and the archive of prerecorded sounds.
Another technical prerequisite for the development of a radiophonic textuality that came in place was devices for switching among, regulating,
and mixing sounds from different sound sources.

By 1940, the development of a radiophonic textuality had not come
particularly far. To a large extent, this lag can be explained with reference
to the available technologies and facilities. So far, weaknesses in many of

the production technologies left much to be desired on behalf of the sound quality. Most productions were live, and the programming output was dominated by monologue verbal formats using the minimal studio/microphone setup. In the case of more complicated productions, such as entertainment programs and radio plays, the number of studios and microphones in use could still be counted on one hand. There were clear limits to the effects of the gramophone recorders on the part of the overall textuality of the radio's programming because they did not allow any post-hoc editing of the prerecorded material. The daily program was still divided into three parts with longish transmission pauses between them. Furthermore, the technical operation of the high-frequency channel caused shorter silences to occur at irregular intervals. The pauses were not felt to be a problem, however, before the idea of the American 'continuity radio' reached the country in the 1950s.

Looking back, it is obvious that it took more than 30 years from the inception of radio broadcasting on Norwegian ground until the medium had adequate production facilities and technologies at its disposal for producing the kind of continuous and diversified output that we have come to perceive of as its identity. When the tape recorders enabling postediting gradually replaced the gramophone recorders in the latter half of the 1940s and the beginning of the 1950s, it meant a veritable revolution to the processing of the radio's sounds (Nyre, 2003). During its first three or four decades in operation, the radio simply did not have the necessary means for creating the kind of textuality that eventually has become its hallmark. What it needed (and what it gradually attained) were tools and methods for catching, reducing, reshuffling, and seamlessly combining and mixing stretches of sounds from various sources—copresent as well as distant ones, live as well as canned ones.

ON THE IMPORTANCE OF BEING SOUND

Historical Context Matters

'There is nothing new under the sky.' True or false? Both, probably. What is definitely true is that many of the things perceived of as new in our near-sighted culture, where all that counts is what is happening right now, they are really not all that new when put in the correct context—in a historical context, that is. A person who has lost her memory does not know who she is. The same goes for a society or a research field. To know something about the old days is to know one's identity (Kjeldstadli, 1999 [1992]).

To see present-day phenomena in their historical contexts is to see that they are not isolated atoms but rather the results of situations and conditions back in time. Our present experience builds on the past without being determined by it in a linear fashion. In today's flurry of claims for multimodality, it is important to examine—and reexamine—its roots.

Listen up!

Electronically processed sounds are important elements in today's multimodal texts and sites. Yet they have not attracted the same amount of attention as their colorful, turning, and twisting images. The reason is probably that sounds and the sense of hearing are taken for granted unless one has a hearing impairment. One does not have to do something like looking in the right direction to catch the sounds. They seem to come to you (Maasø, 2002). Yet these qualities do not mean that they should be left out of the picture. On the contrary, the characteristics of sounds indicate that there is good reason to look more closely at their semiotic functions and communicative effects in today's multimodal and 'digital' media.

Unlike what was the case with the technically strenuous conditions under which sounds were produced in the early days of radio broadcasting, sounds are now easily stored, annotated, archived, processed, and distributed. The use of sounds needs more attention in genre, education, and rhetoric studies, which have focused much on academic writing, lectures, seminar speaking 'skills,' the language of meetings, and so on (see e.g., Swales, 2000 [1990]). We need to learn to listen multimodally, and we also need to learn to sound multimodally (if my readers will pardon the pun).

The next time you get into a shop and become aware of some muzac filling the room or when you come across a Web site throwing all sorts of jingles, tunes, cries, and buzzes at you, will you experience the sounds differently from what you did before reading this chapter? If you do, the chances are that my message has come across.

NOTES

1. All translations from Norwegian are by the author.
2. Because the present chapter focuses entirely on the Norwegian context, a few words on the wider West European context may be essential. Broadcast radio was an international phenomenon between the wars. The ideology of early Norwegian broadcasting has much in common with the visions that John

Reith, the first Director-General of the BBC, had formulated on behalf of British broadcasting. As is well known, BBC's Director John Reith saw the technology of broadcasting as an opportunity to realize the mission of disseminating 'culture' to the general public so as to 'civilize' the masses and incorporate the working classes into the existing social and political order (Syvertsen, 1992). Whether the Norwegian policymakers were directly influenced by Reith's thoughts is difficult to assess. At a certain level of generalization, the major part of my research findings are consistent with findings on programming policies, genre structures, semiotic resources, and production techniques within Swedish and British broadcasting at the time (see Cardiff, 1980; Briggs, 1995; Nordberg, 1998; Åberg, 1999a, 199b; Poulsen, 2006). What is often the case is that the historical timing is delayed by a few years in the Norwegian context, which bears witness to the fact that many impulses were imported from abroad. In fact, Norwegian broadcasting was, to a large extent, formed under the influence of Swedish broadcasting. Whether ideas were fetched directly also from other European broadcasting companies is more difficult to assess, but members of the editorial staff of Norway's first broadcasting company, *Kringkastingselskapet*, traveled quite widely in Europe—in paying several visits to the British BBC and to the German Reichs-Rundfunk-Gesellschaft (Dahl, 1999 [1975]).

3. It should be mentioned in this connection that the growing interest in the historical dimension of media discourse is part of a larger trend in media studies. Empirically, the trend has given rise to the writing of media histories—whether social (e.g., Scannell & Cardiff, 1991; Martin & Wodak, 2003) or institutional (e.g., Dahl, 1999 [1975]; Bastiansen & Syvertsen, 1994; Dahl & Bastiansen, 1999) or pertaining to aspects of media production, media content, and media audiences. Theoretically, the trend is linked to the spread of theories about modernity and modernization processes (von Feilitzen, 1994). In was in the late 1980s that researchers began to draw attention to the fact that relatively little was known about the historical evolution of media formats and in the 1990s that historical and diachronic studies actually started to emerge.

4. For a more detailed presentation of the three text-context models, see Vagle (2005).

5. An exception must be made for the history of the use of sounds in radio drama, which has been described in some detail by Tilman Hartenstein (2001). Furthermore, many observations on the radio's use of sounds and music are made in Nyre's (2003) dissertation on sound media and realism in the 20th century.

6. This is a truth that is not as true as it used to be in early days of radio broadcasting, when the film medium was still in its infancy and television was at the stage of technical experimentation. Since then, moving images structured in *time* as well as *space* have been steadily on the increase.

7. As we are about to see, Crisell (1986) refers to the textual meanings of music as framing mechanisms and cohesive devices. The interpersonal meanings of music are usually called emotional or expressive meanings in the research literature.

8. To carry out this research would take a different kind of approach. See, for instance, van Leeuwen (2005) on the making of semiotic inventories and sound media.

9. The dating refers to the Norwegian context. Because of the state of the art, the dating remains uncertain in many cases. This is signaled with a question mark.

10. I have not been able to establish when this convention was taken into use. Based on Hartenstein's (2001) observation that the realistic sound tradition, which dominated within Norwegian radio drama for decades, was not broken before in the 1970s, my best guess would be the 1970s or 1980s.

11. Station identifications (in Norwegian: *kjenninger*) were used from early on when starting the day's program, when restarting the program after the morning break and then again after the afternoon break. To begin with, they were given verbally as geographical markers, which were coded in the simple form of names ('Oslo,' 'Bergen,' 'Ålesund,' etc.) or as short identifying sentences ('This is Oslo'; in Norwegian: *Her er Oslo*) (Hans Fredrik Dahl, personal communication, June 5, 2000).

12. My English translation is 'sound picture,' but lexically the word means 'picture meant for listening.'

13. In English: *New Norwegian*. To readers who are unfamiliar with the history of the Norwegian language, the names that are used in the present paragraph may seem a bit confusing. The trouble derives from the fact that the names of the two official standards of written Norwegian were changed by Parliament in 1929. *Riksmål* became *Bokmål*, and *Landsmål* became *Nynorsk*. In addition, an unreformed version of *Riksmål* with the status of a private standard also continued to exist.

REFERENCES

Primary sources

Official, contemporary sources:

Hougen, Johannes. (1932a). *Oslo kringkastingselskaps historie. Vol I: I store trekk gjennom de første syv år* (*The History of Oslo Broadcasting Company, Vol. I: Lines of Development Through the First Seven Years*). Oslo: Olaf Norli.

Hougen, Johannes. (1932b). *Oslo kringkastingselskaps historie. Vol II: Programvirksomheten* (*The History of Oslo Broadcasting Company, Vol. II: The Programming*). Oslo: Olaf Norli.

Klæbo, Arthur. (1954/1953). *Dette er Norsk rikskringkasting* (*This Is Norwegian Broadcasting*). Oslo: Norsk rikskring-kasting/Fabritius & sønners forlag.

Unofficial, retrospective sources:

Ormestad, Thor. (1975). *Kringkastingens tekniske utvikling gjennom 50 år* (*The technical development of broadcasting through 50 years*). Unpublished leaflet by NRK's technical department.

Ormestad, Thor. (1993). *Teknisk utstyr brukt til kringkasting i Norge fra 1925. Veiledning til NRKs historiske radioutstilling på Lyd & Bilde '93 (Technical equipment used in broadcasting in Norway from 1925 onwards. Guide to NRK's radio history exhibition at Sound and Picture '93)*. Unpublished leaflet.

Secondary sources

Research literature:

Dahl, Hans Fredrik. (1999) [1975]. *Hallo–hallo! Kringkastingen i Norge 1920-1940 (Hello–Hello! Broadcasting in Norway 1920-1940)*. Oslo: Cappelen.
Dahl, Hans Fredrik, & Bastiansen, Henrik. (1999). *Over til Oslo. NRK som monopol 1945-81 (Over to Oslo. NRK as a monopoly 1945-1981)*. Oslo: Cappelen.
Nyre, Lars. (2003). *Fidelity Matters. Sound media and realism in the 20th century*. Unpublished doctoral dissertation, Department of Media Studies, University of Bergen.
Syvertsen, Trine. (1992). *Public Television in Transition. A Comparative and Historical Analysis of the BBC and the NRK* (Levende bilder No. 5). Oslo & Trondheim: The Norwegian Research Council for Science and the Humanities.

Popular publications:

Andersen, Richard, & Dagfinn Bernstein. (Eds.). (1999). *Kringkastingens tekniske historie (A Technical History of Broadcasting)*. Oslo: NRK.
Hartenstein, Tilman. (2001). *Det usynlige teatret. Radioteaterets historie 1926–2001 (The Unseen Theatre. A History of Radio Theatre 1926-2001)*. Oslo: NRK.

Research publications

Åberg, Carin. (1999a). *Den omärkliga tekniken. Radio-och tv-produktion 1925-1985 (The Unnoticeable Technology. Radio and Television Production 1925-1985)*. Stockholm: Natur & Kultur.
Åberg, Carin. (1999b). *The Sounds of Radio. On Radio as an Auditive Means of Communication*. Unpublished doctoral dissertation, Department of Journalism, Media and Communication, Stockholm University, Stockholm, Sweden.
Åberg, Carin, Vagle, Wenche, & Poulsen, Ib. (1999). 'Radioforskning–en översikt' ('Radio Research—An Overview'). *Nordicom Information*. Vol. 23, No. 3, 59-72.
Barthes, Roland. (1969) [1967]. *Elements of Semiology (Éléments de Sémiologie, 1964)*. Translated by J. Cape Ltd. London: The Chaucer Press.
Bastiansen, H., & Syvertsen, T. (1994). Towards a Norwegian Television History. In Bono, Francesco & Bonderbjerg, Ib. (Eds.). *Nordic Television: History, Politics and Aesthetics*. København: Sekvens. Special Issue.
Berger, Peter, & Luckmann, Thomas. (1966). *The Social Construction of Reality*. London: Penguin Press.
Briggs, Asa. (1995). *The Birth of Broadcasting. The History of Broadcasting in the United Kingdom, Volume I: 1896-1927*. Oxford: Oxford University Press.

Bruck, Peter. (1993). 'The regimen of use of early Canadian radio-news.' *Radiosprache. Medien Journal*. Vol. 17, No. 1, 8-20.

Cardiff, David. (1980). 'The serious and the popular: Aspects of the evolution of style in radio talk 1928-1939.' *Media, Culture and Society*. Vol. 2, No. 2, 29-47.

Crisell, Andrew. (1986). *Understanding Radio*. London & New York: Methuen.

Dahlén, Peter. (1999a). 'Det svenska radioreportaget 1925-1955' ('Swedish radio reportage 1925-1955'). Paper presented at the 14th Nordic conference on media and communication research, Kungälv. JMG, Göteborg University.

Dahlén, Peter. (1999b). *Från Vasaloppet till Sportextra: radiosportens etablering och förgrening 1925-1995 (From 'Vasalppet' to 'Sportextra': The Establishment and Expansion of Radio Sports)*. In series: Skrifter utgivna av Stiftelsen etermedierna i Sverige, Vol. 12. Stockholm: Stiftelsen etermedierna i Sverige. (Writings published by the foundation of ether media in Sweden, Vol. 12. Stockholm: The foundation of ether media in Sweden.)

Eco, Umberto. (1979) [1976]. *A Theory of Semiotics*. Bloomington, IN: Indiana University Press.

Fiske, John. (1985). [1982]. *Introduction to Communication Studies*. London & New York: Methuen.

Goffman, Erving. (1986) [1974]. *Frame Analysis: An Essay on the Organization of Experience*. Boston: Northeastern University Press.

Halliday, Michael. (1990) [1978]. *Language as Social Semiotic. The Social Interpretation of Language and Meaning*. London: Edward Arnold.

Hjelmslev, Louis. (1943). *Omkring Sprogteoriens Grundlæggelse (Prolegomena to a Theory of Language)*. København: Munksgaard.

Jonsson, Åke. (1982). *Den omsorgsfulla ordmålaren: studier i Sven Jerrings radiospråk mot bakgrund av radions allmänna syn på språket under de första decennierna (The Careful Word Painter: Studies in the Radio Language of Sven Jerring in View of the Common Conception of Language During the First Decades)*. Umeå Studies in the Humanities, 48. Stockholm: Almquist & Wiksell International.

Jonsson, Åke. (1991). "Snälla Radiotjänst!" Sex decenniers lyssnarbrev med språkliga synpunkter ('"Dear Radio!" Six decades of letters to the editor from listeners concerning questions of language'). In Brändström, Anders, & Åkerman, Sune. (Eds.). *Icke skriftliga källor (Non-written Sources)*. XXI Nordiska Historikermötet. Umeå: Umeå University.

Kjeldstadli, Knut. (1999) [1992]. *Fortida er ikke hva den en gang var. En innføring i historiefaget (The Past Is Not What It Used to Be. An Introduction to the Study of History)*. Oslo: Universitetsforlaget.

Kjerschow, Peder Christian. (1978). *Musikk og mening (Music and Meaning)*. Oslo: Tanum–Norli.

Larsen, Peter. (2005). *Filmmusikk. Historie, analyse, teori (Film Music. History, Analysis, Theory)*. Oslo: Universitetsforlaget.

Maasø, Arnt. (2002). *'Se-hva-som-skjer!': en studie av lyd som kommunikativt virkemiddel i TV ('Look-what-happens!' A study of sound as a means of communication)*. Unpublished doctoral dissertation. Acta humaniora No. 132. Oslo: University of Oslo/Unipub.

Martin, James. (1992). *English Text. System and Structure*. Amsterdam: John Benjamins Publishing Company.

Martin, James, & Wodak, Ruth. (Eds.). (2003). *Re/reading the Past: Critical and Functional Perspectives on Time and Value. Discourse Approaches to Politics, Society and Culture, Vol. 8.* Amsterdam: John Benjamins.

Matthiessen, Christian. (1993). 'Register in the round: diversity in a unified theory of register analysis.' In Ghadessy, Moshen. (Ed.). *Register Analysis. Theory and Practice.* London & New York: Pinter Publishers. 221-292.

Nordberg, Karin. (1991). 'Skriftligt och muntligt i radion' ('Orality and literacy in radio'). In Brändström, Anders, & Åkerman, Sune. (Eds.). *Icke skriftliga källor. XXI Nordiska Historikermötet.* (Non-written sources. XXI Nordic meeting of historians). Umeå: Umeå University.

Nordberg, Karin. (1998). *Folkhemmets röst. Radion som folkbildare 1925-1950 (The Voice of the Folkhem: Radio as Adult Educator 1925-1950).* Stockholm/Stehag: Brutus Östlings Bokförlag Symposion.

Nordberg, Karin. (2003). *Hör världen! Röst och retorik i radioföredragen. Populärvetenskap på programmet (Listen to the World! Voice and Rhetoric in Radio Talks. Popular Science Programmes).* Svensk sakprosa, rapport nr. 37. Lund: Institutionen för nordiska språk.

Nørgaard, Waldemar, Krebs, Harald & Wolsing, Felix. (1975-1978). *De musiske udsendelser DR 1925-1975: Radioteater, musik, TVteater* (Music Programmes in Denmark 1925-1973: Radio Drama, Music, Television, Theatre). København: Nyt Nordisk Forlag.

Nyre, Lars. (2003). *Fidelity Matters. Sound Media and Realism in the 20th Century.* Unpublished doctoral dissertation, Department of Media Studies, University of Bergen.

Poulsen, Ib. (2006). *Radiomontagen og dens rødder. Et studie i den danske radiomontage med vægt på dens genremæssige forudsætninger (The Radio Reportage and Its Roots. A Study in the Danish Radio Montage With Emphasis on Its Preconditions of Genre).* Roskilde: Roskilde Universitetsforlag.

Rüppel, Inez. (2002). 'Writing the history of texts: A historian's perspective.' In Berge, Kjell Lars. (Ed.). *Teksthistorie. Tekstvitenskapelige bidrag (Text History. Text Scientific Contributions).* Sakprosa–skrifter fra prosjektmiljøet Norsk Sakprosa, No. 6. Oslo: Norsk faglitterær forfatterforening. 73-112.

Scannell, Paddy. (1996). *Radio, Television & Modern Life.* Oxford: Blackwell.

Scannell, Paddy, & Cardiff, David. (1991). *A Social History of British Broadcasting. Vol. I: 1922-1939: Serving the Nation.* Oxford: Blackwell.

Swales, John. (2000) [1990]. *Genre Analysis: English in Academic and Research Settings.* Cambridge, UK: Cambridge University Press.

Vagle, Wenche. (2005). 'From text-context models to discourse-analytical methodologies—three perspectives on radio discourse.' In Berge, Kjell Lars, & Maagerø, Eva. (Eds.). *Semiotics From the North. Nordic Approaches to Systemic Functional Linguistics.* Oslo: Novus. 199-230.

Vagle, Wenche. (2006). 'Interpreting and explaining historical texts—is it possible?' *Nordicom Review.* Vol. 27, No. 2, 205-226.

Vagle, Wenche. (under review). *'I think the listeners would like me to ask you, Mr Prime Minister, ...' The history of texts and contexts in Norwegian radio with emphasis on the early period.* Acta Humaniora no. 317. Doctoral dissertation, Faculty of Humanities, University of Oslo.

van Leeuwen, Theo. (1999). *Speech, Music, Sound.* Basingstoke: Macmillan.
van Leeuwen, Theo. (2005). Introducing Social Semiotics. London: Routledge.
Ventola, Eija. (1987). *The Structure of Social Interaction. A Systemic Approach to the Semiotics of Service Encounters.* London: Pinter Publishers.
von Feilitzen, Cecilia. (1994). 'Den kulturella vändningen, och sedan...? Om tvärvetenskap i medieforskningen under 1980- och 90-talen' ('The cultural turn, and then? On interdisciplinary media research during the 1980s and 1990s'). In Carlsson, Ulla, von Feilitzen, Cecilia, & Fornäs, Johan. (Eds.). *Kommunikationens korsningar. Möten mellan olika traditioner och perspektiv i medieforskningen (Crossroads of Communications: Encounters between Traditions and Perspectives in Media Research).* Gothenburg: University of Gothenburg & Nordicom. 9-14.

CONTRIBUTORS

Andrew Deacon
Centre for Educational Teachnology, CET, University of Cape Town,
    South Africa

Anders Fagerjord
Department of Media and Communication, University of Oslo, Norway

Cynthia Haynes
Department of English, Clemson University, USA

Martin Havnør
Faster Imaging, Oslo, Norway

Maja Kuzmanovic
Director, Foam, Brussels, Belgium

Gunnar Liestøl
Department of Media and Communication, University of Oslo, Norway

Andreas Lund
Department of Teacher Education and School Development, University of
    Oslo, Norway

Sinfree Makoni
Linguistics and Applied Language Studies, Penn State University, USA

Adrian Miles
Royal Melbourne Institute of Technology (RMIT), Australia

Anne Moen
Institute of Health Sciences, & InterMedia, University of Oslo, Norway

Andrew Morrison
InterMedia, University of Oslo, Norway, & Oslo School of Architecture &
    Design, Norway

Palmyre Pierroux
InterMedia, University of Oslo, Norway

Idunn Sem
InterMedia, University of Oslo, Norway

Synne Skjulstad
Department of Media & Communication, University of Oslo, Norway

Ole Smørdal
InterMedia, University of Oslo, Norway

Jane Stadler
Film and Television Studies, University of Queensland, Australia

Dagny Stuedahl
Department of Media and Communication, & InterMedia, University of
    Oslo, Norway

Per Roar Thorsnes
Freelance choreographer, & Oslo National Academy of the Arts, Norway

Wenche Vagle
Department of Teacher Education & School Development, University of
    Oslo, Norway

Even Westvang
Media designer and developer, Bengler Media, Oslo, Norway

AUTHOR INDEX

SUBJECT INDEX

DATE DUE

NOV 2 8 2011	
MAY 1 6 2013	
JUN 1 5 2016	
DEC 1 9 2015	
MAY 3 1 2023	

DEMCO, INC. 38-2971

9 781612 890012